TEXAS

OFF THE BEATEN PATH®

OFF THE BEATEN PATH® SERIES

ELEVENTH EDITION

TEXAS

OFF THE BEATEN PATH®

DISCOVER YOUR FUN

JUNE NAYLOR

Globe
Pequot
Guilford, Connecticut

All the information in this guidebook is subject to change. We recommend that you call ahead to obtain current information before traveling.

Globe Pequot

An imprint of The Rowman & Littlefield Publishing Group, Inc.
4501 Forbes Blvd., Ste. 200
Lanham, MD 20706
www.rowman.com

Distributed by NATIONAL BOOK NETWORK

British Library Cataloguing in Publication Information available

Library of Congress Cataloging-in-Publication Data available

ISBN 978-1-4930-3460-4 (paperback)
ISBN 978-1-4930-3461-1 (e-book)

∞™ The paper used in this publication meets the minimum requirements of American National Standard for Information Sciences—Permanence of Paper for Printed Library Materials, ANSI/NISO Z39.48-1992

Printed in the United States of America

For my parents—
I am grateful for your love and your
abundant Texan legacies.

Contents

Introduction xi

The Brazos-Republic Trail **1**

Heart of Texas 3

State Capital Country 12

The Republic of Texas 24

The Gulf Coast **33**

The Land of Spindletop 35

The Romantic Seaside 46

The Coastal Bend 51

The Coastal Plains 60

The Big Beach 64

The Hill Country **71**

Ranches & Lakes 75

Rocks & Wildlife 83

Exotics, Dudes & Germans 88

South Texas **107**

Missions & Europeans 109

Brush Country 119

The Rio Grande Valley 123

The Piney Woods **131**

Deepest East Texas 133

The 19th-Century Trail 140

Bayous, Lakes & Legends 152

North Texas **160**

    Red River Country 162

    The Big D. 172

    Around Cowtown 179

    Dinosaurs & Hell's Gates 189

The Texas Panhandle **203**

    Fandangles & Rattlesnakes 205

    Cap Rock & Canyons. 215

    The Staked Plains 227

Wildest West Texas **235**

    Forts & the Permian Basin 238

    Big Bend Country. 246

    Trans-Pecos Country 264

Index 273

About the Author

A sixth-generation Texan and Fort Worth native, **June Naylor** has written about food and travel for more than 25 years for publications around Texas and the US. She is currently the food and travel editor for *360 West Magazine* and is a contributor to *Texas Monthly, Texas Highways,* and the *Dallas Morning News.* June is the coauthor of three cookbooks, *The Texas Cowboy Kitchen, Cooking the Cowboy Way,* and *Big Ranch, Big City Cookbook.*

The author of GPP's *Food Lovers' Guide to Dallas and Fort Worth, Quick Escapes from Dallas/Fort Worth, Romantic Days and Nights in Dallas/Fort Worth,* and *Recommended Bed & Breakfasts Southwest,* June has received several writing and photography awards from the Society of American Travel Writers. She is a founder of the nonprofit Foodways Texas and a member of the women's culinary group Les Dames d'Escoffier.

Acknowledgments

Working on the 11th edition of this book was a pleasure, mostly because it allowed me to rediscover the backroads and oft-overlooked corners that make Texas live up to its vast legend. I owe a great debt to the kindly folks who work in tiny museums, cafés, shops, and inns in such towns as Leakey in the Hill Country, Uncertain in the Piney Woods, Marathon in the Big Bend, and Canyon in the Panhandle; it's people like this, in places like those, who make writing about Texas a joyful privilege. I'm also deeply appreciative to my editors at GPP, who make the process of working on books as painless as possible. As for the support at home, I have endless gratitude for my sweet and supportive husband, Marshall Harris, and for all my family and friends who make me keep my sense of humor—and still love me even during those moments when I seem to have misplaced it.

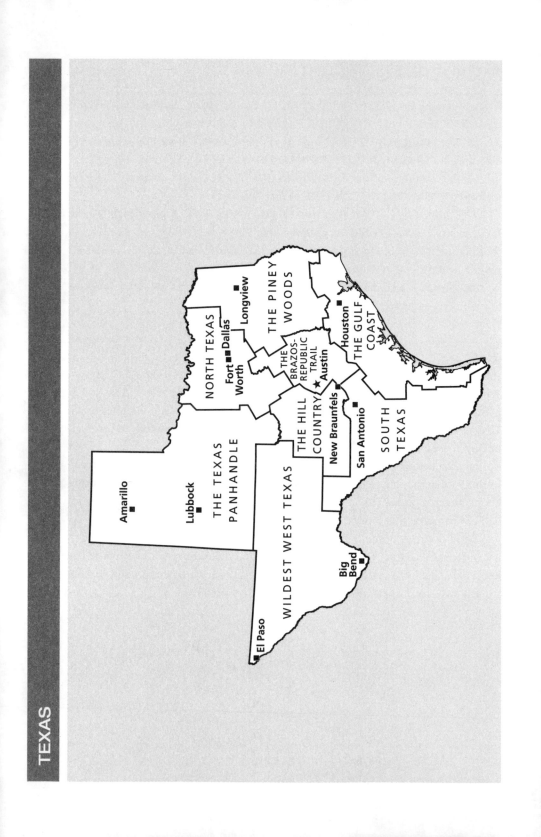

Introduction

John Steinbeck wrote in *Travels with Charley,* "Texas is a state of mind. Texas is an obsession. Above all, Texas is a nation in every sense of the word."

Sam Houston—first president of the Republic of Texas and hero in the defeat of Santa Anna—would have loved Steinbeck.

But for all its staunch independence, Texas is one big welcome mat. Folks coming to call from elsewhere are often taken aback when greeted on the street by total strangers with a "Howdy" or "Hey." There's no catch—Texans are just greeters by nature.

Let's go ahead and dispel some myths: Texas is flat if you don't count those 91 mountains that reach over a mile into the sky; Texas is dry if you ignore 3.07 million acres of inland water made up of streams, rivers, lakes, springs, creeks, and 624 miles of Gulf of Mexico shoreline; and Texas has no trees if you overlook those 23 million acres of woodlands.

Texas's farm-to-market roads serve not only today's farmers but also those wanderers who just want to absorb the gentle, uncluttered environs. The first such road opened in 1937 (redesignated in 1939 as a portion of TX 315), and now there are more than 3,000, making up 41,000 highway miles of the state's total of 79,000. The shortest, FM 742, in McLennan County, is 0.175 mile. Two of the prettiest farm-to-market vistas are in the Piney Woods of east Texas and the Trans-Pecos wilds of west Texas.

When eating in Texas, be aware that Mexican meets southern, Cajun greets soul, and, somehow, dissimilarities welcome one another. From such mingling, southwestern cuisine rides a crest of fame, and country cooking soars higher than ever on all palates.

You can trust places with signs that say If You Leave Here Hungry It's Your Own Fault or pie fixes everything and put your faith in waitresses who are concerned you haven't been eating right and insist you need that piece of pie to keep up your strength. Also, if it sounds absurd, it's probably good; if it sounds French, it probably isn't Texan.

For fried alligator tail, a tender delicacy, look around east Texas lake joints, which also serve up lightly fried catfish with green tomato relish and jalapeño hush puppies. Barbecue, a critical Texas staple, is best from the old places in central Texas's Taylor, Lockhart, and Luling. If you can find barbecued pork or beef ribs, brisket, goat, shrimp, or sausage, eat it up.

How about buffalo? It's a tasty treat, lower in fat and cholesterol than beef, and a wonderful way to eat Wellington, burgers, and steaks. No bull. The best *wurst* turns up in thickly German towns such as New Braunfels and

Fredericksburg, while kolache heaven is spread out over the Czech communities of West and Caldwell.

A word about chicken-fried steak: Sounds weird, but this could be the state food of Texas; go for it only if it's fork-cutting tender and its breading is homemade and light. And whence came chili? San Antonio or Fort Worth? Both claim it. Beef or venison, spicy or mild, beans or no, there's plenty of it for the sampling at cook-offs all year long. Just don't confuse it with chile, which can be a fire-hot stew if eaten on one of Texas's two Native American reservations, or a velvety green or creamy red pepper sauce if found in one of south Texas's Hispanic-infused towns. Now, you'll get plenty of argument from fajita lovers, but the best Mexican eats are breakfast goods—*migas, empanadas* (sweet and savory pastries)—found in cafés and bakeries.

For fruits of the Texas earth, look to Weatherford and Stonewall for peaches, Pecos for cantaloupes, and the Rio Grande valley for citrus. For the nectar of Texas gods, we have dozens of vineyards and wineries, among them international award winners—**Becker Vineyards** in Fredericksburg, **McPherson Cellars** in Lubbock, **Rancho Loma Vineyards** in Coleman, and **Fall Creek Vineyards** in Tow, and more.

As any Texan will tell you, this is one recreation-crazed state. In water action alone, there's rafting, canoeing, and kayaking on Hill Country rivers and the Rio Grande, while sailing and sailboarding are Corpus Christi favorites, surfers flock to Galveston, catamaran rentals are booming business on South Padre Island, and fishing charters and tournaments subsidize the Port Aransas economy.

Texans are always looking for an excuse to have fun. There are festivals celebrating mosquitoes, flowers, berries, hush puppies, rattlesnakes, bluegrass music, fall foliage, and fire ants. Cowboys have a Christmas ball, Native Americans have a championship powwow, and Scottish clans gather in kilts.

When exploring the sprawling state, it's usually helpful to do so by region. Eight easily defined areas—each with its own personality and shape—will keep you busy, to say nothing of intrigued.

In **North Texas,** all Dallas and Fort Worth have in common are a shared river, 30 miles of connecting interstate highway, and one of the largest, busiest airports in the world. Which is just the beauty of the area—in about a half hour you can be someplace drastically different. Dallas is larger, more dashing, and aggressive. It glitters and bustles and has a lifestyle ridden with haute cuisine and couture. Fort Worth defines Texas succinctly: Businesspeople wear boots and make deals over barbecue, and cowboy-hatted police officers ride horses on their downtown beats. Dallas's Uptown neighborhood, Mavericks basketball, Stars hockey, internationally flavored dining, and incomparable shopping bring Fort Worth folks over for visits. Conversely, Fort Worth's restored Stock-yards and world-renowned art museums, the Bass Performing Arts Center, and the family-style Mexican food at Joe T. Garcia's bring Dallasites over in hordes.

East Texas's **Piney Woods** is something of an extension of the Old South, with several of the Republic of Texas's birthmarks. San Augustine and Nacog-doches are vintage towns packed with earliest history, while Jefferson appeals with its old riverboat town and antiques-shop charm. Marshall, a stop on stage-coach and Victorian train lines, has restored mansions and bed-and-breakfasts in lovingly refurbished homes. Train buffs delight in traveling between Rusk and Palestine on the Texas State Railroad's steam locomotives. Approximately one-fifth of all commercial rosebushes in the US are grown in Smith County, and more than half of the nation's rosebushes are packed and shipped from here. Canton brings several thousand people each month to its century-old **First Monday Trade Days.** Four national forests jam the region, and the Big Thicket National Preserve is home to a precious virgin forest where 20 kinds of wild orchids and carnivorous plants and 300 varieties of birds coexist in an impenetrable natural fortress.

Some of Texas's deepest heritage is found in the humid, lush environs of the **Texas Gulf Coast.** Sam Houston's ravaged army rid the Republic of Santa Anna's Mexican troops on a field named San Jacinto, where a breathtak-ing, 570-foot commemorative monument now stands against the backdrop of Texas's largest city. Houston is an oil city, home to the NASA-Johnson Space Center, a vibrant, resurrected downtown, the best dining scene in the entire South, and a sizable selection of theaters, museums, and shops. Like Port Arthur and Beaumont to the east and Rockport and Port Aransas to the south, Houston is rebuilding and rebounding from the utter devastation of Hurricane Harvey in late August 2017.

A short drive east, Galveston remains one of Texas's more significant beach communities. Once known as the Wall Street of the Southwest, the island-city boasts one of the nation's largest collections of restored Victorian buildings. The Strand, the 1894 Grand Opera House, Ashton Villa, and the *Elissa,* a square-rigged tall ship, highlight a long list of attractions. Padre Island is a long, thin finger of sand protecting the Texas coast from Corpus Christi to the Rio Grande. Most of the island's 113-mile stretch is national seashore, populated by more than 400 species of birds, sand dunes, and sea oats. The King Ranch—the largest privately owned ranch in the world—sits inland from the sailboarding, sailing city of Corpus Christi. South Padre Island is a resort town glistening with high-rise hotels and sleek condos, boutiques, and sun-bleached houses. Teens jam the beaches in spring, families ride the waves in summer, and anglers work the bay and beach year-round.

In **South Texas's** Rio Grande valley, the communities of McAllen, Weslaco, and Mission are the heart of Texas's huge citrus industry and the home of Winter Texans, snowbirds from the Midwest. San Antonio, the most common gateway to south Texas, fairly reverberates with the passion of Texas's European origins and the hearty Hispanic culture still enjoying growth. Some explorers make their way down to Langtry, home of revered Judge Roy Bean, whose justice was once the only law west of the Pecos. In this southwestern corner find the world's Spinach Capital, the state's oldest winery, and an opalescent lake shared by two friendly countries.

If the spiritual heart of Texas is to be embraced, it will happen in the **Hill Country.** Spring-fed rivers course beneath limestone cliffs, through rolling hills dotted with live oak and wildflowers. It is a region for escape, for reflection, for rejuvenation. Small towns in the Hill Country embrace a serenity not quite duplicated elsewhere. Fredericksburg and New Braunfels gleam with their German heritage, displayed in the shops, historic lodgings, and plentiful wurst and beer. Kerrville is home to the Y.O. Ranch, and Burnet claims the Vanishing Texas River Cruise.

At the heart of Texas, figuratively and literally, is Austin, the state capital and an integral part of the **Brazos-Republic Trail.** This is an easy city to enjoy, one favored for its music and nightlife, where pleasures unfold from lakes and wooded hills, cultural centers at the University of Texas, and the Lady Bird Johnson Wildflower Center. To the east are more small towns forming the core of the old republic.

John Wayne should have been required by law to make all his westerns in the **Texas Panhandle.** The genuine, traditional Texan style is so thick here you could cut it with a knife. In the High Plains a great treasure is the shockingly beautiful and huge Palo Duro Canyon. An exciting musical drama plays under the stars there in summer, and the city of Amarillo lies at the heart of Texas' stretch of the Mother Road, Route 66.

Texas's western heritage is defined and illustrated with great care at the Panhandle Plains Museum in Canyon and at the Ranching Heritage Center in Lubbock. Another Lubbock asset—wines produced from its sandy but rich land—is offered for sampling at several award-winning vineyards. This part of the Panhandle is responsible for growing more than eighty percent of the grapes used in all Texas' winemaking.

West Texas is a vast area distinguished by attractions as diverse as ancient Native American ruins and pioneer forts, mountains, and unexplained moving lights—this is a region that could take years to truly explore. El Paso is a reservoir of Native American, Hispanic, and Anglo influences characterizing the city's architecture, art, food, shopping, and pastimes.

Due east from El Paso, Guadalupe Mountains National Park contains a wealth of scenery, from McKittrick Canyon and its blazing fall foliage to Guadalupe Peak, Texas's highest point at 8,749 feet above sea level. Fort Davis lies between the Guadalupe Mountains and the Big Bend's Chihuahuan Desert. Home to Fort Davis National Historic Site with its restored cavalry fort, Fort Davis sits beside the Davis Mountains State Park and its romantic Indian Lodge, and it claims the historic Hotel Limpia, a place with restorative qualities; McDonald Observatory, with fascinating "Star Parties"; and miles of cool, clean mountain air and vistas gained by a 74-mile mountain loop road.

The Big Bend is the site of a rugged, 800,000-acre national park, encompassing a wild stretch of the Rio Grande beloved by geologists, naturalists, and outdoorsy types who want to spend a day, week, or month camping and rafting in jagged canyons.

After driving around a spell, you'll notice bumper stickers with the image of the Texas flag emblazoned by the word *Native* or *Naturalized*. Texans, whether born or transplanted here, like to advertise their Lone Star State status.

Such boasts shouldn't detract from the amiable intent—it's simply a friendly state, as the official motto proclaims. It won't take you long to find that out for yourself.

Texas Fast Facts

- Texas is the largest of the contiguous states, with 266,807 square miles.

- Only Alaska has more fresh water than Texas.

- There are four national forests in Texas.

- The King Ranch in Kingsville is the largest ranch in Texas and is slightly larger than the state of Rhode Island.

- Texas has 23.4 million acres of woodland.

- Houston, San Antonio, and Dallas are among the nation's 10 largest cities; and Austin, Fort Worth, and El Paso are in the nation's top 20 most populated cities.

- Texas has more than 500,000 alligators.

- Nearly 28 million people call Texas home, making this the second-most populous state.

- State capital: Austin

- State motto: Friendship

- State nickname: Lone Star State

- State mammal: armadillo (small); longhorn (large)

- State bird: mockingbird

- State tree: pecan

- State flower: bluebonnet

- State dish: chili con carne

- State gem: blue topaz

- State fruit: red grapefruit

- State dance: square dance

- State song: "Texas, Our Texas"

- State plant: prickly pear

- State pepper: jalapeño

- State reptile: horned lizard

- State fish: Guadalupe bass

- State flying mammal: Mexican free-tailed bat

- State grass: sideoats grama

- State insect: monarch butterfly

- State seashell: lightning whelk

- State ship: battleship *Texas*

- State sport: rodeo

Important Dates in Texas's History

1519   Spain is the first of six nations to claim Texas.

1685   France claims the Rio Grande as the western boundary of its Louisiana Territory, based on the exploration of La Salle.

1821   Upon winning independence from Spain, Mexico acquires Texas.

1836   After holding off a Mexican army of thousands for 13 days in the
Battle of the Alamo, 188 "Texans" die. A month later General Sam

Houston leads the Texas army in the successful Battle of San Jacinto to win independence from Mexico.

1845   Texas joins the US as the 28th state.

1861   Texas secedes from the US, joining the Confederates in the Civil War.

1865   Texas rejoins the US.

1901   Oil is discovered at Spindletop.

1917   Miriam A. Ferguson becomes the first woman governor of Texas when she finishes her husband's (James E. Ferguson) term after his impeachment.

1953   Dwight D. Eisenhower becomes the first Texas-born president of the US.

1963   John F. Kennedy is assassinated in Dallas; Lyndon B. Johnson, born in Stonewall, becomes the 36th president.

1965   National Aeronautics and Space Administration (NASA) opens the Lyndon B. Johnson Space Center in Houston.

1966   Barbara Jordan is the first African American elected to the Texas Senate.

1989   George H. W. Bush becomes the 41st US president.

2001   George W. Bush becomes the 43rd US president.

2005   The University of Texas's football team wins its fourth national championship.

2007   The George Bush Presidential Library and Museum opens on the Texas A&M University campus.

2009   The Dallas Cowboys leave Dallas County and begin playing at the team's billion-dollar stadium in Arlington, in Tarrant County.

2010   The Texas Rangers Baseball Club represents the American League in the World Series.

2011   The Super Bowl is hosted by North Texas at the Cowboys Stadium in Arlington.

2011   The Dallas Mavericks win their first NBA title.

2013   All living former U.S. Presidents, including Jimmy Carter, George H. W. Bush, and Bill Clinton, along with President Barack Obama, attend dedication of the George W. Bush Presidential Center in Dallas.

2017   Houston hosts Super Bowl LI.

2017   Hurricane Harvey among deadliest storms in U.S. history.

2017   The Houston Astros win the World Series.

Websites Worth Visiting

Abilene: abilenevisitors.com

Amarillo: visitamarillo.com

Arlington: arlington.org

Austin: austintexas.org

Big Bend: visitbigbend.com

Corpus Christi: visitcorpuschristitx.org

Dallas: visitdallas.com

El Paso: visitelpaso.com

Fort Worth: fortworth.com

Fredericksburg: visitfredericksburgtx.com

Galveston: galveston.com

Houston: visithoustontexas.com

Irving: irvingtexas.com

Jefferson: jefferson-texas.com

Lubbock: visitlubbock.org

San Angelo: discoversanangelo.org

San Antonio: visitsanantonio.com

South Padre Island: sopadre.com

State parks: tpwd.texas.gov

Statewide tourism: traveltex.com

Waco: wacoheartoftexas.com

Speed Limits

The maximum speed limit is 70 miles per hour during the day and 65 at night on all numbered highways in rural areas. Some counties in west Texas have 75- or 80-mile-per-hour speed limits. Lower limits are posted on many highways; limits on urban freeways are from 55 to 70 miles per hour. School zones are strictly monitored at 20 miles per hour, and many cities impose hefty fines for drivers using cell phones while driving through school zones.

Texas State Parks

The Texas Parks and Wildlife Department offers more than 100 parks, state natural areas, wildlife management areas, and historic sites. The State Parks Pass and the Texas State Parklands Passport afford visitors discounted or waived entry fees. Check tpwd.texas.gov for details. The parks department has a centralized reservations office for camping. Call the office at (512) 389-8900 Mon through Fri from 9 a.m. until 8 p.m. and Sat from 9 a.m. until noon.

Texas Travel Information Centers

The Texas Department of Transportation operates travel information centers in 12 locations across Texas. Each center is staffed by professional travel counselors and offers thousands of pieces of free literature, including the excellent *Texas State Travel Guide,* road maps, and lodging guides. All services are free, and the centers are open daily from 8 a.m. until 5 p.m., except New Year's Day, Thanksgiving Day, Christmas Eve, Christmas Day, and Easter Sunday.

Find the travel centers located in Amarillo on I-40; Anthony on I-10 (near the New Mexico state line); Austin at the Capitol Complex; Denison on US 75/69 (near the Oklahoma state line); Gainesville on US 77/I-35 (near the Oklahoma state line); Langtry on US 90 at Loop 25; Laredo on I-35 (near the Mexican border); Orange on I-10 (near the Louisiana state line); Texarkana on I-30 (near the Arkansas state line); Harlingen on US 77 at US 83; Waskom on I-20 (near the Louisiana state line); and Wichita Falls on I-44 (near the Oklahoma state line).

For free road maps and information on travel destinations and road conditions, call the travel consultants at (800) 452-9292, or visit traveltex.com. Throughout the state on major highways, find Safety Rest Areas with clean bathrooms, walking paths, dog-walk areas, playgrounds, and free WiFi.

Texas state roads are designated in this book as Highways, as in Highway 261 and Highway 41. Farm Roads are FR; Park Roads, PR; and Ranch Roads are RR.

Admission Fees

Note that in many cases, attractions are noted with a phrase such as "A small admission fee is charged." Generally this means that admission fees are from $1 to $10 per person. The notation "Admission is charged" usually means that the fee is more than $10.

The Brazos-Republic Trail

A train whistle blows steadily, and soon loudly, through the fragile darkness. Just before dawn a rooster begins its intonation, and moos soon follow. Days begin early in the country, breaking clean and fresh—the sky, grass, and picket fences seem unusually pure along central Texas's Brazos and Colorado Rivers, through a region spreading just to the east of the Balcones Escarpment and the state's fabled Hill Country. German, Scottish, and Czech immigrants made their way to new homes through this rolling corridor, toughing out a life that could become hazardous when conflicts with Mexicans and Native Americans arose. Here, dairy and cotton farmers and horse ranchers carved lives with their families and friends, thanks in part to their own determined spirit and that of the Texas Rangers.

It was through this part of the frontier, once called Tejas by the Mexicans and Indians, that pioneers crafted a republic, a sovereign nation that gave rise eventually to the Lone Star State. Today's explorers find great and lasting remnants of that period in peaceful towns that make wonderful discoveries on the way to someplace else and in a fine capital city whose enduring beauty and character make it a popular place for

people who love art, history, rhythm and blues, comfort food, lakeside scenery, and even bats—yes, the nation's largest urban bat colony lives under the Congress Avenue Bridge spanning the Colorado River in Austin.

Heart of Texas

Hillsboro, resting at the center of Hill County, is a town of about 8,000, established as a trade center and county seat in 1853. People who've passed through remember the *Hill County Courthouse,* built in 1890 to replace the original log cabin structure. The flamboyant, cream-colored design on the town square mixes styles to include classical revival, Italianate, and French Second Empire. A vintage *Saturday Evening Post* story called the courthouse "a monstrosity," while *Harper's* countered with a description declaring the ornate structure "like an outstanding cathedral." The courthouse was destroyed by fire on New Year's Day, 1993; however, the town and some of its powerful children—such as country singer Willie Nelson—rallied quickly to raise funds to restore the masterpiece to its original glory. Work was under way at once, and now the gorgeous creation of Texas limestone reigns over Hillsboro again.

Roughly a block north of the square, at the corner of North Waco and West Paschal Streets, the old jail (1893–1983) is now the *Hill County Cell Block Museum,* (254) 582-8912. Inside find varied Native American artifacts. The museum is open April through October, Sat from 10 a.m. to 4 p.m. Admission is free. Five blocks north of the square on North Waco Street, the Old Hillsboro

JUNE'S FAVORITE ATTRACTIONS

Armstrong Browning Library Waco	**McKinney Roughs** Bastrop
International Festival-Institute Round Top	**Spoetzl Brewery** Shiner
Hill County Courthouse Hillsboro	**Star of the Republic Museum** Washington
Hotel Ella Austin	**State Capitol Building** Austin
Lady Bird Johnson Wildflower Center Austin	**Texas Ranch Life** Chappell Hill

Cemetery is covered with ancient cedar trees and filled with wonderful old headstones and monuments, marking those buried here from 1856 to 1940.

Two blocks from the square, the *1895 Tarlton House* (211 N. Pleasant St., Hillsboro; 254-582-3422, heartoftexasbb.com) is a gorgeous Queen Anne–style Victorian home with 7 comfortable, thoughtfully appointed guest rooms. You'll be tempted to do nothing but sit in a rocker on the front porch and watch the world go by. You'll find plenty of stained glass throughout the lovely bed-and-breakfast, as well as wireless connectivity. This is a great place for girlfriends' getaways and murder mystery weekends.

Take a side trip to *Corsicana,* 41 miles east of Hillsboro on Highway 22. Although established in 1849, the Navarro County seat didn't see much action until oil was accidentally struck here in 1894 when the city was drilling for water. This set off quite a boom, and one of Texas's first refineries was built here in 1897. Today the city of about 23,000 is known far and wide as home to *Collin Street Bakery* (401 W. 7th Ave., Corsicana; 903-874-7477; collinstreet .com), the fruitcake company founded in 1896. Each year more than 1 million fruitcakes are shipped to every state in the US and to nearly 200 foreign countries. You can also find a 10-cent cup of coffee here. Open Mon through Fri from 7 a.m. to 5:30 p.m., Sat 7 a.m. to 6 p.m., and Sun noon to 6 p.m.

Get a little history lesson at Corsicana's *Pioneer Village* (912 W. Park Ave., Corsicana; 903-654-4846), where Navarro County's surviving historic structures, filled with heirlooms, artifacts, and family treasures, make up this living-history village. Grounds include a Peace Officer Museum, a Civil War Museum, the Lefty Frizzell Museum, various archives, an 1870 pioneer home, blacksmith shops, a general store, slave quarters, a barn, a carriage house, and an 1838 Indian trading post (the oldest structure in the park). Open Mon

JUNE'S FAVORITE ANNUAL EVENTS

South by Southwest Music, Film, & Media Conference
Austin, second and third weeks in March

Round Top Music Festival
Round Top, June and July

Wildflower Tours
Brenham, Chappell Hill, and Round Top; throughout March and April

Westfest
West, Labor Day Weekend

Texas Reds Steak & Grape Festival
Bryan, late September

Armadillo/Christmas Bazaar
Austin, early December

through Sat from 9 a.m. to 5 p.m. and Sun from 1 to 5 p.m. A small admission is charged; free for tots under 4 years.

As you return to I-35, bear in mind that the interstate can be particularly crowded, so allow plenty of time for your drive south. A few more miles south of Hillsboro along I-35, watch for exit 358 at the town of **Abbott** (birthplace of Willie Nelson).

Fifteen miles south—at the apex of the lines forming McLennan County—the tiny town of **West** on I-35 at FR 2114 is a town of 2,500 residents rich in Czechoslovakian heritage. The town of West made international news in 2013, when a fertilizer plant explosion killed several firefighters and injured hundreds of people.

First and foremost, West is famous for Czech food, especially **kolaches**—thick, fruit-filled pastries—and homemade sausage, which are sold in packages and are also baked inside pastries called klobasniki. Travelers en route from Dallas or Fort Worth south to Austin and San Antonio invariably stop off in West to fill orders from friends back home who want plenty of kolaches. Consequently, the half dozen or so kolache bakeries on Main and Oak Streets always have pan upon pan ready to box, as well as frozen packages to go.

Right on the interstate are two places offering a quick bite of the local Czech culture. The **Czech Stop** (254-826-4161; czechstop.net) on the access road on the east side of the highway (exit 353), has a convenience store, deli, and Shell station sharing a building with a sister business, Little Czech Bakery. The deli's big cases are filled with kolaches stuffed with fruit fillings, sausage and cheese, or sausage and sauerkraut. There are excellent sandwiches, too, from pastrami and Swiss on rye to egg salad or pimento cheese. You'll almost always find a long line here, attesting to the good food. The bakery next door has an even greater selection of pastries, but the Czech Stop is packed also with gifts and T-shirts; check out the ones in Czech. Bringing roadside competition is **Slovacek's** (214 Melodie Dr., West; 254-826-4525; slovacekwesttexas.com), an enormous and elaborate store, cafe, and butcher shop directly across Interstate 35 from The Czech Stop. In addition to a huge bakery, frozen yogurt bar, beer cave, and gift shop, there's a dog park, too.

If you happen upon West on Labor Day weekend, join in the celebration at **Westfest,** one of Texas's favorite parties. Held at the West Fair and Rodeo Grounds, at Main Street and FR 1858 (254-826-5058; westfest.com), the Saturday and Sunday affair features authentic Czech costume contests, folk dancing, and the music of a nuclear-polka group, Brave Combo. Count on plenty of kolaches, sausages, and other comfort food.

Shortly after heading south again on I-35 from West, start watching for FR 308, 10 miles south of West. You'll exit onto FR 308 and head southwest to reach the **Homestead Heritage Visitor Center** at Brazos de Dios; homesteadheritage.com. Stay on FR 308 for 3 miles, then turn north on FR 933 for 1.5 miles, then turn west on Halbert Lane. This is the center of information for a small farming community where traditional crafts and arts are preserved and practiced. From time to time there are workshops for pottery throwing, basket weaving, soap making, woodworking, quilting, and spinning. At the entrance, check out the cheese shop, offering a dozen kinds of artisan cheeses made on-site, each more delicious than the one beside it. Thoughout **Homestead Craft Village,** find buildings selling early Texas longleaf pine furniture, quilts, wrought-iron fireplace tools, pottery, and soaps (608 Dry Creek Rd., 254-754-9600); it's open Mon through Sat from 10 a.m. to 6 p.m.

Back on I-35, **Waco** is another 7 miles south. A city of 114,000 straddling the historic Brazos River, Waco is a place destined to be noted in history books as one with a diverse heritage. Although Waco remains reminiscent of its cotton-cattle-corn heyday, some people can't help remembering it for being the site of the tragic Branch Davidian episode in 1993 and, more recently and unfortunately, college scandals. Long populated by the Hueco Indians, from which the city took its name, Waco saw its first white explorers when a group of Hernando de Soto's men came through in 1542. Real civilization came when the Texas Rangers established a fort here in 1837, however. The town won the nickname Six-Shooter Junction later, when the Chisholm Trail was brought through the frontier post, but things have calmed down considerably, as the city is best known now for the HGTV phenomenon formally known as *Fixer Upper* and to devotees of the Chip and Joanna Gaines show.

After these TV celebrities and home transformation gurus exploded on the scene with their magnificent makeovers in and around Waco, the charming husband-wife team opened **Magnolia Market at the Silos,** (601 Webster Ave., Waco; 254-235-0603; magnoliamarket.com/silos/) in 2015. Today, fans travel from all over the country to visit their retail complex that covers more than two acres just about three blocks west of the interstate. Two enormous, aged grain silos rise high in to the sky next to the big white barn that houses their store. Inside, find gardening items, flower vases, door mats, locally crafted metal signs laser-cut with sentiments such as, "She designed a life she loved," and "Your mountain is waiting so get on your way." There are books, T-shirts, clocks, kitchen wares, and hundreds of other home décor items, along with locally made jewelry. Outside, there is a vast green space with play areas for kids, a pretty vegetable and flower gardens, a walking path and a stage for the occasional musical concert hosted here. Cookies, cupcakes, and other goodies are stocked inside Silos Baking Co., and there are always at least eight food trucks on property, serving things like fresh crepes, pizza, hot dogs, sandwiches, juices and other edibles. Open Mon through Sat from 9 a.m. to 6 p.m.

Even before the Silos site became such a destination, there was interesting retail to be found in Waco, and now there are more and better shops than ever. Good choices include *The Findery* (501 S. Eighth St., 254-235-1777; the findery.net), housing a collection of shops on two floors of an 1898 brick building. Treasures include vintage industrial furniture and décor, clothes, jewelry and table settings. Nearby, a 1940s building houses *Salvage Sisters* (1708 Austin Ave., 254-235-0735; salvagesisterswaco.com), stocking refurbished and upcycled furniture. *Junque Queens* (1526 Austin Ave., 254-717-9760) also sells restored furniture, as well as clothing for women and kids, jewelry, and gifts for the wine lover.

Travelers enamored with Wild West history will love the *Texas Ranger Hall of Fame and Museum* (Fort Fisher Park, exit 335B off I-35; 254-750-8631; texasranger.org). Inside there's a replica of that 1837 Texas Ranger fort, as well as dioramas and displays detailing the history of the Rangers since Stephen F. Austin founded them in 1823. A firearms collection, Native American artifacts, and western art are exhibited here, headquarters for today's Company F of the Texas Rangers. Camping and picnic sites are available in the 37-acre park. Open 9 a.m. to 5 p.m. daily. A small admission fee is charged for ages 6 and up.

Waco's campiest attraction is the *Dr Pepper Museum and Free Enterprise Institute* (300 S. 5th St., Waco; 254-757-1025; drpeppermuseum.com), housed in the original bottling plant for Dr Pepper, a favorite Texas soda pop. The fountain drink was originally mixed at the Old Corner Drug Store here in the 1880s, when R. S. Lazenby, a Waco beverage chemist and drugstore customer, took interest in the new soda. After working with the formula for two years, he sold it commercially, and the formula is virtually unchanged. The original 1906 bottling plant–museum is on the National Register of Historic Places and features a restored period soda fountain and much Dr Pepper memorabilia, as well as audiovisual enhancement. To accommodate a significant uptick in visitors over the past few years, the museum expanded in 2016 by opening the Emerson Holt-Ted Getterman Exhibit Gallery to showcase more artifacts and visitor space for telling the Dr Pepper story. It's open Mon through Sat 10 a.m. to 4:15 p.m. and Sun noon to 4:15 p.m. A small admission fee is charged for ages 6 and up.

On the campus of *Baylor University*—chartered under the Republic of Texas in 1845, and now the world's largest Baptist university—is the marvelous *Armstrong Browning Library* (700 Speight St., Waco; 254-710-3566; baylor .edu/browninglibrary/). Inside find the largest collection of materials relating to Robert and Elizabeth Barrett Browning in existence, as well as 56 stained-glass windows depicting the famous pair's poetry. Open Mon through Fri from 9 a.m. to 5 p.m. and Sat from 10 a.m. to 2 p.m. Admission is free.

Sports-minded travelers will find the ***Texas Sports Hall of Fame*** (1108 S. University Parks Dr., Waco; 254-756-1633; tshof.org) of interest. Sports greats who competed on the fields, courts, and tracks of Texas are honored, including Shaquille O'Neal, Jackie Robinson, Jack Pardee, and "The Tyler Rose," Earl Campbell, whose high school letter jacket is featured here. There are auto racing uniforms worn by A. J. Foyt and Johnny Rutherford; racing silks; a crop and saddle blanket belonging to Willie Shoemaker; game jerseys worn by Nolan Ryan, Bob Lilly, Mean Joe Greene, and Roger Staubach; and Rogers Hornsby's 1926 St. Louis Cardinals uniform. Highlights from films of college and professional sports are shown in the museum's Tom Landry Theater. Open Mon through Sat from 9 a.m. to 5 p.m. and Sun from noon to 5 p.m. A small admission fee is charged for ages 6 and up.

As interest in Waco has boomed, so has its supply of worthwhile, home-grown food-and-drink options. Immediately north of downtown, ***Lula Jane's*** (406 Elm Ave., 254-366-0862; lulajanes.com) is a charming spot that serves coffee, pastries, and a small lunch menu that changes daily and always sells out before closing. ***Diamond Back's*** (217 Mary Ave., 254-757-2871, diamondback-swaco.com) in downtown looks and feels like a fancy steakhouse, but you're welcome here in boots and jeans for a beautiful T-bone, crab cake sliders, lovely sushi rolls, lobster bisque and wine flights from an award-winning list. ***The Hippodrome*** (724 Austin Ave., 254-296-9000, wacohippodrometheatre .com) is a downtown attraction that's both a handsome, historic movie house—showcasing classics and first-run films—and a restaurant that serves fun and funky burgers and other sandwiches, shrimp, salmon, and tacos. ***Dichotomy Coffee & Spirits*** (508 Austin Ave.; dichotomycs.com) doubles as both cool coffee and cocktail bar in a vintage downtown building. ***The Wine Shoppe*** (1800 Austin Ave., 254-30—7994, wacowineshoppe.com) sits just south of downtown, offering an intimate setting for tasting, sipping and buying wine from a selection of smart boutique choices; watch for delicious bites served gratis at about 6 p.m. One of the great success stories in Texas spirits in recent years is detailed at ***Balcones Distillery*** (225 S. 11th St., 254-755-6003, balconesdistilling.com), maker of single malts and other whiskeys winning international awards; visit for tours, tastings, and bottle sales.

By far, the most beautiful place to rest up in Waco is at ***Migel House*** (1425 Columbus Ave, 254-523-6611, migelhouse.com), a magnificent 1910 mansion made over in recent years to serve as a B&B. The owners spent two paintstaking years renovating the stately home, situated very close to downtown, saving exceptional woodwork, windows, stained glass (some Tiffany creations among

The Oldest Profession

The first legally regulated red-light district in Texas was, of all places, in Waco. It was also the second in the US, as Waco's leaders passed ordinances in 1889 that provided for the licensing of prostitutes and bawdy houses in a specified district called the Reservation or **Two Street.** The women working on Two Street were regularly examined by physicians, but their businesses were shut down after a campaign in 1917, and the last house burned in 1964.

these), fireplaces, light fixtures and much more. Three sizable suites in the main house and a fabulous carriage house with one-bedroom suite and a full kitchen are available, and a full breakfast is included. Among pleasures here is relaxing with coffee in the morning or wine in the late afternoon on either of two huge balconies.

For more information contact the Waco Convention & Visitor Bureau at (800) WACO-FUN or (254) 750-8696, or stop at the Tourist Information Center (take exit 335B off I-35); it's open Mon through Sat from 8 a.m. to 5 p.m. Visit wacoheartoftexas.com.

Outdoorsy types can find Texas's oldest state park within close reach of Waco. Mother Neff State Park, a 259-acre spread in the scenic Leon River Bottom, was founded in 1916. Drive south from Waco on I-35 about 20 miles, then turn west on FR 107 and go another 13 miles. You'll see the park upon reaching Highway 236. There's good hiking in the park's Upland Hills and in ravines with shady rock cliffs. There's good fishing and picnicking here, and photographers frequently find dawn and dusk subjects in raccoons, white-tailed deer, roadrunners, and armadillos. Call the park at (254) 853-2389 or visit tpwd.texas.gov.

Another 55 miles south of Waco on I-35, Salado (suh-LAY-doe) is a bucolic, creek-side stop in Bell County. Although only 2,200 residents call Salado home, it's a well-known jumping-off point for travelers en route to Austin. It was founded on a tract of land along the Chisholm Trail, originally in a grant by the state of Coahuila, Mexico, in 1830.

Scottish colonizer Sterling C. Robertson brought settlers to the area in the 1850s, and it fast became a thriving settlement with the opening of one gristmill inside the town limits and seven others in a 9-square-mile area. After the railroad bypassed Salado near the end of the century, however, 40-year-old Salado College closed, and the town nearly disappeared. Today there are 19 state and 18 national historic markers in town.

The town was named for central Texas's Salado Creek, one of five creeks so named in Texas, and this creek was the state's first designated natural landmark. The lovely waterway is fed by springs that are the northernmost of the huge Edwards Aquifer, surfacing here on the Balcones Fault. Within a few minutes' walk along the creek, it's easy to see why the town has become a retreat for artists, writers, historians, and craftspeople.

Some important folks have passed this way—Gen. Robert E. Lee, Gen. George Custer, and Gen. Sam Houston all stayed at an inn now called the **Stagecoach Inn**, in a shady, six-acre, creekside grove of old oak trees just east of the interstate on Main Street near Royal Street. In fact it was on the inn's front gallery that Sam Houston made one of his impassioned speeches, urging Texans not to secede from the Union.

texastrivia

The Burleson County town of Caldwell, west of Bryan–College Station, hosts the annual **Kolache Festival** in September to celebrate Czech pastries and heritage.

The Stagecoach was the town's reason for surviving when times were toughest, and it's still a destination for travelers. An extensive and recent renovation lasting nearly three years has transformed the 1861 landmark into a showplace once again. Seventy-five guest rooms with private balconies and patios offer a comfortable stay; the significantly renovated restaurant continues to serve Southern-style cooking but with updated twists. Among delicious picks, enjoy deviled eggs, deep-fried bacon, hushpuppies, chicken salad, pork chops, smoked beer can chicken, ribeye steak and, on Friday and Saturday evening, prime rib. Turkey and dressing, a longtime favorite, is served on Sunday. The restaurant is open Wednesday through Sunday at 416 S. Main St., Salado; (254) 947-5111; stage coachsalado.com.

The **Central Texas Area Museum** on Main Street, facing the Stagecoach Inn, is busiest during the **Gathering of the Scottish Clans,** held annually in mid-November; it's open Tues through Sat 10 a.m. to 4 p.m. The building that holds the museum is well over a century old, and exhibits inside detail the history of central Texas. There's also the Wee Scots Shop inside, selling items from Scotland such as kilts and tartans. For information call (254) 947-5232 or try their website at saladomuseum.org.

After lunch or a look through the museum, wander a few yards north to the creek and follow the bank just a bit to the right. Dislocated by a flood in 2010, **Sirena,** a bronze mermaid, now sits on a rock perch beside the stream, where you can see her exquisite and sad face as she eternally tries to remove a hook from her fin. The creek's grassy bank continues east and is traced by a road winding through *Pace Park,* a willow-shaded place to take a picnic and relax with a book.

Bed-and-breakfast accommodations in Salado have soared in number. Among the favorites is the *Rose Mansion* (903 Rose Way, 254-947-8200 or 800-948-1004; therosemansion.com), an 1870 Greek revival home in Victorian Oaks, just off Royal Street. In the main house there are 4 guest rooms, some of which have a private entrance, veranda, and/or fireplace; on the mansion's 2-acre grounds, lodging is also offered in comfortable, thoughtfully outfitted period cottages and cabins. Rates include a full homemade breakfast for two.

Among Salado shops to explore, find a selection in the historic downtown, along Main Street, offering herbal products, antiques, clothing, jewelry, artwork, For a complete listing call the *Salado Chamber of Commerce* at (254) 947-5040, or visit the website at salado.com.

Georgetown, a charming town of 67,000, sits about 20 miles south of Salado on I-35 at Highway 29. The Williamson County seat is home to *Southwestern University,* Texas's oldest private institution of higher learning, founded in 1840. The university's gorgeous stone buildings, immediately east of the courthouse square on University Avenue, are positively European in architecture. The copper-domed county courthouse is its own masterpiece, and the square is lined with more than 50 Victorian era buildings filled with gift shops, antiques stores, art galleries, and cafes. Here's where you'll find everything from a wine tasting room and a Native American hat maker to shops selling jewelry, knitting supplies, home décor, and one-of-a-kind pieces by local artisans. Art aficianados will find interest in the *Windberg Art Center* (7100 I-35 N., Georgetown, 512-869-5588, windbergartcenter.com), featuring original oil works (and prints, as well) by renowned artist Dalhart Windberg. Art classes are offered, as well. Before leaving Georgetown, check out the *Inner Space Cavern* (4200 S. I-35; 512-931-2283; innerspacecavern.com), a maze of fascinating underground rooms 80,000 years in the making.

texastrivia

The middle name of the father of Texas, Stephen F. Austin, was Fuller.

It's not unusual to find Austin-bound travelers staying overnight in Georgetown. When big Austin events, such as the springtime South by Southwest Music Festival and football games at the University of Texas, claim most of Austin's lodgings, people find Georgetown a good option. Among many guest houses and B&Bs, a favorite is *San Gabriel House* (1008 E. University Ave.; 512-930-0070; sangabrielhouse.com), a renovated 1908 mansion by the university. For more information contact the *Georgetown*

Convention & Visitors Bureau at (512) 930-3545 or (800) 436-8696; visit .georgetown.org.

For a memorable barbecue experience, head east from Georgetown on Highway 29 about 17 miles until you reach Highway 95. Turn south on Highway 95 and continue 7 miles to *Taylor*. Your destination is *Louie Mueller BBQ* (206 W. 2nd St., Taylor; 512-352-6206; louiemuellerbarbecue.com), which was, in the 1940s, a tiny tin shack in an alley behind the Mueller family's grocery. They opened the barbecue joint in order to sell meats that didn't move in the store, but before too long another barbecue stand was needed as the farming community grew. In 1959 the third, and present, location opened, and Bobby Mueller took over the business in 1974 when dad Louie retired. Bobby's son, Wayne, took over upon Bobby's untimely passing in 2008, but the legacy remains well-tended. You'll see its long and beloved history on walls plastered with scads of newspaper and magazine articles from across the nation heralding the exceptional food, smoked daily on-site in what can only be called a rustic setting. Meals start at about $9. Open Mon through Fri from 11 a.m. to 6 p.m., Sat 10 a.m. to 6 p.m., "or until we run out of food," which may be as early as 3 p.m. on Fri and Sat.

From Taylor head west on US 79, which takes you back to I-35. From there it's 18 miles south to Austin.

State Capital Country

Just 28 miles south of Georgetown lies *Austin,* the capital city, seat of Travis County, and haven for almost 950,000 people who love to kick back, enjoy great music, and eat some of the best food in the state. But the sun worshippers seen today around Barton Springs, the eternally cool spring-fed pool in Zilker Park, were not the first to find this a great place to hang around. Spaniards decided it was the best place to build a mission in 1730, and that was after Native Americans had been established here for centuries.

The 1800s saw the creation of the fledgling settlement named Waterloo, and new Republic of Texas president Mirabeau B. Lamar liked the place so much he moved the seat of government here. A few ego struggles moved the capital back and forth from the Houston area until 1844, and the town was eventually named for the father of Texas, Stephen F. Austin.

Since 1882, students of higher learning have found the *University of Texas*—with an enrollment today of around 51,000—and the Austin environs a place to stay beyond the traditional four years, thanks to numerous graduate programs and jobs in state government. The *LBJ Library and Museum,* at 2313 Red River St., Austin, which is part of the university, is fascinating even for those who were not fans of the late President Lyndon B. Johnson. Great detail is used in chronicling his career, and personal items are quite interesting: There are early home photos and a fourth-grade report card showing excellent grades but a C in deportment. There are engagement photos of LBJ and Claudia "Lady Bird" Taylor, and there's an intriguing letter on Lady Bird Taylor's letterhead indicating her fear that Lyndon was thinking of a life in politics. The museum (512-721-0200; lbjlibrary.org) is open daily from 9 a.m. to 5 p.m.

Just east of the interstate, the *French Legation Museum,* 802 San Marcos St., Austin, was regarded as ostentatious when built in 1841 for the French ambassador to the Republic of Texas. Today the French provincial cottage of Bastrop pine and French fitments seems modest, but it suited the arrogant Comte Alphonse Dubois de Saligny, if just for a short time. It was learned that the irritable chargé d'affaires held a fraudulent title, and that was after he'd shown great disdain for his Native American visitors and Austin neighbors. He passed most of his time in New Orleans, which he found much more enjoyable, and historians estimate he actually spent eight weeks at most in the Austin home. The museum is undergoing renovations. Be sure to check the Texas Historical Commission website before planning your visit; thc.texas.gov.

A few blocks to the southeast, *Cisco's,* at 1511 E. 6th St. (512-478-2420), is a true Austin institution, especially at breakfast. The Mexican bakery and café has small-town friendliness for regulars and newcomers alike; the eye-opening dishes to look for are huevos rancheros and huevos *migas,* two sassy egg dishes. If you like something a bit heavier, order a basket of *picadillos,* which are homemade rolls stuffed with spicy beef. Lunches include traditional Mexican plates and chicken-fried steak; for a sweet, check out the bakery case in front. It's open daily from 7 a.m. to 2:30 p.m.

Northwest of downtown, the *Elisabet Ney Museum,* at 304 E. 44th St. at Avenue H, Austin, awaits in one of the country's four existing studios of 19th-century sculptors. German immigrant Ney, a staunchly independent artist, came to the US in 1873 and built this studio in 1892, naming it Formosa (meaning "beautiful") after her studio in Europe. Some of her work is displayed

How Sweet It Is

Next time you're in the grocery store buying ingredients for your favorite baked goodies, pick up flavoring from *Adams Extract Co.,* founded in 1909. The Gonzales-based purveyor of good tastes produces more than extracts and flavorings, including the widely famous vanilla, as well as Jamaican rum, butter, almond, peppermint, and lemon—and 95 seasonings. Look for recipes at adamsextract.com.

here, while other pieces grace the Smithsonian National Museum of Art, various European palaces, and the Texas statehouse. Ney's friends and fans transformed Formosa into a museum soon after her death in 1907. It's been restored but retains the rustic nature Ney loved. Art classes and audiovisual presentations are held here throughout the year. Visit the museum Wed through Sat from noon to 5 p.m. and Sun from noon to 5 p.m. Call (512) 458-2255 or visit austintexas.gov for information.

If you need to be refreshed, head west of downtown to 400-acre *Zilker Park,* at Barton Springs Rd. on Lady Bird Lake, home to the renowned *Barton Springs Pool.* The 1,000-foot-long, rock-walled swimming hole—fed by Barton Springs, the fourth-largest natural springs in the state—is an oasis, always a chilly 68 degrees. In warm weather the grassy, shady lawns sloping down to the pool are covered by lounging or Frisbee-tossing sun lovers. Beyond the pool you'll find the city's *Botanical Gardens,* the *Austin Nature and Science Center,* a miniature train, canoe rentals, and the 10-mile-long Lady Bird Hike and Bike Trail. The park is also home to the annual and wildly popular *Austin City Limits* music festival in October. The park grounds are open daily from 5 a.m. to 10 p.m. The pool is closed between late January and mid-March; hours vary by season, but the website is updated annually with proper dates and hours; a small admission fee is charged. Call (512) 472-4914 or visit zilker park.org for pool and park information.

Right in the center of town on the UT campus, the *Harry Ransom Humanities Research Center,* at 21st and Guadalupe Streets, has a remarkable collection of treasures. Visitors may view one of the nation's five complete copies of the Gutenberg Bible, as well as the world's first photograph—shot in 1826 by Joseph Niepce—in the fascinating Photography Collection, which contains more than 5 million prints and negatives. The literary collection includes autographed editions by Dylan Thomas and E. M. Forster, among others; and the Hoblitzelle Theatre Arts Collection exhibits items ranging from Harry Houdini's personal correspondence to some Burl Ives folk recordings. The Ransom Center Galleries are open Tues, Wed, and Fri from 10 a.m. to 5 p.m.; Thurs from 10 a.m. to 7 p.m.; and Sat and Sun from noon to 5 p.m. The reading and viewing rooms are open Mon through Fri from 9 a.m. to 5 p.m. and Sat from 9 a.m. to noon. Call (512) 471-8944 or visit them on the web at hrc.utexas.edu.

Within walking distance of the Harry Ransom Center, the *Blanton Museum of Art* (200 E. Martin Luther King Blvd. and Congress Avenue; 512-471-7324; blantonmuseum.org) is the university's fine arts museum and is counted among the top 10 university art museums in the nation. The permanent collection includes more than 17,000 works spanning the history of Western civilization, from ancient to contemporary periods. The country's largest and most signifi-cant collection of Latin American art and the 20th-century American art col-lection, which includes the Mari and James Michener Collection of American Paintings, are featured. The gallery is open Tues through Fri from 10 a.m. to 5 p.m.; Sat from 11 a.m. to 5 p.m.; and Sun from 1 to 5 p.m. Admission is free on Thurs and the galleries stay open until 9 p.m. on the third Thurs of every month; a small admission fee is charged otherwise.

Just south of the university, ***Capitol Complex Visitor Center*** (E. 11th and Brazos; 512-305-8400; austintexas.gov) is well worth a visit. Built in 1857, the former General Land Office is the oldest government office building in Texas. A massive reimagining of the complex was underway at press time. Open Mon through Sat 9 a.m. to 5 p.m.; Sun noon to 5 p.m. Admission is free.

A few steps away, the ***State Capitol Building*** (11th and Congress Streets; 512-463-0063; tspb.state.tx.us) is a glorious work of Texas pink granite. When the legislature is in session, onlookers can watch policy history in the making. Free tours are given Mon through Fri from 8:30 a.m. to 4:30 p.m., Sat from 9:30 a.m. to 3:30 p.m., and Sun from noon to 3:30 p.m.

Just out of sight is the ***Governor's Mansion*** (1010 Colorado St., Austin; 512-305-8524; gov.texas.gov/first-lady/governors-mansion), which was once the belle of Colorado Street. It has been the cherished home of every Texas governor since 1856. But on June 8, 2008, a devastating fire ripped through the building, causing extensive damage to both the interior treasures and exte-rior beauty of this beloved landmark. After a massive fundraising effort for its restoration, the Mansion reopened for public tours in 2013. Tours lasting 20 minutes are offered on Wednesday, Thursday, and Friday afternoons by reser-vation only.

History buffs will be enthralled with the $80 million ***Bob Bullock Texas State History Museum*** (1800 N. Congress Ave., Austin; 512-936-8746 and 866-369-7108; thestoryoftexas.com). Surrounded by an exterior of six 11x16-foot concrete panels with sculpted bas-relief images that tell the story of Texas, the extraordinary museum is named for the beloved, late lieutenant gover-nor. It houses three floors of exhibits that chart Texas's path. Find artifacts, photographs, art, an IMAX theater, and much, much more. Take extra film to document those sculpted panels, which portray a Native American leading a conquistador through the Palo Duro Canyon, a salute to the Alamo battle's pur-pose, and Texas-size achievements in the worlds of cowboys, trains, cotton, oil, and space exploration. Look for the smallest details, such as the horned toad near the conquistador's horse and the armadillo skittering out from a moon crater. Open Mon through Sat from 9 a.m. to 5 p.m. and Sun from noon to 5 p.m. Admission is charged.

Also downtown is the **Mexic-Arte Museum** (419 Congress Ave., Austin; 512-480-9373; mexic-artemuseum.org), which supports and promotes the Mexican/Latino art community. Exhibitions have shown the work of more than 5,000 artists, including Diego Rivera, Frida Kahlo, Juan Soriano, Jean Charlot, and others. Permanent exhibits showcase prints, photographs, textiles, masks, and artifacts. Open Mon through Thurs from 10 a.m. to 6 p.m. and Fri and Sat from 10 a.m. to 5 p.m., Sun noon to 5 p.m.

One premier downtown music center is the $300 million **Austin City Limits** venue, which matches, if not surpasses, its fancy attached neighbor, the W Hotel. At the corner of West 2nd and Lavaca Streets, you'll see a steady stream of evening traffic flowing up a wide staircase into what looks like nothing more than a tall black box. Upstairs, iconic 1970s lettering tells you you've reached Austin City Limits, now officially called **ACL Live at The Moody Theater** (310 W. Willie Nelson Blvd.; 512-225-7999; acl-live.com). Naturally, Willie Nelson opened the venue with a two-night performance back in 2011 to great acclaim. The venue accommodates 2,750 guests for its music shows and plays host, as well, to *Austin City Limits* tapings for KLRU, the local PBS television affiliate that has made a brand out of the broadcast for more than 40 years. Performing acts have included Tony Bennett, Earth Wine & Fire, Lyle Lovett and many, many more, totaling roughly 60 to 100 concerts per year; KLRU uses the venue another 45 days per year, when tickets for tapings are free for an audience of about 800 people. To get those, you need to know someone or get lucky with drawings posted at acltv.com/upcoming-tapings/. For the live concert schedule, visit acl-live.com.

A few blocks north, at the corner of 7th Street and Congress Avenue, **The Contemporary Austin/Jones Center** (700 Congress Ave.; 512-453-5312) has become the city's ultimate destination for contemporary art exhibits and events. Occupying an 1851 building previously housing a pharmacy, movie theater, and department store, the Arthouse reopened after tripling its space to nearly 21,000 square feet of galleries, a screening room, 2 studios, a mezzanine lounge, and a rooftop event space with BYOB Wednesday-evening gatherings. Natural light and clever architectural innovations that utilize the building's bones offer artful appeal in which to enjoy a schedule of work from emerging and mid-career artists from around the world. Other venues of The Contemporary Austin are at Laguna Gloria and The Art School. Visit thecontemporary austin.org for more info.

When downtown, make your way to dine at **Lamberts Downtown Barbecue** (401 W. 2nd St.; 512-494-1500; lambertsaustin.com). Located inside the historic Schneider Brothers Building, this chic but very comfortable dining spot will win you over with wood-smoked Wagyu beef ribs, prime rib, and coffee-rubbed brisket, as well as dry-aged rib eye steaks, Hawaiian ahi tuna, and desserts like Dr Pepper cake and fried blackberry pie. There's live music upstairs, too.

Another downtown dining venue belongs to superstar chef David Bull, who earned his stripes as one of *Food & Wine's* Best New Chefs in 2003 when he was executive chef at the Driskill Hotel in Austin. Now, his brasserie-type **Second Bar + Kitchen** wins us over with its casual-yet-tony approach to lounge dining, with fine wines on tap (a pneumatic system), beet and goat cheese salad, fried pickles with gor-

gonzola cream, seared diver scallops over braised lentils, and pork belly-blue cheese-date pizza among the delectable choices. Outdoor seating offers a view of the capitol, right up Congress Avenue.(200 Congress Ave., Austin, 512-827-2750; secondbarkitchen.com). Just a few blocks east, **Easy Tiger** (709 E. 6th St., 512-614-4972; easytigeraustin.com) is an especially laid-back joint beloved for its housemade breads, pretzels, corned beef, cheese boards and a fabulous beer garden in which to enjoy those with craft beer and wisely chosen wines and spirits.

Right downtown, the **O. Henry Museum,** at 409 E. 5th St., occupies the quaint Victorian home briefly lived in by the master of short stories and surprise endings. His real name was William Sydney Porter, and he put out an extremely short-lived publication called the *Rolling Stone* from his Austin residence in the 1890s. The museum contains some of Porter's personal effects, including a yellowing original of his *Rolling Stone,* and various period pieces. Writing classes for adults and children are held here from time to time, and each spring brings the O. Henry Pun-Off World Championships, a good time for all. The home is open Wed through Sun from noon to 5 p.m. Call (512) 974-1398 for more information.

Head south from downtown by crossing **Lady Bird Lake** (formerly Town Lake) on the **Congress Avenue Bridge.** If you do so around dusk between March and October, you're likely to run into throngs of often hundreds of people hanging out to watch the millions of Mexican free-tailed bats that take flight from beneath the bridge in search of dinner each evening. In the booming area known as SoCo (South of Congress), just across the bridge, you'll find cool shops such as **Allens Boots** (1522 S. Congress Ave, 512-447-1413, allensboots.com) the flagship location of an iconic store for every manner of fabulous cowboy boots, hats, belts, buckles, jewelry, and more. At ***The Turquoise Door*** (1208 S. Congress Ave., 512-804-0618, theturquoisedoor.com), find beautiful jewelry and folk art from the Southwestern U.S. and Mexico. Visit the district during the evening for First Thursday each month, when all SoCo stores open their doors for a street party.

The coolest digs in town can be found at the ***Hotel San Jose*** (1316 S. Congress Ave., Austin; 512-853-2360 or 800-574-8897; sanjosehotel.com), a stylish inn carved from a 1930s tourist court that had gone to seed. The 40-room motel was turned into a model of retro refinement, with stained cement floors, comfy-modern furniture in the minimalist rooms, Indian cotton print spreads on thick platform beds, and butterfly chairs by the small, soothing pool. Potted cacti are everywhere, taking in the sun that peeks through handcrafted latillas and arbors along patios and walkways. Rooms come with high-speed Internet access, TV, phones, and clock radios with CD players. Guests can get same-day dry cleaning, on-site massage therapy, and beer and wine in the poolside bar after 5 p.m. Dog bowls and dog beds are provided at the front desk for your canine companions. Rates can be pricey, up to about $375 and include a healthful continental breakfast. Some evenings feature a special dinner event, too, and you can always find happy hour in the late afternoon. San Jose owner and hotelier extraordinaire Liz Lambert also owns two more wonderful lodgings in the district, including the ***Hotel Saint Cecilia*** (112 Acadmy Dr., Austin, 512-852-2400; hotelsaintcecilia.com) and the ***Austin Motel*** (1220 S. Congress Ave., Austin, 512-441-1157; austinmotel.com).

For an elegant lodging, visit the lovely ***Hotel Ella*** (1900 Rio Grande Ave., Austin; 800-311-1619; hotelella.com). A small luxury hotel with 48 rooms, this magnificent historic building is an easy walk to the capitol, Bob Bullock and Blanton Museums, and the Ransom Center. Packages can be crafted to include champagne, roses, and spa treatments. The on-site restaurant serves three meals a day in a light-filled room; the bar is cozy and chic, and the grounds are filled with a stunning collection of sculpture works.

To appreciate one of the state's finest sources of pride visit the ***Lady Bird Johnson Wildflower Center*** (4801 La Crosse Ave., Austin; 512-232-0100; wildflower.org), founded in 1982 by Lady Bird Johnson and called by *Texas Monthly* magazine her "visionary gift to Texas." Way back when her husband was still in the White House, Mrs. Johnson began her plan of beautifying America with roadside flowers. Her generous passion gave way to this extraordinary place, which remains the nation's only nonprofit organization committed to the preservation and reestablishment of native North American wildflowers, grasses, trees, shrubs, and vines in planned landscapes. Not only does the Wildflower Center grow more than 800 species of Texas native plants and 70 species of Texas native trees on the property, it also maintains one of the largest collections of information about native North American plants for interested visitors, but it also makes information available to more than 20,000 members across North America as well as landscape professionals and gardeners around the world. The visitor's gallery, research library, and 232-seat auditorium all add to the educational experience of this unique facility.

The grounds are open daily; hours vary according to season. There's a great store and a café on-site, too, also open daily. A small admission fee is charged. Children age 4 and under are admitted free.

Is it time yet to cool off again? If so, drive west from town on Highway 71 about 16 miles to FR 3238 and go south for 13 miles until you see **Hamilton Pool Nature Preserve,** a Travis County park at 24300 Hamilton Pool Road. This stunning, collapsed grotto has been a swimming hole since even old-timers can remember. There are 60-foot waterfalls cascading into the limestone-walled, jade green pool. County conservation authorities now require reservations for visiting the pool daily from Mar through Oct, and on weekends and holidays otherwise. You can picnic and hike there and book a guided nature tour. Open daily from 9 a.m. to 6 p.m.; there is a small admission fee, visitors over 62 enter free. For details call (512) 264-2740; parks.travis countytx.gov/find-a-park/hamilton-pool.

Because Austin calls itself the Live Music Capital of the World, you can count on finding dozens upon dozens of live music venues where you're likely to see groups you'll soon hear on the radio. To find out who's on stage when you visit, pick up a copy of the *Austin Chronicle,* an excellent alternative weekly, which keeps a good calendar online also, austinchronicle .com. Almost any day of the week, the best acts are found at **Antone's** (2015 E. Riverside Dr., Austin; 512-800-4628; antonesnightclub.com), also known as Austin's Home of the Blues; and at **Cedar Street** (208A W. 4th St., Austin; 512-495-9669; cedarstreetaustin.com), where martinis, imported cigars, and live jazz and swing are always served on the shady patio. The **Continental Club** (1315 S. Congress Ave., Austin; 512-441-2444; continentalclub.com) has become an exceedingly hip hangout and a place where the musical mix is decidedly eclectic. There might be a polka band on stage, or there might be a crooner

allnatural

Nature lovers will enjoy the **McKinney Roughs,** a blend of environmental laboratory and nature preserve found between Austin and Bastrop. The park was developed by the Lower Colorado River Authority in 1998 and offers an Environmental Learning Center. The park is at 1884 TX 71, just 8 miles west of Bastrop. Call (512) 303-5073.

singing the sort of lounge music that makes you crave a martini, shaken and not stirred.

To truly lighten up, unwind, and get centered, the destination of choice is the **Lake Austin Spa Resort** (1705 Quinlan Park Rd., Austin; 800-847-5637 or 512-372-7300; lakeaustin.com). A deluxe spa facility in a beautiful setting, the resort offers packages for three, four, or seven nights. Depending on your wants, your visit can include skin and body treatments; personal strength-training sessions; a nutrition consultation and healthy cooking classes; any assortment of fitness classes; body composition analysis; exercise options including kayaking, sculling, canoeing, and yoga; as well as meditation classes.

Widely regarded as one of the nation's finest spa retreats, LAS offers gorgeous suites, cottages, and rooms, many of which have private courtyards and/or porches with lovely views of the lake and hills. Landscaped gardens, a wonderful garden library, and the exquisite 25,000-square-foot Lakehouse Spa ensure comfort and restoration in one of the most unforgettable surroundings in Texas. Inquire about special seasonal offerings, which may include authors' forums, healthful gourmet cooking, and friends and mother-daughter programs. Three-night stays, including meals, fitness programs, and some spa treatments, start at about $1,900–$2,000 per person, based on two people in a room. Expensive, yes, but so well worth it.

Mexican food has been, since the 1920s, a leading reason to visit Austin. And there's such great diversity in the varieties of Mexican food, too. Tex-Mex is most famous, but the foods of Mexico's interiors cannot be overlooked. There are fancy restaurants serving beautiful Mexican dishes, such as **Fonda**

Austin Gone Batty

If Austin loves its wildflowers and live music, it's gone completely wild over its millions of nocturnal winged residents. A stupendous bat colony—now the largest in urban North America—roosting on crevices beneath the Congress Avenue Bridge over Lady Bird Lake has not only attracted a following of devoted observers, it's come under the watchful protection of Bat Conservation International (BCI).

From BCI, Austinites and visitors have learned that these gentle and incredibly sophisticated animals pose no threat to bat watchers—as long as no one tries to handle the bats. In fact on their evening flights from under the bridge, the Austin bats eat from 10,000 to 30,000 pounds of insects, including mosquitoes and numerous agricultural pests. Watching the nightly show of 1.5 million bats drag a flowing black curtain against the sunset is nothing less than spectacular; best viewing is from mid-March until early November, when the bats return to Mexico. As the nights become hotter and drier, the bats emerge earlier in the evening for food.

San Miguel (2330 W. North Loop, Austin, 512-459-4121; fondasanmiguel.com), a place that feels like someone's sophisticated villa deep inside Mexico, where lobster ceviche, grilled baby lamb chops with chile pasilla salsa, grilled beef tenderloin topped with a cheese enchilada and snapper Veracruz are among specialties. Dating from the 1950s, *Matt's El Rancho* (2613 S. Lamar Blvd., Austin, 512-462-9333; mattselrancho.com) is famous for its fajitas, nachos, chile con queso, and chiles rellenos topped with sour cream, raisins, and Texas pecans. At *El Chile Café y Cantina* (1809 Manor Rd., Austin, 512-457-9900; elchilccafe.com) puffy tacos, quesadillas, grilled shrimp and tortilla soup all deserve your attention. An old-school favorite, *Cisco's Bakery* (1511 E. 6th St., Austin, 512-478-2420; ciscosaustin.com) excels at super-simple Tex-Mex breakfast and lunch in the most welcoming, unpretentious setting in town.

Down-home food is found at *Stubb's Bar-B-Que* (801 Red River St., Austin; 512-480-8341; stubbsaustin.com), an outpost of a beloved Lubbock landmark housed within a historic brick building, offering a great deck under the stars. Beef ribs, brisket, chicken, coleslaw, pinto beans, potato salad, and cold beer spell success. Open Mon through Thurs from 11 a.m. to 10 p.m., Fri and Sat until 11 p.m., and Sun until 9 p.m. Meals are about $7 to $15. Two yesteryear burger joint deserve mention, too: *Hut's Hamburgers* (806 W. 6th St., Austin, 512-472-0693; hutsfrankandangies.com) is a 1960s throwback, serving burgers made from Texas beef, along with bison and vegan burgers; and *Dirty Martin's Place* (2808 Guadalupe St., Austin 512-477-3173; dirtymartins .com) is a 1920s relic with a few stools at the counter and picnic tables outside where you tuck into an old-fashioned burger with assorted trimmings, tator tots, Nathan's Famous dogs and a variety of shakes and fountain drinks.

For more information on Austin, contact the visitor bureau at 512-474-5171 or visit austintexas.org. Find the visitor center at 602 E. 4th St.

For some fine Texas barbecue, head east from town, following US 290 to US 183, traveling south about 30 miles to Lockhart, seat of Caldwell County and home to just over 13,500 residents. *Kreuz* (pronounced *krytes*) *Market,* a veritable institution at its location on US 183 (619 N. Colorado St.), is a cultural and gastronomical experience that will be long remembered.

Lines are long before the noon lunch hour, and steady streams of people file through the searing-hot, smoky pit room where your barbecue is cut to order by weight. They'll pile your request for smoked brisket, pork brisket, pork chops, or sausage onto brown butcher paper, along with a stack of white bread, which you then take over to a counter in the lunchroom to get "the fixin's," such as sliced onion, tomato, cheese, avocados, jalapeños, and pickles. If you ask for barbecue sauce, be forewarned that you may insult the proprietors—the meat is so tender and flavorful that none is needed. There are, however, bottles of hot pepper sauce on the tables for fire-eaters. Lunch is usually $5 to $10, plus cheap beer or soda. Kreuz's is open Mon through Sat from 10:30 a.m. to 8 p.m. Call (512) 398-2361 for details or visit kreuzmarket.com.

If it's a typically pretty day, get that barbecue to go. Head east 26 miles on FR 20 to Highway 71 and follow Highway 71 east 8 miles to **Bastrop**, where you can have a quiet picnic at **Bastrop State Park**. There, in 5,900 acres of rolling land studded with the mysterious "Lost Pines," is a tranquil and rich nature sanctuary along Lake Bastrop to be enjoyed for more than a mere day. Fishing, camping, hiking, golf, and nature study are big draws at the park, as are rustic but comfortable cabins, built by the Civilian Conservation Corps and recently restored. The park withstood a horrific fire in 2011 but is rebounding beautifully. Find the park just a mile east of Highway 71's junction with Highway 21. Call (512) 321-2101; tpwd. texas.gov.

The town of Bastrop is the Bastrop County seat and home to about 6,000 residents and several charming shops. The **Bastrop County Historical Museum** at 904 Main St., Bastrop, occupies a storefront on the main drag and houses the town's visitor center, too. Among miscellaneous and interesting manuscripts, pioneer collections, and Native American artifacts are silver spoons that are said to have been crafted from coins taken from Santa Anna at the Battle of San Jacinto. Here you can find information about everything to see and do in town, as well as find good lodging recommendations. Call (512) 303-0904 for information; bastropcountyhistoricalsociety.com or visit bastroptx.com.

The art scene in Bastrop is creating its own niche. At **Deep in the Heart Foundry** (405 S. Jackson St.; 512-321-7868; deepintheheart.net), you can see bronze sculpture in process, which holds fascinating at every step. At **Lost Pines Art Center** (1204 Chestnut St., Bastrop, 512-3218055; lostpinesartcenter .org), you'll see work in several galleries from a vibrant local art community. The **Abri Gallery** (932 Main St.; 512-985-6403; abrigallery.com) houses an unparalleled collection of original Persian and American art, including world-class handmade rugs. Abri's owners also offer **Lost Pines Art Bazaar** (603 Chestnut St.; 512-985-6403; lostpinesartbazaar.com), filled with beautiful Persian rugs and Texas sculpture pieces. Stop in also at **Larryland Music** (601 Chestnut St., Bastrop, 512-321-3325) to see a treasure trove of vintage musical instruments.

There's good dining to be enjoyed in Bastrop, too: **Maxine's on Main** (905 Main St.; 512-303-0919; maxinescafe.com) serves up hubcap-size pancakes, as well as blue-plate specials and great slices of pie. Neighbor's **Kitchen & Yard,** next door to Larry's (601 Chestnut St., 512-988-7036; neighborstx.com) sits on the Colorado River banks and serves up appetizers like black-eyed pea

Mystery Man

Sometimes people are not what they seem to be, even if they offer impeccable credentials. This was certainly the case with **Baron de Bastrop,** for whom the town 30 miles east of Austin was named. Claiming to be Felipe Enrique Neri, an important Dutch nobleman, the "baron" appeared in Texas in 1805; obtained a colony grant; established a freighting business; was named negotiator with the Mexican government for Stephen F. Austin's original Anglo-American colony; was elected representative to the Mexican state of Coahuila, which included Texas; and helped establish the port of Galveston. In reality, he was **Philip Hendrik Nering Bogel,** born in Dutch Guiana to ordinary Dutch parents. He moved to Holland, where he was a tax collector accused of embezzlement before fleeing to Texas for a life as an imposter. When he died in 1827, he didn't leave enough money to cover burial expenses, and there was still a reward offered in Holland for his capture. Interestingly, Bastrop was named for him a full decade after his death.

hummus with tortilla chips, wings in a variety of sauces, and Greek salad, plus assorted sandwiches and pizzas; there's usually live music on tap, too.

East of Bastrop, the **Hyatt Regency Lost Pines Resort** (512-308-1234; lostpines.hyatt.com) offers a vacation in itself. Lying adjacent to McKinney Roughs State Natural Area on the scenic Colorado River, the resort has lovely, comfortable rooms and more outdoor activities than you can imagine. You can opt for a morning of archery and shooting clays, then an afternoon filled with hiking, kayaking, river rafting, horseback riding, treatments at Spa Django, or sensational golf at the Wolfdancer Golf Club, or you can simply lounge by one of three swimming pools. There are five dining venues (enjoy everything from omelets to roasted salmon at Firewheel; burgers, beer, and live music at Shellers; poolside sandwiches and margaritas at Old Buck's Place; exquisite prime filet and Dungeness crab at Stories; and black bean chili at Major Neighbors Grill) and two watering holes at the resort. Just be sure to go sit outside by one of the fire pits after the sun goes down for a little communion with nature under the stars.

If you decide to skip Bastrop, take US 183 south from Lockhart about 30 miles to **Gonzales,** appropriately nicknamed the Cradle of Texas Independence. Founded in 1825, Gonzales is the site where, a decade later, the first shot for Texas's independence was fired. The "Come and Take It" cannon, which fired that fateful shot on October 2, 1835, is displayed at the **Gonzales Memorial Museum,** on East Street at Lawrence Street, a grand structure built for the Texas Centennial and given to Gonzales by the state. Look about five minutes north of the town square for a good lunch at **Baker Boys BBQ** (1404

N. Sarah Dewitt Dr., Gonzales, 830-519-4400), specializing in deeply smoked brisket, sausage and stuffed chicken legs, homemade desserts and, on Friday, fried fish plates.

Birders making the trek this way will want to stop at **Palmetto State Park** (north of Gonzales about 12 miles on US 183; 830-672-3266; tpwd. texas.gov). Part of the Great Coastal Birders Trail, this 263-acre park is on the spring-fed San Marcos River and features natural artesian springs that have been thought for centuries to have healing powers. Numerous nature trails follow the steep banks of the river and wend through a palmetto swamp.

texastrivia

There are 5,000 species of wild-flowers in Texas. The **bluebonnet** is the state flower.

From Gonzales, make a worthwhile detour east via Alternate US 90, driving about 20 miles to **Shiner,** a tiny town in Lavaca County and home to the beautiful old **Spoetzl Brewery.** This is where **Shiner Beer** is "brewed with an attitude," as the slogan goes. Shiner Bock and Shiner Honey Wheat have become extremely popular beers in Texas, and demand across the country is growing. The brewery was founded by Kosmos Spoetzl, one of several German-Czech immigrants who came to this part of the state in 1909. Kosmos brought his Bavarian brewing recipes, and today the brewery produces Kosmos Reserve Lager in his honor.

Brewery tours, which end with complimentary tastings of fresh, cold beer, are given on weekdays at 11 a.m. and 1:30 p.m. or by appointment by calling (361) 594-3852. There's also the Spoetzl Brewery Gift Shop/Museum, where a video offers the history of the brewery. Find them on the web at shiner.com.

The Republic of Texas

To explore deep into Texas's past, begin your journey by driving east on Highway 71, stopping just 32 miles down the road at the hamlet on the mighty Colorado River called **La Grange.** Seat of Fayette County and home to 4,500 residents, La Grange dates to 1831, when the road passing through was simply a buffalo trail. Historical markers abound—at the old railroad depot, the old county jail, the 1890s courthouse, the vintage Episcopal church—and the local historical route called Texas Pioneer Trail courses through town.

Of particular interest is **Kreische Brewery State Historical Site** and **Monument Hill,** 3 miles south of the town center and reached via a beautiful drive on Spur 92 (979-968-5658; tpwd.texas.gov). Vestiges of a stone brewery and home erected by stonemason Heinreich L. Kreische, a German immigrant who arrived in 1840, mark the first commercial brewery in Texas and one that produced more than 700 barrels a year in its prime. Tours of the brewery and ruins are conducted on Sat and Sun; hours vary according to season. A small admission fee is charged in addition to admission to Monument Hill, also part of the state park.

The latter is a resting place of the Battle of Salado martyrs and victims of the tragic Black Bean Episode of the Mier Expedition, all during the Mexican War. The dramatic monument is a 48-foot creation of stone, bronze, and polychrome. There's a visitor center as well as an interpretive trail, a nature trail, picnic sites, and a playground. The monument park is open daily from 8 a.m. to 5 p.m. A small admission fee is charged for adults; it's free for children. For more details call (979) 968-5658.

If it's spring, endless vistas of bluebonnets, orange and yellow Indian paintbrushes, and pink primroses will be your vivid companions as you continue northeast on Highway 159 just 15 miles to **Round Top.** This wide spot in the Fayette County road seems small, with fewer than 100 residents, but it packs a cultural punch. The miniature town was once called Jones Post Office back in 1835, but its new name came from the Round Top Academy, which operated here from 1854 to 1867, with tuition costing $10 per semester.

Today, on what passes for a town square, there's **Royer's Round Top Cafe** (979-249-3611; royersroundtopcafe.com), a lively cottage setting for everything from rack of lamb and red snapper to fabulous homemade pies. Bordering the square's east side, **Henkel Square** is an impressive, growing collection of homes and buildings dating from 1820 to 1870. Furnishings and artistic decor are examples of the period's Anglo and German influences. Under new ownership, the square is now a collection of shops and boutiques where you can find freshly roated coffee, fine art, home décor, candles, crystals, and elegant clothing. Open Wed through Sun at 201 N. Live Oak, Round Top, 979-249-5840; henkelsquareroundtop.com.

Road warriors who love shopping should not miss a visit to the **Junk Gypsy Store** (1215 S. Texas Highway 237, Round Top, 979-249-5865; gypsyville.com), the brick-and-mortar place for the self-style "purveyors of the world's finest junk." Filled with boots, jewelry and furniture, it's an experience unto itself. London native Rachel Ashwell, founder of Shabby Chic, has a couture shop on 46 acres called **The Prairie by Rachel Ashwell** (5808 Wagner Rd., 979-836-4975; theprairiebyrachelashwell.com); it's surrounded by well-appointed B&B cottages and lodges, too. Another combination of shopping and lodging is **The Vintage Round Top** (1450 N. Texas Highway 237, 713-859-5993; thevintage roundtop.com), a pair of cottages that blend elegance and boho, thanks to the owners, who deal in French antiques.

Five blocks north, on Highway 237, **Festival Hill** is the site of the **International Festival-Institute** (248 Jaster Rd., 979-249-3129; festivalhill.org). A concert weekend is scheduled monthly, and summer is devoted to popular performances by institute students with visiting orchestras and string quartets. Festival Hill is occupied by a marvelous array of restored period buildings; even if you're not planning to attend a concert, it's a gorgeous place to explore and photograph.

It's only a 4-mile drive northeast of Round Top on FR 1457 and 2714 to the **Winedale Historical Center,** a picture seemingly realized from Grant Wood's *American Gothic.* Perfectly restored farms, ranch houses, plantation homes, log cabins, smokehouses, and barns represent more of the Anglo and German heritage prevalent in Texas. The center is an extension of the University of Texas, and it's open for tours weekdays by appointment. On Sat tours run at 11 a.m. and 1 and 3 p.m.

Winedale's many events throughout the year include a summer Shakespeare Festival, Oktoberfest, Christmas open house, and spring craft exhibition. Some events cost a few dollars for admission, but others are free. Call (979) 278-3530 or visit cah.utexas.edu for complete information and appointments.

Lodging in and around Round Top has exploded in recent years. There are dozens of B&B choices within a few miles of the town square, ranging from restored period farmhouses to newer cabins and guesthouses built on area farms. Find the selection at roundtop.org. Be warned, however, that lodging is nearly impossible to find on antiques show weekends in late March/early April and late September/early October, when thousands of dealers and buyers descend on this normally quiet burg.

From Round Top, drive north on Highway 237 about 8 miles and turn east on US 290, continuing 16 miles to **Brenham.** Yum—you've reached the home of the **Little Creamery, Blue Bell Ice Cream,** just 2 miles southeast on Loop FR 577 (1101 S. Blue Bell Rd., Brenham; 800-327-8135; bluebell.com). *Time* magazine called it the best ice cream in the world, a small-town giant that now sells ice cream in 19 states. (Though closed for a period during 2015 and 2016 due to a Listeria outbreak, the ice cream makers' loyal fans remained true to the brand.) Visitors are treated to a film and a look at production from an observation deck on weekdays. You can enjoy a scoop in the ice cream parlor and browse the company store, too. It's closed on weekends.

Brenham, seat of Washington County—birthplace of the Republic of Texas—has a charming downtown to explore. In addition to plenty of antiques shops, clothing boutiques, home interiors stores, art galleries, and a silversmith's shop, there are plenty of good places to eat. Favorites include **Funky Art Café** (202 W. Commerce St., Brenham; 979-836-5220; funkyartcafe.com), serving soup, burgers, salads, and crab cakes; and *BT Longhorn Steakhouse* (205 S. Baylor St., Brenham, 979-421-6700; btlonghornsteakhouse.com), with a menu of gumbo, salads, chicken tenders and New York strip in a saloon setting. For more information contact the *Washington County Convention & Visitor Bureau,* 314 S. Austin St., Brenham; (979) 836-3695 or (888) BREN-HAM; brenhamtexas.com.

A moving picture of Texas's past is seen in *Independence,* just an 11-mile drive north of Brenham on FR 50. The Washington County settlement of 150 was founded in 1824 by one of Stephen F. Austin's original 300 families. A town square was designed for the Washington County seat, but Brenham won the hotly contested vote by just two.

Old Baylor Park, ½ mile west on flower-peppered FR 390, holds the ruins of Old Baylor University and the restored home of John P. Coles, the founding settler. Also on FR 390, you'll find the *Sam Houston Homesite,* noted by a granite marker. A few yards away, there's *Mrs. Sam Houston's Home*—one of the earliest surviving examples of Greek revival architecture. Mrs. Houston bought it for herself and her eight children after her husband died in 1863. Sam Houston Jr., other Texas pioneers, and veterans of wars from the American Revolution to World War II are buried in the town cemetery.

It's but another 10 miles east on US 290 from Brenham to *Chappell Hill,* a charming Washington County township of 300 established in 1847 amid rolling pastures of horse farms, wildflowers, and twisting post oak trees. The town, filled with antiques shops, is close to *Washington-on-the-Brazos,* the legendary town where in 1836 the Texas Declaration of Independence was signed and where the constitution of the new Republic of Texas was drafted, also in 1836. From 1842 until 1846, Washington was also the capital of the republic, and the town prospered as a commercial center for the cotton-rich Brazos Valley.

Today that heritage is memorialized at the *Star of the Republic Museum at Washington-on-the-Brazos State Park,* on FR 1155, 18 miles north of Chappell Hill. The museum is indeed star-shaped, and its exhibits offer interpretation of Texas as a separate and exclusive nation as well as its journey to statehood. Seasonal exhibitions, audiovisual presentations, and demonstrations of early 19th-century life are often scheduled. The museum is open daily from 10 a.m. to 5 p.m. Call (936) 878-2461 for details or check starmuseum.org.

The state historical park, which underwent an extensive $6 million expansion, contains a portion of the historic town site; a reconstruction of Independence Hall; the home of Anson Jones, Texas's last president; an outdoor amphitheater; and a pecan grove doubling as a picturesque picnic area. Hours vary for the different sites, and special events are held on the Sunday closest to March 2, Texas's Independence Day. For information call (936) 878-2214 or visit tpwd.texas.gov.

Just south of Chappell Hill sits *Texas Ranch Life* (866-839-2775; texas ranchlife.com), a guest ranch on Lonesome Pine Ranch. Eight historic homes— all expertly restored—and two modern dwellings are situated on 1,600 rolling acres populated by native pecan trees and roamed by herds of longhorn cattle and buffalo. The homes offer something for everyone—a romantic escape or a place where girlfriends or a family can enjoy lots of space to hang together. While on the ranch guests can fish on any of 11 lakes, take riding lessons and head out on trail rides, participate in cattle roundups, enjoy hayrides and chuck wagon meals, hunt dove or quail (in season), go bird watching, or simply enjoy long, quiet walks. Breakfast is included.

From Washington-on-the-Brazos, head north on Highway 90 about 20 miles to the town of *Anderson,* a historic town of just 300, established in 1834 on La Bahia Road, the ancient Indian trail that stretched from Louisiana through Texas and was used by Spanish explorers. There are numerous charming buildings and homes from the post–Civil War and Victorian period, including the delightful 1891 Grimes County Courthouse. Don't miss an opportunity to see *Fanthorp Inn State Historic Park* (936-873-2633; tpwd.texas.gov) in Anderson, a pre–Republic of Texas log inn built in 1834. It's said that Texas notables such as Sam Houston, Anson Jones, Jefferson Davis (who became president of the Confederacy), and generals Stonewall Jackson and Robert E. Lee stayed here. There are stagecoach rides on the second Saturday of each month from 11 a.m. to 3 p.m.; a small admission fee is charged. The inn is open for tours daily. A small admission fee is charged.

From Anderson take FR 244 northwest about 10 miles to TX 30, then head west on Highway 30 another 31 miles to *Bryan–College Station.* Always referred to in hyphenated form, the attached cities spread over the gentle hills of Brazos County. Founded by Stephen F. Austin's colonists between 1821 and 1831, the duo has grown in leaps and bounds with Texas A&M University. Established in 1876 as the state's first public institution for higher education, in 1996 it became the school with the nation's largest undergraduate enrollment, claiming more than 50,000 students.

If the university is College Station's heartbeat, the university's magnificent heart and soul is the *George Bush Presidential Library Center,* dominating the west campus.

Celebrating its 20th anniversary in 2017, this remarkable facility tells a compelling story of the 41st president of the US. Interactive exhibits show his courage and dedication through artifacts such as film, photographs, and documents enhanced by music, sound effects, interactive video, and computerization. War aficionados will be riveted by the World War II Avenger Torpedo Bomber display, while history buffs will be drawn to the 1947 Studebaker and a section of the Berlin Wall. You can sit in a replica of President Bush's Oval Office, walk through his Camp David office, and take part in a National Security briefing in the White House Situation Room. Take time to roam the grounds, too: Just to the left of the entrance of the museum, see a magnificent sculpture work called *The Day the Wall Came Down,* a bronze by artist Veryl Goodnight of five horses (a little larger than lifesize) leaping over actual pieces of the Berlin Wall. President Bush was in office when the wall was breached. Behind the museum-library is the beautiful Barbara Bush Rose Garden, very close to the site where the former first lady was laid to rest in April 2018. For more information and hours, call the center at (979) 691-4000 or visit bush41.org.

Also of significant interest on the Texas A&M campus is the *Sam Houston Sanders Corps of Cadets Center* (979-862-2862; corps.tamu.edu), which offers a look at the history and future of the illustrious Corps of Cadets. Bronzes of seven Aggie Medal of Honor winners and the Metzger Sanders Gun Collection are on permanent display here. The center is open Mon through Fri from 8 a.m. to 5 p.m. Open weekends only for special events. Admission is free.

In Bryan, which is immediately adjacent to College Station on the east, see the marvelous *Carnegie Center of Brazos Valley History* (111 S. Main St., Bryan; 979-209-5630; bcslibrary.org/carnegie/). Built in 1903 with funds from the Carnegie Foundation, it is the oldest existing Carnegie Library in Texas.

A trio of boutique hotels makes overnighting in Bryan-College Station a distinct pleasure now. Thanks to the university's growth and a boom in the local bio-tech industry, the demand for more sophisticated lodgings has been answered. The good news is that though these three hotels bear varying degrees of sophistication, the hospitality is of the downhome sort we look for in the heart of Texas. In Bryan, the *Stella Hotel* (4100 Lake Atlas Dr., Bryan, 979-421-4000; thestellahotel.com) is a 176-room beauty with views to the east at Kyle Field just four miles distant and a view westward at a lovely lake and the *Traditions Club,* a Jack Nicklaus-designed golf course. A midweek farmers market buzzes around Lake Walk, just outside the hotel's front door. The Stella's restaurant Campfire, coffee shop called POV, chic pool setting and comfortable bar Hershel's makes you want to linger for days. In College Station, *Cavalry Court* (200 Century Court, College Station, 979-485-5586; cavalrycourt .com) is a 140-room modern inn paying homage to the university's revered corps with a 1950s American military vibe in the décor. The hotel's Canteen is a casual-hip bar and grill opening onto both a courtyard and a pool. Across the driveway, *The George* (180 Century Court, College Station, 979-485-5638; the georgetexas.com) balances luxury and comfort. Among notable reasons to visit is to see contemporary art, such as the lobby wall fashioned from thousands of red, white and blue book spines arranged to form an image of the Texas flag. The on-site restaurant, Poppy, is an upscale dinner destination bearing a family nickname of President George H. W. Bush.

For an indulgent afternoon head to ***Messina Hof Wine Cellar*** (4545 Old Reliance Rd., Bryan; 979-778-9463; messinahof.com). One of the most awarded premium wineries in Texas, Messina Hof produces numerous wines at its state-of-the-art winemaking facility. The visitor center, which includes a tasting room and deli, is housed in part of the reconstructed former home of Ambassador Williamson S. Howell and is filled with antiques and memorabilia. Next door is the Vintage House restaurant, which is open for lunch from Thurs to Sun and dinner Wed to Sat. Call for the schedule of free tours and tastings daily at the winery. A pretty bed-and-breakfast with 10 private rooms is on-site, too.

For more information on Bryan–College Station, contact the Convention and Visitor Bureau at (979) 260-9898 or (800) 777-8292 or visit experiencebcs .com.

Other Places to Stay on the Brazos-Republic Trail

AUSTIN

Lone Star Court
10901 Domain Drive
(512) 814-2625
lonestarcourt.com
A boutique hotel at the Domain is a fancy version of the vintage motor court, offering 123 retro rooms, luxurious Egyptian linens, free continental breakfast, and an outdoor fire pit.

South Congress Hotel
1603 S. Congress Ave.
(512) 920-6405
southcongresshotel.com
Super contemporary but equally comfortable, this inn offers 71 rooms, and 12 suites with fabulous views of Soco and Travis Heights. Among its attractions is a great lobby bar, all-day restaurant Café No Se, dinner and brunch restaurant Central Standard, coffee-juice-bakery shop called Manana, and the 12-seat omakase restaurant Otoko.

BASTROP

Pecan Street Inn
1010 Pecan St.
(512) 321-3315
pecanstreetinn.com
This eclectic Queen Anne–Gothic home is a century old and is included on the National Register of Historic Places. Each of the 5 guest rooms, 4 of which have private baths, has a fireplace and a coffeemaker. The specialty breakfast dish is pecan waffles with Grand Marnier strawberries.

BRENHAM

Ant Street Inn
107 W. Commerce St.
(979) 836-7393 or
(800) 481-1951
antstreetinn.com
A sensational lodging
that would impress even
the most finicky traveler,
this 15-room inn offers
romance packages, among
many. Exquisite antiques,
upholstery, bed linens,
and attention to detail. A
full breakfast is offered to
guests every night and to
the public on weekends.

GONZALES

St. James Inn
723 Saint James St.
(830) 672-7066
stjamesinn.com
This 1914 Greek revival
home has 3 floors, 0
working fireplaces, 5 guest
rooms, 2 suites, 7 private
baths, and period antiques.
Guests are fed a full
breakfast and can request
candlelight dinners, too.

SHINER

Shiner Country Inn
1016 N. Avenue E
(Business US 90)
(361) 594-3335
shinercountryinn.com
This updated country
motel has a particularly
friendly spirit as well as in-
room phones, high-speed
Internet, and satellite TV.

WACO

Judge Baylor House
908 Speight Ave.
(254) 756-0273
Heartoftexasbb.com
There are 5 guest rooms
available, all with private
baths. Some rooms have
sleeper sofas, in addition
to beds, and kids and
pets are welcome. A full
breakfast is served.

WHITNEY

Arrowhead Resort
Off Highway 22, 106
Arrowhead Rd.,
between Whitney and Lake
Whitney Dam, near
Hillsboro
(800) 412-3044
cabinonlakewhitney.com
Cabins, swimming pool,
volleyball, horse shoes,
and lake sports. Peacocks
roaming the grounds enjoy
being fed by guests.

Other Places to Eat on the Brazos-Republic Trail

AUSTIN

Franklin Barbecue
900 E. 11th St.
Austin
(512) 653-1187
franklinbbq.com
The late Anthony Bourdain
said it was the best
barbecue he'd ever tasted,
and owner-pitmaster Aaron

Franklin won the James
Beard Award for Best Chef
Southwest for his work
here. Lines are notoriously
long and the food sells
out every day by mid-
afternoon. It's a humble
place with rich rewards for
lovers of smoked meat and
craft beer.

La Condesa
400 W. 2nd St.
(512) 499-0300
Lacondesa.com
Not your ordinary Mexican
joint, this stylish, colorful
downtown favorite soothes
with ceviches and thrills
with grilled quail in green
tomato marmalade, duck
in Oaxacan mole, and
handcrafted cocktails.

Scholz Garten
1607 San Jacinto St.
(512) 474-1958
scholzgarten.net
Established in 1866, this
beer garden calls itself the
oldest tavern in Texas.
Regardless, it's great fun.

Threadgill's
6416 N. Lamar St.
(512) 451-5440
threadgills.com
Need some comfort?
Here's the place for
fried Mississippi catfish,
chicken-fried steak, meat
loaf, mashed potatoes,
and country vegetables.
Meals start at about $9.
(Another location is at
301 W. Riverside St.;
512-472-9304.)

BRENHAM

Brazos Belle
Main Street in Burton
(16 miles west of Brenham
via US 290)
(979) 289-2677
brazosbellerestaurant.com
An 1870s-era general
store is now occupied
by a comfortable, casual
restaurant whose owner-
chef is a French native
and a former chef at the
Four Seasons in Houston.
Excellent choices include
steak Delmonico and
cassoulet with duck and
sausage. Open for dinner
on weekends and Sunday
lunch.

CHAPPELL HILL

Bevers Kitchen
Main Street
(979) 836-4178
bevers-kitchen.com
A cute, colorful country
café, this great little
find does good home
cooking, from meat loaf to
cobbler. Reservations are
recommended.

GEORGETOWN

The Monument Cafe
500 S. Austin Ave.
(512) 930-9586
themonumentcafe.com
Exceptional home cooking
includes chicken-fried
steak, pan-fried pork
chops, cheese enchiladas

with two-alarm chili, and a
massive breakfast menu.

ROUND TOP

The Oaks Restaurant
Highway 237 at Warrenton
(979) 249-5909
oaksfamilyrestaurant.com
Informal, friendly family
restaurant offers fried
butterflied shrimp, burgers,
steaks, baby-back ribs,
and pizzas, as well as all-
you-can-eat boiled shrimp
on Sun.

SALADO

Cathy's Boardwalk Café
8 Old Town Rd.
(254) 947-8162
A good shopping stop
for homemade soup,
sandwiches and special like
salmon burger and steak
Diane.

WACO

George's
1925 Speight Ave.
(254) 753-1421
georgesrestaurant.com
Generations of Baylor
alumni can attest to the
worthiness of the burgers,
chicken-fried steak, grilled
chicken sandwiches, and
exceptional cold beer at
this casual hangout, just off
the interstate.

Magnolia Table
2132 S. Valley Mills Dr.
(254) 235-6111
Chip and Joanna Gaines
of HGTV's *Fixer Upper*
fame renovated the former
icon, Elite Café, making
it over into a breakfast,
brunch, and lunch spot.
Sandwiches, burgers, and
pies are among menu
picks.

**Schmaltz's Sandwich
Shop**
105 S. Fifth St.
(254) 753-2332
schmaltzssandwichshop
.com
Small and super-friendly,
this low-key downtown
spot makes delicious
sandwiches in the fashion
of muffalettas, with turkey,
ham, cheeses, or other
varied ingredients.

Vitek's BBQ
1600 Speight Ave.
(254) 752-7591
viteksbbq.com
Since 1915, this family
operation begun as a
butcher shop in nearby
Granger has been a
popular pit barbecue joint
for several generations
of devoted diners. The
signature Gut Pak is a
crazy sandwich of chopped
beef, sausage, beans,
cheese, Fritos corn chips,
pickles and jalapenos on
a bun.

The Gulf Coast

The lengthy, shimmering curve of seashore known as the Gulf Coast of Texas has long been a place of fascination for visitors. The Spaniards arrived in 1528, when Cabeza de Vaca shipwrecked just off Galveston Island; he was followed by conquistadors looking for fabled treasures in cities of gold, and although none was discovered, the Spanish priests established missions as necessary for colonization.

The French came, too, led by the explorer La Salle, who landed in 1685 at Indianola, which became a thriving port—German colonists came through here in the 1840s—but it's now only a ghostly stretch of sand. French buccaneer Jean Lafitte enjoyed a lucrative stay at Galveston Island from 1817 until 1821, when the US government ran him off for making moves on an American ship.

Significant milestones in American history came to pass on this shoreline: Texas's first oil well, the gusher Spindletop, blew in 1901 at Beaumont; NASA astronauts found a new home address in Houston's Lyndon B. Johnson Space Center in the early 1960s; and rock-and-roll legend Janis Joplin was raised in Port Arthur—if not for her, we might never have learned a great hum-along song, "Me and Bobby McGee,"

THE
LAND OF
SPINDLETOP

Beaumont
Port
Arthur

TEXAS
LA.

Houston

Columbus

Colorado R.

Brazos R.

Galveston

Galveston
Island

THE
ROMANTIC
SEASIDE

Victoria
Goliad

San Antonio R.

Matagorda

Matagorda
Peninsula

THE
COASTAL
PLAINS

Beeville

THE
COASTAL
BEND

Fulton
Rockport

Matagorda
Island

Corpus
Christi

Port
Aransas

Gulf of Mexico

Kingsville

Mustang
Island

N

THE
BIG
BEACH

Padre
Island

0   50 mi
0   50 km

Port Isabel

South Padre
Island

written for her by fellow Texan Kris Kristofferson, who hails from the Gulf Coast town of Corpus Christi.

The 624 miles of coastline you find on Texas's Gulf offer everything from a Mardi Gras to symphony concerts, deep-sea fishing to whooping-crane watching, weekends whiled away in Victorian mansions to eating freshly caught seafood on a seaside deck. You may never want to go home.

The Land of Spindletop

As the state's rich forests unwind en route to the Gulf, the land turns to that which has seen massive bursts of industry yet still languishes in woodsy radiance. *Beaumont,* a city of about 115,000 connected to the Gulf by the Neches River, is a pulse point of this section, begun in 1837 as a lumber center that literally exploded onto the energy map in 1901, when the world's first gusher, Spindletop, erupted here. The little settlement of a few hundred suddenly grew to a city of 30,000—literally overnight—and became the birthplace of oil companies such as Exxon, Texaco, and Mobil.

To see just what Beaumont looked like at its moment of glory, pay a visit to *Spindletop–Gladys City Boomtown* (5550 Jimmy Simmons Blvd.; 409-880-1750; spindletop.org). The whole place has been re-created, down to the post office, oil derricks made of wood, blacksmith shop, saloon, surveyor's office, photo studio, and so on. Here, too, is the 58-foot granite monument honoring Anthony F. Lucas's landmark well that blew in at 10 a.m. on January 10, 1901. The boomtown is closed Mon. A small admission fee is charged.

A modern look at the complex petroleum industry is found at the *Texas Energy Museum* (600 Main St., Beaumont; 409-833-5100; texasenergymuseum .org), touted by the Smithsonian Institution as being one of the world's finest. A remarkable parade of exhibits includes robotics and multimedia displays that simulate rig functions. Visit the museum Tues through Sat 9 a.m. to 5 p.m. and Sun 1 to 5 p.m. A small admission fee is charged.

Beaumont's other claim to fame is being home to Babe Didrikson Zaharias (1914–1956), undoubtedly the world's greatest female athlete, some say the most gifted of all American athletes. The *Babe Didrikson Zaharias Museum* (1750 I-10 East, Beaumont; 409-833-4622; babedidriksonzaharias.org) offers tourists a chance to learn more about the woman who was a three-time basketball All-American, double Olympic gold-medal winner in track, and world-class golfer. A wealth of documents, awards, medals, and other memorabilia chronicle her illustrious career and life. The museum is home also to a good visitor center, offering travelers a variety of information on the area. The museum and center are open daily from 9 a.m. to 5 p.m.

JUNE'S FAVORITE ATTRACTIONS

Bayou Bend Collection and Gardens Houston	**Padre Island National Seashore**
	Presidio La Bahía Goliad
Big Thicket National Preserve	
Discovery Green Houston	**Rao's Bakery** Beaumont
Fulton Mansion State Historical Structure Fulton	**The Strand** Galveston
	Tarpon Inn Port Aransas
King Ranch Kingsville	

As you'll find throughout the state, early industrialists built extraordinary, lasting structures that we're fortunate enough to enjoy today. Beaumont is no exception, offering sensational vintage architecture. One such place is the **McFaddin-Ward House** (1906 Calder Ave., Beaumont; 409-832-2134; mcfaddin-ward.org). The 1906 Beaux Arts home is filled with the finery of its day and is open for touring Tues through Sun. Hours vary, so check in advance. A small admission fee is charged. Call for reservations.

Beaumont's **Fire Museum of Texas** (400 Walnut St. at Mulberry Street, Beaumont; 409-880-3927; fmotassn.com) is housed within an early 20th-century fire hall. You'll know it by the enormous fire hydrant out front! The history of firefighting since 1856 is detailed with equipment, machinery, and memorabilia. Open Mon through Fri from 8 a.m. to 4:30 p.m. Admission is free.

A particular pride in Beaumont, understandably, is the **John Jay French Museum** (3025 French Rd., Beaumont; 409-898-0348), an exemplary 1845 home restored to its original Greek revival grandeur. Inside, exhibits chronicle the lives of the French family. Discover more at beaumonthiertiage.org/john-jay-french-house/.com. Closed Sun and Mon. A small admission is charged.

One of the region's best-loved places for good food is **Rao's Bakery** (2596 Calder Ave., Beaumont; 409-832-4342; raosbakery.com), an institution since 1941. Open Mon through Fri for breakfast, lunch, and early dinner and Sat for breakfast and lunch, this is the go-to place for stuffed breakfast croissants and wraps, kolaches, and pecan sticky buns for breakfast and everything from quiche to tomato-mozzarella or Sicilian tuna sandwiches to gelato and fancy coffee drinks the rest of the day. If you simply want sweets, Rao's will load you up with Texas heritage apple pie, fudge-nut brownies, cream puffs, mousse cake, and crème brûlée.

In just a few minutes you can be out in the country enjoying several sites that define this southeasternmost corner of Texas. Head east from Beaumont on I-10 about 25 miles to the town of **Orange,** where the **Shangri La Botanical Gardens and Nature Center** (2111 W. Park Ave., Orange; 409-670-9113; starkculturalvenues.org/shangrilagardens) will awaken your sense of awe with the lushness of nature here along the Texas-Louisiana state line. There's a formal botanical garden with 350-plus plant species, as well as the Cypress-Tupelo Swamp, which you can tour in electric boats. A mile of boardwalk allows you to cross over wetlands.

While in Orange, make it a point to visit the **Stark Museum of Art** (712 Green Ave., Orange; 409-886-2787; starkculturalvenues.org/starkmuseum), one of the most astounding, well-endowed small museums in the nation.

If you still yearn for more of the great outdoors, drive north to the Beaumont city limits, where the nation's biological crossroads—known best as the **Big Thicket National Preserve**—await. Spreading across seven counties, it's the only national preserve and the only place in the US where eight ecosystems coexist. Established in 1974, the Big Thicket National Preserve is the focal point of a tranquil, woodsy region with a deep heritage and plenty of recreational opportunities. Once an ancient, 3.5 million-acre wild forest, it's now an inverted L-shaped, 84,000-acre ecological miracle struggling against the wrecking forces of human nature. The Big Thicket is a refuge for nature supporters who enjoy fishing, hiking, canoeing, and wildlife and wildflower watching. It's also a lab for naturalists and other scientists. The preserve is open daily, but hours vary by section and activity. For details contact the visitor center, 30 miles north of via US 69 and FR 420 at (409) 951-6700, or visit their website nps.gov/bith.

One of the newest and more impressive distinctions related to Beaumont is its importance to the **Great Texas Coastal Birding Trail.** Conceived in 1993, the trail enables birders to get the best possible information about the millions of Neotropical migrant birds flying north to winter, most of them visiting the Texas coast from March through June. The trail includes more than 200 good birding sites along the 500-mile reach of coastline extending from Beaumont to Brownsville. In the Beaumont area, you have easy access to 28 parts of the larger trail. Detailed information on the Great Texas Coastal Birding Trail is obtained from the Texas Department of Transportation's Travel Information office, (800) 452-9292, and from the Texas Parks and Wildlife Department (c/o Great Texas Coastal Birding Trail, 4200 Smith School Rd., Austin). Find interactive maps online at tpwd.texas.gov/huntwild/wildlife/wildlife-trails/.

Just a 17-mile drive south of Beaumont via US 96, you'll find the waterside town of **Port Arthur.** Originally called Aurora in 1840, the town on the shore of coastal Sabine Lake, on the Louisiana state line, changed its name to honor the financier responsible for bringing the railroad to town. The memory of colorful daughter Janis Joplin is honored each year in January with a birthday celebration of concerts, and she's the focus of an exhibit on rock 'n' roll stars at the **Museum of the Gulf Coast** (700 Procter St., Port Arthur; 409-982-7000; museumofthegulfcoast.org). It's open daily.

The oil boom brought prosperity to this town, which has served as one of the state's melting pots. French, Dutch, and early American heritage can be seen in Port Arthur's architecture and museums. A place with a particularly eclectic flair is **Tex Ritter Park**—formerly called La Maison des Acadienne and Dutch Windmill Museum—(just north of town in Nederland; 409-723-1545), where the combined mix of exhibits includes a park dedicated to the memory of country singing star Tex Ritter; a 40-foot reproduction of a Dutch windmill; and a replica house of the French who were forced out of Nova Scotia by the British more than 200 years ago and wound up in Louisiana and Texas. From Mar until Sept the museum is open Tues through Sun 1 to 5 p.m.; after early Sept it's open Thurs through Sun 1 to 5 p.m.

One of the cultural pleasures particular to this corner of the state is of the culinary variety: Barbecued crabs are a delicacy that originated here and can only be found in these parts and in Galveston. Unlike barbecued shrimp found in New Orleans, this unusual creation is its own dish and resembles nothing else. Gulf blue crabs are cloaked in a spicy seasoning mix and quickly fried, then served in a pile on a platter. There's a trick to breaking off the legs from the center of the crab to get good, big bites, and the whole process can be rather labor-intensive—but so worth it. Doused with lemon and enjoyed with a cold beer or soda, barbecued crab is a delicious experience. First served about 35 miles south of Beaumont at a waterside shack in Sabine Pass in the 1940s, barbecued crab are found now primarily at three popular seafood restaurants including **Floyd's Cajun Seafood and Texas Steakhouse** (2290 Interstate 10 South, Beaumont, 409-842-0686; floydsbeaumont.com); **Real Cajun Seafood Restaurant** (7500 N. Twin City Hwy., Port Arthur, 409-853-1818); and **The Schooner Restaurant** (1507 S. Highway 69, Nederland, 409-722-2323; the schoonerrestaurant.com), all great places to enjoy all manner of Gulf seafood.

Newest to this region is the **Golden Triangle Faith Trail,** which connects the myriad places of worship and spiritual enrichment that punctuate the landscape in and around three towns. The trail includes the magnificent **St. Anthony Roman Catholic Cathedral Basilica** (700 Jefferson St., Beaumont; 409-833-6433; stanthonycathedralbasilica.org), dating from 1879; **Temple**

JUNE'S FAVORITE ANNUAL EVENTS

Janis Joplin's Birthday Bash
Port Arthur, mid-January

Mardi Gras
Galveston, weekend prior to Ash Wednesday

Oysterfest
Rockport-Fulton, first weekend in March

Houston Livestock Show and Rodeo
Houston, first two weeks of March

Bayou City Art Festival
Houston, late March

Great Texas Birding Classic
entire coast, mid- to late April

Gumbo Cook-Off
Orange, first weekend in May

Sand Castle Days
South Padre Island, early October

Harbor Lights Festival
Corpus Christi, late November through December

Dickens on the Strand
Galveston, first weekend in December

Emanuel (1120 Broadway St., Beaumont; 409-832-6131; emanuelbeaumont .org), a copper-topped beauty built in 1923; *Buu Mon Buddhist Temple* (2701 Procter St., Port Arthur; 409-982-9319; buumon.org), with a 7-foot gilt-bronze Buddha statue and a lovely garden renowned for its varieties of lotus, water lilies, and bamboo; *First Presbyterian Church* (902 Green Ave., Orange; 409-883-2097; firstpresorange.com), an exquisite pink granite building dating from 1912; and *Our Lady of Guadalupe Church and Shrine* (61st Street at 9th Avenue, Port Arthur; 409-962-6777), an imposing, modern church on the site of a parish dating from 1927. For greater detail on the Faith Trail, check with the *Beaumont Convention & Visitor Bureau* at (800) 392-4401 or (409) 880-3749, or visit beaumontcvb.comf.

History lessons are fascinating at *Sabine Pass Battleground State Historic Site* (15 miles south of Port Arthur via Highway 87, or 34 miles south of Beaumont, 6100 Dowling Rd.; 512-463-7948; thc.texas.gov/historic-sites/sabine-pass-battleground-state-historic-site), which has finally recovered from the devastation delivered by Hurricane Ike in 2008. The park is dedicated to the Confederate forces under Col. Dick Dowling, who managed a victory against staggering odds and much more powerful Union forces in an 1863 battle. In addition to a statue of Dowling, there are picnic areas and a boat ramp. The park is open daily 8 a.m. to 5 p.m., and until 8 p.m, May through August.

While sailboarders and sailors are drawn to *Sabine Lake,* it's the camping, picnicking, nature study, and shell-collecting opportunities that make *Sea Rim State Park* a popular place. The state's only marshland park—spread over 15,109 acres—is 14 miles west of Sabine Pass on Highway 87. Interestingly, the highway splits the park into two separate parts, the southern being the Beach Unit, with stretches of sandy beach and a biologically unique spot where the salt tidal marshlands join the Gulf; and the northern section being the Marshlands Unit, where canoe trails and blinds are found. Bug repellent is a plus here, as mosquitoes can be vicious. Sea Rim is a good place for primitive camping, swimming, fishing, canoeing and kayaking, birding on a boardwalk, and seashell hunting. For information call the park at (409) 971-2559; tpwd.texas .gov/state-parks/sea-rim.

A trip to the nation's fourth-largest city, *Houston,* about 90 miles west of Port Arthur, can seem daunting; the trick is to approach it simply by focusing on a handful of special places. Even though the entire metropolis sprawls across 500 square miles and is home to 4 million people, it is the city's individual elements that make it an intriguing whole. For too many years, the unenlightened judged the city by views from the highways surrounding and running through city, and that's unfair. It's a beautiful city, particularly in the more central areas, thick with green spaces and trees, bayous and streams. The key is to get off the highway and enjoy Houston on its surface streets. You'll avoid aggravating traffic snarls that way, too.

Named, of course, for Sam Houston, the first president of the Republic of Texas, the town was founded in 1836, the year of the republic's birth. A city that boomed with the development of both the oil and the space-exploration industries, Houston has a surprising number of historical and natural attractions.

The first of these, appropriately, is *Sam Houston Park* (1100 Bagby St., Houston; 713-655-1912; heritagesociety.org/sam-houston-park), a 20-acre spread immediately west of downtown Houston containing an array of the city's first buildings, dating from 1823 to 1905. There's a small church, a gazebo, and an early commercial building. On-site there's the Heritage Society, with changing exhibits; and next door, the Long Row, a reconstructed office building, has a tearoom and gift store. Tours are offered Thurs though Sat. Check website for hours. A small admission fee is charged.

Batter Up

In Alvin, a town about 30 miles south of Houston at Highways 6 and 35, you'll find a statue of native Nolan Ryan, retired pitcher from the Texas Rangers, inductee to the Baseball Hall of Fame in 1999, and rancher and namesake for Nolan Ryan Beef. Find the statue at City Hall and check out the *Nolan Ryan Foundation and Exhibit Center,* located at 2925 S. Bypass 35, Alvin; (281) 388-1134; nolanryan foundation.org.

In direct contrast to this historical park is a lively urban park called ***Discovery Green,*** situated smack in the middle of downtown Houston. Opened in spring 2008, the 12-acre park faces the George R. Brown Convention Center and is a boon for both leisure and business travelers, as it's just a short walk away from the basketball scene at Toyota Center and baseball games at Minute Maid Park.

Century-old live oak trees were natural assets around which designers built an expanse that includes the Great Lawn; grand-scale pieces of art; a big pond for boating; and green spaces occupied by a giant fountain (fun for kids to play in on warm days), dog fountains and runs, picnic grounds, a playground, an amphitheater, jogging trails, and places to play bocce ball, horseshoes, and croquet. Whenever you arrive, there may be yoga and dance classes or a festival or concert in progress. The multi-million-dollar project includes restaurants such as The Grove, a Robert Del Grande operation that serves American rustic cuisine with lots of rotisserie specialties; the Treehouse, a supercasual drinks and snacks place; and the Lake House, a fast-casual spot serving burgers, hot dogs, salads, shakes, wine, and beer. *Green* is a keyword here, as all concessions are eco-friendly, utilizing all-biodegradable products. For more information visit discoverygreen.com.

History and art go hand-in-hand at the ***Bayou Bend Collection and Gardens,*** a division of the ***Museum of Fine Arts, Houston*** (1 Westcott Place, Houston; 713 639-7750; mfah.org), originally built as a residence in the 1920s for Will, Mike, and Ima Hogg, the children of former governor Jim Hogg. The paintings, furniture, ceramics, and silver housed here are among the finest collections of American decorative arts in the nation. Guided tours, lasting 90 minutes, are given Tues through Fri; check site for times. Or visit at your own pace Tues through Sat from 10 a.m. to 4 p.m. A small admission fee is charged. Children under 10 are allowed during audio tours only. Be sure to make a tour reservation, as they are required.

Make it a point to visit the ***Orange Show Center for Visionary Art*** (2402 Munger St., Houston; 713-926-6368; orangeshow.org). Its late creator, Jeff McKissack, who hauled oranges during the Depression, began building this monument to the citrus fruit in 1954. Finally, in 1979, it was ready for folks to see. He was quoted as saying that he simply wanted "to encourage people to eat oranges, drink oranges, and be highly amused." What it is, is a patchwork, many-layered labyrinth of sculpture, wagon wheels, tractor seats, flags, tiles, wishing well, observation decks, and whirligigs. It must be seen to be believed. (Recently restored, it was due to reopen by mid 2018 at press time.) It's open Wed through Fri from 9 a.m. to 1 p.m. and Sat and Sun from noon to 5 p.m.—usually. It's best to call first. A small admission fee is charged.

You'll find one of the state's better examples of weird folk art at the **Beer Can House** (222 Malone St., Houston; orangeshow.org/beer-can-house), which was bought by the Orange Show Foundation in 2001. More than 50,000 aluminum cans and pop-tops decorate this little bungalow in a quiet, modest neighborhood. The work was a 25-year effort by the late John Mikovisch, who cut, flattened, and reshaped the cans to cover his house and to make mobiles and sculptures.

Perhaps the most sobering of Houston attractions is the **Holocaust Museum** (5401 Caroline St., Houston; 713-942-8000; hmh.org). Its exhibits and memorials provide testimonials of victims and survivors of one of the darkest eras in history. The museum also has an archives repository and an interactive learning center. Open daily. Admission is free.

Among Houston's profound wealth of arts is the **Children's Museum of Houston** (1500 Binz St., Houston; 713-522-1138; cmhouston.org), housed inside a structure designed by Robert Venturi. This is a great place for kids to explore science and technology, archaeology, agriculture, and the environment. The KID-TV studio features real sound and video production equipment. The courtyard has a greenhouse, pirate's ship, and Victorian playhouse. Open Tues through Sat from 9 a.m. to 5 p.m. and Sun from noon to 5 p.m. Admission is charged.

texastrivia

The proverbial six flags that have flown over Texas include that of Spain, 1519–1821; France, 1685–1690; Mexico, 1821–1836; the Republic of Texas, 1836–1845; the Confederacy, 1861–1865; and the US, 1845–1861 and 1865 to the present.

Other exceptional repositories of art are found at the **Menil Collection** (1533 Sul Ross St., Houston; 713-525-9400; menil.org) and the **Museum of Fine Arts** (1001 Bissonnet Dr., Houston; 713-639-7300; mfah.org). Complete information on these and all attractions is available from the **Houston Convention & Visitor Bureau,** 901 Bagby St., Houston; (713) 227-3100 or (800) 4-HOUSTON; visithoustontexas.com.

Shopping has become a prized pastime in Houston, with good reason— there are superb purchases to be made here that you won't find elsewhere. In addition to the famous Galleria, there are pockets of great boutiques all over town. *Project Runway* fans are flocking to Chloe Dao's **Chloe Dao Boutique** in **Rice Village** (6127 Kirby Dr.; 713-807-1565; chloedao.com) for hot cocktail duds and trendy daywear, plus an on-site hair salon. Although it's been around since 1883, **Hamilton Shirts** (5700 Richmond Ave., Houston; 713-780-8222; hamiltonshirts.com) is hot again, thanks to the young, fourth-generation owners of the haberdashery who have modernized the family business to make it more retail friendly. Lyle Lovett is among famous clientele who stop by (or visit online) to cherry-pick fabrics, cuffs, buttons, and cuts on lovely custom shirts, which are $200 to $400 each. If you have a minimum of $1,400 to spend, Alexandra Knight, former fashion editor at *Allure,* will hook you up with the sort of custom clutches and other accessories—sans hardware or logos—she designs for stars like Rachel Griffiths, Michelle Williams, Sandra Bullock, and Mary J. Blige. Houston local celebrities like Lynn Wyatt are frequently seen at Knight's atelier in the South Hampton neighborhood (by appointment only; 713-527-8848; alexandraknightonline.com).

When you're hungry, Houston will feed you well. Superstar chef Chris Shepherd leads the pack of culinary wizards who have made Houston the most exciting food city in the nation today. At *Georgia James* (1100 Westheimer Rd., Houston; 713-528-9800; georgiajamessteak.com), the James Beard Award winning chef refashions his acclaimed, shuttered Underbelly into a modern, elegant steakhouse serving classic Caesar salad and beautiful cuts of beef, as well as his version of a tasting menu called baller boards. Next door, *Hay Merchant* (1100 Westheimer Rd., Houston; 713-528-9805; haymerchant.com) is a gastropub serving some of Shepherd's classic Underbelly dishes, such as braised Korean goat with dumplings, as well as family-style platters of chicken-fried steak and all the trimmings, crispy tacos, and fried calamari, all washed down with a stunning selection of craft beer in bottles and on tap.

Also in the center of town, find a bastion of Texan culture at *The Armadillo Palace* (5015 Kirby Dr., Houston; 713-526-9700; thearmadillopalace .com), a restaurant, bar and live music venue from the Goode Co. barbecue family. This showplace has a solid saloon spirit and an irresistible menu with standouts like pork-green chile empanadas, a fabulous Mexican seafood cocktail, bacon-wrapped quail over cheddar grits and grilled okra, just for starters. Rib eye steak, heritage pork chop, grilled Gulf red fish and sides like smoked duck-braised greens and creamed corn round out a terrific meal.

The historic *Houston Heights* neighborhood is where you'll find *Coltivare* (3320 White Oak Dr., Houston; 713-637-4095; agricolehospitality.com/ coltivare), a tiny treasure from the genius owners of nearby Revival Market. It's often SRO by 7 p.m., but guests stand around eager for a table to open in the wood-clad space or in the 3,000-square-foot garden outside. Exquisite pizza pulled from a wood-burning oven speaks to owner-chef Ryan Pera's Italian heritage and study in his ancestral home. The vegetable salads speak to his commitment to use products from the restaurant's garden, and the whole fish and especially spicy chicken dish speak to his passion for surprise. Co-owner Morgan Weber crafts a smart cocktail list and maintains an intriguing list of wines and specialty beers.

A few blocks away, the Heights's premier lodging is *Sara's Bed & Breakfast Inn* (941 Heights Blvd., Houston; 713-868-1130 or 800-593-1130; saras .com). Originally a 1-story Victorian cottage, the home was later expanded and now contains 14 guest rooms and suites. Choices include rooms with twin, double, queen, or king beds, and one is a two-bedroom balcony suite with a kitchen. The breakfast, served in the garden room, consists of fruit, homemade breads, and juices.

A visit to the site where Texas finally won its long, tragically difficult fight for independence from Mexico means driving 22 miles east from the city center to La Porte, where *San Jacinto Battleground State Historical Park* (3800 PR 1836, Houston; 281-479-2431; tpwd.texas.gov/state-parks/san-jacinto-battleground) is situated. Sam Houston and his army defeated the forces under Santa Anna in an 18-minute battle here in 1836, and markers on the battlefield detail positions and tactics of both armies. Rising from the park is the magnificent 570-foot *San Jacinto Monument,* honoring all who fought for Texas independence and particularly those at this site. The observation floor allows a view of the Houston Ship Channel and permanent mooring slip for the *Battleship* **Texas,** the sole surviving dreadnought dating to before World War I. The *San Jacinto Museum of History* has exhibits covering 400 years of area history, as well as a theater showing "Texas Forever!", a multimedia presentation chronicling the events pertaining to the Texas Revolution and Battle of San Jacinto. You'll also find a gift boutique, picnic grounds, and concession stand in the park. It's open daily from 9 a.m. to 6 p.m. A small admission fee is charged only for the observation tower.

To gain deep, new appreciation for NASA and its work, pay a visit to *Space Center Houston* (1601 NASA Road 1, Houston; 281-244-2100; space center.org), situated 20 miles south of downtown Houston at Johnson Space Center. The sensational attraction is essentially NASA's visitor center, but the effect is marvelous. Upon arrival, visitors are briefed via continuous NASA update videos and firsthand greetings by Johnson Space Center engineers, scientists, and astronauts. There's a Space Shuttle Mock-Up with flight deck and sleeping quarters to examine; Mission Status Center, where you can see space flight and training activities; *The Feel of Space,* an interactive area where visitors can use computer simulation to land the shuttle or launch a satellite; two theater presentations, including one IMAX show; and a guided tram tour going behind the scenes at Johnson Space Center. Newest among attractions is *Independence Plaza,* where visitors can climb into a shuttle replica and explore the NASA 905 shuttle carrier aircraft on which it's mounted. Fascinating stories of space shuttle development and travel are told on-screen by astronauts, engineers, and pilots. Visitors welcome daily. Admission is charged. Tickets and tour info at space center.org.

Take time while you're in the NASA area to explore one of the more amazing tourist attractions to pop up in Texas. It's called **Kemah Boardwalk,** a creation on Galveston Bay in what was previously a quiet fishing village called *Kemah,* a Karankawa Indian word meaning "wind in the face."

Conceived and built by the owner of Landry's Seafood restaurants, Kemah Boardwalk (kemahboardwalk.com) is a sprawling arrangement of restaurants, amusement rides, landscaping with fountains and palms, and docks for visitors arriving by sailboat and yacht. The **Boardwalk Inn** is a 52-room hotel with a rooftop patio, suites, kitchenettes, retail shops, and plenty of dining.

One of the restaurants at the boardwalk is called **Aquarium,** where dining areas are surrounded by giant aquariums filled with fish from the Caribbean, Hawaii, the South Pacific, and the Indian Ocean. Other dining spots include Landry's Seafood House; Joe's Crab Shack (you can't miss that EAT AT JOE'S sign); Cadillac Bar, a festive Mexican spot; and the Flying Dutchman, a favorite Kemah seafood spot for years.

Adjacent to Kemah Boardwalk is **Old Seabrook,** a cute cluster of antiques shops, seashell stores, a gourmet chocolate boutique, fine-art galleries, and more. For details on Kemah Boardwalk and Old Seabrook, contact the **Bay Area Houston Convention & Visitor Bureau** at (800) 844-5253 or (281) 474-9700, or visit their website, visitbayareahouston.com.

From Kemah or NASA it's a quick trip to **Armand Bayou Nature Center** (8500 Bay Area Blvd., Houston; 281-417-3818 or 281-474-2551; abnc.org), an unusual, 1,900-acre wildlife preserve encompassing forest, bayou, prairie, and marshland ecosystems. Choose one of several trails to hike or join up with a natural-history or boating tour. A re-created farmhouse recalls Victorian days and is designed to illustrate human-and-nature connections. Open Tues through Sat from 9 a.m. to 5 p.m. and Sun from noon to 5 p.m.

If this nature excursion leaves you inspired, you'll want to make time for an even greater communion with wildlife and the outdoors. This involves a journey west of Houston to the area of Eagle Lake, about an hour's drive west on I-10, then southwest on FR 3013 to Colorado County, near the river of the same name. First you'll find the **Attwater Prairie Chicken National Wildlife Refuge** (FR 3013, Eagle Lake; 979-234-3021; fws.gov/refuge/attwater_prairie _chicken/). If you make your visit to the 8,000-acre reserve for the odd and endangered species between late February and early May, listen for the male's resounding mating call and watch the mates' ritualistic dance. The refuge is open daily from dawn until dusk.

If you're not heading to the beach, look northward for a place to be pampered. Just north of Houston on Lake Conroe, **La Torretta Lake Resort's** Spa Terre has plenty of space—17,000 square feet, to be exact, with 20 treatment rooms—in which to indulge you. Attached to a 10,000-square-foot gym, with yoga, Pilates, and spin classes, the spa's specialties include the Milk and Honey Body Wrap, including an exfoliating sugar scrub and Vichy shower; Balinese Massage, incorporating acupressure and rhythmic strokes to encourage relaxation; and the Essence of Thailand, a body massage and scrub combined with foot and facial massage. There's more, too: All spa guests can avail themselves of the *hamam,* the steam-eucalyptus bath said to boost circulation and rid the body of toxins. Packages at the all-suite resort can include golf and spa options. Just head to 600 La Torretta Blvd., Montgomery; (936) 448-4400; latorrettalakeresort.com.

The Romantic Seaside

The utterly Victorian island-city known as **Galveston,** population about 50,000, is roughly an hour's drive south from Houston via I-45. Plan to spend a few days here, because you'll be reluctant to leave.

Galvestonians lived lavishly in the mid-19th century: In 1858 alone they bought 23 grand pianos, almost $2,500 worth of silverplate, more than 3,600 gallons of French wine, and nearly 800 gallons of brandy.

Galveston was the largest city in Texas, the second-wealthiest city in the nation, and the busiest port in the Southwest. Cotton was king, ships called from around the world to the deep natural harbor, and deals were made by the hundreds on **The Strand,** the waterfront banking center dubbed the Wall Street of the Southwest and today's tourism magnet.

The opulent era of the island-city was characterized by full-scale mansions built by the local gentry; even an average family was housed quite comfortably in a pretty frame house profuse with gingerbread trim. These are generally viewed on walking and driving tours in the **Silk Stocking and East End Historical Districts.** Several homes are showcased annually during the first two weekends of May on the **Historic Homes Tour.** Brochures from the Galveston Visitor Center (2027 61st St. or 2215 Strand) have maps of these neighborhoods; see more on the annual tour at galvestonhistory.org/events/.

An abrupt and terrifying end to the glamour came upon the dawn of the 20th century: On September 8, 1900, a devastating hurricane claimed 6,000 lives and most of the city's structures, leaving Galveston in a deathly stillness. The event still ranks as the worst natural disaster in US history. To gain a deeper understanding of the devastation of the 1900 hurricane, see *The Great Storm* (Pier 21 Theater, Pier 21 at Harborside Drive, Galveston; 409-763-8808; galveston.com/pier21theatre/). The multi-image documentary experience lasts about 30 minutes and provides actual accounts from diaries and letters of survivors of the storm.

In reconstruction, a 4.5-mile seawall was built, and for seven years silt was pumped onto the land to raise the city's grading. The resilience of Galveston and its people was remarkable. Yet business moved in the meantime 50 miles north to Houston, and commerce on the Strand dwindled while countless stately Victorian homes lapsed into sickly states of disrepair. The Galveston Historic Foundation gathered its energy just in time, and wonderful vestiges of a golden era were saved from the wrecking ball in the 1970s.

The island city was hammered again, however, when Hurricane Ike swept in on September 13, 2008, damaging more than 75 percent of the island. Many businesses reopened within 6 months to a year, and cruise ships began sailing from the busy Galveston port again in 2009. Today you find a city that sparkles more than before, thanks to the hard work and diligence of its people.

Ashton Villa, a redbrick Italianate mansion at 2328 Broadway, Galveston, was a primary salvage from threats of demolition in 1971. Built in 1859, the exquisite home is no longer a tour house but provides shelter to the *Galveston Visitors Center* (409-765-7834; galveston.com). The greatest of Galveston's historic structures, the *Bishop's Palace* (1402 Broadway, Galveston; 409-762-2475; galvestonhistory.org), has a prestigious reputation among architectural experts, who compare its ornate design to the Biltmore House in Asheville,

Moody Gardens

It might seem easy to dismiss *Moody Gardens* in Galveston as a prettified theme park, but that would be doing a disservice to the respect this facility pays to nature. Kids love it because there is a world of hands-on stuff to do, and it gives little ones and grown-ups alike options—from swimming and playing on the sand to watching 3-D films.

Among diversions at Moody Gardens: a 10-story Rainforest Pyramid with an amazing bat exhibit; a blue lagoon and white sand at Palm Beach; an IMAX 3-D "Ridefilm" theater; the Aquarium Pyramid starring creatures from worldwide waters; a 4-D special-effects theater; and a very cool penguin exhibit with close encounters of the cute kind.

North Carolina. Crafted from Texas granite, limestone, and red sandstone, the Bishop's Palace is the only Texas creation included on the list of 100 outstanding buildings in the US by the American Institute of Architects. Completed in 1893, its great pitched roofs, cupolas, gables, and cast-iron balustrades bear the mark of famed architect Nicholas J. Clayton. It's open for tours Memorial Day through Labor Day, Mon through Sat from 10 a.m. to 4:30 p.m. and Sun from noon to 4:30 p.m.; open daily noon to 4:30 p.m. the remainder of the year. Admission is charged.

The National Historic Landmark Strand District contains one of the nation's larger collections of restored Victorian buildings and is once again a vibrant and colorful mercantile center fixed within the old wharfside business zone. Great revelry invades during early spring for a massive Mardi Gras and again in December for a very British Dickens on the Strand celebration.

The *Mardi Gras Museum* (2309–2311 Ship's Mechanic Row, Galveston; 409-765-5930; mardigrasgalveston.com) helps you see how Galveston's Mardi Gras has become the third-largest in the nation, behind those in New Orleans, of course, and Lafayette, Louisiana. Costumes and historical memorabilia are displayed with models of the Arches created for Mardi Gras. There's a Mardi Gras gift shop here, too. Open Mon through Fri from 10 a.m. to 8 p.m., Sat from 10 a.m. to 10 p.m., and Sun from 10 a.m. to 6 p.m. Admission is free.

The 19th-century banking buildings and cotton warehouses along the Strand now hold a trove of shopping and entertainment. For a list of options, visit galveston.com.

Centerpiece for the *Texas Seaport Museum* is the *Elissa,* Texas's tall ship and another National Historic Landmark. The 1877 iron barque, built in Scotland, provides an exciting look at Galveston's seafaring past. The ship and adjacent museum, with superb exhibits and a dramatic film, are open daily from 10 a.m. to 5 p.m. at Pier 21, near the Strand at the foot of 22nd Street. For information call (409) 763-1877 or visit galveston.com/texasseaportmuseum.

Three blocks from the Strand, the *Grand 1894 Opera House* is a distinctive, lavishly decorated theater whose stage has been graced by dignitaries from Anna Pavlova and John Philip Sousa to Hal Holbrook and Ray Charles. Found at 2020 Post Office St., the Grand continues to offer a full schedule of renowned entertainers. For information call (409) 765-1894 or (800) 821-1894 or visit thegrand.com.

Between the Strand and the Seawall, find the *Bryan Museum* (1315 21st St., Galveston; 409-632-7685; thebryanmuseum.org), an astonishing collection of some 70,000 artifacts chronicling the history of Texas and the Southwest. Its creator and namesake is oilman J. P. Bryan, a noted historian and art collector and a descendant of Stephen F. Austin, the father of Texas. Bryan chose the handsome 1895 Gothic Revival mansion that once housed an orphanage to house his collection of swords, guns, saddles, tools and rare books, along with maps and documents pertaining to Native American, Spanish, missionary, and other early cultures that weave through the tapestry of Texas heritage. Visit Fri through Mon.

One of the most popular Galveston attractions is ***Moody Gardens*** (1 Hope Blvd., Galveston; 800-582-4673 or 409-744-4673; moodygardens.com). Here a massive ***Rainforest Pyramid,*** recently upgraded to the tune of more than $25 million, houses thousands of exotic plants, mammals, birds, butterflies, and fish in a rather fantastic tropical setting with waterfalls, cliffs, caverns, wetlands, and forests. The on-site 3-D, 4-D, and Ridefilm IMAX theaters offer a selection of extraordinary multimedia films, while Palm Beach provides a white-sand beach with a blue lagoon, a 30-foot Yellow Submarine with octopus tentacle slides, a periscope, and water guns for kids. There's a fantastic penguin exhibit, too, which survived Hurricane Ike's devastation through a generous contribution of ice from donors from across the state. Open Sun through Fri from 10 a.m. to 6 p.m. and Sat from 10 a.m. to 8 p.m. Admission is charged.

The island has 32 miles of beaches to explore, with ***Stewart Beach*** and ***R. A. Apffel Park*** among busy city areas with concessions, and ***Galveston Island State Park*** (FR 3005 near 13 Mile Road; 409-737-1222; tpwd.texas.gov/state-parks/galveston-island), where people go for bird-watching, nature walks, and camping. Admission fees are charged at some beaches, and entry to the state park is $5 per person over 13 years of age. Be watchful on the sand at all beaches for tar deposits generated by offshore oil rigs, and jellyfish—two sure vacation dampers.

Old-fashioned rest and relaxation are obtainable in Galveston's several historic hostelries. ***The Hotel Galvez,*** a Spanish-style stucco mansion built in 1911 and spiffed up for its centennial, faces the gulf at 2024 Seawall Blvd., Galveston (409-765-7721 or 800-WYNDHAM; hotelGalvez.com). ***The Tremont House,*** built in 1872 and located a block off the Strand at 2300 Ship's Mechanic Row, Galveston (409-763-0300 or 800-WYNDHAM; thetremonthouse.com), has impressive and sophisticated appointments that shine anew after a multimillion-dollar renovation. Take a loaner bike from the Galvez, available also to Tremont House guests, to cruise the historic neighborhoods and see the

texastrivia

Whence came the margarita? Published reports have credited a bar in Tijuana, Mexico, in 1930, and a hotel in Puebla, Mexico, in 1936. Another story says it came from a Galveston bartender named Santos Cruz, who made the drink in 1948 for singer Peggy Lee.

tree sculptures, created by local artists after Hurricane Ike destroyed dozens of stately old trees (galveston.com/treesculpturetour/).

Charming and genteel bed-and-breakfast lodgings are numerous; for information contact the Convention and Visitor Bureau (409-763-4311 or 800-351-4237; galveston.com/bedandbreakfastinns/). A good one to consider is **Coppersmith Inn** (1914 Avenue M, Galveston; 800-515-7444 or 409-763-7004; coppersmithinn.com), a Queen Anne mansion built in 1887 and outfitted with gingerbread trim; a double veranda; turret tower; winding staircase of teak, walnut, and curly pine; stained glass; fireplaces; and beautiful grounds with an herb garden. Among the guest rooms are Clara's Country Cottage, a private cottage nestled in the back garden; the Carriage House; and 3 main-house rooms, each with shared baths. Guests enjoy afternoon wine and cheese, elaborate breakfasts, and the option of dinner catered in guest rooms.

Dining has become a favorite reason to make escapes to Galveston. **Gaido's** (3828 Seawall Blvd., Galveston; 409-762-9625; gaidos.com), founded in 1911, remains a place for good fried blue crabs, five kinds of baked oysters, and homemade pepper cheese bread. It serves lunch and dinner daily. More contemporary is the very popular **Saltwater Grill** (2017 Post Office St., Galveston; 409-762-3474; saltwatergrill.com), with an open kitchen and chic decor. High marks go to Asian soba noodles cradling seared rare tuna and to the grilled red snapper draped in crabmeat. Prince Edward Island oysters are a big hit, too, at lunch and dinner. Very hip and casual is the **Mosquito Cafe** (628 14th St., Galveston; 409-763-1010; mosquitocafe.com), with a divine breakfast quiche of bacon and mushroom, and lunches of grilled shrimp salad. Weekend dinners are also a great idea. The oldest place in town, **Sonny's Place** (1206 19th St., Galveston; 409-763-9602; galveston.com/sonnys), is also a hangout for the local medical students. Sort of a dive, Sonny's food is pretty cheap and good, the service can be a little surly, and the beer's cold. Try the oyster mug, an off-the-menu specialty of freshly shucked oysters with lots of cocktail sauce. A favorite place for breakfast, brunch and lunch is **Farley Girls Café** (801 Postoffice St., Galveston; 409-497-4454; farley girls.com), a sister-owned spot with a good patio for drinking mimosas.

Diners swoon over the Central American ambience and menu at **Rudy and Paco** (2028 Post Office St., Galveston; 409-762-3696; rudyandpaco.com).

texastrivia

Texas covers 275,416 square miles of land, inland water, and submerged tidelands to three leagues—enough to fit 15 of the 50 states and still have 1,000 square miles left over. The state extends 801 miles from north to south and 773 miles from east to west.

Empanadas (Latin turnovers) stuffed with spicy meats, hearts-of-palm salad, and grilled vegetables are all huge hits at lunch and dinner.

The Coastal Bend

The tricky aspects of following Texas's jagged coastline southward are fully realized on wildly meandering drives from Galveston Island down to the Coastal Bend. Travelers making just this journey will pass through Brazoria, Matagorda, and Calhoun Counties, skirting the coast's series of inward-jutting bays, driving 200 miles southwest on Highway 35.

Plan to spend time exploring *Matagorda Bay,* which was largely ignored by all but its residents before the 1995 discovery of La Salle's 17th-century shipwreck in these waters, roughly 100 miles north on the Texas shore from Corpus Christi. Nature lovers, however, are finding good reason to make their way here, thanks to that rarest of commodities on the coast—unspoiled, undeveloped waterfront. Word is starting to spread about the cool 1,600-acre *Matagorda Bay Nature Park* (6420 FR 2031, Matagorda; 979-863-2603 or 800-776-5272, ext. 4740; lcra.org/parks/), a Lower Colorado River Authority operation that opened in 2007. As Matagorda County boasts the most coastal frontage of all counties along the Gulf of Mexico, this park gives you the best opportunity to experience the outdoors at its purest. When guests arrive they are greeted by one of the most remarkable pieces of sculpture found anywhere along the Texas coast. This 1-ton shiny scrap metal artwork, welded in the shape of a roseate spoonbill, was crafted by the Lower Colorado River Authority rail fleet and stands outside the park headquarters. Inside you can get information on the extraordinary bird watching to be done around here—some 230 different species were noted during the 2007 Audubon Christmas Winter Bird Count—and you'll find out about the wondrous monarch migration that comes through here in mid-spring.

On the park's long jetty pier, fishers show up around sunup to cast for saltwater cat, striped and speckled trout, and whiting. By midmorning, families are playing on the beach, and by afternoon the picnic tables and grills are busy. The most fun, however, is had on the monthly 4-hour, guided kayaking trips in the east bay's estuaries. After a few minutes of paddling instruction, you're off with guides, learning about the ecosystem, wetlands, and birds and looking in the shallow water for rays and other inhabitants.

Twenty miles inland at Bay City, the *Matagorda County Birding Nature Center* (TX 35, west of Bay City; 979-245-3336; mcbnc.org) is still another destination for birders and kayaking fans. The 34-acre refuge on the Colorado River covers former farmland with nature trails, butterfly and hummingbird gardens, deer habitats, waterfalls, flower gardens, and wildflower fields. There's a launch area for kayaking, and Kayaking 101 is typically offered in late spring.

For a good night's rest between all the encounters with nature, book a room at the historic ***Stanley-Fisher House Bed & Breakfast*** (107 Saint Mary's St., Matagorda; 979-863-2920; stanley-fisher.com). Built in 1832 by Samuel Rhodes Fisher, one of Stephen F. Austin's 300 colonists and one of the signers of the Texas Declaration of Independence, the imposing 4,000-square-foot, 2-story home has been restored by its new owners to show off intricate detail. Owners Peggy and Rik Stanley updated the home with modern, private bathrooms and central air; their ample hospitality includes lavish breakfasts. Look also for nice vacation rentals on or near the water; look for condos, cottages, bungalows, and homes at matagordabaytexas.com/matagorda-vacation-rentals/. And for ideas about good dining and shopping, check out the community site, matagorda baytexas.com.

A great detour en route south to Corpus Christi is found just shy of the LBJ Causeway, the portion of Highway 35 spanning ***Copano Bay.*** At the tiny unincorporated community of Lamar—it's too small even to be listed on the state highway map—you'll find PR 13, which leads to ***Goose Island State Park*** (361-729-2858; tpwd.texas.gov/state-parks/goose-island), a 320-acre recreation area covering a little peninsula and an assortment of islands in the waters where Aransas, Copano, and St. Charles Bays meet. You can fish from a 1,620-foot lighted pier, bird-watch, take nature and wildlife walks, swim, and camp, and you'll have a chance to see a historical Karankawa Indian meeting site, the ***Big Tree of Lamar.*** This coastal live oak is possibly 2,000 years old and measures more than 35 feet around, 44 feet tall, and 89 feet at its crown span. Note that some parts of the park are closed due to Hurricane Harvey damage.

If you'd like to hang a while around Lamar, book one of four simple but comfortable cabins at the ***Habitat*** (164 4th St., Lamar; 361-790-3732; txhabitat .com). This quiet retreat sits beside a lovely pond, framed by palmettos, fan palms, live oaks, and little else. A kitchenette allows you to fix basic meals, and there's a screened porch where you'll want to have coffee in the morning and wine in the evening. Breakfast and snacks are included, and you're in easy reach of St. Charles Bay, Goose Island State Park, and the Aransas National Wildlife Refuge.

If you have plenty of time to spare, there's a great side trip inland nearly 60 miles to the town of ***Victoria.*** One of the first three towns incorporated by the Republic of Texas, Victoria's history dates to its 1824 founding by 41 Spanish families. Among the sites and sights is the ***Texas Zoo*** (110 Memorial Dr. in Riverside Park; 361-573-7681; texaszoo.org), a 6-acre spread with 200-plus animals indigenous to this area. In September the zoo hosts an annual South

Texas Beautiful Burro Pageant, awarding prizes to the most beautiful, most congenial, best-dressed, and most obstinate burro. Open daily from 9 a.m. to 5 p.m. A small admission fee is charged.

There's also the **Nave Museum** (306 W. Commercial St., Victoria; 361-575-8228; victoriaregionalmuseum.com), a Greco-Roman–style building erected by the widow of artist Royston Nave to exhibit his Texas landscape and portrait paintings. Open Tues through Sun from 1 to 5 p.m. Admission is charged.

When you decide to head on down to the Corpus Christi area, you'll stay on Highway 35, cross the LBJ Causeway, and find yourself at the other end in the adjoining towns of **Rockport** and **Fulton.** On August 25, 2017, this was ground zero of Hurricane Harvey's devastation. The eye of the Category 4 storm passed over this area and the slow-moving system sat atop the towns and surrounding communities for a couple of days. The wind damage (an estimated 150 tornadoes were dispatched by the hurricane) and storm surge destroyed hundreds of homes, putting some 6,000 county residents on the street. The community has pulled together to rebuild, but much government assistance went to the flooded Houston areas. Restoration has been slow but steady. Within six months, it was easy to find signs claiming, "Harvey – we won." Rockport, the Aransas County seat and home to a seaside art colony of about 8,000, is a quiet community fostering its cultural growth in places like the **Rockport Center for the Arts** (106 S. Austin St., Rockport; 361-729-5519, rockportartcenter.com). The center offers a main gallery for exhibition of invited and curated artwork, a pair of parlor galleries dedicated to member artists, and the Sculpture Garden on Aransas Bay, where artwork includes *Lighthouse Fountain* and *Interlocking* by Jesus Moroles, *Rites of Spring* by Kent Ullberg, and *Return of Ancient Wisdom* by Leo Osborne. Closed Sun; free admission.

Barely 5 miles away in Fulton—also on Highway 35 and not far from the exotic-looking windswept leaning trees, twisted by constant winds—is the **Fulton Mansion State Historical Structure** (Fulton Beach Road at Henderson Street, Fulton; 361-729-0386; visitfultonmansion.com). Suffering Hurricane Harvey damage, the center is undergoing extensive renovations, but the mansion is open for tours all the while. A 4-story showpiece dating to 1876, the innovative home was uniquely outfitted with central air-conditioning and hot and cold running water at its beginning. A French Second Empire garden design surrounds the 30-room mansion, which was restored by the state parks department. Visitors are asked to wear soft-soled shoes to protect the floors, and you're advised to call ahead in summer to find out if touring lines are long. The home is closed Mon; a small admission fee is charged.

One of the nicest inns along the entire coast, **The Inn at Fulton Harbor** (215 N. Fulton Beach Rd., Fulton; 361-790-5888; innatfultonharbor.com) reopened three months after the storm, and it's better than ever. Each of the 44 guest rooms and the inn's cottage were thoroughly rebuilt from the studs with new sheetrock, cabinetry, beds, floors—the works. The owner couldn't bear to see the century-old live oak trees ravaged by the storm be hauled off to a dump, so he had a local sawmill make benches from these giant beauties. The benches are in each guest room, standing as testament to Rockport's durability. Across the street from the inn, ***Charlotte Plummer's Seafare Restaurant*** (202 N. Fulton Beach Rd., Fulton; 361-729-1185; charlotteplummers.com) is also back in business, serving spicy grilled shrimp with crabmeat dressing and crab Louis. Get a seat on the upstairs deck to enjoy the sea breeze.

Rockport and Fulton most often host nature enthusiasts visiting ***Aransas National Wildlife Refuge*** (fws.gov/refuge/aransas/) from November to March, prime months for viewing the rare whooping cranes, which numbered only 14 in 1941. The US and Canada have joined together in a sensational effort for more than 50 years to save these remarkable migratory birds, who journey annually from Canada in October and November to spend winter in these nesting grounds. The 55,000-acre asylum, home now to some 140 whooping cranes, is operated by the US Fish and Wildlife Service for protection and management of around 300 species of birds, including Canada geese, sandhill cranes, and pintail and baldpate ducks, as well as white-tailed deer, javelina, and raccoon. You can view the wildlife from an observation point or from one of several boat tours along the intracoastal canal from Rockport.

Information on the refuge, situated 37 miles north of Rockport and reached by car via Highway 35, FR 774, and FR 2040, is available by calling the visitor center at (361) 286-3559 or (361) 286-3533; the refuge is open daily from dawn to dusk, and the visitor center is open daily from 8:30 a.m. to 4:30 p.m. Boat tours departing Rockport cost about $65 per person; the most popular trip is

Victoria's Windmill

Unlike most of the windmills seen around Texas on farms and ranches, Victoria has a distinctive claim to a Dutch windmill. Located on Memorial Square in Victoria, it was built by two German immigrants, Fred Meiss Sr. and Otto Fiek, on a farm in the county around 1870. Made from hand-hewn logs and assembled with wooden pegs and homemade nails, it's thought that the windmill also contains machinery and millstones from a pre–Civil War windmill over in Goliad County. Interestingly, Henry Ford tried to buy the windmill in 1935 to exhibit at his Greenfield Village in Dearborn, Michigan, but the offer was declined. The Victoria Morning Study Club, a women's group, inherited the windmill and moved it to Memorial Square. See it at E. Commercial and De Leon Streets.

with Captain Tommy and his crew aboard the Skimmer, departing daily from the Fulton Harbor (877-TX BIRDS or whoopingcranetours.com). For all touring information, contact the **Rockport-Fulton Chamber of Commerce** at (361) 729-6445 or (800) 242-0071 or visit rockport-fulton.org.

Fourteen miles southeast of Rockport via Highway 35, **Port Aransas** can be reached via free ferry—which departs from a huge dock in Aransas Pass—operated 24 hours daily by the state highway department. For decades the little beach community fondly called Port A, at the northern tip of Mustang Island, has been a vacation spot where families spend days or weeks deep-sea fishing and body surfing in the Gulf and shell collecting on the hot sand. While it was once known as a lazy town, better access spurred the growth of multistory condos, beachwear boutiques, and nightspots. Note that Port Aransas was devastated by Hurricane Harvey, as well. The town was hit hard but the beaches and much of Mustang Island are just fine.

Now as then, however, Port A, population 4,000, is a place meant for dawdling—if not feasting on fresh shrimp and crab, taking long walks on the shore, horseback riding, or Jet-Skiing. Children and grown-ups get a kick out of clinging to the rail and watching for porpoise acrobatics during the 5-minute ferry trip to the island. The other island access is at the southern end, where a highway connects Corpus Christi on the mainland to Mustang and to Padre Island, adjacent to the south.

At either end of the ferry run are several brightly painted shacks selling fresh seafood. Here people buy shrimp at bargain prices to cook for supper in their rented cottages or for icing down in a take-home cooler.

Mustang Island was one of Texas's barrier islands frequented by Jean Lafitte and his buccaneer buddies in the 1820s. Now and then island romantics, perhaps with the help of a little grog, set out in search of a legendary Spanish dagger that is said to mark the spot of a buried pirate treasure. The most common booty, however, is a wealth of sand dollars and varied seashells found just after high tide on the light brown sand. The island's 18 miles of beach are cleaned daily, and the tar deposits are usually fewer than those at Galveston. Cars are not given free rein of the beaches, as they were until the 1980s, but are limited to a narrow path alongside the dunes. You can rent dune buggies to explore the beach, book a sailing charter, sign up for kiteboard and surfing lessons, go on guided fishing, birding and kayaking tours and even take a tour from the air on a sightseeing flight. Check out your many options at portaransas.org.

Crowds are naturally drawn to **Mustang Island State Park** (on Highway 361; 361-749-5246; tpwd.texas.gov), almost 3,500 acres decorated with sand dunes, sea oats, and morning glory. The park, just 14 miles south of the town of

Port A, has 5 miles of Gulf-front beach, and it offers camping, picnicking under arbors, a nature trail, a fish-cleaning station, and showers. The park is open daily from 8 a.m. to 10 p.m. for day use and at all times for campers. A small admission fee is charged. For a more private, open expanse of white sand, hop the Jetty Boat for an 8-minute ride to *San Jose Island* (Fisherman's Wharf, 900 Tarpon St., Port Aransas; 800-605-5448; wharfcat.com)—or, as the locals call it, St. Jo. The uninhabited beach reserve is known for excellent shelling along 21 miles of shoreline, and it's an ideal place to take a picnic, fresh water, and some fishing gear for a real getaway. The passenger-only ferry (you can take bicycles with you) operates 10 times daily from 6:30 a.m. to 6 p.m.; fares are $12 for adults and $6 for children. Learn more about San Jose Island at sanjose islandtexas.org/.

texastrivia

The *lightning whelk* is the state seashell. It's unique in that its aperture is on the left instead of the typical right.

Mostly, though, people come to Port A to see what they can find in the water. The town calls itself the place "where they bite every day," and fishing for redfish, speckled trout, flounder, and drum is free in the surf from the south jetty and the Station Street Pier. Group fishing aboard party boats such as the *Island Queen* gives anglers a chance to reel in bigger game fish for just $40 per person, which includes rod, reel, and tackle. Private charters, which can cost in the hundreds, go in search of tarpon, sailfish, marlin, kingfish, mackerel, bonito, red snapper, amberjack, barracuda, yellowfin tuna, wahoo, and shark. Call the chamber of commerce (361-749-5919 or 800-452-6278) for a list of charter companies or visit portaransas.org.

People who just want to look at sea life can go to the *University of Texas Marine Science Institute* (Cotter Street, opposite Port Aransas Park; 361-749-6711; utmsi.utexas.edu). The research facility has seven habitat aquariums as well as impressive shell displays. It's open daily from 8 a.m. to 5 p.m. during summer months and Mon through Fri from Sept through May. Note: At press time, the facility remained closed due to Hurricane Harvey damage.

Because travelers want to simply stay and stay once they've arrived in Port A, comfortable condos have become plentiful without being congestive—and most are reasonably priced and many have reopened since the hurricane. Some of the high-rises are a bit south of town, while many of the 2-story complexes are close to the commercial area, and everything's on the beach. Generally, condos are individually owned and well maintained and have large pools, tennis courts, cable TV, and landscaped boardwalks reaching across the dunes to the beach. For a step back in time, check out the *Tarpon Inn* (200 E. Cotter

St., Port Aransas; 361-749-5555 or 800-365-6784; thetarponinn.com), which at press time was still under renovations, post-Hurricane Harvey. Originally built in 1886 by a boat pilot and lighthouse keeper who used surplus lumber from nearby Civil War barracks, the inn burned down and then its replacement was destroyed in a hurricane. Today's version is a renovation of the 1920 structure, and it remains popular with anglers. A list of noted guests includes Franklin D. Roosevelt, and the inn is included on the National Register of Historic Places.

texastrivia

Texas is second only to Alaska in volume of inland water, with more than 5,175 square miles of lakes and streams.

For a complete listing of lodgings, including cottages, B&Bs, motels, and condos, contact the **Port Aransas Chamber of Commerce Tourist & Convention Bureau** at (800) 45-COAST or portaransas.org.

The Crazy Cajun restaurant (303 E. Beach St., Port Aransas; 361-749-5069) offers a Louisiana-style shrimp and crawfish boil: hot fresh shrimp, crawfish, stone crab claws, new potatoes, corn on the cob, and smoked sausage. The gumbo and sourdough bread are good, too. It's open Mon through Fri for dinner only, and Sat and Sun for lunch and dinner, closed Mon.

Other worthy Port A eating spots include **Shell's Pasta and Seafood** (522 F. Avenue G, Port Aransas; 361-749-7621), serving blue crab ravioli in red bell pepper cream sauce (open daily, except Tues, for lunch and dinner); and **Seafood & Spaghetti Works** (710 Teas Highway 361, Port Aransas; 361-749-5666).

Just across Corpus Christi Bay, which laps at Mustang Island's western shore, is the same-name city with almost 300,000 residents. The Nueces County seat, **Corpus Christi** is reached on a half-hour drive inland from Mustang Island and is the most common arrival spot for travelers flying to Texas's Coastal Bend area.

Corpus is thought to have first hosted a European in 1519, when explorer Alonzo de Pineda made a visit. Today the city is separated from the Gulf by a lengthy seawall, which was designed by sculptor Gutzon Borglum of Mount Rushmore fame. Just a few years ago eight gazebolike *miradors*—Spanish for "lookouts"—were added to the seawall; the brilliant white miradors, capped by pointed, barrel-tile roofs and complemented by Victorian-style street lamps, function as both resting spots and wedding sites.

The shining star in Corpus remains the **Texas State Aquarium** (2710 N. Shoreline Dr., Corpus Christi; 361-881-1200 or 800-477-4853; texasstateaquarium .org), an outstanding aquarium featuring hundreds of species of aquatic plants and animals. Newest is the Caribbean Journey, opening in 2017 to double the size of the aquarium. Within you'll see that more than 350,000-plus gallons of seawater are required to support all the Gulf of Mexico life on exhibit, as well as an artificial reef created by the legs of an oil derrick, providing a home for rays, sharks, and tropical fish. Turtle Bend is a pool and beach area where several rare species live, including the endangered Kemp's turtle. Open Memorial Day through Labor Day weekend, daily from 9 a.m. to 6 p.m. The rest of the year it's open daily from 9 a.m. to 5 p.m. An admission fee is charged.

Since 1992, when the World War II aircraft carrier **USS Lexington** opened as a museum in the port near the aquarium, naval history has been observed as never before on the Texas coast. Only the fourth carrier to make such a conversion, the *Lexington*—nicknamed the Lady Lex—was commissioned in 1943, participated in all major Pacific battles from Tarawa to Tokyo, collected 11 battle stars, and was the first to enter Tokyo Bay in September 1945. Among 16 decks to explore are the cavernous hangar area, where immense elevators carried fighters and attack planes from the landing deck for maintenance; and the landing deck, where volunteer guides—mostly retired naval officers—show center lines and arrest and catapult areas and explain the complications that go into running a small oceantop landing strip where planes land as often as every 30 seconds. The USS *Lexington* is open seven days a week from 9 a.m. to 5 p.m.; from Memorial Day through Labor Day, the museum stays open until 6 p.m. An admission fee is charged, and military discounts are offered. Call (361) 888-4873 or (800) LADY-LEX or try their website at usslexington.com.

Near the soaring Harbor Bridge, don't miss the **Art Museum of South Texas** (1901 N. Shoreline Blvd., Corpus Christi; 361-825-3500; artmuseumof-southtexas.org), an austere white building whose interior is acclaimed for its huge picture window looking over the water. Traveling exhibits have included such varied works as those of Remington and Warhol. A major addition designed by Mexican architect Ricardo Legorreta features 13 rooftop pyramids and a noteworthy infusion of color and light. Open Tues through Sat from 10 a.m. to 5 p.m. and Sun from 1 to 5 p.m.; the museum also charges a small admission fee.

Heritage Park (361-826-3410), on Bayfront, provides an opportunity to look at various historic homes all conveniently situated on a single block. The structures are among the best of old Corpus Christi, dating back to 1851. Among them are elaborate designs, such as the colonial revival Victorian Lichtenstein House and the ornate Queen Anne Sidbury House, as well as simpler cottages. The homes have been painstakingly restored and are open for tours.

Texas's oldest federal military cemetery is Corpus Christi's **Old Bayview Cemetery** (Ramirez Street at Waco Street; cclibraries.com/localhistory/

oldbayview/), laid out by US army engineers while Gen. Zachary Taylor was encamped in Corpus Christi in 1815. Seven of Taylor's soldiers are buried there, as are many pioneer settlers, veterans of the American War of Independence, the Mexican War, Indian campaigns, and the Civil War. You'll find a Texas Historical Marker.

Learn still more about the city's early history at **Centennial House** (411 N. Broadway St., Corpus Christi; 361-882-8691; ccahs.org/), the oldest existing structure in Corpus Christi. Built in 1849–50, the spectacular building and Texas Historical Landmark served as a Confederate hospital, a hospital and officer's mess for the federal army, and a citizen's refuge during desperado and Indian raids during the 1870s. Open the first Sun of the month from noon until 4 p.m.

For a change of pace, there's the **Asian Cultures Museum** (1809 N. Chaparral St., Corpus Christi; 361-881-8827; asianculturesmuseum.org), focusing primarily on Japanese history, religion, and art. Exhibits feature Kabuki masks, shrine replicas, a large collection of costumed Hakata dolls, and a wonderful Buddha statue dating to the 1700s. Open Tues through Fri from 10 a.m. to 4 p.m. A small admission is charged.

Thrusting seaward from the huge seawall is the city marina, bustling within the shadows of tall downtown buildings. Watery diversions found in the marina vary from sailboat and sailboard rentals to fishing excursions. People arrive in droves in the afternoon to make cheap buys from fishermen of live shrimp and blue crabs. For information, visit corpuschristimarina.com.

Corpus Christi's status as one of the breeziest cities in the nation makes it a hot spot for those sailing and sailboarding fans. Sailboat regattas are held each Wednesday evening on Corpus Christi Bay. The variety of waterways, from open Gulf beaches to protected coves, including the Laguna Madre, Gulf of Mexico, Corpus Christi Bay, and Bird Island Basin, make this appealing to beginners and experts alike. Rentals and lessons are readily available.

Some places to consult are the **Corpus Christi Yachting Center** (at the marina on Cooper's Alley L-head, Corpus Christi; 361-881-8503; harrisonslanding .net), with services for beginner, intermediate, and advanced sailors, by captains licensed by the US Coast Guard, and **Wind & Wave Water Sports** (10721 South Padre Island Dr., Corpus Christi; 361-937-9283; windandwave.net), offering sailboarding lessons for beginner and advanced, individual or group instruction, as well as sailboard, surfboard, stand-up paddle board and boogie board and kayak rentals.

Fishing enthusiasts may call the **Corpus Christi Visitor Office** at (800) 566-2322 for information on charter companies, or visit visitcorpuschristitx.org.

At the south end of town, Corpus Christi Bay meets Laguna Madre at the JFK Causeway, the connection to **Padre Island National Seashore**. The legendary narrow island extends 113 miles southward nearly to Mexico and is the longest of all barrier islands on the Texas coast. No commercial development is allowed on the 80-mile mid-island stretch, but National Park Service rangers provide information on camping and four-wheel-driving areas. Beachcombing and shell collecting are the national seashore's primary attractions, but federal law forbids taking flint points, coins, or anything that might be considered historical. Daily programs offered in summer by National Park Service rangers at *Malaquite Beach* include a 1 p.m. daily walk (and also at 11 a.m. on weekends). Rangers also conduct fireside talks at dusk on Friday and Saturday on a variety of island topics. For information call the National Park Service's Padre Island office at Malaquite Beach, (361) 949-8173. Or you can visit the website at nps.gov/pais.

The Corpus Christi area also features sites on the *Great Texas Coastal Birding Trail*, a $1.4 million effort with more than 300 marked spots along nearly 700 miles of coastline reaching from Beaumont to Brownsville. Some 500 species of birds have been documented on the isles of Texas, including sightings of brown pelicans, the rare masked duck, and the endangered whooping crane. A good birding information source is the *Coastal Bend Audubon Society* (361-885-6203; coastalbendaudubon.org).

Two favorites for seafood sit next to each other under the JFK Causeway that links the mainland to Padre Island. *Doc's Seafood & Steaks* (13309 S. Padre Island Dr., Corpus Christi; 361-949-6744; docsseafoodandsteaks.com) is a destination for sunset views, waterside dining and platters of fried fish, along with red snapper, blackened redfish, grilled mahi mahi, and chili cheeseburgers. Another favorite for many years, *Snoopy's Pier* (13313 South Padre Island Dr., Corpus Christi; 361-949-8815; snoopyspier.com), is a waterside joint on Laguna Madre with excellent fried shrimp, oysters on the half shell, cheeseburgers, and ice cream. It's also cheap and open for lunch and dinner daily.

For more information log onto corpuschristicvb.com.

The Coastal Plains

An excursion from Corpus that won't easily be forgotten is the one to *Goliad*, a deeply historic spot northwest about 78 miles via US 181, US 77, and US 183. There you'll find the most fought-over and exemplary Spanish fort in Texas and the state's true birthplace. A metal plaque outside the heavy chapel doors at *Presidio La Bahía* seems to glow with the poignancy of the words it bears:

HERE FELL THE MEN IN MARTYRED DEATH TO GAIN THE FREEDOM AND INDE-
PENDENCE OF TEXAS; AND HERE FOR CENTURIES TO COME GENERATIONS OF MEN
WILL GATHER IN REVERENCE AND APPRECIATION OF LA BAHIA'S GLORIOUS PAST.

The rough-hewn building dates to 1749 and is the nation's only completely restored inland fort. Among several important roles the presidio played is one from the Republic of Texas, one wrought with utter tragedy: The stillness of the tiny chapel here continues to emanate the desolation of Palm Sunday morning, 1836, when Col. James Walker Fannin and 352 Texas volunteers were held captive before being marched out and shot under orders of Mexican dictator Santa Anna. The death toll was twice that of the Alamo's.

The first flag of Texas independence, emblazoned with a bloody arm wielding a saber, is still flown here in remembrance of La Bahía's stature as the place where independence was first planned and where the Declaration of Texas Independence was signed on December 20, 1835. A museum in soldiers' quarters and officers' barracks details nine levels of civilization uncovered in artifacts, as well as artifacts from the revolution. Behind the presidio you'll find the Fannin Monument and Grave. The presidio, on US 183 about 2 miles south of Goliad, is open daily from 9 a.m. to 4:45 p.m. Admission is charged; call (361) 645-3752 or visit presidiolabahia.org for more information.

Across the San Antonio River from La Bahía rises the white-walled majesty of **Mission Espiritu Santo de Zuñiga,** once New Spain's finest outpost north of the Rio Grande. The mission is now contained within **Goliad State Historical Park,** also on US 183, just a quarter mile south of modern Goliad. Espíritu Santo functioned as a mission for 110 years and was the home of Texas's first large cattle ranch. Within the old mission building is a superb if small museum detailing Spain's attempt to colonize the New World. You'll find wonderful pictures and detail at tpwd.texas.gov/state-parks/goliad.

The surrounding 180-acre park has wonderfully scenic shaded picnic and camping areas, interpretive nature trails, and river fishing. Across the highway, a junior-Olympic swimming pool is operated by the city of Goliad. Park admission is $3 per person; for information call (361) 645-3405.

The Goliad town square surrounds a grand limestone courthouse, built in 1894, and an enormous live oak known as the **Hanging Tree.** Court was held here during the mid-19th century, and the guilty were hanged, as many as five men at a time. Wonderful old Victorian and Texas pioneer buildings line the square. Nearby, at Franklin and Market Streets, **Fannin Park Plaza** contains a cannon from the revolution and a memorial to Fannin and his men.

If it's springtime, and especially in March, you'll want to make a detour from Goliad southwest on US 59 to **Beeville,** seat of Bee County, where wildflowers create a great big buzz in spring. A favorite route outlined in *Southern Living* magazine follows US 181 south from Beeville about 10 miles to the town of Skidmore, where you'll turn right on FR 797 and then loop into FR 1349 back to Beeville. Your drive's reward will be stunning vistas of tall, crimson

Indian paintbrush next to purple-topped thistles, lemony blooms on prickly pear cactus, pink primrose and white prairie larkspur, burgundy-colored wine cups, and delicate crochet blankets of Queen Anne's lace.

From Goliad it's an easy, 95-mile path south via US 183 and US 77 to **Kingsville,** home of still more pure Lone Star heritage. Riverboat captain Richard King established the legendary **King Ranch** in 1853 in the southeast Texas coastal plains by purchasing Mexican and Spanish land grants totaling approximately 68,500 acres, originally naming it Rancho de Santa Gertrudes for the rare creek running through it. That the ranch succeeded in such an uninhabited place and time is as profound as the modern accomplishments that would happen in the next dozen decades. It's come to be known as the birthplace of American ranching.

Ranch workers and King's family fought off armed attacks by Mexican bandits on numerous occasions; the towers from which guards kept watch remain the most notable design element on the ranch's oldest structure, a big white commissary built in the 1850s. Visitors straggled through the area without much regularity, but King and his wife, Henrietta, took in overnighters. One guest is said to have been Jesse James, who gave a gray stallion to King after the captain admired it; today, ranch lore holds that all gray horses are descendants of James's horse.

King brought some longhorn cattle to Texas from Mexico, luring entire Mexican villages to come along and work the livestock for room and board. Some of the descendants of these *kiñeos,* or king's men, continue to work for King Ranch today.

By the early 20th century, 1.2 million acres with departmentalized operations formed an empire that would be known worldwide as innovative in the cattle and horse industries. Today the spread measures 825,000 acres and reaches over Nueces, Kenedy, Kleberg, Brooks, Jim Wells, and Willacy Counties. Its fences, if placed in a straight line, would reach from the plains near Corpus Christi to Boston. The ranch is larger than the state of Rhode Island and home to 50,000 head of cattle, 1,000 horses, and 300 artesian wells reaching 600 feet or more into the earth.

Tours aboard minibuses take travelers around the Loop Road on King Ranch, through the brushy landscape, and guides point out the romantically named vegetation that characterizes this challenging corner of the world. The anaqua, or sandpaper tree, often grows up to 50 feet high, guides explain, and the sprawling, low-lying lantana brightens the terrain with a rainbow of colored flowers. In addition to persimmon, yucca, hackberry, and prickly pear, you'll find fragrant purple sage at home on the King Ranch range. Mesquite, that most defiant of Texas trees, gave the Kings plenty of problems, so a massive root-digging plow was invented expressly to clear mesquite from the King Ranch. One of the hostile, fanged machines is displayed with other model equipment near a cattle pen.

During the daily, 90-minute tour, travelers can see where Santa Gertrudis cattle—the first beef breed developed in the US—are worked, as well as the horse areas, famous for having contributed to American quarter horse development. You will also see the auction arena, horse cemetery, ranch homes, and workings of the modern ranch,

A much-photographed building is the 1909 livery stable, a classic blend of western and Victorian influences. The only real disappointment is not being able to see the interior of the fabulous main house. A video of the interior is available to see or purchase at the *King Ranch Museum.* Birding tours are becoming extremely popular here. The scissortail flycatcher, whose males sport beautiful orange breasts, is one of 350 species living on the ranch. Call for tour rates and schedules. For details contact the King Ranch at (361) 592-8055 or (800) 282-KING or check king-ranch.com.

The adjacent town of Kingsville was created in 1904 when King's widow, Henrietta, deeded 853 acres of the ranch for a town to be built. An interesting stop after ranch exploration, it's home to the *Connor Museum.* Situated on the campus of Texas A&M–Kingsville, the Connor has a unique collection of horns, arrowheads, game trophies, spurs, and such that is strange and almost creepy, but a collection that's worth a stop. Also at the Connor, "The Living Mosaic" is a polished educational TV production illustrating the Texas coastal plain and its natural resources and history. The photography of plant and animal life, especially wildflowers, is nothing but absolutely stunning. Open Tues through Sat from 9 a.m. to 5 p.m.; call (361) 593-2810 or visit tamuk.edu/artsci/museum/ for more information.

The *King Ranch Museum* (405 N. 6th St., Kingsville; 361-595-1881; king-ranch.com/museum), housed in a renovated 1907 icehouse, exhibits a wonderful, award-winning photographic essay by Toni Frissell depicting life on King Ranch in the early 1940s. Also of interest are fabulous collections of antique coaches, vintage cars, and saddles. Open Mon through Sat from 10 a.m. to 4 p.m. and Sun from 1 to 5 p.m. A small admission fee is charged.

The *King Ranch Saddle Shop* (6th and Kleberg Streets, Kingsville; 361-595-5761 or 877-282-5777; krsaddleshop.com) is the place to spend big dollars in a short time, although it takes a few hours to really see the spectacular inventory. A very sophisticated boutique, its pale hardwood floors and rough wood walls are adorned with artfully composed displays and beautiful Indian saddle blankets and rugs. Custom-made goods include leather backpacks, "gunpowder" shoulder or belt bags, antler candlesticks, Running W collector's china, a gift crate of mesquite, cactus and jalapeño jellies, and jewelry, including sterling-silver cuff links bearing the King Ranch's Running W brand against prickly-pear cactus.

The Big Beach

From Kingsville it's a little more than a 2-hour shot straight south to Texas's most famous spread of sand. To reach *South Padre Island,* just follow US 77 down to Los Fresnos, then turn east on Highway 100, which ends at the state's southernmost beachfront.

The only reason to pause even for a moment before hitting the beach is to stock up on supplies in Port Isabel. Certainly there are legions of stores on the island, but you'll save money by shopping for groceries and fresh-caught fish in the placid little fishing village.

While you're at it, take note that the smallest state park in Texas is right here—the *Port Isabel Lighthouse State Historic Park* (Highway 100 and Tarvana Street at the Causeway; 956-943-2262; tpwd.texas.gov). The only lighthouse on the Texas coast open to the public, it cast its light 16 miles out on the Gulf from its erection in 1853 until it was closed in 1905. Those in shape can scale the winding 70-plus steps to the top to gain a view of Port Isabel, the Causeway, South Padre Island, and the Gulf of Mexico.

texastrivia

The largest county in Texas is *Brewster,* in west Texas, measuring 6,193 square miles, an area larger than the state of Connecticut. The smallest of the 254 counties is *Rockwall,* in north Texas, at 147 square miles.

Can't wait to get to the waves? Then head east, crossing the great blue Laguna Madre Bay on the *Queen Isabella Causeway,* Texas's longest bridge, stretching just over 2.5 miles. The center span rises 73 feet above the mean high tide, allowing ships heading to sea to pass below; its strength will withstand threefold hurricane-force winds.

The lower end of long, skinny Padre Island gained its name, South Padre, when the Mansfield Cut—about 35 miles north of this developed tip—was created by state engineers in 1964, chopping the island in two. *Padre Island National Seashore* (profiled in the Corpus Christi section) is north, and this megaresort area is south.

From a scattering of simple beachy bungalows in the 1960s grew a city of high-rise hotels and condominiums in the 1980s known for its powerful tourism magnetism. South Padre's 34 miles of coastline and beaches, music, volleyball, and dance clubs bring 125,000 college kids to the beach from more than 125 colleges and universities in the US and Canada during spring break, from early March to early April. Unless you're among this notorious crowd, it's best to visit South Padre Island any other time of the year.

State and world fishing records are frequently set in South Padre's bay and Gulf waters—and no wonder, with the bounty of whiting, drum, flounder, trout, redfish, kingfish, wahoo, tuna, marlin, and sailfish here. Half-day and full-day trips in the Laguna Madre Bay and the Gulf of Mexico cost as little as $25 or as much as $1,000, depending on skill, budget, and how far offshore you venture. Find out more about conditions and booking a trip by visiting spadre.com/fishing.htm.

Fly-fishing in the clear, pale aqua Laguna Madre has become possibly the favorite pastime of all. For a fly-fishing experience that includes lodging, contact the **Kingfisher Flyfishing Company** (36901 Marshall Hutts Rd. in Rio Hondo; 956-371-8801; lagunamadre.net), which offers guided fishing trips and bed-and-breakfast stays on the Arroyo Colorado, about 45 minutes from South Padre Island.

The Laguna Madre Bay also is recognized as one of the world's top sailboarding destinations. The sailing season off South Padre runs from September through May. Water depth varies from 3 to 5 feet; daytime winds average 18 miles per hour. Novices and pros come to sail the bay, the Jetties, Boca Chica, and the Ditch. For complete information on conditions, accommodations, equipment, and rentals, contact the **South Padre Island Convention and Visitor Bureau** (610 Padre Blvd., South Padre Island; 956-761-6433 or 800-767-2373; sopadre.com).

Horseback riding is a great way to enjoy the beach. **Island Adventure Park** at north of the city limits at the end of Park Road 100; 956-415-0851; southpadreislandadventures.com) offers a variety of horseback rides, as well as a petting barn and zip-lining.

An unforgettable experience is a dolphin tour with an outfit called **Fins to Feathers** (at Sea Ranch Marina, South Padre Island; 956-299-0629 or

The Aplomado Falcons' Comeback

Thanks to the Peregrine Fund's 1986 breeding program, **Aplomado falcons** are making a promising comeback at the **Laguna Atascosa National Wildlife Refuge.** Almost extinct since the end of World War II, the Aplomado are nesting at the refuge after being captured in Mexico and released in the south Texas sanctuary, where they are safe from the pesticides and loss of habitat that threatened their existence.

956-761-7178; fin2feather.com). Guides maintain a respectful relationship with several families of bottlenose dolphins in the Laguna Madre, taking only small groups to conducts tours in the most eco-conscious manner. Birding tours and photo safaris are another option with Fins to Feathers. Scarlett Colley runs the **Dolphin Research and Sea Life Nature Center** at 110 N Garcia, South Padre Island (956-299-1957; spinaturecenter.com), another conscientious tour company taking small groups out to see dolphins in the wild. Birders can get information and maps there.

Nature lovers will enjoy visiting **Sea Turtle Inc.,** an endeavor begun years ago by the Turtle Lady, the late, beloved Ila Loetscher. Her successors continue to welcome visitors Tues through Sun to raise money for the preservation of the nearly extinct Kemp's ridley sea turtle and other endangered turtles. Several of the rehabilitating specimens are observed, and the staff offers information about these marine creatures. Visit Sea Turtle Inc. at 6617 Padre Blvd., South Padre Island. Call (956) 761-4511 or visit seaturtleinc.org for a schedule. A small admission fee is charged.

The internationally acclaimed environmental artist simply known as **Wyland** picked the South Padre Island Convention Centre (7355 Padre Blvd.) as his canvas for **Whaling Wall No. 53.** The giant mural, featuring a pod of orcas (commonly known as killer whales), covers three walls of the Convention Centre. The life-size whales are illustrated in full color and are accompanied by other local sea life. Wyland's purpose for painting giant murals—he plans 100 during his career—is to raise awareness of the dangers facing these wonderful creatures. In addition to his Whaling Walls, Wyland is recognized for his outstanding ability as a fine-arts painter and sculptor.

Next to the Convention Centre and Whaling Wall No. 53, the **Laguna Madre Nature Trail** is a 1,500-foot boardwalk that extends across 4 acres of wetlands. Containing informative signs about dune systems and bird species that frequent the area, the nature trail provides visitors with the opportunity to observe many species of birds and other wildlife in their natural habitat. Both the Whaling Wall and the nature trail are always open to the public free of charge and can be accessed through the circle driveway leading up to the Convention Centre, located at 7355 Padre Blvd. at the north end of town.

The **University of Texas Pan American Coastal Studies Lab** (in Isla Blanca Park at the south end of the island; 956-761-2644; utpa.edu) has aquarium displays of fish and other

texas*trivia*

Clute, a coastal town in Brazoria County, celebrates the **Great Texas Mosquito Festival** annually in July. Special tribute is paid to Willie Manchew, "the world's largest mosquito."

marine life indigenous to the area as well as an extensive shell collection. It's open Sun through Fri from 1:30 to 4:30 p.m. Admission is free.

The area's largest nature exhibit is found at the **Laguna Atascosa National Wildlife Refuge,** a 45,000-acre federal preserve for wildlife and bird watching, located about 15 minutes away on the mainland across the Laguna Madre from South Padre Island. The largest protected area of natural habitat left in the Rio Grande valley, it's home to redhead ducks, snow geese, sandhill cranes, and white-tailed hawks, as well as ocelot, white-tailed deer, mountain lion, javelina, ground squirrel, long-tailed weasel, coyote, various snakes, and other animals and reptiles. The refuge is open daily from sunrise to sunset and offers nature hikes, kayaking, fishing and much more. The visitor center at the refuge is open from 10 a.m. to 4 p.m. A small admission fee is charged. For more information and detailed driving directions, contact the refuge at (956) 748-3607 or (956) 748-3608 or visit fws gov/refuge/laguna_atascosa/.

Birders are flocking to a lovely retreat called the **Inn at Chachalaca Bend,** a small bed-and-breakfast lodge in the town of Los Fresnos, which is about 20 minutes from South Padre Island and convenient to Laguna Atascosa. Guests wake to the call of the wild chachalacas, native to south Texas and the nearby reaches of Mexico, which live on the grounds and wander between aged Texas ebony and honey mesquite trees. Nature lovers roam the walking trails to viewing platforms and towers and to butterfly gardens or sit by the outdoor fire pit to watch the soothing resaca, or oxbow, that feeds a nearby river flowing to the Gulf of Mexico. The renovated home features beautifully used mahogany and teak and holds seven lavishly decorated bedrooms, all with beautiful private baths. A full breakfast is included. The inn is located at 20 Chachalaca Bend Dr., Los Fresnos (956-233-1180 or 888-612-6800; chachalaca.com).

There's so much good food on South Padre Island that it seems a shame to mention only a few restaurants. For excellent ahi tuna, Gulf oysters and flounder, shrimp done every which way, and seafood enchiladas, try **Sea Ranch Restaurant and Bar** (33330 State Park Road 100, South Padre Island; 956-761-1314; searanchrestaurant.com), open for dinner only. For the island's own home brew, check out **Padre Island Brewing Company** (3400 Padre Blvd., South Padre Island; 956-761-9585; pibrewingcompany.com), where the hot-hot chicken wings, peel-and-eat shrimp, beer-battered shrimp, snapper, and other fish are good.

As South Padre has boomed, so has its nightlife. Some of the most happening places include **Kelly's Irish Pub** (101 E. Morningside St., South Padre Island; 956-433-5380); **Boomerang Billy's** (2612 Gulf Blvd. at the Surf Motel, South Padre Island; 956-761-2420; boomerangillysbeachbar.com); and **Wanna Wanna Beach Bar & Grill** (5100 Gulf Blvd., South Padre Island;

956-761-7677). All, by the way, are open during the day, too, if you need to relieve that sunburn.

Finding a place to stay on South Padre Island can be an overwhelming task, with more than 5,000 condos and hotel rooms to consider. For help with finding the condo or beach house you'd like, there are several reservation agencies on South Padre Island.

For a complete list of rental agencies and visitor information, contact the ***South Padre Island Convention and Visitor Bureau*** at (800) SO-PADRE or visit sopadre.com.

Other Places to Stay on the Gulf Coast

CORPUS CHRISTI

Omni Corpus Christi
900 Shoreline Blvd.
(361) 887-1600
omnihotels.com/hotels/
corpus-christi
Facing the bay, this hotel has comfortable rooms, a very nice bar and fine-dining restaurant on the top floor.

GALVESTON

Mermaid & Dolphin Resort
1103 33rd St.
(409) 762-1561 or
(888) 930-1866
mermaidanddolphin.com
An impressive 1866 home underwent extensive renovation to become this luxurious inn with 8 suites and private baths with Jacuzzi tubs, CD, DVD and

and book libraries, bicycles, hot tub, spa massage therapy, tropical gardens, and wedding chapel.

HOUSTON

Hotel Derek
2525 West Loop South
(713) 961-3000
destinationhotels.com/
hotel-derek
Excellent location near the Galleria also puts you near River Oaks and Upper Kirby. Chic and modern, the hotel has good spaces for work and reading in guest rooms. Good bar off the lobby, too.

Hotel Granduca
1080 Uptown Park Blvd.
(713) 418-1000
granducahouston.com
When it's time to splurge, this is the place. Elegant and very European, the all-suite property offers an equipped kitchenette in each of its gorgeous rooms. Afternoon noon and

dining are first-rate. It's a dog-friendly hotel, too.

La Maison in Midtown
2800 Brazos
(713) 529-3600
lamaisonmidtown.com
Intimate and lovely, this boutique inn in Midtown is close to dining in Montrose and the Texas Medical Center and museums, too. A beautiful breakfast is included with your stay.

PORT ARANSAS

Cinnamon Shore
5009 Highway 361
(866) 639-9919
cinnamonshore.com/rentals
A contemporary real estate development bears the look of a Nantucket village. While many of the homes are for permanent residents, there are numerous options for vacation rentals, from one-bedroom condos and three-bedroom townhomes to five-bedroom homes. Some face the beach,

while others are an easy walk to the sand. Note that some require minimum stays of two to five nights.

ROCKPORT

La Quinta Rockport-Fulton
2921 Highway 35 North
(361) 727-9824
laquintarockport.com
The very contemporary, bright and cheery hotel offers a friendly breakfast area and nice rooms and suites.

Other Places to Eat on the Gulf Coast

BEAUMONT

J Wilson's
4190 Gladys Ave.
(400) 899-0080
jwilsons.com
Upscale bistro with chef-driven dishes that include steaks, jambalaya, shrimp tamales, and more. Excellent wine list.

Tia Juanita's Fish Camp
5555 Calder Ave.
(409) 434-4532
Crab cakes benedict and Mexican breakfast dishes are great for brunch. Fried shrimp, gumbo, fish tacos and boudin quesadillas are great anytime.

Willy Burger
5535 Calder Ave.
(409) 892-3400
willy-burger.com
You'll know it by the Airstream out front. Fantastic burgers include the Kung Fu, topped with Asian slaw, bacon strips, jalapenos and pepperjack. Chili, grilled tuna steak, and fried pork chop sandwich are also on the menu.

CORPUS CHRISTI

Hester's Café & Coffee Bar
1714 S. Alameda St.
(361) 885-0558
hesterscafe.com
Inspired, inventive dishes include omelets, breakfast paninis, Belgian waffles, and much more. Bakery goods are worth blowing a diet.

FULTON

Moondog's Seaside Eatery
100 N. Casterline Dr.
(361) 729-6200
Sitting right on the harbor where you can watch shrimping and oyster boats bringing in the day's catch, this happy bar and grill serves great burgers, seared ahi tuna salad, oyster dishes, and cold adult beverages.

GALVESTON

Leon's World's Finest In & Out BBQ House
5427 Broadway
(409) 744-0070
leonsbbq.com
This old house serves well as a great barbecue joint, where you can have a brisket or sausage sandwich, or ribs, chicken, and other smoked meats by the pound or with turnip greens (this is the South, you know), coleslaw, potato salad, Leon's "rice stepped up" beans, green beans, and pies. Rum cake and sweet-potato pie are super desserts. Open daily for lunch and Fri through Sun for dinner (until 8:30 p.m.).

Sunflower Bakery & Café
512 14th St.
(409) 763 5500
thesunflowerbakeryandcafe.com
A sunny, welcoming place brings in a steady crowd for avocado toast and fried eggs, corned beef hash and quail and grits at brunch; and brisket tacos, red snapper and fish and chips at lunch. The bakery offerings range from beautiful pies and cakes to cookies and pound cake.

HOUSTON

Backstreet Cafe

1103 S. Shepherd Dr.
(713) 521-2239
backstreetcafe.net
Balancing acts include
meat loaf with garlic
mashed potatoes and
roasted beet–goat cheese
salad. Setting is a pretty,
old house with a shady
patio and overall comfort.
Serves lunch and dinner;
reservations are advised.

Killen's Barbecue

3613 E. Broadway (in
Pearland)
(281) 485-2272
killensbarbecue.com
About a 20-miinute drive
from downtown Houston,
this place could be the
best barbecue stop in all
of Texas. Owner Ronnie
Killen is a classically trained
chef, but his first love was
BBQ. He's serving it in an
old school cafeteria, and
it's worth the long wait in
line (you'll be treated to a
free beer for your trouble)
to enjoy his giant beef ribs,

deeply flavored brisket,
special creamed corn,
and incredible barbecue
sauces.

ROCKPORT

The Groove

2001 N. Highway 35
(361) 729-3663
thegrooverockport.com
Upscale dining in a casual
setting has created a loyal
clientele. Pizzas, fresh
seafood and steaks come
from a wood-burning oven,
and there's a primo wine
list, too. Live music on
weekends.

Paradise Key Dockside Bar & Grill

165 Cove Harbor North
(361) 729-6000
paradisekeydockside
barandgrill.com
A sprawling food and drink
gathering spot on the water
brings in huge crowds for
strong margaritas, crunchy
fried shrimp and oysters,
blackened drum and
redfish, and live music.

SOUTH PADRE ISLAND

Café on the Beach

At the Palms Resort,
3616 Gulf Blvd.,
(956) 761-2703
palmsresortcafe.com/café-
on-the-beach
At breakfast, eggs benedict
and migas; shrimp cocktail,
crab cakes, tortilla soup
and seafood bisque,
coconut shrimp, blackened
mahi mahi and grilled tuna
at lunch and dinner.

Dirty Al's

33396 State Park Rd.
956-761-4901
dirtyalspi.com
Blackened lobster, fish
tacos, ceviche and oysters
are specialties.

Yummie's Bistro

700 Padre Blvd., Suite J
(956) 761-2526
Waffles with fruit is a
good breakfast pick, as
is the California benedict.
Sandwiches and salads are
other good meals.

The Hill Country

Visualize two-lane roads, twisting and climbing, leading to an antique borough here, a winery there. Imagine hills, soft and scrubby, green valleys, limestone cliffs. Conjure up ranches and communities of German heritage, farmers markets and fields of wildflowers, sparkling rivers lined with cypress and oak.

Ah, the Hill Country realized. To some it's the state's greatest natural resource. No big cities, no bustle. Just cafes with country cooking, rivers and lakes for fishing and inner tubing, and old places with timeworn comfort.

Raised by the Edwards Plateau, the hilly region extends west from I-35, which follows the edge of the Balcones Fault. You can find this land of escape below US 190 and above US 90. Wander alone or take the whole family to this beautiful part of Texas. But don't venture too far west of US 83, where the hills—and the Hill Country—taper off. Just go armed with plenty of time to stop and take photos.

Spring—when Texas is blanketed in glorious wildflowers—is by far the most popular time to wander through the Hill Country. Experts at the Lady Bird Johnson Wildflower Center in Austin are deluged with calls every year in early March, when

JUNE'S FAVORITE ATTRACTIONS

Blackchalk Laundry & Home Fredericksburg	**Luckenbach General Store** Luckenbach
Camp Comfort Comfort	**Pedernales Falls State Park** near Johnson City
Enchanted Rock State Natural Area near Fredericksburg	**Vanishing Texas River Cruise** Lake Buchanan
Fall Creek Vineyards Tow and Driftwood	**Wimberley Pie Co.** Wimberley
Farm Road 337 Vanderpool	**Y.O. Ranch** near Kerrville

travelers are begging for information as to when the bluebonnets, the state flower, will sprout their colorful hats.

These experts manage to patiently explain time and time again that everything depends on whether fall and winter rains reached the wildflower seeds after germination, whether sunshine followed, and whether Mother Nature decides to cooperate. In other words, blooming is just too hard to predict.

While there's no guarantee for abundant *Lupinus texensis* (the bluebonnet's proper name), you'll usually find plenty of opportunities to pose children amid the colored country fields for an Easter portrait. What the country's wildflower authorities will promise is that they'll pass along to you whatever bluebonnet and other flower information they have. Call the center at (512) 232-0100 or the highway department's hotline at (800) 452-9292 for information about the best highway routes in Texas for wildflower watching; that's also the phone number to check out road conditions during inclement weather.

As the deeply blue carpet spreads northward from south Texas, we cross our fingers in hopes that the sapphire blooms—mixed in with the palette of Mexican hat, Indian paintbrush, black-eyed Susans, primroses, and hundreds of others—will make a timely appearance in the Hill Country for a scattering of festivals. The Hill Country's upper reaches, called the Highland Lakes for the 150-mile, sparkly string of seven lakes formed by the Colorado River, are particularly vibrant for two weeks in spring when the Highland Lakes communities throw out floral welcome mats during the annual bluebonnet celebrations.

From late March through mid-April, it's easy to spend a day or a weekend at a medley of arts and crafts fairs, featuring works by more than 500 artists in all, as well as related musical events, children's events, street parties, cook-offs,

Texas Wildflowers

The Texas Department of Transportation buys and sows some 30,000 of wildflower seeds along the roadsides each year to attract toursts from around the nation, who travel to Texas to see our bounty. Here are some of the wildflower facts shared by the highway department.

More than 5,000 species of wildflowers grow in the state of Texas.

TxDOT nurtures them through their carefully planned mowing policies, caring for 800,000 acres of right-of-way.

All species of the bluebonnet are considered the State Flower. There are also white bonnets and pink bonnets. These will not necessarily bloom the next year true to color if they are mixed among bluebonnets. This is due to their being pollinated by bees and if the bee goes from a bluebonnet to a white bonnet and pollinates the white bonnet, then it could come back as a bluebonnet.

More than 20% of wildflowers are in the sunflower family.

Indian Paintbrush comes in colors ranging from orange to yellow to purple.

Goldenrod—often confused with ragweed, which causes hayfever—is not a wind-pollinated plant. It is pollinated by bees.

Prickly poppies have branched, prickly stems and are an abundant supplier of pollen for insects. They come in white, red, and pink colors.

Sideoats Grama is the State Grass of Texas. It is a warm season grass growing from July to September.

Little Bluestem has an extensive root system.

Buffalograss is excellent for erosion control and can survive short mowings.

Sand Lovegrass is sometimes called "Ice Cream Grass" because livestock love to eat it and the tops of it look like ice cream.

and fishing tournaments. Waterside pastimes—golf, tennis, and hiking among them—are handy, too, on cliff-lined lakes that offer more total shoreline than even the whole Texas coast. Stay the night at a lakefront resort, waterfront cabin, or bed-and-breakfast inn. Just pick your pace and do a self-guided tour aided by a free Bluebonnet Trail brochure and map. Call the chamber of commerce of any town the trail winds through, including Buchanan Dam, Burnet, Lampasas, Llano, Marble Falls, or Kingsland, or visit the umbrella website at highlandlakes.com.

Before you begin touring, you may want to note on your map the Hill Country's best lanes for spring wildflowers and year-round scenery. They include US 281 from Lampasas south to San Antonio; Highway 16 from Llano south to Medina; US 290 from Austin to west of Fredericksburg; Highway 71 from Austin northwest to Llano; Highway 29 from Burnet west to Llano; and Highway 46 from New Braunfels to just east of Bandera.

Ranches & Lakes

There's no better place to begin the Hill Country tour than in *Johnson City,* found about 50 miles west of Austin at the junction of US 290 and US 281. The seat of Blanco County, the town of about 1,600 residents and its nearby neighbor, *Stonewall* (just across the Gillespie County line, 16 miles west on US 290), lay in relative obscurity for a hundred peaceful years before one of the most colorful men in political history became president suddenly in 1963. Lyndon Baines Johnson was profoundly attached to his roots and made his family ranch in Stonewall, just 14 miles west of his Johnson City birthplace, the Texas White House.

The Lyndon B. Johnson National Historic Park, with units on US 281 in both Johnson City and Stonewall, and adjacent Lyndon B. Johnson State Park do a fine job of detailing the heritage of this larger-than-life figure and his land. The national park visitor center has a multimedia program on the illustrious LBJ and Johnson City history as well as a gift shop. There's also the president's boyhood home, a humble 1886 frame house where LBJ's parents moved in 1914; it's been restored and furnished to 1920s style.

The park's ranch unit spreads along the serene *Pedernales River* and is where LBJ retired. Since the passing of Lady Bird Johnson, scheduled bus

JUNE'S FAVORITE ANNUAL EVENTS

Bluebonnet tours/festivals
Burnet, Llano, Buchanan Dam, Lampasas, Marble Falls, and Kingsland; early April

Bandera ProRodeo
Bandera, late May

Folk Festival
Kerrville, late May and early June

Grapestomp
Fredericksburg and area, early to mid-August

World Championship Barbecue Goat Cook-Off
Brady, early September

Oktoberfest
Fredericksburg, early October

Fall foliage
Lost Maples State Natural Area, early November

Wurstfest
New Braunfels, first two weekends in November

tours onto the LBJ Ranch are no longer necessary. You can now pick up a free permit at the LBJ State Historical Park Visitor Center and drive onto the ranch in your private vehicle and tour the ranch home, also called The Texas White House, for $3 per person.

While you're on the grounds, be sure to take photos of the cattle, family cemetery where LBJ is buried, and a reconstruction of the president's birthplace. Also on the site are a living historical farm; small church cemetery; two furnished, pioneer dogtrot-style houses; swimming pool; and tennis court spread about the parks, but its riverside picnic areas shaded by ancient live oaks provide unparalleled peace.

For details on the state park, call park headquarters at (830) 644-2252 or (830) 644-2241 or visit tpwd.texas.gov. For national park information call (830) 868-7128 or visit nps.gov/lyjo.

It's not just about history in Johnson City, however; here and there, you'll find various diversions, such as the *Benini Foundation Galleries and Sculpture Ranch,* immediately west of town (377 Shiloh Rd., Johnson City). Here's where you'll be able to view work by the Italian-born Benini, whose contemporary paintings and sculpture have been the focus of 160 one-man exhibitions around the world. He lives and works here, where the studios and galleries can be seen Thursday through Sunday and by appointment; call (830) 868-5244 or visit benini.com. *Chantilly Lace Country Inn* (625 Nugent Ave., Johnson City; 830-660-2621; chantillylacesoaps.com) sits on 6 acres that include a lavender farm, of which you'll see plenty in this area these days. The handsome historic stone house holds 6 suites with king-size beds, private baths, refrigerator, microwave, and coffeepot; 2 suites have whirlpool tubs. One of the suites is a two-room cabin on the property that accommodates up to 4 guests. All stays include a big breakfast. The innkeepers also produce a line of all-natural soaps, as well. Lodging starts at $145.

Pedernales Falls State Park, about 10 miles east of Johnson City via FR 2766 (830-868-7304; tpwd.texas.gov), is a stunning spread of nearly 5,000 acres of former ranch land with 6 miles of spectacular riverfront for tubing, swimming, fishing, hiking, and camping. It's wise to arrive early in the day, as rangers close the park when parking lots are full. The park is open daily and charges a small admission fee.

Another detour for naturalists is to *Westcave Preserve,* a 30-acre nature reserve northeast of Johnson City, near the Pedernales River. A Lower Colorado River Authority property, Westcave is first seen as upland savannah, replete with wildflower meadows, before it descends to a verdant canyon formed hundreds of centuries ago when a huge limestone cave collapsed. As you hike along, you'll find an amazing development: A spring-fed creek meanders for a while before sharply turning into a 40-foot waterfall spilling into a radiantly green pool. Sensational bird watching and wildflower spotting can be had in the preserve. Tours are given Sat and Sun on a first-come, first-served basis and you reserve your place on a tour in person with payment. Admission is $7 for Upland Trails access and $15 for the Canyon Tours. You can reach Westcave by driving north on US 281 from Johnson City about 12 miles, turning east on RR 962, and continuing another 12 miles. For information call (830) 825-3442 or check westcave.org.

From Johnson City it's also easy to make a side trip to **Blanco,** south just 14 miles on US 281. A bucolic burg of the first order, this is the place to go to spend idle hours on the Blanco River banks. Named the Blanco County seat upon organization in 1858, the town of 2,000 lies about 45 miles north of San Antonio. A lovely little state park is in Blanco, too, offering nice riverside picnic spots.

The town's centerpiece is the old **Blanco County Courthouse,** a Second Empire design built in 1886 but then abandoned when the county seat moved to Johnson City in 1890. After an impressive restoration effort, it is open to the public. For tour information call the Blanco Chamber of Commerce at (830) 833-5101 or visit blancochamber.com.

Throughout the town, century-old limestone buildings are a testament to the German colony that settled in the river valley, and some of the best historic buildings line the courthouse square. Businesses here now include a covey of antiques shops with some funky collectibles; a tiny library; and a handful of cafés. A café to note is **Redbud Café** (410 4th St., Blanco, 830-833-0202, redbud-café.com), occupying an old hardware store. Enjoy soups and salads of simple and elaborate descriptions, along with live music. The owners are potters, too, with a gallery next door to the café, where they also sell lavender products. Nearby, **Old 300 BBQ and Back Forty Event Hall** (318 4th St., Blanco, 830-833-1227, old300bbq.com) is a great hangout for eating barbecue and listening to music while sipping cold beer.

A funky, fun spot to grab a bite to eat in town is on the north side of the square and in a somewhat unlikely location. Inside the **Blanco Bowling Club Cafe** (310 4th St., Blanco; 830-833-4416; blancobowlingclub.com), you can bowl a few frames and tuck into a fine, juicy burger, too. There's also mile-high meringue pie, as well as giant cinnamon rolls with coffee in the morning.

After your Blanco diversion, it's time to journey from Johnson City north on US 281 to the **Highland Lakes.** You'll first reach **Lake Marble Falls** in Burnet County, about 25 miles north of Johnson City. Overlooking the lake is a town of the same name, at US 281's junction with RR 1431, one of the Hill Country's most scenic highways. **Marble Falls,** with 6,500 residents, is home to **Granite Mountain,** situated just west on RR 1431, an 860-foot-tall dome of rusty-red granite sprawling across 186 acres. It's this rock source from which the spectacular state capitol in Austin was built more than a century ago. You can see it from the highway, but the quarry isn't open to the public.

A good reason to stop in Marble Falls is to eat at the **Bluebonnet Cafe** (211 US 281, Marble Falls; 830-693-2344; bluebonnetcafe.net), a very popular country diner since 1929, serving Texas and southern specialties, such as chicken and dumplings, cobbler, catfish, chicken-fried steak, steaks, and all-day breakfasts. It's open for breakfast, lunch, and dinner Mon through Sat and through lunchtime on Sun. There's pie happy hour (when you see the pies, you'll understand) on weekday afternoons.

The best scenic drives from Marble Falls can easily fill a morning or afternoon. Try heading northwest on Highway 71 for a 32-mile jaunt to Highway 16; or go west on RR 1431, which unwinds 18 miles through the tiny towns of Granite Shoals and **Kingsland** before its intersection with Highway 29. This latter route follows the lakes trail, as the Colorado River meanders past dams creating Lake LBJ and then Inks Lake and **Lake Buchanan Dam.**

If you reach Kingsland during bluebonnet weekends, handcrafted items are exhibited and sold at the **Kingsland House of Arts and Crafts** (112 Chamberlain St., Kingsland; 325-388-6159; kingslandcrafts.com).

A turn-of-the-20th-century railroad hotel has been renovated and reopened as **The Antlers Inn** (RR 1431 at Kingsland; 325-388-441 or 800-383-0007; the antlers.com). First opened in 1901 by the Austin & Northwestern Railroad, the inn now offers 6 suites, each accommodating up to 3 people; one room for 2

A Taste of the Grape

The tiny town of Stonewall, just outside of Fredericksburg, is home to numerous wineries. At **Grape Creek Vineyards,** the motto is "where wine is a pleasure, not a party." The property's buildings evoke thoughts of Tuscany. Reservations for tours are a good idea, and taking a tour is required if you want to eat at the winery's lovely restaurant, **Stout's Trattoria;** 10587 East US 290, Fredericksburg, (830) 644-2710; grapecreek.com. Nearby, **Kuhlman Cellars** offers a special tasting by reservation that pairs special noshes with five specially selected wines; 18421 E. US 290, Stonewall, (512) 920-2675, kuhlmancellars.com.

For more information about these and all Hill Country wineries, visit texaswinetrail .com. Visit this site also to read about upcoming events—of which there are many—throughout the Hill Country wineries much of the year. You can plan entire weekends around these visits, so it's smart to consult the website frequently for new additions to the calendar.

Joy to the Fishes in the Deep Blue . . . Lake

Inks Dam National Fish Hatchery features scientific ponds in which thousands of fish are bred for stocking lakes across the nation. One of its functions is that of restoring Gulf Coast striped bass to the northern Gulf of Mexico. It's open weekdays from 8 a.m. until 4 p.m. and until noon on weekends and is located at FR 2342 at PR 4—look for signs—(512) 793-2474.

people; and 8 cabins, housing between 2 and 10 people each, equipped with kitchens and porches. There are also restored train cars that you can stay in, each accommodating 4 guests. All lodgings have private baths; rates start at $170. The 15 acres of wooded grounds have nature trails, a fruit orchard, and 1,500 feet of waterfront on Lake LBJ. Good dining is in the immediate area, as is a cocktail lounge and even a massage studio. Spend time in the area riding bicycles, fishing, and playing in the lake.

Lake LBJ, immediately west of Lake Marble Falls, lies on the line shared by Burnet and Llano Counties and is probably the best liked of the Highland Lakes in terms of recreation and scenery. The 6,300-acre impoundment of the Colorado River is shielded from winds by tree-cloaked bluffs and granite cliffs and is consequently a big lake for waterskiing, sailing, Jet-Skiing, and fishing.

Some travelers who make Lake LBJ their destination settle in at **Horseshoe Bay Resort** (200 Hi Circle North, Horseshoe Bay; 877-611-0112; hsbresort.com), which recently underwent a $60 million renovation. Guests stay in hotel rooms, condos, or town houses and spend time playing golf on three 18-hole courses (all Robert Trent Jones Sr. championship designs). The full-service marina makes available pontoon boats, WaveRunners, and paddleboards. There's also a beach, indoor and outdoor tennis, and stables, along with a selection of good dining and cocktail venues. If you feel like some pampering, book a treatment at the resort's Bayside Spa and Fitness Center. Among them, the Essence of Hill Country Vineyards gives you a full-body exfoliation with cocoa extract, red wine grape body wrap, accompanied by a scalp massage and mini anti-aging facial, and a light body butter application. Just to be sweet, the spa throws in wine-inspired locally handmade truffles. The Sweet Hill Country Escape includes the signature Sugar Honey Pecan full-body scrub, hydrating honey-based, glazed body wrap, scalp and foot massage, and a body butter massage all over.

Your traveling path will likely take you from Marble Falls 12 miles north on US 281 to **Burnet** (pronounced BURN-it), seat of Burnet County and home to about 6,000 residents. Frontier Fort Croghan was established here in 1849, and the town grew up around it. Today Burnet—known as one of the most interesting geologic spots in the world—is a magnet for rock hounds as well as professional and amateur geologists.

Longhorn Caverns State Park (south on US 281, 5 miles to PR 4; 830-598-CAVE or 877-441-CAVE; tpwd.texas.gov/state-parks/longhorn-cavern or longhorncaverns.com) is a remarkable, 11-mile underground maze of caves and passages a million years in the making. What's odd about this cavern is that it was the site of big speakeasy parties during Prohibition. Guided tours are offered daily. The snack bar and souvenir shop are better than some. Tour hours vary; admission is charged.

Another Burnet stop is the *Fort Croghan Museum* (703 Buchanan Dr., Burnet; 512-756-8281; fortcroghan.org). The museum offers more than 1,200 items pertaining to early central Texas history plus 6 pioneer cabins. Open Apr through Oct Thurs through Sat from 10 a.m. to 5 p.m. There's no admission, but donations are welcome.

Just west of Burnet, head along 29 to Lake Buchanan and the *Canyon of the Eagles Lodge & Nature Park,* found on a 940-acre spread at the northern tip of the lake at the end of RR 2341, which you'll follow north from Highway 29 (16942 Ranch Road 2341, Burnet, 512-334-2070; canyonoftheeagles.com). This nature lovers' retreat, with a 61-room lodge, is perfect if your interests include hiking, canoeing, kayaking, fishing, and birding—and traveling with your pet. Enjoy kayaking and canoeing outings, nature walks and hikes lets by naturalists, group dog walks, special programs for kids, along with nightly stargazing. The long-popular *Vanishing Texas River Cruise* is boarded near the lodge; regularly scheduled tours take you on Lake Buchanan in fall and winter to look for great blue herons, osprey, red-tailed hawks, American white pelicans, and, with any luck at all, a bald eagle, roosting in trees along the shoreline or gliding overhead. In spring and summer the cruises give you a chance to see wildflowers, deer, and other samples of Mother Nature's gifts. To book cruises call (512) 756-6986 or log onto vtrc.com.

texas**trivia**

Texas is the number one bird-watching destination in the US, and the Rio Grande valley is the number one bird-watching area in Texas. Nearly 500 species of birds, including 35-plus species found nowhere else in the country, have been spotted in Texas. Most can be found in the Rio Grande valley.

After the cruise continue on Highway 29 west to *Inks Lake State Park,* just an 8-mile reach from Burnet, (512) 793-2223; tpwd.texas.gov. This

1,200-acre spread—one of the smaller but prettier lakes in Texas—is perfect for anybody who wants beautiful surroundings in which to read, sketch, or write postcards, and it affords camping, picnicking, fishing, and hiking. The park is open daily and charges a small admission. Inquire about canoe tours to the Devil's Waterhole.

Just 5 miles west of Inks Lake via Highway 29, across the line into Llano County, is the town of ***Buchanan Dam*** (pronounced buck-ANN'n), sitting on the lovely Lake Buchanan. Only 1,600 people call it home, but it's a busy place in mild weather and spring flower time. The 2-mile-long dam is a work of arches and is likely the largest multi-arch dam in the nation. Built in the 1930s, it holds the Colorado River and forms the highest and largest of the Highland Lakes. One of the better places to view the lake and dam is at the Buchanan Dam visitor center office, on Highway 29 in the observation building at the dam. Call the ***Llano County Chamber of Commerce*** at (325) 247-5354 or visit highlandlakes.com/Llano for more information.

texastrivia

Guadalupe Peak, at 8,749 feet, is the state's highest mountain. That's more than 2,000 feet higher than North Carolina's Mount Mitchell, the highest point east of the Mississippi River.

From the town and lake, it's an easy, 14-mile side trip up to the town of Tow, on the lake's northwestern shore, to visit ***Fall Creek Vineyards*** (1820 County Road 222; 325-379-5361; fcv.com), founded in 1975. One of the more successful wineries in the state, Fall Creek offers an impressive visitor center, guided tours, a tasting room, and a gift shop. Tasting fees are charged, and hours vary. Fall Creek has opened a second winery location, as well, at Driftwood, which is detailed later in this chapter.

From Buchanan Dam the Hill Country tour continues 17 miles west again on Highway 29 to ***Llano,*** seat of Llano County. Nearly 3,500 folks find Llano a comfortable place to live, and it's largely due to an undisturbed array of historic buildings. You'll want to explore the town one afternoon—it's easy to see on foot—to have a look at places such as the ***Llano County Courthouse*** (Main and Ford Streets), built in 1892; ***Acme Dry Goods*** (109 W. Main St., Llano), dating to the same time; the ***Southern Hotel*** (201 W. Main St., Llano), built in 1881 and housing a century-old hardware business; and the ***Old Llano County Jail*** (Oatman Street, northeast of the courthouse), today occupied by a museum. All details about these and some B&Bs in town are available from the ***Llano County Chamber of Commerce*** at (325) 247-5354 or llanochamber.org.

Llano is extremely popular with deer hunters in late fall and with rock hounds year-round. As the county is on the 1.5 billion–acre ***Llano Uplift,*** described as a geological phenomenon, the ground is riddled with sensational finds of amethyst, azurite, dolomite, galena, garnet, quartz, serpentine, gold, and llanite, a brown granite with blue crystals and pink feldspar unique to this area.

People have been known to drive quite a way to eat Llano's barbecue. *Cooper's,* just west of Highway 16 on Highway 29 (604 W. Young St., Llano; 325-247-5713; coopersbbq.com), produces outstanding smoked ribs, brisket, pork, chicken, sausage, and *cabrito* (baby goat), with a fine pot of beans and savory barbecue sauce. It's open daily for lunch and dinner.

The wildflower period in spring signals a show and sale of paintings, sculpture, drawings, weavings, pottery, and more at *Llano Fine Arts Guild Gallery* (503 Bessemer Ave., Llano; 325-247-4839; llanofineartsguild.com).

Llano is the best place to strike out for a side trip to *Colorado Bend State Park.* Reach it by driving north on Highway 16 for 16 miles, then, inside San Saba County, turn east on RR 501 for 15 miles. More out of the way than many parks, it can feel like a private Eden for travelers. Beautiful scenery unwinds along the banks of the Colorado River, where primitive camping sites, hiking trails, and picnicking areas are scattered. Anglers say the fishing is unsurpassed, and cave tours are offered on weekends. One is a walking tour through *Gorman Cave,* while the crawling tour explores smaller caves suited to the most dedicated spelunkers. Call for tour fees and times. The park is open daily and charges a small admission. For information call (325) 628-3240 or visit tpwd.texas.gov.

Wine lovers will want to make time to visit *Fiesta Winery* (5 miles west of Bend at 18727 West RR 580; 325-628-3433; fiestawinery.com). This winery produces a number of sweet and dry red, white, and blush wines, paired with small plates to enjoy in the tasting room and on the patio. Call ahead to find out when tours and tastings are offered. The winery also has tasting rooms in Fredericksburg.

Just 18 miles northwest of Bend, visit the town of *San Saba*—easily worth an overnight. Deep into pecan-growing country, where rugged stretches of landscape are interrupted by lazy rivers lined by green cactus-strewn meadows, this sleepy town has sprung back to life on the backs of two lively wineries. *Wedding Oak Winery*'s tasting room (316 E. Wallace St., San Saba; 325-372-4050; weddingoakwinery.com), housed in a handsome 1926 stone building in the vintage downtown invites you to cozy up at the bar or relax out on the Spanish tile patio to enjoy wines by the bottle or flight of five pours (the whites include an albariño). Two doors down, *Old Man Scary Cellars* (302 E. Wallace St., San Saba; 325-372-6071; oldmanscarycellars.com) is newer, opened with help from the Wedding Oak winemakers. Order in a charcuterie platter from neighboring *Oliver & Co.* to enjoy on the back porch with a bottle of Dolcetto, a light-bodied red with hints of berry and spice, made from Texas High Plains grapes. Upstairs, the *Dofflemyer Hotel* (108 S. High St., San Saba; 325-372-5614; dofflemyerhotel.com) is a 1913 inn recently and thoroughly renovated with all modern notes in six rooms. Find locally made jewelry, antique tables, and early Texas signage downstairs again at *J.C. Campbell Mercantile* (318 E. Wallace St., 325-372-5865). Buy boots and cowboy hats across the street at *Harry's* (403 E. Wallace St., San Saba; 325-372-3636; harrysboots.com). All along the main drag, find shops selling olive oils, coffees, locally made jams, and plenty of pecan goodies. If you're up for a break from wine, check out *Bar D Brewhouse* (213 N. High St., San Saba; 325-372-1798), a hangout where the owners make 11 craft beers, easily sampled in a tasting flight. Follow that with a dinner of bacon-wrapped quail and juicy, mesquite-grilled rib eye steaks at old-fashioned *Diggs Restaurant & Club* (1035 E. U.S. 190, San Saba; 325-372-3010)

Just to the east of downtown via U.S. 90, find a lovely chain of parks filled with streams, rock, trees and green spaces. *Mill Pond Park* is one of these, with good places to walk, picnic, and feed the ducks. Across the road, *San Saba River Nature Park* is perfect for a morning or afternoon walk. You'll see ruins of the city's stone waterworks, a birding blind, and places to unwind.

Rocks & Wildlife

From Llano, point your car northwest on Highway 71 to *Brady.* It's a 54-mile drive to the seat of McCulloch County, home to 5,400 residents, and the town closest to the geographic center of Texas—hence the appropriate nickname, the Heart of Texas.

Any Texan who holds Lone Star foods near and dear to the heart can tell you Brady is the site of the *World Championship Barbecue Goat Cook-Off,* held annually on Labor Day weekend. Don't laugh—the competition draws more than 200 teams from around the US and abroad, cooking a total of 5,700-plus pounds of goat The weekend brings plenty of entertainment and unique contests, all held at Richards Park on Commerce Street, just west of downtown. Admission is free; for details call (325) 597-3491 or visit worldchampionship-goatcookoff.com and bradytx.com.

For a look into the past, check out the *Heart of Texas Historical Museum* (High and Main Streets; 325-597-0526), a converted old jail that rises 3 stories into the sky and resembles a castle. You'll see exhibits on area history and the background of the jail cells and gallows. Open Fri through Sun afternoons only; admission is free.

You're in barbecue country, remember, and the most popular place to go in town is *Fat Boys BBQ* (2010 S. Bridge St., Brady; 325-597-1111), specializing in brisket and rib plates, cabrito, pork chop, and rib eye steak (the latter on Friday). Surprises include bacon-wrapper asparagus and poppers—those are stuffed, smoked peppers—filled with your choice of chicken, shrimp, or quail.

Anyone who finds romance in history—and has a soft spot for animals—will want to stop in *Mason,* 28 miles south of Brady via US 377. The seat of Mason County—home to just 2,000—took its name from Fort Mason, built in the early 1850s as one in a chain of army posts established to protect against Indian attacks between the Red River and the Rio Grande.

Mason was unusual among Texas towns in that it endured an internal war in the 1870s when cattle rustlings and prejudices between German and Anglo settlers stirred up angry emotions; more than 10 men were killed in ambushes and lynchings before the Texas Rangers were summoned to reestablish peace in the community. For more information about the town, call the local chamber of commerce at (325) 347-5758 or visit masontxcoc.com.

You can explore the fort and town history at *Fort Mason* (204 West Spruce Street, Mason,; 325-347-5758). Among the illustrious soldiers who were once stationed at the fort were George Armstrong Custer, Albert Sidney Johnston, and Robert E. Lee. Today's fort is a reconstruction on the original foundation, and a miniature of the fort is among the exhibits. The museum is open daily, but it's best to call ahead for hours. You can read much more, and follow a wonderful journey through the forts that fill the area, at this Texas Historical Commission site, texasfortstrail.com.

If you read the book or saw the film *Old Yeller,* you probably never stopped crying long enough to wonder where its author, Fred Gipson, was from; Mason, it turns out, was his hometown. Gipson and other local notables are detailed in the local library, found at Post Hill and Schmidt Streets.

Rather unexpectedly you'll come upon the *Seaquist House* (400 Broad St., Mason, seaquist.org/), a sensational, 3-story Queen Anne Victorian mansion. Remarkable are its 22 rooms, 15 fireplaces, beautiful wooden staircase constructed without nails, galleries wrapping around 2 stories on the exterior, and third-floor ballroom. The house was started in 1891, then renovated in 1919 by a Swede who made his fortune in boots. The home is not open to the public, but it is a wonderful example of Victorian architecture.

There's no shortage of down-home, country stays in the Mason area: *Hasse House* (east from town square 6 miles on Highway 29; 325-347-6463), a spacious place on a 300-acre working ranch; another is *Fort Mason Outpost Guest House*(304 Pecan St., Mason, 325-347-6021). See a full list at masontx coc.com.

Right in the middle of town is a particularly comfortable stay for just $60 to $70. The **Mason Square Hotel** (122 Fort McKavett St., Mason; 325-347-7829; masonsquarehotel.com) is a4-room inn with private bath, kitchenette, sunroom, and a balcony overlooking the town square, all above a law office. Dining on or very near the square includes **Mason Burger** (205 San Antonio St.), Square Plate (212 Fort McKavette St.), and **Willow Creek Café** (106 Fort McKavett). Finally, rock hounds will be thrilled at the area's fantastic variety of minerals and rocks located in the geologic outcroppings. Specifically, blue topaz, the state gem—a rarity in North America—is found here. The public can hunt topaz at the **Seaquist Ranch** (325-347-5413; masontxcoc.com/topaz.html) just northwest of Mason. They charge fees but permit camping. All Mason info can be found through the local chamber of commerce, masontxcoc.com.

Continuing along the Hill Country trail, turn southwest on US 377 and go 39 miles through big deer-hunting country to **Junction,** the seat of Kimble County, home to about 2,600 people and more flowing streams than any other Texas county.

Most people who cite Junction as a destination do so for its wildlife watching and other outdoorsy pursuits. **South Llano River State Park** (4 miles south of town on US 377; 325-446-3994; tpwd.texas.gov) is just the right place for these, as animals often seen here include white-tailed deer, wood ducks, fox squirrels, rock squirrels, javelina, and the Rio Grande turkey. The turkeys roost in bottomlands; this site is closed to visitors from October through March. At the park enjoy camping, hiking, picnicking, canoeing, and inner tubing between wildlife sightings. The spring-fed river is simple pleasure itself. A small admission fee is charged.

Historians are wise to make two detours from Junction before exploring the remainder of the Hill Country. Thirty miles due north of Junction is the town of **Menard,** seat of Menard County, with a population of about 1,600. Established during the pioneer and cattle-driving days near the ruins of the 18th-century Spanish mission **Santa Cruz de San Saba,** Menard tells its story in a little county museum in the old train depot, designed in the Mission Revival style in 1909, at 100 Frisco Ave. (325-396-2365; menardchamber.com/the-chamber/).

Rather intriguing is the sight of ruins on the city golf course. There, by the eighth hole, are the ancient walls of the Spanish presidio built to protect the mission. The mission was attacked in 1758 by Comanche and other Native Americans; the presidio soldiers weren't numerous enough, and the presidio was abandoned in 1769. Learn details about the town and its annual outdoor musical drama in June by calling the local chamber of commerce (above).

About 20 miles west of Menard, in the southwestern corner of Menard County, *Fort McKavett State Historic Site* (RR 864; 325-396-2358; thc.texas .gov/historic-sites/fort-mckavett-state-historic-site) presents yet another portrait of rugged Texas history. Established as Camp San Saba in 1852, the fort was one of the most important in west Texas pioneer history; 15 restored buildings include an officers' quarters, barracks, hospital, and a cluster of interpretive exhibits pertaining to military history and historic archaeology. Throughout the year, the park is open daily from 8 a.m. to 5 p.m.

On the road again, prepare yourself for spectacular scenery. From Junction, take US 83 south, making a 57-mile journey to *Leakey* (LAY-kee), the Real County seat and a town of 450 tucked into an especially picturesque corner of the Edwards Plateau. About 12 miles shy of town, you'll be happy if you packed a picnic lunch, because there's a particularly good roadside park with superb scenery right there.

Although you won't see Comanches and Apaches living in the area around Leakey as did the Spanish explorers, you will find flocks of registered Angora goats from which area ranchers harvest mohair. This, too, is a popular hunting ground for white-tailed deer, mourning dove, quail, wild turkey, and javelina.

Consider taking a day or two to revel in the surroundings, putting your feet up at one of the comfortable retreats in this bucolic setting. Your dreams of rest and relaxation will be fulfilled at one of the cabins or private vacation homes booked through *Rio Frio Lodging* (throughout Uvalde Country; 830-966-2320; friolodging.com), which offers riverside abodes with fireplaces and full kitchens. At *River Haven Cabins* (RR 1120; 830-232-5400; riverhavencab-ins.com), the two-bedroom log cabins sitting on 6.5 acres along the Frio River are equipped with full kitchens, fireplaces, and satellite TV, and the grounds have barbecue pits, basketball goals, a playground, and picnic tables.

An appealing park in the area is *Garner State Park,* on the Frio River just inside Uvalde County, a 9-mile drive south of Leakey via US 83. Here the fun in warm weather is all about settling into a big inner tube and floating down the clear, cold Frio, surrounded by limestone shelves and shady cypress lining the way. Stone-and-timber cabins at the park offer a comfortable night's rest; call (830) 232-6132 or visit tpwd.texas.gov for reservations. Other diversions include pedal boats, miniature golf, camping, hiking, fishing, and grocery facilities. (*Note:* Spring break crowds tend to be big and lively.) The park is open daily, and a small admission is charged.

If the park is full, check out *Neal's Vacation Lodges,* right on the Frio and near the park (830-232-6118; nealslodges.com). This collection of rustic cabins and motel-style kitchenettes—which also have televisions—has been a Hill Country favorite since opening in 1926. Also on-site are a grocery, laundry facility, country store, and cafe, the latter serving breakfast, lunch, and dinner. During the summer Neal's offers wildlife excursions, hayrides, and fishing, along with inner-tube rentals and shuttles for floating the river.

From Garner State Park, your next destination is east on FR 1050—one you'll always remember for climbing views of bluffs and valleys and blooming cacti—15 miles to **Utopia,** an appropriately named town if ever one existed. The farming-ranching hamlet—population just 360—in Uvalde County was established on Sabinal Creek in 1852 and is a second home to hunters and campers; spring wildflowers and fall foliage bring plenty of fans, too.

Sparkling spring-water drinkers have likely heard of Utopia by now—the crystal liquid is bottled here and shipped around the world. Notice how at the post office, the general store, and the café, all those friendly people seem unusually happy? It must be the water.

Simple country cooking is the pride at **Lost Maples Cafe** (in the middle of town on RM 187; 830-966-2221; lostmaplescafe.com). Chat with the local game warden, park rangers, neighboring farmers, and outgoing staffers over Frisbee-size pancakes or fresh, made-to-order chicken-fried steak, enormous baked potatoes, and barbecue.

People who want the restoration found in long, breathtaking drives come to the Leakey-Utopia area to see where the Frio, Nueces, and Sabinal Rivers etched vividly shaded canyons, from which hills and mesas rise between 1,500 and 2,400 feet. The specific drives from Leakey that attract photographers, painters, and other artists of the soul are FR 337 west to Camp Wood, past wooded rises and lonely, green valleys colored purple in spring with mountain laurel; and FR 337 east into Bandera County to **Vanderpool,** then north on Ranch Market 187.

Lost Maples State Natural Area is on every Texas fall foliage fan's list as a must-see, but be assured the park is roaring with beauty in all seasons. These bigtooth maples are said to be lost because they're far from any other stands of their kind, which are scattered over the western US and northern Mexico. The brilliant orange, red, and gold peak is usually in early November, and crowds tend to be staggering.

There are more than 90 plant families in the park, represented by more than 350 species. The bird population is healthy as well, with the golden-cheeked warbler among uncommon finds. Camping and hiking are the park's other big draws, and reservations are a good idea; call (830) 966-3413 or visit tpwd.texas.gov. The park is open daily, and admission is charged.

The town of Vanderpool, population 20, is 4 miles south of the park on Ranch Market 187. You'll find accommodations here, including **Foxfire Cabins** (1 mile south of the park facing the Sabinal River; 830-966-2200 and 877-966-8200; foxfirecabins.com) offering log cabins.

Exotics, Dudes & Germans

From Vanderpool journey north on FR 187 for 19 miles to Highway 39, then eastward on Highway 39 for 26 miles, through the town of Ingram to the intersection of Highway 27; take this highway just another 7 miles east into *Kerrville,* the seat of Kerr County, the largest city in the Hill Country, and home to more than 21,000 people.

Easily the spiritual center of the Hill Country, Kerrville straddles the peaceful *Guadalupe River* and captures all that Texans treasure about this agreeable region—clean air, clear water, limestone bluffs, and pure repose. Kerrville owes its success to developer Charles Schreiner, who became a Texas Ranger at age 16 and later served as a captain in the Civil War, and whose grandson brought the Texas longhorn breed back from the brink of extinction.

An enduring foundation of the area, Schreiner's *Y.O. Ranch Headquarters,* 26 miles west on I-10 and Highway 41, is a top working ranch and a top attraction in the state. Forty thousand acres remain of Schreiner's 550,000 acquired in 1880; the ranch came under new ownership in 2015 and it remains open to visitors who want to see herds and herds of longhorn, sheep, and goats, plus free-ranging animals from around the globe; this is considered North America's largest collection of exotic wildlife.

In all there are some 10,000 animals of 58 species, including wildebeest, oryx, addax, Japanese sika, aoudad, black buck antelope, ostrich, giraffe, zebra, and Watusi cattle, to name a few. Most day-trippers come for a wildlife tour that includes lunch, or horseback ride. Overnight guests can stay in a cabin or a ranch house, enjoy time in the pretty swimming pool, and share a chuckwagon dinner with other guests. For details and reservations call the ranch at (830) 640-3222 or visit yoranchheadquarters.com.

You may spend a day seeing the Y.O.'s animals, but you won't want to miss a weekend in town, where culture and cowboys prevail. Kerrville's a bastion of artistic diversity, with folk music and folk-art festivals in May. For details contact the *Kerrville Convention & Visitor Bureau* at (830) 792-3535 or visit kerrvilletexascvb.com.

Kerrville is also home to possibly the nation's only museum dedicated to the work of a single group of living artists. The *Museum of Western Art* features the paintings and sculptures of about 30 members, some of whom are considered the country's foremost artists of Western American Realism. The building itself is wonderfully artful, incorporating light Mexican brick in bóveda domes that need no supporting forms or wiring. The museum charges admission and is just south of downtown on Highway 173; call (830) 896-2553 or visit museumofwesternart.com for more information. The museum is open Tues through Sat.

For a lovely sunset drive, head west from Kerrville on **RR 1340,** which winds its way through the scenic communities of Ingram and Hunt. The ribbon of road twists and turns, repeatedly crossing the Guadalupe River, passing a scattering of summer cottages, boys' and girls' summer camps, and deer-hunting country. In the middle of one field, you'll see a Stonehenge replica, of all things.

Among several good places to find rest in Kerrville, start with the **Inn of the Hills Resort** (1001 Junction Hwy., Kerrville; 830-895-5000 or 800-292-5690; innofthehills.com), a spreading complex with motel rooms, suites, and condo apartments. The 4 pools, pretty landscaping, games and activities for kids in summer, 3 restaurants, an exercise facility with sauna and whirlpool, bowling lanes, a putting green, bike and boat rentals, fishing in a stocked lake, and lighted tennis courts make this a full-service resort.

The **Y.O. Ranch Hotel** (2033 Sidney Baker Blvd., Kerrville; 830-257-4440 or 877-977-3767; yoranchhotel.com) is a charming hotel accented with western design. The huge lobby is lighted with chandeliers crafted from branding irons and is dominated by a bronze of a mounted cowboy working to bring a longhorn back to the herd. Room furnishings continue the theme.

Lazy Hills Retreat (west on Highway 27, just past Ingram; 830-367-1445; lazyhillsretreat.com) has shifted gears from a dude ranch offering to a family getaway destination with miniature golf, beach volleyball, kayaking,

The Wine Trails

Of the roughly 450 producing wineries in Texas, more than 50 are in the Hill Country/Central Texas region. Fredericksburg and Stonewall claim their fair share of those, and many more are in easy reach in towns like Johnson City, Mason, Comfort, and Sisterdale. In other words: There's a lot of wine to be tasted around here—and everyone seems to be on top of it.

You'll be wowed by swarming crowds at the **Becker Vineyards** (830-644-2681; beckervineyards.com) tasting room, but you won't be surprised that this spot in Stonewall, about 5 minutes east of Fredericksburg, has become a popular destination. Producer of some very nice wines, including a dandy viognier and best-selling chardonnay, Becker wines have been noted in the Wine Spectator and Wine Enthusiast, and they've been poured at at least two White House dinners in the past few years. This winery has become so popular, in fact, that the Beckers have opened a tasting room also in the heart of Fredericksburg, as have other wineries on what's now called Fredericksburg's Urban Wineries Trail. You can learn more about the region's wineries at texaswinetrail.com and about those in the immediate Fredericksburg area at visitfredericksburgtx.com/food-wine.

zip-line adventures, hiking and biking trail, and more in a beautiful hilly setting. The stone lodges have been spiffed up; rooms start at about $100 nightly.

Next stop after Kerrville is found north on Highway 16, 24 miles away in **Fredericksburg,** seat of Gillespie County, population 11,500 and climbing all the time. Texas's cache of German heritage is a miniature Bavarian treat with a proliferation of bed-and-breakfast lodgings, the backbone of Old World touring. In Fredericksburg, guests have the state's largest selection of places to spend rest periods off the road in quaint historic homes and inns, much more appealing to some than sleeping in cookie-cutter hotels.

Start your visit with a stop inside the **Fredericksburg Visitor Information Center,** 302 E. Austin St. (1 block off of Main Street; 888-997-3600 or 830-997-6523; visitfredericksburgtx.com). Here, you'll find information on Fredericksburg and the Hill Country, along with large public restrooms and plentiful parking, which gives you easy access to the National Museum of the Pacific War, across the street, and to Main Street shopping, dining, and entertainment. There's free wireless access at the visitor center, too.

If you haven't been to this burg recently, you'll have plenty of surprises in store. Yes, the deep German influence of its founders still prevails, but there's much more to this town than the sausage-beer-knickknack stop that became so popular in the early 1990s. Sure it's still a handy romantic getaway town, thanks to more than 350 guesthouses, but the level of sophistication that permeates the town today means that that signature "country-cute" appeal lingers only as a fading memory. Today you'll find a real wine country with requisite gracious dining to satisfy discerning palates, as well as galleries and shopping of a higher caliber than in the past. Travelers from the East Coast are finding this is an area for visiting and relocating, and developers have built million-dollar vacation homes on golf courses. In early summer you can wander the lavender trails, winding through farms blooming along the Pedernales River, and all spring and summer and parts of the fall, there are myriad weekend wine events hosted by area vineyards.

If you've come for the wine experience, you'll have plentiful ground to cover: There are more than 30 wineries in Gillespie County and another dozen or so within driving distance (consult wineroad290.com for details on these). On Main Street, you'll find several custom wineries (you create your own labels), tasting rooms, and wine bars. The Fredericksburg-based **Texas Wine Tours** lets you leave the driving to them when you sign up for half- and full-day winery tours (call 877-TEX-WINE or visit texas-wine-tours.com). It's just one of many tour companies operating in the area now. Find a full list at visitfredericksburgtx.com/food-wine-categories/. Note that bachelorette parties

Lincoln Street

One spring weekend I took my mom and her friends Vicki and Juanita on a girl-friends' getaway to Fredericksburg—a pastime that's now the most popular visiting demographic around town. We whiled away our days shopping—naturally—and wandering around the scenic countryside. In town we wound up an afternoon at what's become my favorite hangout—a place called **Lincoln Street,** a wine bar and market just off Fredericksburg's Main Street. Everyone gathers around a communal table, grabs comfy armchairs, or perches somewhere on the arbor-covered patio to kill an hour or two over wine from an impossibly diverse, global list. The staff exhibited infinite patience with our foursome as we mulled over the wine choices, all of which are available by the bottle for taking home, too. Ordering a cheese-olive board for two as a snack, we soon realized our enormous platter of exquisite edibles would render dinner plans completely unnecessary. We loved watching the locals drift in and out, some of them cowboys in hats and boots, dropping in for a glass of cabernet before heading back to the ranch. See more at lincolnst.com.

have become popular on the winery-touring circuit in this area, which can be fun for some visitors and less so for others. It's wise to check ahead of time to see which wineries do and don't accept such tours, and which tasting rooms require reservations.

Descriptions of the numerous guesthouses vary widely, from tiny, cute places to larger, rambling Victorian homes in town, to remote cabins and historic stone buildings in the countryside. Some are luxuriously decorated and command higher prices. All include breakfast, of course, which can mean anything from breads, fruits, and juices left for guests to have when they choose to formal feasts served at a large dining room table. A good searchable database is found at visitfredericksburgtx.com. While in Fredericksburg take time to explore history a bit. The town was the 1885 birthplace of Adm. Chester W. Nimitz, commander in chief of the Pacific fleet during World War II. A tribute to him and other heroes of that war is found at the **National Museum of the Pacific War** (340 E. Main St., Fredericksburg; 830-997-8600; pacificwar museum.org). Now a museum of national standing, the complex began with an old hotel building that houses exhibits on Nimitz's life and the restored ballroom. The vastly expanded George H.W. Bush Gallery, now measuring 33,000 square feet and costing $15.3 million, opened more recently. Detail on the Pacific War is astounding, and the Pacific War education programs extend to include African Americans and Hispanic Americans serving there. Be sure to leave time to walk through the Japanese Garden of Peace. The museum is open daily; admission is charged.

Shoppers can spend considerable time (and money) at the 100-plus boutiques and stores along *Fredericksburg's Main Street,* which offer everything from books, candles, quilts, primitive antiques, bath goods, and herbal remedies to peach jam, wine, pewter mugs, dulcimers, jewelry, clothing, and fine art and folk art.

Newer in the entertainment realm, the *Rockbox Theater* (109 N. Llano St.; 830-997-7625; rockboxtheater.com), just a block off Main Street, presents four live musical comedy shows every weekend in its 392-seat space. There's a new show each weekend, featuring music from the 50s, 60s, and 70s. At the *Fredericksburg Brewing Company* (245 E. Main St., Fredericksburg; 830-997-1646; yourbrewery.com), visitors tour the area's largest brew facility, housed in an 1890s rock building. There's a restaurant, lodgings, and a beer garden on-site, too.

A newer attraction for anyone who loves food and wine is the cooking class program inside *Das Peach Haus,* a culinary center sponsored by *Fischer & Wieser,* longtime Fredericksburg maker of jams, sauces, and other goodies (1406 S. U.S. 287, Fredericksburg; 866-997-89609; daspeach haus.com). The evening cooking demo-dinner program is led by chef and cookbook author John DeMers, who whips up a fabulous four-course dinner while you watch. A winemaker is on hand to pour wines chosen to pair with each dish. It's an entertaining, informative, and delicious experience. Check the schedule, as some classes are hands-on for those wanting to roll up their sleeves. Make reservations well in advance; find schedule and details at fwcookingschool.com.

Among favorite dining spots in Fredericksburg is *Navajo Grill* (803 E. Main St., Fredericksburg; 830-990-8289; navajogrill.com), a sophisticated sprawl of dining rooms inside a renovated cottage; and *Otto's German Bistro* (316 W. Austin St., Fredericksburg; 830-307-3336; ottosfbg.com), serving duck schnitzel, mussels, pan-seared rockfish, and inspired craft cocktails. For casual meals head to *Hondo's on Main* (312 W. Main St., Fredericksburg; 830-997-1633; hondosonmain.com) for grilled flat-iron steak, barbecued pork ribs, and mesquite-grilled burgers on sourdough buns. At lunch, a good bet is *Woerner Warehouse* (305 S. Lincoln St., Fredericksburg; 830-997-2246; woernerware house.com), where pizza and salads are delightful.

That's next door to one of two beautiful home furnishings stores, *Carol Bolton Hicks Antiquities* (301 S. Lincoln St., Fredericksburg; 830-997-5551; carolhicksbolton.com), a warehouse space that brims with distressed doors, cabinets, wrought-iron tables, books, beds, fabrics, and lighting, all imported from France. Across the street, *Blackchalk Home and Laundry* (306 S. Lincoln St., Fredericksburg; 830-998-1556) occupies a century-old commercial laundry. The clay brick building is stocked now with a colored assortment of handpainted dishes from Turkey, handmade wooden tables for Texas artisans, Italian lamps, and pillows from the Middle East.

A favorite side trip from Fredericksburg is the jaunt to **Enchanted Rock State Natural Area,** 18 miles north of town on RR 965. The park surrounds an otherworldly, huge, monolithic dome of pink granite, rising 600 feet into the sky—a challenge perfect for ambitious hikers. Climb it if you have stamina, good athletic shoes, and the foresight to have arrived early enough to find a parking space inside the park, as the annual visitor count now tops 350,000. The surprising vegetation up top is as impressive as the views, particularly in the first light of day. On summer nights the huge rock creaks and moans as it cools down, an occurrence the Comanches understandably found to be of a powerfully spiritual nature. Clever visitors can pack a picnic to be enjoyed on the rock as the sun is preparing to set. Just be sure to take a flashlight for the hike back down. The park is open daily and charges a small admission; get details by calling (830) 685-3636 or visiting tpwd.texas.gov.

For an explosion of color at any time of year, head to **Wildseed Farms,** 7 miles east of Fredericksburg on US 290 (800-848-0078; wildseedfarms.com). Wildseed Farms harvests up to 400,000 pounds of wildflower seeds annually and seems to be forever expanding its production. There are some 600 acres blooming in the Fredericksburg area, and the farm center allows visitors to see planting, harvesting, and flowers in various stages on 200 acres. The market complex, crafted from hand-cut Texas cedar and native stone, sells fresh-cut flowers, dried flowers, herbs, and hundreds of gifts, including housewares and clothing, pertaining to herbs and flowers. A beer garden offers refreshments and a butterfly garden demonstrates a biological system that butterflies inhabit during their lives. A vineyard is now planted, producing grapes, and Wedding Oak Winery, based in nearby San Saba, operates a tasting room here, too.

Make Your Own Way

When Waylon Jennings sang, "Let's go to Luckenbach, Texas, with Willie an' Waylon an' the boys," he knew instinctively how to get there. He had to, because there's no sign indicating where it is. The tiny burg of 25 people became so famous for its spontaneous concerts and parties in the 1970s that souvenir hunters kept swiping the signs. The highway department dutifully replaced them for years, just to have them stolen again and again. It finally gave up, deciding visitors who really wanted to find the place would do so. And they do.

The most famous detour of all is *Luckenbach,* population 25, reached by driving 6 miles east of town on US 290, then turning south (right) on RR 1376; continue on this little road about 5 miles till you see signs. If you cross the creek, you've gone too far—maybe it's time to stop and ask directions, as signs to Luckenbach just don't last long, thanks to souvenir hunters.

"In Luckenbach, Texas, ain't nobody feelin' no pain" is how the song goes, and honestly, everybody feels fine when they're in Luckenbach because it's mostly a state of mind. It isn't even a town, but a little pocket of peace where the population is really just the number of people sitting around drinking longnecks on the porch of the eternally unpainted general store, playing dominoes, or pitching horseshoes. There's live music nightly in the dance hall, where you can join folks two-steppin' to the likes of Gary P. Nunn, who stops in occasionally to entertain the idea of going "home with the armadillo" in his song "London Homesick Blues."

An 1850 German settlement, Luckenbach was unremarkable for more than a century, with the exception of Jacob Brodbeck, who—years before the Wright brothers—invented an airplane powered with coiled springs. He abandoned the project after a discouraging crash in 1865.

Then in the 1970s humorist-writer and legendary Texas character Hondo Crouch invited like souls to share in Luckenbach's bucolic remoteness, laced with bluebonnets and pioneer flavor. This made it a place where "everybody's somebody," as prescribed by Waylon Jennings and Jerry Jeff Walker, in the song that propelled the tiny spot in the road into fame.

You can find great T-shirts, postcards (stamped with a Luckenbach postmark), jewelry, snacks, beer, and plenty of conversation in the general store; a barbecue stand next to the dance hall is generally open on weekends. Someone is always on stage for the weekend dancehall crowd, and there are frequent picking sessions for folks who just want to join in. For information call the general store at (888) 311-8990, or visit luckenbach texas.com.

From Fredericksburg the tour continues south on US 87 to *Comfort,* a 23-mile drive. Barely inside the Kendall County line, the borough of almost 2,400 was settled in 1854 by free-thinking German intellectuals, some of whom later joined Union forces in the Civil War; you'll see the Treue Der Union Monument, a tribute to them, on High Street between 3rd and 4th Streets.

Comfort is also known for being batty: The *Hygieostatic Bat Roost,* 1.5 miles east on Ranch Road 473, was a 1918 experiment; a century later, the bats still use it. Sunset is the time to watch for them here and at the Old Railroad Tunnel, 14 miles north via FR 473 and Old Highway 9, where several thousand bats live in a tunnel abandoned in 1942.

Take a stroll down *High Street* to have a close-up look at one of the state's more complete 19th-century business districts still intact. The Chamber of Commerce office, at 7th and High Streets, (830-995-3131; comfortchamber .com), has free, helpful guides. If you're into shopping, High Street has places of interest, such as *The Elephant Story,* a store promoting elephant conservation in Asia by selling assorted free-trade products—including jewelry and clothing and wooden home décor items—from that region (723-725 High St., Comfort; 830-995-3133; the-elephant-story.com).

Around the corner, there are additional fun finds at *8th Street Market,* revealing a treasure trove of architectural pieces, like beautiful, distressed antique doors and wrought iron patio furnishings, as well as carved antique wooden mirrors, 1950s bar sets and assorted garden accessories (523 8th St., Comfort; 830-201-0214; the8thstreetmarket.com).

The old *Faust Hotel,* which had operated as the Comfort Common B&B and then an antique collective, is now a lodging under its original name again (717 High St., Comfort; 830-995-3030; hotelfaust.com). A state historic landmark, the lovely old limestone building and other structures on the property offer a total of six suites, a one-bedroom cabin, and a two-bedroom cottage, all with every modern convenience and a mix of antique and contemporary furnishings. The courtyard behind the main building brings everything together, offering a pretty outdoor space for gathering.

Cozy sleepovers can be had, too, at *Meyer Bed & Breakfast* (845 High St., Comfort; 830-995-2304 or 888-995-6100; meyerbedandbreakfast.com), a historic and charming hotel complex with a swimming pool and fishing behind the complex in Cypress Creek. The main building was a stage stop in Comfort's earliest days. A new favorite place to stay is *Camp Comfort,* a collection of cabins and suites built atop an old bowling alley and community

The Camel Corps

It is known as the great failed camel experiment. In 1856 the US Cavalry placed an outpost at **Camp Verde,** where Texas Rangers had already fought off Comanches in what was known as the Bandera Pass. Secretary of War Jefferson Davis chose the site for an Army experiment, using camels as pack animals. The idea was that the camel corps would be useful in communication and transportation through the arduous west to Fort Yuma, California. While there was some success, Confederate troops took over the fort in 1861, and many of the camels were allowed to wander off or simply die. At least one of the descendants of the camel corps lives at a ranch near Camp Verde, but visitors can see a camel theme in the Camp Verde General Store in the form of camel wind chimes and other gift items.

gathering house. Décor is modern but exceptionally comfortable, and construction includes lots of reclaimed wood. Thoughtful appointments in each of the quarters make you think of summer camp in only the best ways. Each comes with a private bath, lounge area, and kitchenette, and all the guests share a common area for continental breakfast and for playing board games or playing cards (601 Water St., Comfort, 830-995-2356; camp-comfort.com).

There's good eating and drinking in Comfort, too: An excellent meal is had at **Comfort Pizza** (802 High St, Comfort; 830-995-5959), which occupies a former corner gas station. From a wood-fired oven came super-thin, crisp pizza topped with goods like artichoke hearts, local smoked sausage, goat cheese and fresh basil. It's such a popular place that guests need to call ahead to reserve pizza dough; that way the staff will make enough of the fresh stuff each day. There's a good brunch, lunch, and dinner at **814: A Texas Bistro,** (713 High St, Comfort; 830-995-4990, 814atexasbistro.com); and The **Wander'n Calf Espresso Bar & Bakery** inside 8th Street Market (above) serves a fine French press carafe of coffee with beautiful, fresh scones. You can also get a great cappuccino, meat loaf sandwich, or fresh cookies at **High's** (726 High St., Comfort; 830-995-4995).

Bending Branch Winery, found on a hilly estate just outside of town (142 Lindner Branch Trail, Comfort; 830-995-2948; bendingbranchwinery.com), offers tastings and tours, as well as live music on weekends. In town, the winery's **Branch on High** (704 High St., Comfort; 830-995-3394) invites you to taste the winery's numerous award-winning wines and enjoy paired snacks. Delicious sipping is found also at **Texas Hill Country Distillers** (723 Front St., Comfort; 830-995-2924; hillcountrytxdistillers.com), where a friendly bar staff whips up cocktails made with spirits distilled on-site, many of them crafted from prickly pear cactus. The Rosemary Gin Fizz, made with the distillery's Texas Revenge Gin, lemon juice and fresh rosemary, is refreshing.

Camp Verde, west of Comfort 17 miles via Highway 27 and then RR 480, is barely a wide spot in the road. The community has only 40 residents but a Texas-size heritage. At its heart is **Camp Verde General Store & Restaurant,** operating as a store since 1857 (285 Camp Verde Road East, Camp Verde; 830-634-7722; campverdegeneralstore.com). Inside the retail part of the operation, which is the original general store, you'll find T-shirts, gift baskets, Hill Country jams and jellies, wood carvings, cookbooks, and home decor items. The new and sizable addition to the store is a restaurant, serving a lunch menu of soups and salads, burgers and deli sandwiches, and comfort dishes like meat loaf and pork chops. The store is open daily; the restaurant is closed on Sunday.

If you're ready to kick back at the ranch, head south on Highway 173, about 15 miles to **Bandera,** the Bandera County seat and home to a population of nearly 900 in town and far more in the county. It claims the title Cowboy Capital of the World not just for its cattle-drive and ranching heritage but also for the record number of National Rodeo Champions who lived there or still do. And, what travelers most like to find, Bandera is home to seven terrific guest ranches.

Long before would-be dudes began showing up in Bandera, several hundred Comanches ambushed about 40 Texas Rangers here in 1841. Peace eventually prevailed, and settlers arrived in 1852, finding the cypress-and-live-oak–laden banks of the Medina River a good place to put down roots. The primitive countryside about 45 miles west of San Antonio still holds that appeal, and vacationing cowboys and cowgirls have all the western-style fun they want.

The guest ranches each offer family lodging in bunkhouses or cabins, horseback riding and hayrides, trick-roping and snake-handling (!) demonstrations, rodeos, country-western dancing, chuck wagon meals on the trail, swimming, fishing, and inner tubing on the river. Some are more specialized than others, offering fitness programs, golf, and the occasional spa treatment.

Dixie Dude Ranch (9 miles south of town on RR 1077; 830-796-7771 or 800-375-9255; dixieduderanch.com) has been in the family for more than 50 years, and now the fourth generation is running the 700-acre spread. The place is nothing if not homey, and guests find themselves making friends from all over the globe during fried chicken suppers, poolside cookouts, and Saturday-night barbecues. The ranch hands—especially good at matching riders with mounts—lead trail rides through a wild terrain, pointing out historic sites along the way. Lodgings include 20 rooms in cabins and a lodge.

Mayan Dude Ranch (1.5 miles northwest of town via Main and Pecan Streets; 830-796-3312; mayanranch.com) is more like summer camp with 68 rooms in cottages and lodges; it's an all-year affair for 100 or more guests of all ages. Days begin with cowboy-made breakfast on a trail beside the Medina River and usually continue in the saddle or in the Olympic-size pool. Nights are never dull—each one brings a different theme and activity, such as a Mexican fiesta, a ghost-town trip and steak fry, or a cocktails-barbecue-and-ice-cream party. The *Flying L Hill Country Resort* (1.5 miles south on Highway 173; or 800-292-5134; flyingl.com) has cabins, villas, and condos, a water park, golf and tennis facilities, lots of nightly programs for family, along with horseback riding. There are three restaurants, snack and coffee bar, and two watering holes on the premises.

If you're on your own for meals, the *OST*—named for the Old Spanish Trail, on which Bandera lies—(305 Main St.; 830-796-3836) will do you right with its chicken-fried steak, biscuits and gravy, Mexican food, and grilled steaks. A full list of places to eat is found at banderacowboycapital.com.

On Wednesday evenings, the *11th Street Cowboy Bar* (307 11th St., Bandera; 830-796-4849; 11thstreetcowboybar.com) hosts Wednesday steak night, in which you bring your own slab of meat—or chicken, fish, veggies skewers, or whatever you can pick up from the local grocery stores—and cook your own steak over one of several charcoal grills set up and readied for you. There are marinades and seasonings in a common pantry for all to use, and for $7 per person, you get a plate loaded with salad and sautéed veggies to augment your grilled item. Beer, wine, and soft drinks are sold, and a country band plays for your dancing pleasure. Most every other night, the bar's stage features a country band of local, regional, or national renown.

Even people just passing through Bandera should take just 30 minutes or so to have a peek at one of the funkier collections ever assembled: *The Frontier Times Museum* (506 13th St., Bandera; 830-796-3864; frontiertimes museum.org) exhibits more than 40,000 items, including bottles from Judge Roy Bean's saloon; 500 bells from around the world; antique firearms and saddles; and spear- and arrowheads.

On Thursday, Friday, and Saturday, you can enjoy a wine flight and cheeseboard at *Mulberry's* (823 Main St., Bandera; 830-796-9463), a wine bar with a surprisingly good selection. A cigar shop and smoke room is adjacent.

Immediately southwest of Bandera is *Hill Country State Natural Area* (830-796-4413; tpwd.texas.gov), reached by driving south of Highway 173 to RR 1077, which you'll follow to the west for 10 miles. This 5,370-acre spread—once the Bar-O Ranch—is cloaked with oak and juniper and offers 40 miles of trails shared by hikers, mountain bikers, and equestrians. The 23 marked trails are often used by trail-riding guests at the nearby guest ranches, as these pathways take in sensational springs, waterfalls, creeks, and hilly vistas. The park is absolutely primitive, so backcountry camping is the only option. The park is closed on Tues and Wed; entry is $3 per person over 12 years of age.

Another appealing place in the Bandera area is the *Hill Country Equestrian Lodge,* about 10 miles outside of town just off RR 1077 (830-796-7950; hillcountryequestlodge.com). Unlike the other guest ranches around, this one gives you a chance to take private riding lessons or even bring your own horse. Guests who don't want to ride can amuse themselves by hiking, birding, fossil hunting, mountain biking (bring your own wheels), or spending the day fishing, inner tubing, or kayaking on the nearby Medina River.

The lodge offers cabins crafted from native limestone and rough cedar, with fireplaces, sleeping spaces for 4 or 6 guests, one or two bathrooms, full kitchens, and great decks from which to watch the sun rise or set. Breakfast goodies are supplied for you to fix your own.

All details on lodging, dining, shopping, and other diversions in Bandera are easily obtained at the **Bandera Convention & Visitors Bureau** (Highway 16 South, a half-block from Main Street; 800-364-3833; banderacowboy capital.com).

If you drive about 15 miles northwest from Bandera on Highway 16 to the town of **Medina,** you'll be in the **Apple Capital of Texas.** Be sure to stop in the **Apple Store,** where you'll find delicious bakery goods, ice cream, coffee with apple strudel flavoring, apple jelly, cider, and saplings. Find it at **Love Creek Orchards** (14024 TX 16 North), which grows 11 apple varieties, lets you pick your own fresh fruit, starting with blackberries in May and June; apples in July; and figs in August. Contact the store at (800) 449-0882 or visit lovecreekorchards.com.

After living the ranch life, it may be time to search for more of that German Hill Country; you can do that by driving east on Highway 46, 23 miles from Bandera to **Boerne** (BURN ee), seat of Kendall County, with a population of about 15,000. The cerebral Germans who settled the town in 1851 named it for Ludwig Boerne, one of their fellow countrymen who was a political satirist, journalist, and refugee. You may run into day-trippers from San Antonio, just 30 miles southeast, while out browsing through the charming antiques shops—packed with great little finds—or at one of the pleasant restaurants in town. The places to enjoy along historic Main Street grow in number all the time, with art galleries, home goods, décor, clothing, jewelry, wine, and gifts among great finds. A full list is found at visitboerne.org, which also includes plentiful info on dining and lodging.

You can't go hungry in Boerne, that's certain. A favorite is **Po Po Family Restaurant** (at I-10, 7 miles west of Boerne, at the Welfare exit; 830-537-4194.), in an old stone house and former dance hall decorated with an array of at least 1,000 china plates on the wall, serving solid American and southern fare. It's open daily for lunch and dinner.

The town's lodging of choice is **Ye Kendall Inn** (128 W. Blanco, Boerne; 800-364-2138 or 830-249-9954; yekendallinn.com). Opened in 1859 as a stagecoach stop for travelers heading west from San Antonio, this handsome landmark with state and national historical markers has 34 restored rooms, suites, and cabins. It's a showplace, with 22-inch-thick limestone walls and old-fashioned verandas, all sitting on 5-plus acres on the Cibolo Creek and the town's fairy-tale plaza. An art gallery is on-site. Good dining is had at the inn's **Peggy's On the Green** (128 W. Blanco St., Boerne; 830-572-5000; peggysonthegreen.com), where steaks, seafood, and salads are good choices.

A special place to visit in Boerne is the **Kuhlmann–King Historical House** (402 E. Blanco St., Boerne; 830-249-2030). Built in the late 1880s by

German physicist William Kuhlmann, the 2-story house offers a look into life in that period. The separate Archives Building houses historical documents of the area. Call for tour times. A $2 donation is welcomed. It's one of several sites listed on the town historical walking tour; visit visitboerne.org for the route and any other Boerne information.

Spelunkers will be happy to know that two caves open to the public are nearby. The larger is *Cascade Caverns* (3 miles south on I-10 to Cascade Caverns Road; 830-755-8080; cascadecaverns.com), fascinating for its 90-foot interior waterfall, crashing from an underground stream. Tours last 45 minutes; a nice park with campsites, picnic areas, dance pavilion, swimming pool, snack bar, and bunkhouses is outside the cave. Admission is charged; open daily from 9 a.m. to 6 p.m.

The smaller cave in the area is simply known as *Cave Without a Name* (FR 474 east 6 miles to Kreutzberg Road, 5 miles along this road to the cave; 830-537-4212; cavewithoutaname.com), so called because the 1939 contest held to give it a title was won by a local boy who declared the cave "too pretty to name." The cave, 98 percent still active, is enormous—it takes from about an hour to 90 minutes to tour—and is filled with stalagmites and stalactites, "soda straws," "strips of bacon," "gnomes," and all sorts of mushrooming formations. Open every day except Thanksgiving and Christmas. Check cavewithoutaname .com for maps, photos, and admission prices, as well as special events such as Summer Solstice celebrations and musical events held underground.

Guadalupe River State Park (Highway 46 and PR 31, 16 miles east of Boerne; 830-438-2656; tpwd.texas.gov) occupies 1,900 acres where cypress, limestone bluffs, and natural rapids blend to make a place of beauty on the gracious Guadalupe River. Canoeing, fishing, hiking, camping, and nature study are all available. Open daily; a small admission fee is charged.

Just in case you haven't had enough of Texas's rich German heritage, more awaits in *New Braunfels,* a 43-mile drive east of Boerne on Highway 46. The

Conserve History

Conservation Plaza is where you'll go in New Braunfels to see priceless historic structures, including the Lindheimer Home, the Rose Conservatory, the Church Hill School, the Jahn Cabinet Shop, the Buckhorn Barber Shop, and the Wagenfuehr Home. The local conservation society's work is also seen in the Baetge House, built 26 miles from town but dismantled and relocated in the downtown plaza to display its fine example of *fachwerk* (half-timbered) construction, done in 1852 by a German engineer.

Summer Fun

An oldie but goodie, *Schlitterbahn* is a splashy, 65 acre spread in New Braunfels. Known for German-like castles and more than 40 attractions, such as waterslides, hot tubs, uphill water coasters, inner-tube chutes, and water playgrounds, this favorite sits on the beautiful Comal River. New are the private Cabanas and BBQ Palapas, for groups of six to ten, that you reserve in advance. Ask also about lodging at the resort. Open all summer, Schlitterbahn is located at 400 N. Liberty St., New Braunfels; (830) 625-2351; schlitterbahn.com.

seat of Comal County, New Braunfels has about 74,000 citizens and a history that was almost very romantic.

The story goes that the town was settled in 1845 by a German prince and 200 immigrants; the prince named his establishment for the town in Germany where his castle stood. He was to build a new castle for his fiancée, Princess Sophie, but she refused to come to this rough, unknown land, so he returned home to marry her and never saw Texas again. This and the remaining history of New Braunfels are told at the *Sophienburg Museum*—named for her anyway—at 401 W. Coll St., New Braunfels; (830) 629-1572; sophienburg.com.

One of the state's lovelier places to rest is the *Prince Solms Inn* (295 E. San Antonio St., New Braunfels; 830 312-5387; princesolmsinn.com), a luxury bed-and-breakfast hotel filled with antiques and housing a day spa. The historic *Faust Hotel & Brewing Company* (240 S. Seguin St., New Braunfels; 830-625-7791, fausthotel.com) is restored and filled with antiques. On property, enjoy a brewery and restaurant (faustbrewing.com).

If you happen upon New Braunfels in the fall, plan to dance a polka and drink a stein or two to the oompah-pah in Wursthalle, as the town hosts well over 100,000 people each year at *Wurstfest,* an enormous German party held over the first two weekends in November. A generous schedule of events is always offered, as are food and drink. For details call (830) 625-9167 or (800) 221-4369 or check wurstfest.com. For a good overview of places to stay, eat, and visit in New Braunfels, check out innewbraunfels.com.

For anyone looking for a little watery excitement, head north a couple of miles to the restored town of *Gruene* (north on I-35 to FR 306, west about 1.5 miles to Hunter Road, then follow the signs; gruenetexas.com). There, on the Guadalupe River, several river outfitters (call 830-625-2385 for a list) offer trips lasting anywhere from 3 to 5 hours. If it's late spring or early summer, the river will probably run high and fast, so do as the instructors say and paddle like crazy through the little rapids. If it's late in summer and there hasn't been much rain, you're likely to have a slow trip. For a lonely, peaceful trip, tackle the river on a weekday, when high-spirited rafters and tubers won't be clogging the waters.

While in Gruene, plan to spend time poking around *Gruene Historic District,* a quaint 1870s cotton-gin town containing what is now the oldest dance hall in Texas; restored buildings housing antiques shops, clothing boutiques, woodwork, leather goods, and pottery shops; a winery tasting room; and good restaurants, starting with the *Gristmill* (1287 Gruene Rd.; 830-625-0684; gristmillrestaurant.com), purveyors of excellent fried catfish, grilled chicken, steaks, burgers, and frosty margaritas. On weekend nights there's live music on the patio under the stars. The primary reason most people visit Gruene, however, is to see live music shows at *Gruene Hall,* said to be the oldest dance hall in the state (1281 Gruene Rd., New Braunfels; 830-606-5077; gruenehall.com). Legendary acts still play the stage, as do up-and-coming musicians. It's a great experience, no matter when you visit.

Next door to the Gristmill, *Gruene Mansion Inn* (1275 Gruene Rd., Gruene; 830-629-2641; gruenemansioninn.com) is a gorgeous Victorian home overlooking the Guadalupe River and operating as a bed-and-breakfast inn.

texastrivia

Texas Hill Country native Lyndon B. Johnson was the first American president to host a barbecue on the White House lawn. He usually served Texas-style barbecued ribs at official parties and receptions.

From New Braunfels head north on I-35 just 16 miles to reach *San Marcos,* seat of Hays County and home to nearly 62,000 residents. The headwaters of the San Marcos River are here, where Native Americans are thought to have lived some 12,000 years ago, making this one of the oldest continuously inhabited places on the continent. Springs forming the river come from the Edwards Underground Reservoir, pushing up through the Balcones Escarpment limestone at a rate of at least a million gallons daily. It's known as one of the largest artesian springs in the world.

The Meadows Center for Water and the Environment, formerly called Aquarena Springs (512-245-9200; www.meadowscenter.txstate.edu/Explore SpringLake.html) was long the primary reason folks visited San Marcos. In 1994, however, Texas State University in San Marcos—whose wonderful red-topped spires are seen on a hill above town—purchased Aquarena Springs and closed the resort. Today the center focuses on research for clean, abundant water. Visitors can ride the famous glass-bottom boats or take a kayak or stand-up paddleboard tour; enjoy Discovery Hall, with its 1,000-gallon aquarium; and follow a self-guided tour on the Wetlands Boardwalk. There are fees for the boat tours, guided Wetlands tours; and parking. Hours vary, so call ahead.

To see another set of Hill Country caverns, head to **Wonder World** (1000 Prospect St., San Marcos; 512-392-3760; wonderworldpark.com). There's a 120-foot-tall observation tower and tour of the million-year-old limestone cave. Hours and fees vary according to season.

Canoeing is a hugely popular activity on the fabulous San Marcos River. Outfitters include **T.G. Canoe Livery** (512-353-3946; tgcanoe.com). Floating the river on inner tubes is another great way to pass a warm day; call **Lions Club Tube Rental** in summer, (512) 396-LION; tubesanmarcos.com. For all information on dining, lodging, outdoor attractions, and more, visit toursan marcos.com.

From San Marcos you're in for a day in shopping heaven and a charming bed-and-breakfast night at **Wimberley,** a 15-mile drive west of San Marcos via RR 12. It's a small town—population 3,000—but its stature is large, indeed, among the enlightened.

Here's a mini-resort town that happens to rest between two of the prettiest little streams in Texas—the Cypress Creek and the Blanco River. It's a hub of shopping activity on weekends, when dozens of pottery studios, art galleries, antiques shops, and boutiques are open for business. The **Blue Hole,** on Cypress Creek, is one of the state's primo swimming holes, and most guests at resorts, ranches, and B&Bs spend a few lazy hours floating under the clouds.

If you're in the humor for shopping, Wimberley is a great place to exercise those credit cards. On the square, which

texastrivia

The vast Texas highway system encompasses 77,133 miles of highways, of which 40,985 are paved farm and ranch roads.

isn't square-shaped at all, you'll find art galleries, boutiques, wine shops, and much more. Wimberley has become a prime place to unwind with expert help. **Serenity Farmhouse Inn & Resort** offers a full menu of spa services, as well as dining and lodging (888-882-8985; serenityfamhouseinn.com).

Sweet tooths will have a heyday at **Wimberley Pie Co.** (on RR 12 just south of the square; 512-847-9462; wimberleypie.com), where you'll be wowed by aromas of 70 or so pies. Pie varieties include buttermilk, black bottom cherry cheesecake, key lime, and pecan. It's open Wed through Fri from 9:30 a.m. to 5:30 p.m., Sat from 10 a.m. to 5 p.m., and Sun noon to 4 p.m.

The most popular lodging in town is probably **Blair House Inn** (100 Spoke Hill Rd., Wimberley; 512-847-1111; blairhouseinn.com). There are 3 rooms in the main lodge, 3 rooms in the Pond Cottage, 2 rooms in the Honeysuckle Cottage, and 3 individual Archangel Cottages, all of which are impeccably outfitted for a luxurious stay. The dining room serves elaborate breakfasts daily and 5-course feasts (by reservation only) on Saturday night. A cooking school and day spa are on-site, too. Rooms begin at $160.

For all lodging, dining, shopping, and entertainment information relating to Wimberley, visit Wimberley.org or call the chamber at (512) 847-2201.

A good night's rest is needed to prepare you for a drive on the **Devil's Backbone,** the wildly twisting RR 32, reaching from RR 12 immediately south of Wimberley almost 25 miles toward Blanco. This, a dramatically nicknamed route, is easily a contender for the state's most scenic drive, cutting a winding path along a sharp ridge through the hills; be on the watch early or late in the day for white-tailed deer. It's spectacular at any time, but with spring wildflowers or autumn foliage, it's the ultimate.

Another pair of diversions in this neck of the woods lies north of Wimberley about 13 miles at the hamlet of **Driftwood**. The wide spot in the road became famous years ago, and remains rightly so, for a destination called **The Salt Lick BBQ** (18300 Farm Road 1826, Driftwood, 512-858-4959; saltlickbbq .com). Just a little stone cottage serving smoked meats when it opened in 1967, the operation has grown significantly to accommodate hundreds of customers at once on its rolling, bucolic grounds. Open daily for lunch and dinner, it's a good place from deeply smoked brisket, pork ribs, sausage, and turkey, with all the trimmings, and you can enjoy cold adult beverages on-site, too. The Salt Lick has added a winery to its attractions; **Salt Lick Cellars** makes tempranillo and mourvedre with grapes grown on property, and there are lovely decks for enjoying a glass (512-894-3117; saltlickcellars.com).

Across the road from Salt Lick is **Fall Creek Vineyards**' second location (18059-A Farm Road 1826, Driftwood, 512-858-4050; fcv.com/driftwood). The beautiful estate offers a tasting hall for its numerous wines, with reservations required for groups of six or more. A menu of noshes to accompany the tastings includes artisanal cheeses, a charcuterie board, duck pate plate or an elegant grilled cheese on sourdough. A few steps away, you can book the Wine Country Inn, Fall Creek's lodging with two master suites, beautiful rock fireplace in the living room and a full kitchen. Once the winery closes for the evening, you have the gardens to yourself. That's a true Hill Country pleasure.

Other Places to Stay in the Hill Country

BANDERA

Rancho Cortez
872 Hay Hollar Rd.
(830) 796-9339 or
(866) 797-9339
ranchocortez.com
Half dude ranch and half fitness camp, this ranch south of town and next to a vast state park attracts couples and families from around the world. There's a pool, plenty of exercise and health-improvement options, and beautiful views.

BLANCO

Beckmann Lane Guest House
Off RR 32, two miles southeast of Blanco
(512) 644-8424
beckmannlaneguesthouse.com
A restored 1900s farmhouse makes a fine place for a smaller family reunion or girlfriend or romantic getaway. There are three bedrooms, two bathrooms, two fireplaces, full kitchen, and room to spread out.

FREDERICKSBURG

Inn on Baron's Creek Spa & Conference Center
308 S. Washington St.
(830) 990-9202 or
(866) 990-0202
innonbaronscreek.com
Close to Main Street, this resort has 89 suites, including 6 on the creek. Serenity Spa is on-site, along with a fitness center. Spa package deals start at about $350.

Outlot 201 Guest Houses
2015 W. Live Oak St
(830) 456-6555
homeaway.com
Three modern farmhouses on 10 acres, about five minutes from downtown, offer peace and quiet, lovely surroundings, kitchenette and living room, patio, and continental breakfast.

Rose Hill Manor
Upper Albert Road
(877) ROSE-HIL
rose-hill.com
Elegant inn on a hilltop in the countryside east of town offers 4 large suites in the main house, as well as a scattering of private cottages on the grounds. A lovely restaurant is on-site as well. Rooms start at about $159.

NEW BRAUNFELS

Kuebler-Waldrip Haus B&B
1620 Hueco Springs Loop
(830) 625-8300 or
(800) 299-8372
kueblerwaldrip.com

SAN MARCOS

Crystal River Inn
326 W. Hopkins St.
(512) 396-3739 or
(888) 396-3739
crystalriverinn.com

WIMBERLEY

Cypress Creek Cottages
1004 Scudder Lane
(512) 847-5950
cyrpesscreekcottages.com
Twelve cottages with private hot tubs, fireplaces, kitchens, and gas grills. Pet-friendly, too.

Other Places to Eat in the Hill Country

BANDERA

Busbee's Bar-B-Q
339 Main St.
(830) 796-3153
Pork ribs, beef brisket, and peach cobbler are among the favorites.

TJ's at the Old Forge
807 Main St.
(830) 796-9990
tjsoldforge.com
Fried pickles, fried mushrooms and bacon cheddar fries are among appetizers; entrees include pecan-crusted chicken, honey-glazed salmon, and steaks.

FREDERICKSBURG

August E's
203 E. San Antonio St.
(830) 997-1585
august-es.com
Asian pumpkin–asparagus soup, sushi, glazed grilled quail, and sushi are among offerings. Thai Tuesdays are popular, as is dining at the bar.

Cabernet Grill
At Cotton Gin Village
Just south of Fredericksburg on TX 16
(830) 990-5734
Cabernetgrill.com
Serving steaks and seafood, this restaurant offers a Texas-only wine list.

The Peach Tree Tea Room
210 S. Adams St.
(830) 997-9527
peach-tree.com
This lovely shop offers lunches of salads, soups, sandwiches, pasta, and desserts Mon through Sun.

JOHNSON CITY

The Hill Country Cupboard
at the junction of US 290 and US 281
(830) 868-4625
Hillcountrycupboard.com
Specialties are plate lunches and dinners, plus fresh bakery goods.

KERRVILLE

Francisco's Restaurant
201 Earl Garrett St.
(830) 257-2995
Franciscos-restaurant.com
Cilantro-lime chicken, chipotle shrimp, poblano pasta, and Veracruz nachos are among specialties in this art-filled space in a historic downtown building. Open for lunch and dinner; closed Sun.

Grape Juice
623 Water St.
(830) 792-9463
grapejuiceonline.com
Cozy wine bar serving small plates for pairing with choices from a great list, as well as a good selection of craft beer.

SAN MARCOS

Texas Reds Steakhouse
120 Grove St.
(512) 754-8808
Texasreds.com

WELFARE

Welfare Cafe
223 Waring Welfare Rd.
(830) 537-3700
A charming old post office and general store building houses a terrific restaurant. The grounds are enjoyable to roam, too. Pork tenderloin in dried cherry-molasses glaze, chicken sautéed with peaches, and crab cakes with smoked-jalapeño tartar sauce stand out. Serving dinner Thursday through Sunday and lunch Saturday and Sunday.

WIMBERLEY

The Leaning Pear
111 River Road, suite 110
(512) 847-7327
leaningpear.com
Subtitled "Hill Country-inspired cuisine," this contemporary space with cozy, comfy furnishings serves a menu made from seasonal, local ingredients. The menu features dishes like pecan-black currant-tuna on rye, stacked vegetable enchiladas, chicken and grits, and pizzas from a wood-burning oven.

South Texas

Resting beneath the Hill Country's lower reaches, San Antonio is indisputably the gateway to vast south Texas—often a lonely, wide open region. Long, unhurried drives impart views that must have been overwhelming to early settlers, so endless are the fiercely blue sky and the ferocious and scrubby land.

The Spaniards came to colonize the new land, doing so mightily in the San Antonio area with their missions, and other Europeans eventually followed. Fanning southward from the great Alamo City are settlements reflecting varied origins, from Alsatian to Polish and, of course, Hispanic.

Only a few communities in south Texas are heavily populated, but most towns have surprising depth of character. In between are protracted stretches of road, ranch land, and thickets of mesquite—a tough tree if ever one lived. For an hour or more you'll see nothing piercing the horizon other than clumps of cacti, fence posts, an occasional telephone pole, a very rare windmill, and that tenacious mesquite. For anyone who appreciates truly raw beauty, this might be heaven.

Along the Mexican border various small settlements still simmer with Texas's Old West heritage, and all are permeated by a binational spirit that flows alongside the Rio Grande as it

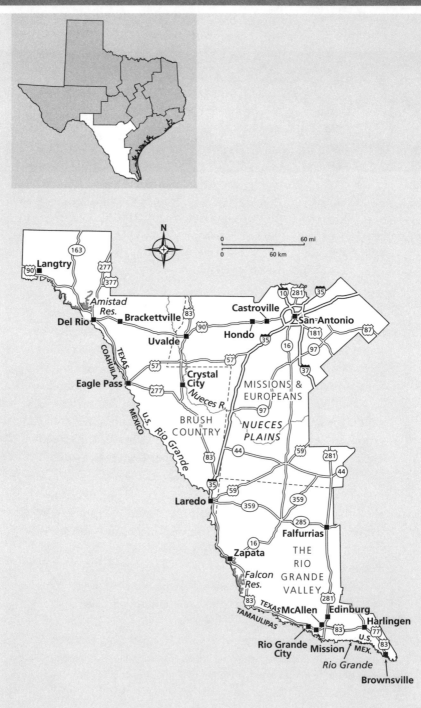

continues quietly and at length to the Gulf of Mexico. It's easy to picture, right there in your mind's eye, pioneer ranchmen of a century ago surveying the border, hoping somehow to tame a hopelessly wild land.

Missions & Europeans

Kaleidoscopic vistas of bluebonnets, Indian paintbrush, and other wildflowers frame US 281, Highway 16, and I-35 as you approach San Antonio in spring and summer, a subtle prelude to the year-round symphony of sights waiting in this cultural paradise. Get ready, because this vast storehouse of heritage and diversion knows how to entertain.

San Antonio, the nation's seventh-largest city with 1.5 million residents, boasts healthy German and Native American influences, but Hispanic culture dominates the city. This Mexican-American accord will always be part of San Antonio, as the city was part of colonial or independent Mexico for nearly 150 years. It celebrated its TriCentennial in 2018.

No written records tell us much of the area's early Native American period, but writings show that in the late 1690s resourceful Spaniards camped on the San Antonio River, which they called Rio San Antonio de Padua. Six Spanish missions were established in the early 1700s, but only five were successful. The first was Mission San Antonio de Valero in 1718, best known later under its nickname, *the Alamo.*

The Alamo mission doubled as a fort, where Davy Crockett, Jim Bowie, and William B. Travis were among the patriots who gave their lives for the

JUNE'S FAVORITE ATTRACTIONS

Casa de Palmas
McAllen

Fort Clark Springs
Brackettville

Institute of Texan Cultures
San Antonio

Lake Amistad
near Del Rio

The Pearl
San Antonio

Seminole Canyon State Historical Park
Comstock

Southwest School of Art
San Antonio

Spanish Governor's Palace
San Antonio

Texas Iwo Jima War Memorial
Harlingen

World Birding Center
Mission

Texas Revolution. For 13 days in late February and early March 1836, 187 men were surrounded and then crushed by the Mexican army. The would-be liberators managed to deplete Santa Anna's forces considerably before falling, enabling the Texans to win the Battle of San Jacinto and the revolution.

Heavy doors bearing bullet holes still front the Alamo, which sits before one of four Spanish plazas downtown, all connected by winding streets. Some people are disappointed to find the landmark to be such a small place, but its size doesn't diminish its significance. Inside, find collections of varying descriptions, including that donated in 2014 by British rock star Phil Collins, a devoted fan of the Alamo whose passion for artifacts resulted in a stunning collection. The Alamo, at 300 Alamo Plaza downtown, is open daily from 9 a.m. to 5:30 p.m. and until 7 p.m. in summer; call (210) 225-1391 or visit thealamo.org for more information.

Behind the Alamo, in the elaborate RiverCenter Mall, there's an **IMAX Theatre** presenting an excellent, 42-minute docudrama entitled *Alamo: The Price of Freedom* on a 6-story-tall film screen (849 E. Commerce St., Sutie 800, San Antonio). Historians double as actors in this production, telling a more factual story than the classic John Wayne movie version. For show schedule and ticket information, call (210) 247-4629 or (800) 354-4629 or visit shoprivercenter.com; an admission fee is charged.

Mission San Jose (6701 Mission San Jose Dr. at Mission Road, San Antonio; 210-932-1001), founded two years after the Alamo, is the most interesting of the four still functioning as churches. The mission, noted for its rare and opulent hand-sculpted rose window, is home each Sunday to a lively mariachi mass at noon. Today San Antonio is the only US city with as many missions within its city limits, and the five erected here comprise the **San Antonio Mission National Historic Park** (2202 Roosevelt Ave., San Antonio; 210-534-8833); missions are open daily in summer from 9 a.m. to 6 p.m. and in winter from 8 a.m. to 5 p.m. Visit nps.gov/saan for more information.

The Alamo Trolley offers a 1-hour narrated tour, stopping at the Alamo, HemisFair Park, Tower of the Americas, River Walk, La Villita, Market Square, San Fernando Cathedral, the Mission Trail, and the IMAX 3D Theatre. Your ticket (about $25) provides unlimited reboarding at the Alamo Trolley Hop Stops with your Hop Pass. You can buy tickets at the San Antonio Visitors Center on Alamo Plaza (210-247-0238; thealamotrolley.com).

The biggest of Texas's parties is **Fiesta San Antonio,** begun as a festival honoring visiting president Benjamin Harrison. Everyone had such a good time they didn't notice that the prez was a no-show, and the bash—now in its second century—is repeated annually. Fiesta, put on by some 50,000 residents, covers a 10-day period in the latter part of April and includes 150 events.

JUNE'S FAVORITE ANNUAL EVENTS

Texas Citrus Fiesta
Mission, late January

Charro Days Fiesta
Brownsville, mid- to late February

Washington's Birthday
Laredo, second or third weekend in
February

Alamo Irish Festival
San Antonio, second weekend in March

Fiesta
San Antonio, mid-April

Texas Folklife Festival
San Antonio, second weekend in June

Candlelight Posada
McAllen, first weekend In December

Among the flashier are the Battle of Flowers Parade, the King's River Parade, Fiesta Night Parade, and A Night in Old San Antonio. There's also a king's coronation, Alamo pilgrimage, arts fair, and *charreada,* or Mexican rodeo. For information call the Fiesta office at (210) 227-5191 or (877) 723-4378 or visit fiesta-sa.org.

A rather bizarre cultural assemblage is that found at the *Buckhorn Saloon and Museum* (318 E. Houston St., San Antonio; 210-247-4000; buckhorn museum.com). See the museum's 118-year-old gallery of animal horns and antlers, plus hundreds of fish, bird, and large mammal trophies, combining to deliver visual overload. There's also a remarkable collection of antique and custom made firearms, plus a wax museum that chronicles Texas history in figures from Cabeza de Vaca to Teddy Roosevelt. And finally, there's the preserved San Antonio home of the writer O. Henry. Open daily from at least 10 a.m. to 5 p.m., and closes later on other days; check the website calendar for the daily closing time. The museum charges admission.

Kids will find plenty to entertain them in San Antonio. For starters there's the *San Antonio Children's Museum* (305 E. Houston St., San Antonio; 210-212-4453; thedoseum.org). This entertaining, hands-on museum appeals to kids ages 2 to 10 and makes learning fun with all kinds of interactive educational exhibits. Open daily, the museum charges admission.

HemisFair Park (Alamo Street, I-37, Durango, and Market Streets; hemis fair.org) is home to the 750-foot Tower of the Americas, the symbol built for the 1968 World's Fair. A glass elevator whisks you to the top in less than a minute, and the sky-high restaurant makes one revolution per hour. On the ground there's a pleasant configuration of walkways, ponds, and waterfalls. There are splash pads, sand play areas, climbing structures, swings and much more for kids. Festivals are frequently staged here. Story time activities, yoga and other fitness classes, live music and other programming is typically on tap.

The park is home to the *Institute of Texan Cultures,* by far one of the nation's superior ethnic history museums and now associated with the Smithsonian Institution. Exhibits focus on the people of 26 ethnic and cultural groups of Texas; the multimedia show and museum store are also superb. Open Mon through Sat from 9 a.m. to 5 p.m. and Sun from noon to 5 p.m. Admission is charged. Call (210) 458-2300 for information or check texancultures.com.

From the HemisFair area, head west to *Market Square* (514 W. Commerce St., San Antonio; 210-207-8600; sanantonio.gov/marketsquare), a re-created Mexican *mercado.* Time and money easily disappear among the bustle of mariachis, whir of margarita machines, and come-ons from vendors in hundreds of booths packed with arts, crafts, jewelry, and produce and other foods.

While you're there, *Mi Tierra* (210-225-1262; mitierracafe.com) is the place to find good Tex-Mex eats 24 hours daily—and the bakery case is where you'll satisfy that sweet tooth.

Near Market Square see what the National Geographic Society once called one of San Antonio's most beautiful buildings. The *Spanish Governor's Palace* (105 Plaza De Armas, San Antonio; 210-224-0601) was the former home of officials who governed the Spanish Province of Texas; over its entrance is the original keystone on which is carved the double-headed eagle of the Hapsburg coat of arms and the inscription in Spanish, "finished in 1749." Distinguishing features include the period furnishings and a spacious cobblestone patio with fountain and luxurious foliage. Open Mon through Sat from 9 a.m. to 5 p.m. and Sun from 10 a.m. to 5 p.m. A small admission fee is charged.

An extraordinary source of pride for more than 70 years is the *Witte Museum* (3801 Broadway St., San Antonio; 210-357-1900; wittemuseum .org). The exciting regional museum features history; science; the humanities; hands-on exhibits of Texas history, natural science, and anthropology; changing exhibits; and family programs. Expansions have been many in recent years: In 2012 the *Robert J. and Helen C. Kleberg South Texas Heritage Center* opened in the historic Centennial building next to the original Witte Museum; it houses new exhibits on Texas history and art. The former H-E-B Science Treehouse is now the *H-E-B Body Adventure,* said to be the first interactive health experience in the United States. In 2014 the *B. Naylor Morton Research and Collections* opened to offer more than 300,000 artifacts in visible storage, as well as offer research space for scholars, archivists and school children. The *New Witte Museum* and the *Zachry Family Acequia Garden* opened in 2017 with a new H-E-B Lantern, Valero Great Hall, Naylor Family Dinosaur Gallery, McLean Family Texas Wild Gallery and Kittie West

Nelson Ferguson People of the Pecos Gallery. The museum is open Mon through Sat from 10 a.m. to 5 p.m. (9 p.m. on Tues) and Sun from noon to 5 p.m. Admission is charged for visitors ages 4 and older.

Art is another of San Antonio's considerable strengths. The *McNay Art Museum* (6000 N. New Braunfels at US 81, San Antonio; 210-824-5368; mcnayart .org) is the former estate home of Marian Koogler McNay and now repository of Impressionist and post-Impressionist paintings (van Gogh, Monet, Picasso, Matisse, O'Keeffe, Goya, Renoir, and Bourdelle), early New Mexican arts and crafts, plus gothic and medieval collections and one of the nation's largest theater-arts collections. A highlight of the McNay is its charming patio and gardens and the excellent museum store. Open Tues through Sat from 10 a.m. to 5 p.m. and Sun from noon to 5 p.m. Donations are accepted.

national treasures

In 2015, Texas received its first UNESCO World Heritage Site award, with San Antonio's historic missions making the elite international list. Only 22 such landmarks existed in the United States at that point, and San Antonio's cultural treasure earned a lofty status alongside the Statue of Liberty, Independence Hall, and the Grand Canyon. The five limestone missions (Mission Concepcion, San Jose, San Juan, Espada, and the Alamo) constitute the largest collection of Spanish colonial architecture in North America. Each is a museum in its own right and, with the exception of the Alamo, continues to serve as a church parish. Learn more at nps.gov/saan/.

The *San Antonio Museum of Art* (200 W. Jones Ave., San Antonio; 210-978-8100, samuseum.org) is housed inside the remarkable former Lone Star Brewery's castlelike building. Art collections range from ancient art to the most contemporary, including magnificent Greek and Roman sculpture and Latin American folk art. The Asian section has been expanded to include Asian sculpture as well as Chinese, Japanese, and Korean art. The museum is listed in the National Register of Historic Places. Open Tues from 10 a.m. to 8 p.m., Wed through Sat from 10 a.m. to 5 p.m., and Sun from noon to 6 p.m. A small admission fee is charged.

With one of its entrances marked by a dramatic trail drive sculpture right on the River Walk, *The Briscoe Western Art Museum* is a new repository for beautiful remnants from Texas' western heritage and bold artworks honoring that very past. Unfolding partially within a repurposed 1930s library building, its architectural finery glows from loving restoration. Adjoining the vintage building is a complementary new structure by Austin's award-winning Lake-Flato firm. Together the museum's three levels offer nine galleries; Check out Santa Anna's gilded sword, Pancho Villa's ornate saddle, a magnificent collection of spurs, a Frederic Remington painting and more. Find the Briscoe at 210 W. Market ST., San Antonio; (210) 299-4499; briscoemuseum.org.

Two galleries worth seeking out are the *Blue Star Contemporary Art Center* (116 Blue Star St., San Antonio; 210-227-6960; bluestarart.org) and *ArtPace* (445 N. Main St., San Antonio, 210-212-4900; artpace.org). Blue Star is a very stylish, contemporary gallery in a fashionably renovated warehouse area, featuring such works as mixed-media paintings, papier-mâché sculptures, and videos. It's open Wed through Sun from noon to 6 p.m. Housed inside a renovated 1920s auto dealership, ArtPace features contemporary art that ranges from hand-tinted photos to mixed media from international artists. This gallery is open Wed through Sun from noon to 5 p.m.

The *Southwest School of Art* (300 Augusta St., San Antonio; 210-224-1848; swschool.org) occupies a former girls' school established by the Ursuline Order. The old convent and beautiful courtyard are the settings for classes, workshops, exhibitions, special events, and a restaurant. Artistic craftspeople create, exhibit, and sell a variety of items on-site, from weaving and macramé to pottery and wood carvings. Numerous classes are offered on a year-round schedule. Gallery hours are Mon through Sat from 10 a.m. to 5 p.m. and Sun from 11 a.m. to 4 p.m. Admission is free.

Just south of downtown, the *King William Historic District* (on and around King William Street; kingwilliamassociation.org) is a trove of wonderful mansions built by the city's German gentry. Walking and cycling this area on spring or fall days is a pleasure that will be long remembered, but you can have a look inside, too. The *Steves Homestead* (509 King William St., San Antonio; 210-227-9160) is a century-old Gothic revival mansion on the San Antonio River containing period antiques owned and maintained by the San Antonio Conservation Society; a small admission fee is charged, and the home is open daily from 10 a.m. to 4:15 p.m.

Make it a point to visit *Guenther House* (205 E. Guenther St., San Antonio; 210-227-1061 or 800-235-8186; guentherhouse.com) in the King William Historic District. Inside you'll find historic items related to the development of Pioneer Flour Mills, an impressive collection of Dresden plates, a gift shop, and a restaurant. Museum and gift shop hours are Mon through Sat from 9 a.m. to 4 p.m. and Sun from 8 a.m. to 3 p.m. The restaurant is open from 7 a.m. to 3 p.m. daily. Admission is free.

The city is chock-full of art galleries, clothing boutiques, gift shops, craft markets, and the like. Those accessible on foot are found on the flagstone banks lining the *River Walk,* or *Paseo del Rio,* sitting beneath street level downtown and following the river's twisting contours. Arbors of palms, olive trees, cottonwoods, cypress, and willows shade sidewalk cafes, and pots of flowers are set between doors to shops, galleries, boutiques, hotels, bistros, and watering holes. Beware that crowds on weekends can be crushing.

River barges cruise the Paseo's 21 blocks, allowing visitors to review the retreats, unique retail shops, restaurants, and nightclubs. This 35- to 40-minute historical tour can be reserved by calling the Rio San Antonio River Cruise Tours at (210) 244-5700 or (800) 417-4139; riosanantonio.com. Special breakfast, lunch, or dinner cruises can be arranged, as well.

La Villita Historic Arts Village (418 Villita, facing the Convention Center, San Antonio; 210-207-8610; lavillita.com) is an unusual arts-and-crafts community adjacent to the River Walk. Working artists in 26 shops as well as three restaurants and a post office are within. You're likely to find irresistible creations such as Oaxacan rugs and Peruvian tapestries at Village Weavers; mixed-media paintings at Artistic Endeavors; stoneware and porcelain pottery at the Village Gallery; colorful Oaxacan animal sculptures at Casa Manos Allegres; and all manner of supplies at Bonsai Arbor. You'll also find the Old San Antonio Exhibit (located in Bolivar Hall), housing a small collection of art objects and artifacts relevant to San Antonio's earliest days. Open daily; admission is free.

The River Walk has expanded to include the deftly and extensively renovated *Pearl Brewery* (303 Pearl Pkwy., Ste. 300, San Antonio; 210-212-7260; atpearl.com), complex, which is reachable by river taxi, too. Found about a mile and a half north of the Alamo, on what is called the Museum Reach of the San Antonio River, the Pearl sits along the riverfront with a landscaped park, amphitheater, plentiful shopping, and dining and cultural experiences. Among favorite destinations at Pearl, the *Culinary Institute of America* (312 Pearl Pkwy.; 800-285-4627; ciachef.edu)—this is only the second outpost outside of New York—offers day, weekend, and weeklong cooking programs, along with its 2-year schedule for professional chefs. There's also an *Aveda Institute,* where you can enjoy a makeover, and a fabulous Saturday farmers' market, too. Among restaurants not to miss, *La Gloria* (100 E. Grayson St.; 210-267-9040; chefjohnnyhernandez.com) brings the best dishes from the heart of Mexico; and *Osteria Il Sogno* (200 E. Grayson St.; 210-223-3900) will spoil you for antipasto forever. Leave time to shop at *Melissa Guerra Tienda de Cocina* (303 Pearl Pkwy., Ste. 104, San Antonio; 210-293-3983; melissaguerra.com), a spectacular kitchenware store. Find more details by going to atpearl.com.

Even if you're not staying at *Hotel Emma,* it's a stunning showpiece of the Pearl and well worth an hour of exploration. The hotel that occupies the main brewery building and pays homage to the city's deep German roots is named for Emma Koehler, who kept the brewery afloat during Prohibition after her husband's death. The ornate 1894 Second Empire grandeur survives everywhere, from the lobby throughout the old brewhouse engine room, with its soaring ceilings. Designers repurposed original brass fittings, using them in stairway railings, and converted giant brewing tanks into lounge seating areas. Upstairs, 146 guest rooms are magnificent with original concrete and tile floors, bare brick walls, and furniture made from Mexican saddle leather and native white oak. Best are rooms overlooking the pool or river, and those with fireplaces and balconies. Restaurants and bars in and around the hotel are among the best in town. 136 E. Grayson St., San Antonio; (210) 448-8300; thehotelemma.com.

simplybatty

Although everyone expects Austin to hold this honor, it's actually a spot about 20 miles north of San Antonio that is home to the world's largest bat colony. Austin is the largest urban colony. The **Bracken Cave Colony** is a population of some 20 million to 40 million bats, thought to be the largest congregation of mammals anywhere, eating some 250,000 pounds of insects nightly during summer months. Learn more at batcon.org/Bracken.

San Antonio's sightseeing and shopping are nothing if not exhausting, so it's probably time to check into the **Menger Hotel** (204 Alamo Plaza, San Antonio; 210-223-4361 or 800-345-9285; menger hotel.com), outfitted with the Alamo Plaza Spa, where an old-fashioned 2-hour treatment includes steam bath, sauna, and herbal scrub. The Menger, next door to the Alamo, was a splendid hotel at its 1859 opening, and its claim to fame is that Teddy Roosevelt came to this wild and raucous city and this very hotel in 1898 to recruit his Rough Riders—or so the story goes. It's still a good hotel with choice rooms in the older section, and the bar has a friendly, comfortable feel.

Travelers will have to look long and hard to find better Mexican food anywhere else. The first of two favorites is **Los Barrios** (4223 Blanco St., San Antonio; 210-732-6017; losbarriosrestaurant.com), a delightful family operation with hearty Mexican and South American dishes of beef, chicken, and soups. Open for lunch and dinner daily, prices start at about $12. More elaborate in decor and menu, **La Fogata** (2427 Vance Jackson at Addax Street, San Antonio; 210-340-1337; lafogata.com) continues to pull people in droves to its rambling patios and its unbeatable chiles rellenos, flaming cheese, enchiladas, and possibly the best salsa anywhere. Open for lunch and dinner daily, meals average about $15 to $20.

Keep in mind that the Alamo City grows ever more popular: Polls conducted by a national travel magazine show San Antonio ranking consistently in the top 10 favorite US destinations. Between 10 million and 11 million people visit annually, so don't think you can just show up and get a room in the central area without a reservation.

Another hotel that serves as much as a window to history as a lovely place to vacation, the **St. Anthony** sits in the heart of downtown. The 1909 beauty had fallen on hard times but was lovingly rescued in recent years and turned back into a supremely regal space. Palatial qualities include the exquisite terrazzo flooring, hand-painted tiles, restored fixtures, and a 1927 Steinway grand piano originally made for the Russian Embassy in Paris. Corner rooms have been turned into stunning suites. The ground floor features a swanky restaurant and a bar, the latter called Haunt in honor of the ghosts said to reside in the hotel. 300 E. Travis St., San Antonio; (210) 227-4392; thestanthonyhotel.com.

Small and luxurious, the **Oge House** on the River Walk (209 Washington St., San Antonio; 210-223-2353 or 800-242-2770; ogecinn.com) is another fine choice. Located in the King William Historic District, this gorgeous and extensively refurbished 1857 home is packed with period antiques and offers 9 rooms, many with fireplaces.

A relatively quiet River Walk lodging is the **Hotel Havana,** a 1914 downtown national historic landmark, renovated by the owners of the Hotel San Jose and the Saint Cecilia in Austin. Period Cuban music seeps from unseen speakers throughout the vintage-chic, 27-room hotel, whose design features hardwood floors, high ceilings, Persian area rugs, and a dark, sexy bar. A restaurant is on-site, as well. Find this hideout at 1015 Navarro St., San Antonio, (210) 222-2008; havanasanantonio.com.

Complete information is offered by the **San Antonio Convention and Visitor Bureau,** (210) 270-6700 or (800) 447-3372; a handy visitor center is situated steps from the Alamo at 317 Alamo Plaza, San Antonio. It's open daily from 8:30 a.m. to 6 p.m. Call (210) 207-6748 or visit the website at visitsan antonio.com.

Texas Ghost Town

About an hour southeast of San Antonio in Karnes County lies the ghost town of **Helena,** population 35. Established in 1852 near the famed Chihuahua Trail and the Indianola–San Antonio Road, the rowdy frontier town saw plenty of shoot-outs—one too many, it seems. When 20-year-old Emmett Butler, an area resident, was killed during a saloon gunfight in 1884, his wealthy rancher father, Col. William Butler, vowed to kill the town that killed his son. By donating land miles away, he persuaded the railroad being built across south Texas to bypass Helena. Helena lost its county seat status, and the townsfolk moved away. The old courthouse, a post office, and a jail can still be seen.

Head to **Castroville,** 20 miles west on US 90, a town of just more than 2,500 in Medina County. It became the Little Alsace of Texas after founder Henri Castro brought a band of Alsatian settlers with him from that region of France. It's the only Alsatian community in the country, and it has clung tightly to its heritage; it's a lucky visitor who comes across descendants of those settlers, especially those who can speak the original, unwritten dialect, which is more German than French.

For a look into Alsatian history, visit **Mount Gentilz Cemetery** (US 90 and Alsace Street), also called Cross Hill. Here you'll have a far-reaching view of the Medina Valley, and you can see the burial spot of Amelia Castro, Henri's wife. Also see **St. Louis Catholic Church** (US 90 and Angelo Street), built in 1868–70 next to the colonists' original chapel, constructed in 1846. The big, 3-story building is the **Moye Center,** a convent erected in 1873 for the Sisters of Divine Providence.

Travelers will be pleased to find the Alsatian community's **Landmark Inn State Historic Site** (Florence and Florella Streets, Castroville; 830-931-2133; visitlandmarkinn.com), a hotel on the San Antonio–El Paso road when built in 1863; it's said that Robert E. Lee was among its guests. Now it's the only historic inn run by the state, which restored it to a 1940s look. A visitor center and an old gristmill are here, too.

Continue west from Castroville on US 90, traveling another 20 miles to **Hondo,** which became the seat of Medina County after the Southern Pacific Railroad bypassed Castroville in the 1880s. Today it's a community of 6,000 known best for attractions of the four-legged kind.

Much older and far more exotic, **dinosaur tracks** cast in stone are easily viewed in Hondo Creek's bed, almost 24 miles north of town via FR 462. Scientists speculate these were made by 15-ton, 40-foot herbivores called trachodons.

Forty-two miles farther west on US 90, **Uvalde,** seat of the same-named county and home to 15,000 residents, is known as the crossroads of two roads spanning the whole country—US 90 and US 83—and a fat little pocket of Old West and US history.

In the 1880s, J. K. King Fisher and Pat Garrett—two unforgettable lawmen of their day—lived in Uvalde. Fisher was an outlaw who became a deputy, though some said he was both at the same time, and Garrett was the man who killed Billy the Kid in nearby New Mexico in 1881.

Uvalde's John Nance Garner served as vice president of the US from 1933 to 1941; his life is chronicled in detail at the **Briscoe-Garner Museum** (333 N. Park St., Uvalde; 830-278-5018; cah.utexas.edu/museums/garner.php). Garner went to Congress in 1903 during Teddy Roosevelt's administration, served as

Speaker of the House, and stayed in Washington, serving as the number two man under FDR. It's said that his signature Texan candidness earned him the nickname "Cactus Jack." The museum is housed in his former home, a beautiful building; Garner died shortly before his 99th birthday and was buried at the west end of *City Cemetery* (on US 90 West). The museum is open Tues through Sat from 9 a.m. to 4 p.m.

Take time to look at *Uvalde Grand Opera House* (104 W. North St. at N. Getty Street, Uvalde; 830-278-4184; uvaldeoperahouse.org). A building befitting its name, this 2-story creation seated 370 patrons and is now partially occupied by a museum. Open Mon through Fri from 9 a.m. to noon and 1 to 5 p.m., Sat from 10 a.m. to 3 p.m. Admission is free.

With big skies and pretty rivers nearby, Uvalde's fine for hanging around for a couple of days. Several options for lodging are available just 24 miles north via US 83 in Concan. Check with the Uvalde Convention and Visitor Bureau at 300 E. Main Ave., Uvalde. Call 800-5-UVALDE or visit visituvalde.com for details.

Brush Country

From Uvalde, proceed 40 miles west on US 90 to reach *Brackettville,* seat of Kinney County. Be assured that this is the epitome of isolation: There's only one other town in the county. Sadly, Alamo Village (film site of the John Wayne classic *The Alamo*) has closed. On the town's eastern edge on US 90, however, find *Fort Clark Springs,* a resort resting on old Fort Clark, one of the country's best-preserved cavalry posts. Built in 1852 to protect settlers against Indians and banditos, the fort is famous for having been the training ground for 90 years for several infantry units, including the Ninth and Tenth Infantry's black Buffalo Soldiers and almost all of the army cavalry units. Others stationed at Fort Clark included generals George S. Patton Jr. and George C. Marshall. Historic buildings remain, some of which have been restored. The Old Guardhouse contains a small museum, and the resort offerings include a motel in old limestone barracks; two restaurants; a large spring-fed pool; tennis courts and golf courses; and a fitness center. Call (800) 937-1590 or (830) 563-2493 or visit fortclark.com for details.

At *Seminole Indian Scout Cemetery,* 3 miles south of town on FR 3348, you'll find the burial sites of several scouts hired by the army to help in campaigns against the warring Apaches. These Seminoles were descended from escaped Georgia slaves who intermarried with Florida Native Americans and moved west. Four of those buried here received the prestigious Congressional Medal of Honor, and some of the Seminole offspring still reside in Brackettville, working at ranching or farming.

From Brackettville, keep steady on US 90 another 32 miles to *Del Rio,* the seat of Val Verde County and nicknamed "Queen of the Rio Grande." In this corner of dry, hot south Texas, Del Rio is a blessing, as it rests atop bubbling San Felipe Springs, the outlet of an underground river pouring forth 90 million gallons of crystal-clear water daily. That's why you see so many ranches around—the irrigation opportunity is abundant for those prospering in sheep and Angora goat ranching nearby.

One look at the ornate, gothic 1887 *Val Verde County Courthouse* is to understand the wealth and depth of history in this town. Stop by the Del Rio Chamber of Commerce (1915 Avenue F, Del Rio; 830-775-3551; drchamber .com) and pick up the walking guide and map of 34 historic homes, buildings, and sites, many dating to a romantic, if tumultuous, time in Texas history.

Another gaping surprise out here is *Lake Amistad,* home of *Amistad National Recreation Area,* 10 miles northwest of town via US 90. This 67,000-acre, vividly blue impoundment on the Rio Grande is a perfect example of the unity enjoyed today between Mexico and the US, and particularly Texas. As the US shares the river with Mexico, it also shares the dam creating the mesmerizing binational lake, which stretches 75 miles upriver and offers 1,000 miles of shoreline. Fishing permits are offered by both countries, and there are dozens of other diversions, including camping, boat rentals, picnicking, and bow hunting. The dam is topped by a 6-mile road that connects the lake's two sides. For information contact the National Park Service office on US 90 West, just at the Del Rio city limits, at (830) 775-7491.

One of the best hideouts in south Texas is *The Lodge at Sanders Point,* found about 20 minutes northwest of Del Rio on the Devil's River arm of Lake Amistad (830-774-2422; thelodgeatsanderspoint.com). The humble lodge is made up of several native rock and rough-wood apartments with either one or two bedrooms, full-size kitchens, bath and living areas, barbecue grill, all kitchen utensils, and linens. Try to get a unit with a big porch overlooking the water. It's not a fancy place, but it's clean and the setting is magnificent.

Another look into history is discovered at *Val Verde Winery* (100 Qualia St., Del Rio; 830-775-9714; valverdewinery.com), Texas's oldest winery, begun in 1883 by Italian immigrant Frank Qualia. It's still in the same family, whose members offer free tours of the vineyards, storage vats, aging room, and bottling processors. Among eight wines made here, one is the Lenoir, the first wine produced more than 110 years ago. Tasting and buying opportunities follow the tour. It's open Mon through Sat from 10 a.m. to 5 p.m.

Set aside ample time for two outstanding side trips from Del Rio, which can be done on the same drive northwest of the city along US 90. The first stop

George West

Leaving San Antonio, the land flattens out considerably and reveals a thick carpet of mesquite, prickly pear, and occasional lechuguilla. Cruising past Three Rivers, a jumping-off spot for the oasis that is Choke Canyon State Park, stop some 80 miles south of the Alamo at *George West,* the seat of Live Oak County and birthplace of legendary writer J. Frank Dobie, resting along the Nueces River. On the courthouse lawn you'll see Geronimo, a rather mangy stuffed version of the 2,200-pound steer who had his own pasture on the giant local ranch. Since 1927, Geronimo has displayed his 9-foot, 6-inch horn span behind glass in his own small stone building; he left, however, for a time in 1976 when he went with an Americana tour to Moscow. Just outside of town, in the median along a four-lane stretch of US 281, is the biggest live oak in this part of the state, surely thousands of years old.

is *Seminole Canyon State Historical Park,* 45 miles from Del Rio and about 9 miles past the village called Comstock. The rugged setting of desert and canyons showcases a collection of Indian paintings and pictographs thought to be more than 8,000 years old. Look in Fate Bell Shelter, just below the park's interpretive center, for the most brilliant pictographs. Discoveries of other human artifacts—possibly 12,000 years old—and the drawings have combined to give scientists some ideas of daily life all those millennia past, which are illustrated in a life-size diorama at the visitor center. Call to inquire about ranger-led tours, usually offered on weekends. The park is open daily from 8 a.m. to 10 p.m. and at all times for campers. Admission is $2 per person 13 and older; call (432) 292-4464 or visit tpwd.texas.gov.

The second side trip from Del Rio is *Langtry,* only 20 miles beyond Seminole Canyon on US 90, still in Val Verde County. The desperately lonely Wild West outpost was founded in 1881, when the railroad came through, representing the junction of eastbound and westbound construction. How the town's name came about is still up for debate: Some historians believe that the civil engineer, a man called Langtry, who directed a crew of Chinese railroad laborers, is the source, but romantics stick with the story of Judge Roy Bean, who said he named the town for his favorite actress, the Jersey Lily, Englishwoman Lillie Langtry.

Worth the trip alone, the *Judge Roy Bean Visitor Center* is the preserved site of the infamous, unforgettable Law West of the Pecos, whose 1880s rule was a masterful blend of wit and bravery. Travelers find the rustic saloon, courtroom, and pool hall that was Bean's, along with a visitor center staffed by counselors and stocked with loads of free brochures, maps, guides, and varied information. Outside there's a cactus garden with indigenous southwestern plant life. Open daily from 8 a.m. to 5 p.m., the center's phone number is (432) 291-3340; learn more about this site and others in the area at the Texas Pecos Trail website, run by the Texas Historical Commission, texaspecostrail.com

Notice on your way to Langtry, about 18 miles east of town, there's a terrific *Pecos River Canyon scenic overlook*, offering a stunning view of the formidable canyon. This is an ideal place to stretch your legs, and a picnic area is right there if you've brought lunch along.

From Del Rio, you can begin making tracks to the southeast along the Rio Grande, traveling 56 miles on US 277 to *Eagle Pass,* the seat of Maverick County and home to 20,650 residents. An early US settlement during the Mexican War, it's where the government founded Fort Duncan in 1849 and remains a gateway to Mexico today.

Have a look into that window of history at the *Fort Duncan Museum* (on Bliss Street between Monroe and Adams Streets; 830-758-1445), housed in the old headquarters. There are archaeological exhibits, as well as details on the Kickapoo tribe nearby, and 11 surviving buildings. The history told here is of the post's closing in 1900, then reopening in 1916 during the Mexican Revolution, and its use as a World War I training base. Among famous officers who spent time here were Phil Sheridan, James Doolittle, and Matthew Ridgway. Open Mon through Sat from 1 to 5 p.m.

From Eagle Pass, travel 50 miles east on US 277 and east on FR 191 to *Crystal City.* It may seem odd, but this seat of Zavala County and town of 8,000 is home to a big *statue of Popeye the Sailor,* found in front of city hall on the square. Well, it's not so strange after all—this town calls itself the Spinach Capital of the World for its huge production of spinach. Look also for farmers selling watermelons, tomatoes, onions, carrots, and peppers from their pickup trucks.

It's 92 miles straight south on US 83 from Crystal City to *Laredo,* seat of Webb County, with more than 175,000 residents. Rich in history and culture, Laredo is the place for more of that beloved binational experience. Since its founding by Don Tomás Sánchez, a captain in the Spanish colonial army, on May 15, 1755, Villa San Agustín de Laredo has served as everything from a raiding site for Lipan Apaches and Comanches, a cattle and sheep ranching community, and an outpost for the expanding New Spain to capital of the Republic of the Rio Grande and an international commerce center.

Here you'll find numerous historic neighborhoods and buildings. While you're looking around downtown, be sure to pay attention to *San Agustín*

Plaza, bordered by Grant, Zaragoza, Flores, and San Agustín Streets; here you'll see the beautiful *St. Agustín Church,* a Gothic revival masterpiece, and several remarkable buildings in designs ranging from Mexican colonial and Mexican vernacular to Victorian and neoclassical revival, dating from the 1700s.

Facing the plaza, *La Posada Hotel* (1000 Zaragoza, Laredo; 956-722-1701 or 800-444-2099; laposada.com) occupies the former Laredo High School, built in 1916. The hotel is nothing short of lovely, with an exquisitely blue-tiled pool surrounded by a lush courtyard. The food is fair to good in the hotel's restaurants, the best being the *Tack Room,* upstairs in an adjacent building that was once the town's telephone exchange. You'll find big steaks, spareribs, chicken, and fish on the menu.

Laredo's supply of Mexican and other restaurants will keep your motor running. Start your day with mango crepes, chilaquiles, or croquet madame at *La Finca* (1713 E. Del Mar Blvd., Laredo; 956-568-0162; lafincabruncheria .com). At *La Carreta Carnes Asadas* (9209 McPherson Rd., Laredo; 956-796-0338), try red chile enchiladas, fajitas, ribs, and sausage.

If you happen upon Laredo in February, you may be in for a real treat during *George Washington's Birthday Celebration,* a two-week party held annually since 1898. The fiesta includes parades, pageants, fireworks, dances, a jalapeño festival (one contest challenges brave souls to gobble as many jalapeños as possible in 15 minutes!), carnival, *charreada* (Mexican rodeo), and an occasional bullfight.

The Rio Grande Valley

Back on the road, it's another 49 miles south on US 83 to *Zapata,* seat of Zapata County and home to 4,800 Texans. Named in honor of Antonio Zapata, the renowned Mexican pioneer and tough Indian fighter, the town is mostly a supply point for outdoor enthusiasts embarking on an adventure at *Falcon State Park* (28 miles south on US 83, FR 2098, and PR 46; 956-848-5327; tpwd .texas.gov). The shores of the enormous international lake, impounded on the Rio Grande, offer more than 500 acres for camping, picnicking, fishing, and swimming. There are groceries at the park, too, as well as a snack bar. Admission is $2 per person; the park is open daily.

From Zapata, it's 51 miles south on US 83 till you reach *Rio Grande City,* seat of Starr County, with a population of nearly 12,000. The town came about in 1848 when Gen. Zachary Taylor established Fort Ringgold, which was named for Maj. David Ringgold, the first army officer killed in the Battle of Palo Alto, opening the Mexican War. The fort remained active until 1944 and was home to Col. Robert E. Lee when he commanded the Department of Texas prior to the Civil War.

Travelers will want to pause in Rio Grande City just to stay at *La Borde House* (601 E. Main St., Rio Grande City; 956-487-5101; labordehouse.com), the 1899 home and border mercantile built by a French merchant and riverboat trader who had the house designed in Paris, then refined by San Antonio architects. Renovated about 35 years ago, the home was made into a hotel and contains sublime Victorian furniture and antiques. With shaded verandas, courtyard, patio, parlor, guest rooms, and restaurant, it's the rare showplace along this part of the Rio Grande. Ghostly activity is explained on the website's paranormal videos.

Continuing south on US 83 just 12 miles, watch for FR 886, which you'll turn right onto for 2 miles until you reach the Rio Grande and a sight found nowhere else on a US border. The *Los Ebaños Ferry* is a wooden, two-car ferry hand pulled by a Mexican staff using ropes. Rumors of its replacement by a bridge seem to be unfounded, as it has been restored to prime condition. Its operation is from 8 a.m. until 3:30 p.m. daily, but service suspends during the month of April, when irrigation in the Rio Grande valley brings the water level too high in this area for the ferry to run. Fares are $2.50 per vehicle and 50 cents per pedestrian. For details, call (956) 485-1084.

Another 14 miles south on US 83, *Mission* is an 1824 settlement where the Rio Grande valley's famous citrus industry was begun, possibly by the original priests. Today the town of 45,000 in Hidalgo County is Home of the Grapefruit, specifically the famous Texas ruby red. Mission is not only the citrus center but also the state's poinsettia center and home of the nation's only all-poinsettia show, held annually in December. Most Texans— and all Rio Grande valley residents—will also proudly tell you that Mission is the birthplace of Tom Landry, the first (and 30-year) coach of the Dallas Cowboys. See his mural on a building downtown at Conway Avenue at Tom Landry Street.

Should you join other Winter Texans for a January stay in the valley, rest up for the more than 70-year-old *Texas Citrus Fiesta,* held the last week of the month all over the area. The bash consists of a grand parade, barbecue cook-off, carnival, dances, citrus judging, arts and crafts show, sporting events, and a spectacular citrus products costume style show. For information call the *Mission Chamber of Commerce* at (956) 585-2727 or (800) 580-2700, or visit missionchamber.com.

La Lomita Chapel (on FR 1016, 3 miles south of town) was first an adobe way station dating to 1865 for Oblate padres traveling on horseback upriver from Brownsville. The present, rebuilt version, erected in sandstone in 1889,

The End of the Road

Highway 4 leads east from Brownsville in a slightly curving path 24 miles to the Gulf of Mexico. **Boca Chica** is the name given to the end of the road, where motorists will find a stop sign at the point where the road ends, meeting the sand. There's the beach, period. Apparently the stop sign is meant to keep you from driving straight into the ocean.

is a tiny structure with original floors, rough beamed ceilings, and an outdoor beehive oven. It sits in a 7-acre park with picnic areas, barbecue grills, restrooms, walkways, and historic site signs.

For still more outdoors, head for **Bentsen–Rio Grande Valley State Park** (6 miles southwest on US 83, FR 2062, and PR 43; 956-585-1107; tpwd.texas .gov), 760 acres of land along the Rio Grande with excellent bird watching, especially for the Audubon's oriole, hooded oriole, zone-tailed hawk, and red-eye cowbird. At the park office, pick up lists and booklets on these, as well as mammals, herbs, plants, butterflies, and other flora and fauna to be seen on nature trails. Camping, picnicking, and boating are options, too. The park is open daily. A small admission fee is charged.

The Bentsen RGV park also functions as the headquarters for the wonderful **World Birding Center,** the most exciting nature facility to open in south Texas. The spectacular buildings, along with exhibits, trails, bird-viewing blinds, and bird-feeding and watering stations, cost roughly $7 million. You'll find more great birding information than you ever thought possible, as well as a good gift shop and snack bar. Read more at theworldbirdingcenter.com.

texastrivia

The south Texas town of Luling hosts an annual **Watermelon Thump** in June, a 4-day festival celebrating the annual crop and the traditional thumping to test the melon's readiness.

McAllen, 10 miles east along US 83, also lies in Hidalgo County and is home to 106,000 residents. The hub of activity in the lower Rio Grande valley, McAllen appeals to retirees from the Midwest and Canada who spend entire winters here in the subtropical environs.

McAllen International Museum of Art & Science (1900 Nolana St., McAllen; 956-682-1564; theimasonline.org) has a wonderful Mexican folk-art mask and textile collection, as well as contemporary American and regional prints, sculptures, and oils from 16th- to 19th-century Europe. Open Tues through Sun; check website for hours. A small admission fee is charged.

The citrus season lasts from October through April; to pick some citrus for yourself or buy your own crates, head over to **Bell's Farm to Market** (116 S. Ware Rd., McAllen; 956-630-1015 or 800-798-0424; bellsfarm.com), a great place to buy fruits to be shipped home. Gift packs are sold, and an adjacent garden center offers exquisite tropical foliage.

If you find yourself in McAllen around the holidays, try to catch the lovely **Candlelight Posada,** typically held the first full weekend in December in Archer Park. You'll see traditional Christmas entertainment and caroling in the burnished glow of luminarias, and you'll be moved by the beautiful Mexican posada, or candlelit posada, that represents the journey of Mary and Joseph as they look for a place to rest so that the Christ child can be born. For details contact the McAllen Convention and Visitors Bureau at (956) 682-2871 or visit mcallen.org.

Close to downtown and the lovely **Casa de Palmas** hotel you'll find an exquisite Mexican dinner at **Costa Messa Restaurant** (1621 N. 11th St., McAllen; 956-618-5449; costamessargv.com). Painted in serene shades of blue and coral, the dining room is a relaxing place in which to feast on grilled steak with enchiladas, seafood soup, and an excellent chile relleno stuffed with shredded beef. Don't miss the appetizer of grilled onion with bacon and jalapeño. Open for lunch and dinner.

A side trip to take if you have a free morning or afternoon—and if it's not too awfully hot—is to **Santa Ana National Wildlife Refuge** (US 83 east to Alamo, south on FR 907, 7 miles to US 281, and east to the entrance; 956-784-7500; fws.gov/refuge/santa_ana/). Here 2,000 acres of subtropical foliage provide a habitat for an astounding variety of bird species, some of which aren't found elsewhere in the US. The species list of nearly 400 can be picked up at the visitor center, and three nature trails are offered. In the winter a tram tour is available. Trails are open daily from sunrise until sunset, and the visitor center is open daily from 9 a.m. to 4:30 p.m. Admission is free, but tram tours, which run Thurs through Mon, cost $3 for adults and $1 for children. **Note:** Use insect repellent before going out on trails.

Head north of McAllen 8 miles on US 281 to **Edinburg,** the Hidalgo County seat, on Saturday night to see a proud Texas tradition, the rodeo. The **Sheriff's Posse Rodeo** is a weekly offering, with cowboys demonstrating calf roping, bull riding, and quarter horse racing. The rodeo arena is 2 miles south of town on US 281. Admission is free.

Just a couple of miles east of McAllen via US 83, the San Juan exit delivers you to the doors of the **Shrine of La Virgen de San Juan del Valle** (US 83 and Raul Longoria Road; 956-787-0033; olsjbasilica.org). This impressive church was built to the tune of $5 million—mostly paid for by small contributions—after the elaborate 1954 original was destroyed when a plane was deliberately crashed into it. The wooden La Virgen statue wasn't harmed, and now it has a special place at the center of a 100-foot wall. Open daily from 6 a.m. to 8 p.m.

It's but 30 miles east from McAllen on US 83 to **Harlingen,** a town of nearly 80,000 in Cameron County named for a city in the Netherlands. The town was called Sixshooter Junction for a wild time around 1910 and during the Mexican Revolution, when frequent bandit raids necessitated the peace-keeping efforts of the Texas Rangers and mounted patrols from US Customs. The National Guard was eventually brought in to help the Rangers when, it's said, there were more firearms than citizens in town.

A somewhat unexpected treat is found at Harlingen's **Marine Military Academy and Texas Iwo Jima War Memorial** (320 Iwo Jima Blvd., Harlingen; 956-423-6006; mma-tx.org/About-Us/The-Campus/Iwo-Jima-Monument). The Public Affairs Office will tell you if any parades or activities are scheduled that offer the chance to see a US Marines–style private academy at work. On the campus is the original working model for the Iwo Jima Memorial bronze statue at Arlington National Cemetery, donated to the academy by sculptor Dr. Felix W. de Weldon in 1981. The figures are 32 feet high, the M-1 rifle is 16 feet long, the flagpole is 78 feet long, and the canteen could hold 32 quarts of water. The pole flies a cloth flag. The Marine placing the flagpole in the ground was Corp. Harlon Block from nearby Weslaco, who was later killed in battle.

A good surprise in Harlingen is the excellent Thai food at **Lil Rita's Grill House** (410 E. Tyler Ave., 956-425-6242; lilritasgrillhouse.com), where authentic soup, salad, and rice dishes thrill the tongue. If your mouth waters for huge platters of fajitas, however, head to **Los Asados** (210 N. US 77/Sunshine Strip, Harlingen; 956-421-3074; losasados .com). Just south of Harlingen in San Benito, try **Longhorn Cattle Company** (3055 W. US 83, San Benito; 956-399-9151 or 956-399-4400; longhorncattle company.com). Smoked beef brisket, sweet pork ribs, and all the fixin's are served while you watch longhorn cattle graze out in the pastures. Open for lunch and dinner Tues through Sun; prices start at about $8.

texastrivia

McAllen in the Rio Grande valley is called the **Square Dance Capital of the World.** Each fall some 10,000 square dancers swing their partners during winter months in the warm climate.

The final leg of the valley tour is a 26-mile stint south from Harlingen on US 83/US 77 to **Brownsville,** seat of Cameron County and city of 140,000 Texans. While it's a pleasant place near the ocean and a popular gateway to Mexico, Brownsville's past is tumultuous.

In 1846 President James K. Polk ordered Gen. Zachary Taylor to build a fort at this spot, and the Mexicans understood this to be an act of veiled aggression. Soon the Mexicans invaded Texas here, igniting the Mexican-American War, which counted among early casualties a Maj. Jacob Brown, for whom the fort and city were eventually named. Two important battlefields are found near town, the first being the **Palo Alto Battlefield,** north of town at FR 1847 and FR 511, home to a small but beautiful new visitor center (956-541-2785, ext. 233; nps.gov/paal). The other is **Resaca de la Palma Battlefield** on FR 1847 between Price and Coffeeport Streets; a leader in this battle was 2d Lt. Ulysses S. Grant.

Another significant battle site—this in the Civil War—is **Palmito Ranch Battlefield,** about 14 miles east of downtown via Highway 4. The fight was won by Confederate forces who hadn't heard that Lee had surrendered at Appomattox a month earlier. When the Rebels learned of the South's concession, the victors were taken prisoner by the prisoners.

For a much more modern and nature-oriented attraction, look no further than the **Gladys Porter Zoo** (at Ringgold and 6th Streets; 956-546-7187; gpz .org). Widely considered one of the top 10 zoos in the nation, this one is special for having no bars or cages. Animals in the 31-acre spread are kept separated by moats and waterways and have room to roam. There are some 1,800 birds, mammals, and reptiles representing five continents. A children's zoo offers petting opportunities and an animal nursery. There's a half-hour, narrated tour aboard a miniature train on Sunday. Open Mon through Fri from 9 a.m. to 5:30 p.m. and Sat and Sun from 9 a.m. to 6 p.m. Admission is charged.

A favorite among purists, **Vera's Backyard Bar-B-Q** (2404 Southmost Rd., Brownsville; 956-546-4159) is a 1955 relic, still producing old-school barbacoa over wood. This Mexican specialty (tender meat from the cow's head) is wrapped into soft, handmade tortillas; it's often sold out daily at 2 p.m. For a big selection in breakfast tacos and traditional Rio Grande Valley Mexican plates, check out **El Pato** (2425 Paredes Line Rd., Brownsville; 956-547-9100; elpatomexicanfood.com), where fillings inside soft tortillas include spicy, stewed beef; potatoes; chicken; cheese; avocado; beans; and *chorizo,* a spicy Mexican sausage.

texastrivia

Country-western musician and singer *Freddie Fender* was born Baldemar G. Huerta in San Benito.

If you've a hankering for some crashing waves, head just 22 miles east of town on Highway 4 to **Brazos Island State Park,** also known as Boca Chica. There's nothing but ocean and a little swatch of sand—it's completely undeveloped, and no facilities are available, so take your own water, drinks, ice chest, snacks, towels, and sunblock. If you're so inclined, feel free to swim, camp, surf, picnic, hunt for seashells and sand dollars, or just stroll the dunes. For Gulf fishing, there's a ½-mile-long stone jetty at the northern end of the beach.

Other Places to Stay in South Texas

BROWNSVILLE

Residence Inn
3975 N. Expressway 83
(956) 350-8100
On the north end of town, this nonsmoking hotel has suites with kitchens. There's a hot breakfast buffet daily and a social hour Mon through Thurs.

DEL RIO

Whispering Palms Inn
1300 Veterans Blvd,
(830) 488-6270
whisperingpalmsinn.com
A former motor lodge has been renovated, with 48 guest rooms, continental breakfast, and swimming pool with waterfall.

LAREDO

Embassy Suites
110 Calle Del Norte
(855) 605-0319
Two-room suites, complimentary afternoon cocktails, and full, made-to-order breakfast make this a preferable choice.

MCALLEN

Renaissance Casa de Palmas
101 N. Main St.
renaissance-hotels.marriott
.com/casa-de-palmas-
renaissance-mcallen-hotel
(956) 631-1101
This century-old Texas Historical Landmark has 165 rooms and a bar, restaurant, shops, art gallery, and sauna.

SAN ANTONIO

The King William Manor
1029 S. Alamo St.
(800) 405-0367 or
(210) 222-0144
kingwilliammanor.com
An 1892 Greek revival home and adjacent 1901 guesthouse in King William District offer 11 guest rooms with Victorian antiques and reproductions. Full breakfast is included.

Mokara Hotel & Spa
212 W. Crockett St.
(866) 605-1212
mokarahotels.com
A truly luxurious offering, the swanky spot with 99 rooms and suites offering a fabulous spa and good dining right on the River Walk was previously the Watermark Hotel and Spa. The spa is simply beautiful, and dining on the rooftop pool deck is a treat.

Hotel Contessa
306 W. Market St.
(210) 229-9222
thehotelcontessa.com
Exposed brick warms up the spaces inside 265 suites. An elegant hotel, this one has a rooftop pool and, right along the river, the Cork Bar.

Omni La Mansion del Rio
112 College St.
(210) 518-1000
omnihotels.com/hotels/san-antonio-la-mansion-del-rio
Occupying the former St. Mary's Academy and, later, St. Mary's University Schoolf Law, this exquisite hotel is full of romance, artfully designed spaces, comfortable rooms with balconies overlooking the River Walk, and San Antonio heritage. Dining and drinking here are legendary.

Other Places to Eat in South Texas

BROWNSVILLE

1848 BBQ
5 Avalon Dr
(956) 504-1848
An old office building now houses a simple barbecue joint where you can enjoy brisket, pulled pork, ribs and creative sides on a covered patio.

LAREDO

Charlie's Corona
3902 San Bernardo Ave.
(956) 725-8227
Longtime town favorite, this is the place for garlic-slathered steak with grilled onions and chicken-fried steak in rich gravy. Live music and happy hour are popular, too. Open for lunch and dinner; closed Sun.

Obregon's
303 Market S.
(956) 462-5298
Breakfast tacos in a former gas station are beloved for handmade flour tortillas stuffed with beef stew, eggs, beans, or potatoes. At lunch, there are enchiladas and tostadas.

MCALLEN

Taco Palenque
1000 S. 10th St.
(956) 994-8950
Part of a solid mini-chain, it's a great destinatinon for delicious tacos in homemade tortillas and a fresh salsa bar.

SAN ANTONIO

Biga on the Banks
203 S. St. Mary's St.
(210) 225-0722
biga.com
Biga features upscale fusion (Asian–southwestern–New American) dishes. Steaks, fish, chops, vegetables, salads, and soups receive thoughtful treatments and preparations that command medium to high prices for dinner, Mon through Sat.

Cured
306 Pearl Pkwy.
(210) 314-3929
curedatpearl.com
Bustling eatery with top-notch charcuterie and crafty cocktails is one of the most respected restaurants in Texas.

Liberty Bar
1111 S. Alamo St.
(210) 227-1187
liberty-bar.com
Longtime favorite for salads, soups, steaks, seafood, pasta, and fowl. Open daily for lunch and dinner; prices start at about $12.

La Fonda on Main
2419 N. Main Ave.
(210) 733-0621
lafondaonmain.com
Situated in a 1930s house, this is a destination for some of the finest margaritas ever made, along with plates of steak topped with enchiladas, ceviche made with mahi mahi and avocado, chile-rubbed trout, and shrimp in garlic and butter.

UVALDE

Evett's Barbecue
301 E. Main Ave.
(830) 278-6204
A local favorite for smoked brisket and barbecue sandwiches. Open Tues through Sat for lunch and dinner.

The Local Fix
2001 E. Main St.
(830) 900-7183
Thelocalfix.com
Espresso and cappuccino choices start the day, along with protein or fruit smoothies, breakfast tacos, toasted bagel sandwich, and pancakes. Burgers, sandwiches, wraps, soups, and salads all with fresh preparations make this a place of note.

The Piney Woods

East Texas's Piney Woods region defies many myths held by those who don't truly know Texas: It's generously green, frequently hilly, and always lush. There are majestic millions of acres of forest—four national forests, to be exact. Rich in ancient pines, cypress, and plenty of hardwoods, this is where Texans make annual pilgrimages in autumn to see fall blazing in its radiant glory. In spring, country paths in and out of the forest lands are sensational with brilliant explosions of magenta azaleas, frilly pink and white dogwoods, and evening primroses blooming across wild fields in lavender profusion. Amid the legions of trees pushing skyward are lakes and more lakes, small places and big spreads of water, where lifelong lake residents share space and stories of honey holes with anglers hoping to catch even a little one—shimmering lakes where sailing and waterskiing and watching sunrises are the most important events that occur in a day, places where timeless Native American legends tell of the Great Creator's work in watery, woodsy artistry.

Everything in the Piney Woods seems fresh and new, though the area has history dating to Texas's origins as a republic and as a state. Vestiges of the life of Sam Houston—whose

THE PINEY WOODS

later years were spent serving his adopted, beloved Texas—are found here, and the state university in Nacogdoches, a wonderful Piney Woods town, is named for the Father of Texas, Stephen F. Austin. A healthy population of Native Americans, the people of the united Alabama and Coushatta nations, lives on a reservation near one of the state's great pioneer living-history museums. Travelers to the Piney Woods can ride restored 19th-century railroads or buy baskets that have been made here for more than 100 years and pottery that has been crafted by generations of the same families, families that helped settle the region. There are no amusement parks or major league athletic teams or 4-story shopping malls in the Piney Woods, but you will find a rose garden with 500 varieties that supplies a third of the nation with its commercial roses; the state's antiques capital; Victorian man-

texastrivia

From late February into early March, the prettiest blooms in East Texas are those at **Mrs. Lee's Daffodil Garden,** a 28-acre bright yellow sweep of blooms on a 900-acre farm just outside of Gladewater (call for directions; 903-845-5780; daffodilgarden .com).

sions made over into bed-and-breakfast homes, some rumored to be staffed by resident ghosts; and towns offering the World's Richest Acre, the nation's first drill team, a biblical airplane, and some of the best fried alligator tail you could ever hope to savor. That's just a small taste of the Piney Woods.

Deepest East Texas

Begin this journey in **Huntsville,** an hour north of Houston, the Walker County seat and home to 35,000 east Texans. Settled in a very pretty setting of rolling, forested terrain at I-45 and US 190, Huntsville was founded as a trading post in 1836, the same year Texas won its independence from Mexico. Now home to Sam Houston State University (SHSU), the city is better known as the place to learn more about the life of Sam Houston himself. The **Sam Houston Memorial Museum Complex** (on the SHSU campus at 1836 Sam Houston Ave., Huntsville; 936-294-1832; samhoustonmemorialmuseum.com) is a 15-acre spread that belonged to the Texas hero and now holds two of his homes, the furnished Woodland Home and the Steamboat House, the latter of which was the site of his death in 1863. Other buildings there include a law office, kitchen, and blacksmith shop displaying, among other things, some of Houston's possessions, as well as Mexican items taken at the defeat of Santa Anna at San Jacinto. Pack a lunch for this visit, as the grounds have a spring-fed pond with

JUNE'S FAVORITE ATTRACTIONS

903 Handmade
Tyler

Caddo Lake

High Hill Farm
Arp

Kiepersol Estates
Tyler

Lafitte's Landing Guest Quarters
Uncertain

Municipal Rose Garden
Tyler

New Zion Missionary Baptist Church
Barbecue
Huntsville

Oak Grove Cemetery
Nacogdoches

Stanley's Famous
Tyler

Texas Basket Company
Jacksonville

Texas State Railroad
Rusk and Palestine

Turning Basin Riverboat Tours
Jefferson

picnic facilities. Open Tues through Sat from 9 a.m. to 4:30 p.m. and Sun from noon to 4:30 p.m. Free admission.

There's no better testimony to Houston's huge bearing on Texas than the enormous, 67-foot-tall *statue of Sam Houston,* dedicated in October 1994. Called *A Tribute to Courage,* it's the world's tallest statue of an American hero. Made from 30 tons of concrete and steel, artist David Adickes created the monument from his life-size (6-foot, 6-inch) model, which is seen in the library at Sam Houston State University. See Big Sam at 34000 US 75, off I-45 at exit 109. There's a visitor center with a gift shop; it's open Mon through Fri from 10 a.m. to 5 p.m., Sat from 10 a.m. to 5 p.m., and Sun from 11 a.m. to 5 p.m. Call (936) 291-9SAM for more details.

You can visit Houston's burial site at Oakwood Cemetery, Avenue I and 9th Street. *Sam Houston's Grave and National Monument* is marked by a tomb bearing Andrew Jackson's sentiment, "The world will take care of Houston's fame." Always open, there is no admission charge.

An entirely different kind of attraction is found at the *Texas Prison Museum* (491 SH 75 North, Huntsville; 936-295-2155; txprisonmuseum.org), where exhibits include the history of the Texas prison, with Bonnie and Clyde's rifle collection; Old Sparky, the electric chair; relics from the Carrasco prison siege; memorabilia from the famous, defunct Texas Prison Rodeo; and music and art projects by inmates. Open Mon through Sat from 10 a.m. to 5 p.m. and Sun from noon to 5 p.m. A small admission fee is charged.

Barbecue of the soul-food variety is had at *New Zion Missionary Baptist Church* (2601 Montgomery Rd., Huntsville; 936-294-0884), a shade-tree stop of sorts. Sausage, chicken, brisket, and ribs are smoked on-site and served from 11 a.m. until 6 p.m., Thurs through Sat. Don't overlook the buttermilk pie.

To begin your tour of Texas's thick forest country, drive east on US 190 just 2 miles from Huntsville, and you're in *Sam Houston National Forest* (936-344-6205; fs.usda.gov/ddetail/texas/about-forest/). Covering 160,000 acres in Montgomery, San Jacinto, and Walker Counties, this forest contains 27 miles of the 128-mile *Lone Star Hiking Trail.* To reach this National Recreation Trail, find the trailhead off FR 1725 just northwest of the town of Cleveland on the forest's southern edge. For a map see the forest ranger's offices either at Cleveland or at New Waverly, 13 miles south of Huntsville. There is a $3 parking fee per vehicle. Also in the forest, *Stubblefield Lake* is on the West Fork of the San Jacinto River about 12 miles north and west of New Waverly; there you can go camping ($12 per night) and picnicking.

From the forest head east on US 190; you'll immediately see *Lake Livingston,* 52 miles long and lined with 452 miles of wooded shoreline with every sort of recreation. The 640-acre state park on the east shore of the lake offers campsites, screened shelters, group trailers, boat ramps, a store, floating docks and gas docks, showers, and hiking-nature trails. Fishing, swimming, and waterskiing are the most popular pastimes on the lake. For details call the state park at (936) 365-2201 or visit tpwd.texas.gov. Admission is $3 per person for day users and $2 per person for overnight users 13 and older. Groceries,

JUNE'S FAVORITE ANNUAL EVENTS

First Monday Trade Days
Canton, weekend prior to first Monday of each month

Texas Blueberry Festival
Nacogdoches, early June

Dogwood Trails Festival
Palestine, third and fourth weekends in March and first weekend in April

Azalea and Spring Flower Trail
Tyler, first weekend in April

Historic Pilgrimage
Jefferson, first weekend in May

Tomato Fest
Jacksonville, early June

Great Texas Balloon Race
Longview, last weekend in July

Uncle Fletch Hamburger Festival
Athens, mid-September

Fire Ant Festival
Marshall, mid-October

Wonderland of Lights
Marshall, Thanksgiving weekend-New Year's weekend

restaurants, and all supplies are available in the town of Livingston, the Polk County seat, 7 miles east of the park.

About 40 miles east of Lake Livingston, watch for **Heritage Village Museum** (right on US 190; 409-283-2272; heritage-village.org). This reconstructed pioneer village contains old shops, homes, and vehicles, while photographs, documents, maps, and other aids show the difficult lives of early settlers. A log cabin built on this site in 1866 still has its peg windows and wooden door hinges. Also on the site is a rebuilt 1911 Cherokee church, which was moved from the Cherokee Dies community, northwest of Woodville, in 1990. Open daily from 9 a.m. to 5 p.m.; admission is charged.

Don't miss the chance to eat at the nearby **Pickett House** (409-283-3371), a re-created boardinghouse with family-style offerings including fried chicken, chicken and dumplings, homegrown veggies, stone-ground corn bread, freshly made biscuits, and homemade preserves. Hours for daily lunch and early supper on weekends can vary according to season, so call ahead.

Spend a little time moseying around **Woodville,** a town of about 3,000 residents and the Tyler County seat, 90 percent of which is covered in forest. This is another good jumping-off place to explore the Big Thicket National Preserve (see Gulf Coast chapter) and a pleasant place to hunt for antiques.

Back near Lake Livingston, **Davy Crockett National Forest** is 11 miles west from the lake on US 190, then north on FR 356, 12 miles northwest to Sebastopol, where you'll pick up FR 355 and go 14 miles north. This forest, like the other three national forests in Texas, was ravaged early in the 20th century yet has made remarkable recovery in its hardwood and pine populations. The Davy Crockett is 161,000 acres in Houston and Trinity Counties, containing the Big Slough Canoe Trail and Wilderness Area on the Neches River, and the Four C Hiking Trail, a 19-mile path linking the Neches Bluff and Ratcliff Lake.

texastrivia

The first oil well was drilled in Texas in 1886 near Nacogdoches. By 1928 Texas was the leading oil-producing state in the US, a position that's never been relinquished.

That lake has camping, picnicking, and swimming areas, plus screened shelters and canoe rentals. For maps and facilities go to the ranger station at Ratcliff (936-655-2299;fs.usda.gov/ddetail/texas/about-forest/) on FR 227 just off Highway 7, or Apple Springs (936-831-2246), in the forest on Highway 94.

While you're in the neighborhood, make a detour to the town of **Crockett,** about 10 miles west of Davy Crockett Forest via Highway 7. Naturally the town—the Houston County seat—was also named for the Alamo hero, and it's said he stopped en route to the Alamo to camp at the springs found at the intersection of Highways 7 and 21, now marked by a historical plaque. Spend some time poking around the quaint town, filled with more antiques shops. When you're hungry, consider stopping in to eat at **Doc's BBQ** (1277 East Loop 304, Crockett; 936-546-7743; docssmokedmeats.com), a good place for smoked chicken and brisket, honey-glazed ribs, pork chops wrapped in bacon, and sausage.

At the **Texas Forestry Museum** (1905 Atkinson Dr., Crockett; 936-632-9535; treetexas.com) in **Lufkin,** 12 miles east of the forest on Highway 94, the state's lumber industry is detailed, as well as the impact the forestry-products business has had on the region. Also there's a moonshiner's still, a fire lookout tower, a blacksmith's forge, and a logging train. Open Mon through Sat from 10 a.m. to 5 p.m. and Sun from 1 to 5 p.m. Admission is free, but donations are welcome.

From Lufkin head 22 miles southeast on US 69 to the **Angelina National Forest,** a 152,000-acre preserve spreading across Angelina, Jasper, Nacogdoches, and San Augustine Counties and wrapping itself around vast **Lake Sam Rayburn.** The lake, exceptionally popular with bass and catfish anglers, has 560 miles of shoreline with numerous marinas and campgrounds. The pine- and hardwood land gives shelter to deer, squirrel, and turkey, some of which can be seen on the Sawmill Hiking Trail, a 5.5-mile path following the Neches River and stretching from Bouton Lake Park to the Old Aldrich Sawmill and Boykin Springs. Along the way you'll find ruins of an old tram line, logging camps, and bridges. Several parks line the lake, offering various concessions. For maps and information, as well as ranger-led activities, check at the ranger office next door to the Texas Forestry Museum in Lufkin (listed earlier); call (936) 639-8620.

After a day on Lake Sam Rayburn, you can rest easy at a pleasant little inn in **Jasper,** 15 miles south of Angelina National Forest via Highway 63. Jasper has several unique gift shops and an outstanding art gallery downtown. The **Belle-Jim Hotel** (160 N. Austin St., Jasper; 409-384-6923; belle-jim.com) is right there, too; the 1910 structure offers private baths and homemade breads for breakfast. There's a café on-site, too, that offers weekday lunches of soups, salads, and sandwiches.

From the Angelina forest, head for the **Sabine National Forest** by following Highway 147 to its intersection with Highway 103, which leads east to this last of Texas's four national forests. At nearly 158,000 acres, covering ground in Jasper, Sabine, San Augustine, Newton, and Shelby Counties, the Sabine hugs the 65-mile-long **Toledo Bend Reservoir,** which Texas shares with Louisiana. Along the lake, in the shade of southern pines and hardwoods, are seven different parks with offerings ranging from picnicking, camping, and swimming to boating areas and nature trails.

Fishing on Toledo Bend is a big attraction to anglers in search of bass, catfish, bluegill, and crappie. Check at the ranger offices for maps, concessions, and activities in Hemphill, in the forest on Highway 87 (409-787-2791; toledo bend.com).

San Augustine is conveniently found just 8 miles west on Highway 21. A town of nearly 3,000, San Augustine is known as the Cradle of Texas and was settled officially in 1832, although it was a community on the Spaniards' Old Road to San Antonio, also called El Camino Real, even earlier. Because a mission was established here in 1716 (and abandoned just 20 years later), San Augustine claims to be the oldest town in Texas. Important historical residents included Sam Houston, who was a San Augustine resident while seeking the republic presidency, and J. Pinckney Henderson, Texas's first governor.

Although much of the town burned in 1890, there are some good sites still standing, such as the **Ezekiel Cullen House** (207 Congress St., San Augustine; 936-275-5110). The home belonged to a judge and Texas House of Representatives member who fought for public-school lands funding. This Greek revival house was built in 1839, given to the Daughters of the Republic of Texas by Cullen's family, and is headquarters for an annual tour of homes in April. Call ahead for hours and admission fees. For more on the town, visit sanaugustinetx.com.

From San Augustine continue your tour for 36 miles on Highway 21 to **Nacogdoches** (NACK-ah-DOE-chez), the town generally credited with being the oldest in Texas. The settlement is historically believed to have had hospitable Native Americans—the Caddo people—when the Spaniards came through en route to Mexico, probably around 1541 or 1542. The first permanent European settlement, however, is dated at 1716, when Father Margil founded the Mission of Our Lady of Guadalupe of Nacogdoches; it was abandoned in 1773, when the settlers were ordered to move to San Antonio.

Several weren't happy and moved back with Antonio Gil Ybarbo to Nacogdoches; in 1779 he laid out the town and built a stone house and trading post there, which survives as the **Old Stone Fort,** the town's most heritage-packed site. An exact replica of Ybarbo's structure sits today on the Stephen F. Austin State University Campus, at Griffith and Clark Streets (936-468-2408; sfasu .edu/stonefort). Its long and colorful history includes its service as a fort and a prison, as well as government headquarters during many attempts to establish the Republic of Texas; its function as offices for the first two newspapers published in Texas; and the place where Jim Bowie, Thomas Rusk, Sam Houston, and Davy Crockett were administered the oath of allegiance to Mexico. Nine different flags have flown over the fort, including those from three failed revolutions. Now a museum, the Old Stone Fort offers exhibits detailing this

Bizarre Texas Stuff

A plague known far too well among most Texans is that of the fire ant. But the good folks in Marshall exhibit a perverse but contagious sense of humor with their annual *Fire Ant Festival,* held the second weekend every October in honor of the insidious little insect with a burning bite. Some 50,000 celebrants have been known to gather on and around the downtown courthouse square to join in the zany festivities. Among the events are fire ant costume contests, fire ant calling contests, a chili cook-off (recipes must call for the inclusion of one fire ant), a giant parade, and much more.

tumultuous past and the people who left an indelible mark on the republic and the state. Open Tues through Sat from 9 a m to 5 p.m. and Sun from 1 to 5 p.m. Admission is free, but the museum welcomes donations.

Nacogdoches is fairly flooded with historic sites directly related to the Republic of Texas. One that must not be missed is the **Sterne-Hoya House** (211 S. Lanana St., Nacogdoches; 936-560-5426; ci.nacogdoches.tx.us/696/Sterne-Hoya-House-Museum-and-Library), built in 1828 by Adolphus Sterne, a prominent landowner who raised $10,000 to outfit a volunteer company to serve in San Antonio. Sam Houston was baptized there in the Roman Catholic faith in 1833 as Mexican law required at the time to become a Texas citizen. Today the home is a memorial library and museum of Texas history since colonization. Open Tues through Sat from 10 a.m. to 4 p.m. Admission is free.

Nearby **Oak Grove Cemetery,** at Lanana and Hospital Streets, is where four of the signers of the Texas Declaration of Independence are buried. One is Thomas Rusk, secretary of war in the republic, San Jacinto hero, commander-in-chief in Sam Houston's army, and one of the first US senators from Texas. Another is William Clark, the great-grandfather of this author's maternal grandmother. The cemetery is always open, and there is no admission charge.

Today Nacogdoches—seat of the same-named county—is home to nearly 29,000 residents, some of whom have worked to make a success of several worthy downtown antiques shops, as well as the showplace known as **Millard's Crossing,** at the north end of town (6020 North St., also US 59 North, Nacogdoches; 936-564-6631; millardscrossing.org). Numerous 19th-century homes and commercial buildings have been relocated here in a village setting. Among them is the first Methodist parsonage (1900) and its chapel (1843); a rustic stone-and-log cabin (1830); and the Millard-Burrows House (1840), graced with enormous holly bushes and an iron fence with fleur-de-lis detail. Tours are given Mon through Sat from 9 a.m. to 4 p.m. and Sun from 1 to 4 p.m. Admission is charged. For all Nacogdoches information, call (888) 653-3788 or visit visitnacogdoches.org.

The recently renovated and updated *Fredonia Hotel* turned this 1955 lodging into a fashionable stay. Mid-century modern appointments in public areas and guest rooms, a new fitness center, and a firepit next to the swimming pool all add to the charm. Three restaurant/bar venues and a cute shop off the lobby earn praise, too. Find it downtown at 200 North Fredonia St., Nacogdoches; (936) 564-1234; thefredonia.com.

Do plan to relax for a few days at the *Llano Grande Plantation Bed and Breakfast,* a complex of three historic homes sheltered deep in the woods immediately south of town. The centerpiece is the Tol Barrett house, a pioneer farmhouse dating to 1840, named for its original owner, the oilman credited as being the first to drill a producing well west of the Mississippi. It's rustic, but most guests find it comfortable. Its front is framed by myriad wildflowers, and the interior is filled with period pieces. Guests cook their own breakfasts of venison sausage and homemade breads (in the stocked kitchen, of course) in this private house; other guests stay in one of the two other lovingly restored houses, within walking distance of the Tol Barrett. Guests find their hosts to be hospitable and friendly historians. Reservations and directions must be obtained in advance by calling (936) 569-1249. Visit the website at llanogrande.com.

Another countryside retreat is *Pine Creek Country Inn,* 10 miles west of Nacogdoches via FR 225 and FR 2782 (936-560-6282; pinecreeklodge.com). The Pitts family has owned the hilly, 140-acre farm near Lake Nacogdoches off and on since before World War II and developed it into a bed-and-breakfast in 1995. Rustic buildings contain a total of 17 guest rooms filled with handmade furniture, and each has a king-size bed, sitting area, small refrigerator, private bath, and a basket of candies and fruit. There are terry robes for guests to wear to the hot tub, and a swimming pool is on-site. A full breakfast buffet is offered daily in the main lodge, where guests are welcome to borrow videos and help themselves to popcorn, coffee, tea, and hot chocolate. The on-site Creekside Restaurant is open Fri and Sat from 6 p.m. to 8 p.m.; it's BYOB for now. Visit their website at pinecreeklodge.com.

The 19th-Century Trail

From Nacogdoches head west on the very scenic Highway 21—once the famed El Camino Real—25 miles to the town of Alto, where you'll head north on US 69 for 12 miles to reach *Rusk.* More than 5,000 people live in the Cherokee County seat, cited for having the nation's longest footbridge, measuring 546 feet, located in Footbridge Garden Park, 1 block east of the town square on E. 5th Street. The town was also the birthplace of Jim Hogg and Thomas Mitchell Campbell, the first and second native-born Texans to serve as governor.

Most visitors come to Rusk with a single purpose, that of riding the **Texas State Railroad,** which has one of its two depots here. The parkland surrounding the train terminal here is spread with 100 acres of pines and hardwoods. Not only can you catch the scenic train ride here, but you can camp, hike on trails, picnic, rent paddleboats and rowboats, turn the kids loose in a playground, play tennis, and cast for catfish, bass, and perch in the 15-acre stocked lake. The park is 2 miles west of town on US 84; call (877) 726-7245 or visit texasstaterailroad.net/ for information.

The Texas State Railroad, formerly an operation of the state parks, came under private ownership in 2007. Established in 1881, it's an antique train that transports passengers along 26 miles of track between Rusk and **Palestine.** Passengers ride in vintage coaches powered by antique steam engines through gorgeous forestlands, decorated with pink and white dogwood blooms in spring and rust, scarlet, and gold tapestries in fall. There's a snack bar aboard the train and short-order restaurants at both terminals. The train trip is exceptionally popular, and reservations are a must. The train operates year-round. Call (877) 726-7245 in advance for reservations, schedules, and fares, or see the monthly train schedule online at texasstaterailroad.net/.

In Palestine, the Anderson County seat and home to 18,000 Texans, your sightseeing opportunities are varied. The **Howard House Museum** (1011 N. Perry St., Palestine; 903-729-5094) has been established in an 1851 home and offers a doll collection, an array of antique photos depicting early residents and events, and good period furniture. The home is shown by appointment but is usually open during Palestine's **Dogwood Trails Festival,** a popular event among Texans from around the state, as it is a prime opportunity to see the delicate pink and white blooms cover the forests in a dainty blanket. The event is usually held in late March and early April and features tours of historic homes, a parade in historic downtown, an arts and crafts festival, a chili cook-off, a community theater play, trolley tours, and a car show. The festival has a link on the Palestine Convention and Visitor Bureau website at visitpalestine .com. More on these and other regional interests can be found at the Texas Historical Commission's Texas Forest Trail site, texasforesttrail.com.

Once back in Rusk via the Texas State Railroad, you can continue your journey by driving north on US 69, 14 miles to **Jacksonville,** another Cherokee County town. Known 50 years ago for its abundant tomato crop, the modest city of 12,000 residents today is known for baskets. The **Texas Basket Company** (100 Myrtle Dr., Jacksonville; 903-586-8014; texasbasket.com) is one of a handful of such companies still in operation in the nation. Established in 1924, this outfit still uses original equipment to make baskets crafted entirely from wood cut within 200 miles of town, including sweet gum, black gum, birch, hackberry, elm, cottonwood, and sweet bay. Between 6,000 and 10,000 baskets are produced daily for shipment to all 50 states, as well as to Canada, Germany, and Puerto Rico. Visitors can watch craftspeople at work, and most will want to spend some shopping time in the large store, stocked with thousands of baskets in every imaginable shape and size. Open Mon through Sat from 8:30 a.m. to 5 p.m. Admission is free.

While you're in Jacksonville, be sure to eat at *Sadler's Kitchen* (101 S. Bonner St., Jacksonville; 903-589-0866), which, Thurs and Fri, is a good place to lunch on anything from deluxe sandwiches and salads to pot roast and grilled chicken. And on Thursday, Friday, and Saturday nights, it's open for lovely dinners of pecan-crusted rainbow trout and shrimp with spinach fettuccine. Check out specials on margaritas, too. For more information about Jacksonville, call the chamber of commerce at (903) 586-2217 or visit jackson villetexas.com.

Travelers who enjoy a leisurely drive filled with exquisite scenery will rejoice in the countryside surrounding Jacksonville. Take a picnic to *Love's Lookout Park,* on the roadside 5 miles north of town on US 69. Or just take a few soft drinks and soak in the hilly vistas of forest and water on FRs 747 and 2138 wrapping around Lake Jacksonville.

For a lake of greater import, follow US 175 from Jacksonville 17 miles west to Frankston and catch Highway 155 north, which crosses *Lake Palestine,* a 25,500-acre impoundment on the Neches River in this rolling timberland. Anglers especially will want to spend time here, as the lake is known for record catches, such as a 12-pound striped bass and a 12-pound largemouth bass. Waterskiing is popular here as well. Marinas and campgrounds surround the lake, as do numerous catfish restaurants serving up the freshest local catches.

From the east side of Lake Palestine, continue north on Highway 155 another 13 miles to *Tyler,* the Rose City of Texas. The Smith County seat, Tyler has nearly 105,000 residents. After the Civil War, nurserymen found the sandy soil and rainfall ideal for growing fruit trees and roses. The fruit trees became diseased before the turn of the 20th century, so the rose business carried these growers happily into the 1900s. Today over a third of the nation's commercially grown rosebushes are raised within a 50-mile radius of Tyler.

Visitors revel in the glory found at Tyler's *Municipal Rose Garden* (420 Rose Park Dr., Tyler; 903-531-1213; visittyler.com/tylerrosegarden), where more than 30,000 rosebushes in 500 varieties fill a 14-acre park—making it the country's largest municipal rose garden. The blooming season peaks in mid-May and continues through November. The garden is open daily, 24 hours a day. Admission is free.

This huge rose business gives rise to the **Texas Rose Festival**, a giant celebration held every October, complete with the crowning of a Rose Queen, a rose show featuring more than 100,000 roses, and parades, balls, antiques shows, crafts fairs, and more. Call the chamber of commerce at (903) 592-1661 for details, or visit texasrosefestival.com.

Tyler is well known for its **Caldwell Zoo** (2203 Martin Luther King Dr., Tyler; 903-593-0121; caldwellzoo.org), begun in 1938 as a backyard menagerie. Today it's a 35-acre spread with wonderful, lush settings for elephants and giraffes, birds, bears, alligators, flamingos, and numerous ducks from around the world. There's a monkey island, an aquarium, and a native Texas exhibit. Open daily from 9:30 a.m. to 6 p.m. A small admission fee is charged.

Should you find yourself in Tyler and starving for performing arts, check out the schedule at the **Cowan Center** on the University of Texas/Tyler campus (3900 University Dr., Tyler; 903-566-7424; cowancenter.org). Typical playbills include the Vienna Boys' Choir, the Russian National Ballet, and Hal Holbrook in his Mark Twain show.

You also might consider a visit to the **Tyler Museum of Art** (1300 S. Mahon St., Tyler; 903-595-1001; tylermuseum.org). Exhibits featured here have included one on Latin American textiles and another titled *Self-Taught Artists of the Twentieth Century*. Open Tues through Sat from 10 a.m. to 5 p.m. and Sun from 1 to 5 p.m. Admission is free.

The sweetest place to stay in Tyler is the **Rosevine Inn** (415 S. Vine Ave., Tyler; 903-592-2221; rosevine.com). A 1930s-style home in a bricked-street area becoming well-known for good antiques shops, the inn is surrounded by a white picket fence with well-manicured grounds. The interior is thoughtfully

Busy brewery

The craft beer scene has found a happy home in Tyler, evidenced at *ETX Brewing Co.* pulling in crowds Wednesday through Saturday. When it's nice outside and the garage doors are up, you're sitting in a sidewalk beer garden, watching the street traffic go by as you sip brews made on-site. Because the choices are so many, we enjoy getting a flight that lets us sample several short pours. Among choices, I especially like Red House Wheat, an unfiltered red wheat beer that hints of orange; Downtown Cherry Brown, a brown ale bearing notes of tart cherry; Hitching Post, a mellow amber ale with a faint caramel influence; and Coffee City Stout, a dark beer made with a little locally roasted coffee and Belgian chocolate. Find it in the bustling new downtown area called Off the Square, 221 S. Broadway Ave., Tyler; (903) 630-7720.

decorated, its cozy corners and comfortable rooms scattered with antiques and country decor. Each of the 6 rooms has a private bath, and there's a hot tub on the patio. The inn also offers extended-stay suites in assorted 1930s homes nearby. Breakfasts are gourmet affairs.

Another excellent choice is the ***Woldert-Spence Manor*** (611 W. Woldert St., Tyler; 903-533-9057 or 800-WOLDERT; woldert-spence.com), an 1859 home built by a German immigrant and civil engineer. The home has been added on to over the years, and today it's an elegant inn with original stained-glass windows, chandeliers, several porches and fireplaces, and 5 guest rooms. A full breakfast is served on antique china.

Tyler's dining is improving steadily. Though it's been around for decades, ***Stanley's Famous Pit BBQ*** (525 S. Beckham Ave., Tyler; 903-593-0311; stanleysfamous.com) keeps pulling in new customers with its progressive barbecue scene approach. There's old-fashioned, pecan-smoked beef brisket, ribs, chicken, turkey and sausage, as well as stuffed potatoes and Frito pie. But vegetarians find happiness, too, thanks to tacos stuffed with guacamole and other non-meat goodies. Indulgences include the Mother Clucker, smoked chicken thigh meat with spicy mayo, cheddar and fried egg on jalapeno cheese sourdough at lunch or dinner, as well as the morning specialty, the Breakfast Brother-in-Law, a grilled hot link with cheese and scrambled eggs on a bun. There's live music here, as well as a list of delicious cocktails (make mine the Whiskey Smash, a blend of bourbon with fresh lemon, mint, and simple syrup), best enjoyed at a picnic table on the upper deck.

Nearby in the Midtown Corridor, close to the reinvigorating downtown, ***Roast Social Kitchen*** (1125 E. 5th St., Tyler; 903-202-0295; roastsocialkitchen .com) comes from the Stanley's folks—but don't look for barbecue here. Instead, a brick oven produces exceptional pizza, the super-thin variety made from handcrafted dough and fresh ingredients roasted on-site. Try the Bee's Knees, topped with roasted garlic, a variety of cheeses, sopressata, Italian sausage, local spicy honey and fresh thyme. Light dish choices include the roasted beet salad, tossed with baby spinach, caramelized onion, Haute Goat chevre (from Longview), candied pecans, and lemon Dijon vinaigrette. In the bar, find wine, beer and cocktails on tap, including Rose's Night Out, blending vodka with rose syrup and lemon for light effect.

Dependable places also include ***The Diner*** (7924 S. Broadway Ave., Tyler; 903-509-3463), good for waffles and omelets at breakfast and sandwiches and salads the rest of the day. Or you can dine at the place the locals prefer for steak and seafood, ***Bernard Mediterranean Cuisine*** (212 Grande Blvd., Tyler; 903-534-0265; bernardstyler.com), where specialties include baked brie, crab cakes, tortellini, and rib eye Provençale.

When roaming the downtown area, check out the ***Off the Square neighborhood,*** known for a growing bevy of interesting shops. You'll be tickled pink at all the fun finds in ***903 Handmade*** (253 S. Broadway Ave.), where tables and shelves nearly overflow with gift items, and you'll want most for yourself. There are fabric cosmetic bags in vibrant designs and colors, fun socks (decorated with yetis, caution tape, flamingos, buffalo and watermelons), hand-crafted jewelry (with beads or keys or letter-stamped metal discs) and handy little leather cord keepers. The fabric-covered passport sleeves in a dozen or more designs are a steal at $10 each. Neighboring ***El Guapo Records*** (257 S. Broadway Ave.) serves as a window to the past, with equal doses of nostalgia and chill groovy vibes. Old vinyl finds range from Michael Jackson to the *Midnight Cowboy* soundtrack to Grateful Dead, and there's much to be discovered among the CD collection, too. If you're looking for a turntable or other stereo needs, they're probably here. DJs spin records on some Wednesday evenings, and there's spoken word open mic nights, too. Another few doors away, ***Moon Rivers Naturals*** (265 S. Broadway Ave.) helps us take better care of ourselves. The line of skin care products made with essential oils and other natural ingredients—many of which smell divine—includes several kinds of soaps and moisturizers. Coconut milk face wash, peppermint-lava salt hand and body wash, coffee-grapefruit scrub, rose-geranium bath soak and myriad incense varieties add up to a lot of irresistible purchases. There's even beard oil for guys, too.

Tyler is a central location for various east Texas side trips. One to keep in mind is a jaunt to ***Edom,*** 15 miles west of Tyler via Highway 31 and FR 279. A tiny artists' enclave, Edom has become known for its extraordinary annual arts and crafts show held in September, with juried works drawing artists from around the nation. Several artists—mostly crafters of pottery, leather, and brass—keep shops in town right on the main street, which is FR 279. These shops don't keep regular hours, so you will have to take your chances. Next to one row of shops on the road is ***The Shed,*** a simple country café serving huge lunches and dinners, with specialties such as pork chops, chicken-fried steak, catfish, and enormous coconut, banana cream, and chocolate pies. The café's phone number is (903) 852-7791, or you can visit the website at theshedcafe.com.

Slightly southeast of Tyler, near the burg of Bullard, ***Kiepersol Estates*** (21508 Merlot Ln., Tyler; 903-894-3300; kiepersol.com) has become a popular destination for weekend escapees from Dallas, Houston, and Louisiana. Doing quadruple duty as an elegant B&B inn, restaurant, winery, and cattle business, this impressive operation offers 5 lush suites with private porches and hot tubs. The restaurant offers fancy preparations of duck, sea bass, lamb, and hand-cut steaks, along with a tempting wine list. Reservations should be made well in advance.

East of Tyler toward Kilgore, there's a beautiful retreat called **High Hill Farm** (12626 County Road 217, Arp; 903-730-5055; highhillfarm.com). Stay in a collection of pastel-colored cottages sitting next to a vineyard; relax on your private patio with a bottle of wine and a good book; take a swim in a pool surrounded by potted roses and rosemary; and dine on locally grown beef and seasonal veggies. There's a pretty cocktail bar next to the dining room, and local artwork throughout the main building where the restaurant and bar are situated. Ask about spa treatments, too.

Another option is an excursion to **Kilgore**, 25 miles east of Tyler via Highway 31. Crude, classics, and kicks aren't what most people expect in an east Texas town of 11,000. Home to the **World's Richest Acre**, Kilgore has the mammoth success of the Great Texas Oil Field discovery in 1930 to thank for its prosperity, but the community is best known as giving the world its most famous classical pianist, Van Cliburn, who now resides in Fort Worth; it's also responsible for the phenomenon known as the drill team.

First the oil business: Head to the corner of Main and Commerce Streets, a small area with one life-size derrick and 23 miniderricks representing the oil boom days when more than a thousand wells were jammed into the downtown area and 24 wells, claimed by six different operators, were crowded onto a 1-acre site, creating the World's Richest Acre, which produced more than 2.5 million barrels of crude oil.

To see the industry explained in an interesting manner, visit the **East Texas Oil Museum** (Henderson Boulevard at Ross Street on the Kilgore College campus, Kilgore; 903-983-8295; easttexasoilmuseum.com), and see how a town grew from 800 to 8,000 residents in 24 hours. There's a working oil rig out front, with a 70-foot wooden derrick, steam boiler, rotary table, and draw works. A realistic model of a 1930s street is created inside, complete with a car stuck in the mud, board sidewalks, post office, barbershop, general store, sounds of a thunderstorm building overhead, and music from a period radio. Firsthand accounts of boomtown existence can be heard through headphones; a 15-minute film of actual footage is shown in a "town theater," with the theater rumbling during a gusher; and an elevator takes riders to the center of the Earth. This just scratches the surface of the museum's offerings; see for yourself Tues through Sat from 9 a.m. to 4 p.m. (Apr through Sept, Tues through Sat from 9 a.m. to 5 p.m.) and Sun from 2 to 5 p.m. A small admission is charged.

For something radically different, and certainly more frivolous, walk down the street a block to the **Rangerette Showcase**, also on the Kilgore College campus, at Broadway and Ross Streets (903-983-8265; rangerette.com). In this little corner of east Texas is yet another worldwide attention getter, born 10 years after the oil boom began. The Kilgore Rangerettes formed their first high-kick line in 1940, and the showcase tells the story of this famous precision-and-drill dance team of Kilgore College. Some may say it is sexist, but many will argue it's just Texas camp. Red Grange called them the "sweethearts of the nation's gridiron," and they perform annually on New Year's Day at the Cotton Bowl halftime, their painted red lips matching their shirts, contrasting with little blue skirts and white boots and cowgirl hats. The group responsible for putting showbiz on the football field is chronicled through an assemblage of displays with historical films and videos and decades of newspaper clippings illustrating the team's global reach. The showcase is open Mon through Fri from 9 a.m. to 4 p.m. and Sat from 10 a.m. to 4 p.m. Admission is free.

Even if these attractions don't draw you to Kilgore, the **Country Tavern,** on Highway 31 just on the western outskirts of town, probably will. Most patrons are from all over Texas, and many will argue that this unassuming beer joint serves the best pork ribs in the state. A jukebox and dance floor are good for dancing the Texas two-step, and blue-jeaned waitresses are good for friendly local color. For more than 30 years, this place has served up the biggest platter of ribs in memory, with sides of tasty potato salad, onions, and pickles. Open Mon through Sat for lunch and dinner, the tavern's phone number is (903) 984-9954.

Still another side trip from Tyler is **Mineola** (minny-OH-lah), north 27 miles on US 69. An impressive collection of antiques shops brings folks to Mineola, but it's the **Munzesheimer Manor** (202 N. Newsom St., Mineola; 903-569-6634; munzesheimer.com) that makes them stay. The remarkable 1906 home—with stained-glass windows, seven fireplaces, wraparound porch, and footed tubs—has been thoroughly restored and decorated with English and American antiques. It's a huge, comfortable home with 7 guest rooms, perfect for settling in with a cup of tea and a good novel. Breakfasts during the week are continental, while weekends are full affairs with such treats as fresh berries and German pancakes.

Amid Mineola's antiques shops, a wonderful find is **Kitchen's Hardware & Deli,** at the corner of Pacific and Broad Streets. Part museum and part retailer, the vintage store has old auger bits and ancient tools on display, as well as new stuff, ranging from plumbing supplies and Case knives to American flags and Marshall pottery. In front there

texastrivia

Produce is popular here: East Texas hosts festivals for the tomato in Jacksonville, the hot pepper in Palestine, the blueberry in Nacogdoches, and the yam in Gilmer.

are some picnic tables where you can lunch on the deli's roast beef sandwiches, German sausage plate, homemade chili, or specials such as corn bread, beans, and greens. Or get an old-fashioned root beer float to go.

About 14 miles east of Mineola on Highway 49, find **Pine Mills Pottery** (5155 FR 49, Mineola; 903-857-2271; pinemills.com), a studio and gallery showing and selling some exceptional work by artists Gary C. Hatcher and Daphne Roehr Hatcher. The depth and breadth of their artistry is remarkable. It's generally open daily from 10 a.m. until 5 p.m., but it's wise to call in advance to be sure.

Fishing enthusiasts will want to linger in this area, as 27,000-acre **Lake Fork** (fewer than 10 miles west of Quitman, via Highway 182) is where record-setting bass are caught annually. The lake is surrounded by marinas where you'll find good fishing guides, while **Lake Fork Lodge** (at the intersection of Highways 17 and 515, Alba; 903-473-7236; lakeforklodge.com) offers everything including comfortable rooms, hot tubs, a game room, bass boats, licensed guides, dog kennels, fishing pier, and full breakfasts with your stay. Your next destination is **Canton;** head west of Tyler 40 miles on Highway 64, and you'll wind up directly at the Van Zandt County Courthouse Square, just a few yards beyond your actual destination, **First Monday Trade Days.** If you arrive early and are lucky, you may be able to find a parking spot on the square or nearby, then just walk the block east to the 100-acre fairgrounds, where some 5,000 vendors are spread out with their goods for sale. This, of course, occurs the Friday, Saturday, and Sunday preceding the first Monday of each month. Since the middle of the 19th century, country folks have been traveling here to buy and sell everything from kitchenware, clothes, farm equipment, furniture, and toys to baby carriages, jewelry, homemade jellies and jams, and books. Collectors of Depression glass, quilts, iron beds, and china find this a great place to hunt bargains. Food booths are set up everywhere, too, selling burgers, barbecue, pastries, and cold drinks. It's a colorful experience well worth taking in, even for visitors who aren't in the market to buy anything. Trade Days gates open at 7 a.m. and close at dark; for information call the chamber of commerce at (903) 567-2991 or visit firstmondaycanton.com.

But even if you reach Canton on a non–First Monday weekend, there's good reason to slow down and look around. The town has a growing farmers' market, a water park called Splash Kingdom, golf courses, an alligator-wildlife park, Christmas tree farms, regularly scheduled bluegrass music festivals, and much more. Check with the **Canton Visitors Bureau** by calling (877) 462-7467 or visiting visitcantontx.com.

Buttermilk's On the Square (100 W. Dallas St., Canton; 903-567-3287; buttermilkscanton.com) is the go-to for scratch cooking. Pecan-cranberry chicken salad, fried green tomatoes, jalapeno-cheddar burger, chicken-fried steak and buttermilk chess pie are favorites.

From Canton head south on Highway 19 almost 30 miles to the town of **Athens,** known to masters of American food trivia. Proof that Athens is birthplace of the hamburger is found on a historical marker on the north side of the Henderson County Courthouse Square, next to the 1927 First National Bank Building. It explains that on this site in the late 1880s, a café owner named Fletcher Davis (1864–1944) created the first hamburger sandwich. He took his invention to exhibit at the 1904 St. Louis World's Fair, in fact. Family members and local friends, as well as the resources of McDonald's Hamburger University, support this story. The **Uncle Fletch Hamburger Festival** is held here in the fall.

Athens has become nationally famous in the past couple of years for its proximity to the **Cleveland Armory Black Beauty Ranch** (18 miles east of town off Highway 31, via FR 1803 and County Road 3806; 903-469-3811; fund foranimals.org). Open to the public only for special events and tours (check their website for dates), the ranch is a setting for modern-day miracles in the form of a 1,620-acre refuge for abandoned and abused animals of all sorts, from chimpanzees, burros, and elephants to dogs, cats, and horses. Founded in 1979 by the late author Cleveland Amory and the Fund for Animals, the ranch is operated as a nonprofit facility supported primarily by donations. Today several hundred animals are guaranteed a healthy, safe home for their lifetimes at this extraordinary sanctuary. Call ahead to have a guide show you some of these wonderful, living stories.

In Athens be sure to take the kids to visit the **Texas Freshwater Fisheries Center** (5550 Flat Creek Rd., Athens; 903-676-BASS; tpwd.texas.gov), a 106-acre operation of the Inland Fisheries Division of the Texas Parks and Wildlife Department. You'll learn about the "sharelunker" program, designed to increase the production, size, and quality of Florida largemouth bass in Texas waters.

The massive visitor center—named for Athens native Edwin L. Cox Jr., a former chairman of the Parks and Wildlife Foundation of Texas, rancher, and conservationist—presents an introduction to this intriguing aquarium and hatchery complex, which houses some 300,000 gallons of fishy representatives of more than 40 species from the state's freshwater streams, ponds, and lakes. Among hundreds of things to see (and often, to catch) are some of the heftiest largemouth bass in the world and the American alligator. The fisheries center is open Tues through Sat from 9 a.m. to 4 p.m. and Sun from 1 to 4 p.m. Admission is charged.

About 30 miles north on Highway 155 and then 10 miles east on US 80 is the **Antiques Capital of East Texas,** seen on the map as **Gladewater,** a town of 6,500 in Gregg County. It is home to more than 250 antiques dealers scattered around in 16 antiques malls and 16 individual shops. Most of the shopping is concentrated in Gladewater's vintage downtown area, all within easy walking distance from one point to another.

Slow down long enough to enjoy lunch at *The Central Station* (103 N. Main St., Gladewater; 903-374-4700; gladewatercentral.com), housed in a 1930s Texaco station. Margherita pizza, prosciutto-wrapped pork tenderloin, Caribbean chicken tacos, ribeye steak, root beer floats and a menu of craft beer and cider make this a terrific surprise. From Gladewater continue to *Longview,* 13 miles east on US 80. The unassuming town of 73,000 is the Gregg County seat and has a heritage of railroad, agriculture, lumber, and oil businesses that left it somewhat undistinguished. This has changed, however, as the popularity of the *Great Texas Balloon Race* has skyrocketed. For a 3-day weekend in mid-July, hundreds of brightly colored hot-air balloons can be seen scattered throughout the sky in early morning or evening as pilots from around the nation compete in tests of skill. The contest involves a pilot's ability to maneuver the balloon between points and drop a marker on a designated target—all of which is determined by the winds. Besides the flights, there are on-ground events during the festival, such as arts and crafts fairs, aircraft exhibits, evening concerts, and other fun for spectators. The party is held at the Gregg County Airport; information is available from the chamber of commerce by calling (903) 237-4000 or visiting greattexasballoonrace.com. Admission is free, but parking fees are charged.

If you've worked up an appetite, head for *Bodacious Barbecue,* at 227 South Mobberly and five other locations in Longview (903-753-8409), an east Texas institution famous for its chopped-beef sandwiches as well as sliced beef brisket, ribs, and spicy links. Open Mon through Sat 10 a.m. to 7 p.m.

New and delightful, *Haute Goat Creamery* (1908 Esat U.S. 80, Suite 2, White Oak; 430-558-8020; hautegoatcreamery.com) is a small but wonderful shop selling French-style artisan cheeses, made on site with milk from local goats. The selection is surprising, and the owner generously shares recipes for making dishes with her cheeses.

With bellies full, try to find the strength to push on to *Marshall,* 23 miles east on US 80. The Harrison County seat, with almost 24,000 residents, has a deep southern heritage imbued with plantations and Civil War history—in fact, more than 150 historical markers are found throughout Harrison County. So strong is its legacy that newsman Bill Moyers, Marshall's favorite son, hosted a PBS broadcast titled "Marshall, Texas; Marshall, Texas" in his *A Walk Through the 20th Century with Bill Moyers.*

Downtown Marshall is energized by ongoing restoration of century-old buildings, bringing residents and visitors alike to the sidewalks day and night.

The Weisman (211 N. Washington St, Marshall; 903-934-8836; theweisman .com) is a marketplace in the Washington Square District will a collection of antiques, art, jewelry, and gifts on three floors. Central Perks is a coffeehouse on the premises with a vegan menu. Next door, *Blissmoor Valley Ranch Company Store* (208 N. Washington St., Marshall; 903-472-4550) is a shop selling antiques, fudge, gifts, home goods, and a lunch spot called the Blue Frog.

The *Michelson Museum of Art* (216 N. Bolivar St., Marshall; 903-935-9480; michelsonmuseum.org) is a small treasure house of works by Impressionist painter Leo Michelson (1887–1978). His work is also displayed in museums in Baltimore, Jerusalem, Paris, San Diego, and Tel Aviv, among others. Traveling exhibits fill the gallery as well. The museum has grown to accommodate the Gloria and Bernard Kronenberg Collection of early 20th century American art, as well as the Ramona and Jay Ward Collection of African Masks. Open Tues through Fri from noon to 5 p.m. and Sat and Sun from 1 to 4 p.m. Admission is free.

warbetween thestates

In the spring of 1864, a place called *Camp Ford* had a stockade holding some 6,000 Union troops, making it the largest prisoner-of-war compound west of the Mississippi. You can see a historical marker noting the place in a rest area on US 271, about 2 miles northeast of Tyler.

Winter is prime time for visiting Marshall, when the town lights up like a Christmas tree—literally. The *Wonderland of Lights* is focused on the historic county courthouse, which is covered with 4.5 million tiny white lights, and area businesses and homes are aglow as well, from Thanksgiving until New Year's Day. For information on special events, call the chamber of commerce at (903) 702-7777 or (800) 953-7868 or visit marshalltexas.net.

Look in Marshall's beloved Ginocchio Historic District for the *Three Oaks Bed and Breakfast* (609 N. Washington Ave., Marshall; 903-935-6777 or 800-710-9789; threeoaks-marshall.com). The 1895 historic landmark offers 4 guest suites decorated with antiques, each with its own private bath and free wireless access. A full breakfast is included. Music fans will find a worthwhile detour 31 miles south of Marshall, via US 59, in the town of *Carthage.* In the summer of 1998, Panola County residents welcomed the new *Texas Country Music Hall of Fame* at the *Tex Ritter Museum* (300 W. Panola, Carthage; 903-693-6634; tcmhof.com/). The first inductees were the late Jim Reeves, whose nearby grave is noted with a Texas Historical Marker, as well as Gene Autry and Tex Ritter. The museum is filled with honorees' guitars, stage clothing, gold records, and photographs. Hours vary according to season, so call ahead.

Bayous, Lakes & Legends

From Marshall you need travel only 14 miles northeast on Highway 43 to find one of the state's greatest natural assets, **Caddo Lake.** The only lake in Texas not created artificially, the 35,400-acre lake is characterized by seven-century-old cypress trees draped in an ethereal manner with heavy curtains of Spanish moss. The effect nature has wrought is one of haunting beauty, appropriate for a place whose creation is a mystery. One legend holds that the reservoir was formed when a resident Caddo Indian chief was warned by the Great Spirits to move his people to higher ground or watch them die in a terrible earthquake and flood. It seems he ignored them and chose to take his warriors hunting; they returned to find that a mighty shake had occurred and their village had been replaced by a huge lake. Some part of the story could be true, as recorded history shows that an earthquake in 1811 in New Madrid, Missouri, is estimated to have had a force that would register 8.9 on today's Richter scale—and it's possible that that tremor created a logjam in the Red River that dammed Caddo Lake, lapping a bit across the Louisiana state line.

Naturally, photographers and painters are captured by Caddo's ancient beauty, best seen on boat tours led by lake experts. These sloughs and canals are terribly confusing to anyone unfamiliar with its shrouded paths, but the fishing and wildlife watching are far too wonderful to pass up. Inquire about guides at **Caddo Lake State Park** on Highway 43 by calling (903) 679-3351 or visiting tpwd.texas.gov.

At the state park, on FR 2198, just 1 mile east of Highway 43, several rock cabins—which have been completely remodeled and updated—are available for rental, but they are reserved for weekend stays up to 90 days ahead, so call the state park early or try for a weeknight stay. Shaded by towering pines near the water, these are nice places to kick back for a while. Canoe rentals are offered in the park, as are camping, fishing, hiking, picnicking, and nature study. One of the canoe outfitters to try is **Caddo Lake Tours** (903-431-1673). For guided flat-bottom boat tours, which are great for individuals or very small groups, check out **Caddo Outback Backwater Tours** (903-789-3384). **Big Cypress Tours of Caddo Lake** (903-570-3319) is still another option for guided trips with experts who help you spot gators and beautiful water birds. The former Graceful Ghost Steamboat Company is now **Captain Ron's Swamp Tours** (903-679-3020; captronswamptours.com), an outfit taking you aboard a 28-foot pontoon boat for a narrated tour providing detail on Caddo's history and unusual ecosystem.

The best dining close to the park is **Big Pines Lodge** (903-679-3655; bigpineslodge.com), rebuilt after a huge fire and far nicer than ever. Order a mountain of fried catfish and fried alligator tail, as well as hush puppies. Another popular choice, **River Bend Restaurant** on Caddo Lake (211 Private Road 2422, Karnack; 903-679-9000) is a destination for fried catfish and shrimp, steaks and baked sweet potatoes, and hushpuppies.

Adjacent to the park is the tiny community of **Uncertain**—and no one's certain how the name came about. One theory is that when the hamlet was contemplating incorporation, a poll was taken to choose a town name, and "Uncertain" was frequently listed on the third-choice line. Of one thing you can be sure, there is a cluster of little businesses offering rustic accommodations, marina and fishing guide services (helpful in navigation and landing big catfish and bass), cafés, and good humor. Among those offering accommodations are **Shady Glade** (903-789-3295) and **Uncertain Inn** (FR 2189, on the lake; 903-789-3292). You'll find these and many more at cityofuncertain.com.

Newer lodging worth a good look is **Lafitte's Landing Guest Quarters** (843 Cypress Dr., Uncertain; 903-789-3269; caddolodging.com/lafittes), a collection of new cottages made to look exactly like historic houses in and around New Orleans. They're exceedingly comfortable, sitting near the water. There's a community kitchen for all guests to use, but each cottage has its own kitchenette, living room, bathroom, and porch. Down the road a short walk, check out Lafitte's Caddo Grocery and Cafe, owned by the cottage proprietors, who serve pecan-smoked pulled pork, pork ribs, sausage, and chicken.

A little side trip into history from Caddo is a short drive away at **T. C. Lindsey and Company General Store,** found by following FR 134, 13 miles east in

June's Texas Anecdotes

One chilly spring afternoon, I let Caddo Lake guide George Cox talk my husband and me into taking one of his mud-boat tours to search for alligators. Meeting George at the appointed spot in the fading daylight, setting out for the shallow areas that only flat-bottom boats can access, we are steered into darkly shaded stretches that we wouldn't dare venture ourselves; who could ever find the way out of the twists and turns and dead-ends? Every log looks like an alligator. I'm terrified that in my jitters I'll simply fall out of the boat and instantly become supper. Finally George turns into Alligator Bayou, and as the name promises, he points toward a gator silently slipping through the water. Possibly 10 to 12 feet long, the gator keeps an eye on us as we keep a respectful distance. George cuts the motor and we just drift, watching the alligator submerge and resurface. "I was hoping to show you the 15-footer, the biggest one we've ever found on the lake," George says of his favorite gator sighting. "Maybe next time." We agree; we're game. Another time, though, we're not disappointed with this outing in the least.

the town of Jonesville. In business since 1847, it's still a family-owned, no-frills country store. With high ceilings and creaky wooden floors, this general store is obviously the real McCoy. Shelves are stacked with groceries, fabrics, and feed, while a room off to the side is now a makeshift museum. You'll find farm tools, old hunting traps, horseshoes, massive iron skillets, and other relics from another time. Glass cases in front hold antique eyeglasses, glass bottles, toiletries, and household items used by our grandparents and great-grandparents. Snacks, candies, cold drinks, and slices from a massive wheel of cheese will tide you over until supper. The store is open Tues through Sat from 8 a.m. to 4 p.m. Admission is free; call the store at (903) 687-3382.

From Caddo Lake your next destination could be the old bayou town of *Jefferson,* a town packed with charm and romance, 13 miles west of the lake on FR 134. The Marion County community of 2,200 is rapidly growing in stature around the state for its perfect balance of historical preservation and hospitality.

A good place to call home during a few days of relaxation and exploration is the *Excelsior House* (211 W. Austin St., Jefferson; 903-665-2513; the excelsiorhouse.com). The second-oldest hotel in Texas, the Excelsior has been in continuous operation since 1858 and has hosted dignitaries such as Ulysses S. Grant, Rutherford B. Hayes, W. H. Vanderbilt, Oscar Wilde, and Lyndon B. and Lady Bird Johnson. A beautiful place with ornate furniture and heavy, baroque French frames around paintings, crystal chandeliers, Oriental carpets, a grand piano, Italian marble mantels, and pressed-tin ceiling, it's a showplace as well as a delightful setting in which to have a plantation breakfast—by reservation, of course. The 14 rooms and suites are in demand on weekends, so call ahead or try for a midweek visit.

The Excelsior's 1961 restoration spurred revitalization throughout the town, which had fallen into a quiet decline after its riverboat days were long past. In the 19th century, steamboats churned the waters of the Big Cypress Bayou from Jefferson, via Caddo Lake and the Red River, all the way south to New Orleans. Today's visitors can still tour the bayou aboard the *Turning Basin Riverboat Tours,* an open-air boat departing Jefferson Landing four times daily in spring, summer, and fall for 1-hour, narrated tours. Call (903) 665-2222 for hours and rates, or visit jeffersonbayoutours.com.

Another way to see the water and woodsy environs is aboard the *Jefferson and Cypress Bayou Railroad,* a narrow-gauge railroad powered by an antique steam locomotive winding along the bayou on a scenic, 5-mile route; this is another great way to gain an overview of the town. Tours are offered on weekends. Call (866) 398-2038 for details and schedule updates, or visit jeffersonrailway.com.

The haunted Jefferson tours are extremely popular, and not just a little bit scary. If you're brave enough, sign up for the tours with local historian Jodi Breckenridge, owner of *Jefferson Ghost Walk* (903-665-6289; jeffersonghost walk.com).

For more background on the town and area, head for the *Jefferson Historical Society Museum* (223 W. Austin St., Jefferson; 903-665-2775; jefferson museum.com), where history lessons are made fun. Housed in a former federal courthouse and post office (1888), this big red gem of the past contains three floors of the historical society's collected memories. More than 30,000 visitors come annually to see the dress Lady Bird Johnson (from nearby Karnack) wore to a state dinner for the West German chancellor; sterling silver flatware that belonged to Whistler's mother; and personal belongings of Sam Houston and Annie Oakley. Open daily. Admission is charged.

For a great, fresh lemonade or scoop of ice cream, visit *Jefferson General Store* (113 E. Austin St., Jefferson; 903-665-8481; jeffersongeneralstore.com) where books and all sorts of souvenirs and gifts are sold.

Dozens of antiques shops are found along the brick streets of downtown in historic commercial buildings. Some beautiful 19th-century homes are open for tours year-round, while eight homes are chosen annually to be on show during the *Jefferson Pilgrimage,* held the first weekend in May. The weekend features not only the homes but also the *Diamond Bessie Murder Trial,* a wonderful melodrama based on the story of a former prostitute who was thought to have been murdered by her rich diamond-merchant husband. For pilgrimage information contact the chamber of commerce, (903) 665-2672, or the Jessie Allen Wise Garden Club, event hosts, at the Excelsior Hotel, (903) 665-2513, or visit theexcelsiorhouse.com/tour.htm.

An expansive, 1920s home now serves as a five-room bed-and-breakfast inn called the *Delta Street Inn* (206 East Delta Street. 1-877-665-2929; deltastreetinn.com), a few blocks from downtown Jefferson. Filled with antiques, the inn is refined yet unfussy. Each of the guest chambers has its own fireplace, king-size bed, TV with DVD option, sitting hardwood floors and updated bathroom; ask for one of the rooms with a balcony. Common areas include a spacious living room, front porch, sprawling lawn with a gazebo and finally, where you'll mingle with fellow guests over a filling breakfast, a big dining room.

Jefferson's dining options are numerous. Some of the very best barbecue in all of Texas is found at *Joseph's Riverport Barbecue* (201 N. Polk St., Jefferson; 903-665-2341), popular for smoked beef brisket, pork ribs, sausages, and unexpected finds like hot-water cornbread, and "swamp fries," a plate of french fries covered in onion, chopped barbecue, and cheese. A lively spot for nachos and beer is *Auntie Skinner's River Boat Club* (107 W. Austin

St., Jefferson; 903-665-7121), while the town's most elegant dinners of grilled veal chop, red snapper, and dessert soufflés are served at ***Stillwater Inn*** (203 E. Broadway St., Jefferson; 903-665-8415; stillwaterinn.com). Easily the most popular breakfast spot in town, ***Bayou Bakery and Café*** (201 W. Austin St., Jefferson; 903-665-2253) serves a breakfast sandwich on raisin toast, as well as lunchtime plates of chicken-fried steak, barbecued chicken, and chicken pot pie.

For complete details on Jefferson, call the Marion County Chamber of Commerce at (903) 665-2672 or (888) 467-3529 or visit jefferson-texas.com.

For a detour into curiosity, take an hour's drive north from Jefferson on US 59 to ***Texarkana***, sometimes called the State Line Cities, as it's part Texas, part Arkansas—hence, the name. Of particular interest here is the ***Perot Theatre*** (at 221 Main St., Texarkana; 903-792-4992; trahc.org), an Italian Renaissance theater opened as the Saenger in 1924. Seating 1,600 patrons, it was among the most famous showplaces in a four-state area in its heyday. In the late 1970s, Texarkana native Ross Perot donated $2 million to restore the theater to its former magnificence with glistening chandeliers, royal blue and gold interiors, and marble floors. A symphony series, plays, musicals, and pop music concerts are staged here from September through May. Tours are by reservation, depending on scheduled events.

Most unusual in Texarkana is the ***Bi-State Justice Center*** (100 N. State Line Ave., Texarkana; 903-798-3153), a building straddling the Texas-Arkansas line and, therefore, shared by two cities, two counties, and two states. It is thought to be the world's only post office and federal building with a state line bisecting it. As was appropriate, the building was crafted from both Texas pink granite and Arkansas limestone. The building is open Mon through Fri from 8 a.m. to 5 p.m.; tours are free and by appointment.

Take Flight

The modest town of Pittsburg is regionally famous for possessing the ***Ezekiel Airship,*** a replica of a 1902 flying craft that, while undocumented, is said to have been airborne a year before the Wright brothers made their first flight. Its inventor was an inspired, sometime-Baptist preacher who took his idea of an airship from the prophet Ezekiel, who described in the Bible an apparatus that flew. The preacher raised $20,000, sold stock in his company, and built his ship. Unfortunately it was destroyed during shipment to the St. Louis World's Fair in 1904. The 26-by-23-foot replica was for many years displayed at a restaurant in Pittsburg. Now it's on view at the ***Depot Museum,*** 204 W. Marshall St.; (903) 856-1200; pittsburgtxmuseum.com.

From Jefferson there is still much to be seen in the way of outdoor beauty. To sample this bounty drive west from Jefferson on FR 729 for 17 miles and you'll find yourself at the shores of shimmering *Lake o' the Pines,* surrounded by lush hardwoods and pines, a scene that's splendid in autumn, as the leaves make quite a show of changing to crimson, burnt orange, and amber. The lake is 18,000 acres, with excellent fishing for largemouth, white, and spotted bass; swimming, waterskiing, and sailing are favorites here, too. Campsites abound, as do picnic areas and nature trails. The Army Corps of Engineers, at (903) 665-2336, offers more information. For more information about all services and attractions, visit lakeothepines.com.

About 10 miles north of the lake via US 259, the town of *Daingerfield,* is on the way to one of the prettiest state parks in Texas. At *Daingerfield State Park,* immediately east of town on Highway 11, 550 acres of pine-blanketed land surround a lovely, 80-acre, spring fed lake. Photographers have traveled from around the state to capture the color riot in autumn, and spring's demonstration is just as dramatic, as redbuds, dogwoods, and wisteria explode in shades of pink and purple. Hiking trails, fishing, camping, cabins, playgrounds, and picnic areas make this a place to stay for more than a day. For information and reservations call the park office at (903) 645-2921 or visit tpwd.texas.gov.

From Daingerfield, travel west 16 miles on Highway 11 to *Pittsburg,* the Camp County seat and home to 4,000 residents. Its economy is based on a significant poultry business—Pilgrims Pride alone produces more than 600 million pounds of chicken yearly.

The chicken business may be big here, and there is a Spring Chick Festival held in Pittsburg in late April, but the primary food found here is the *Pittsburg Hot Link.* The not-too-spicy sausage made from beef and pork is, appropriately, served up hot at the *Pittsburg Hot Links Restaurant* (136 Marshall St., Pittsburg; 903-856-5765; pittsburghotlink.com). Patrons place their orders at the counter in back, ordering by the link or choosing from other specialties, such as beef stew, chili, burgers, or chicken-fried steak. The restaurant is open Mon through Sat from 8 a.m. to 6 p.m.

timber

The Piney Woods reaches southward from the Red River to within 25 miles of the Gulf Coast and receives about 40 to 55 inches of rainfall each year. With millions of acres of pine forests, the Piney Woods is the source of nearly all of Texas's larger commercial timber productions.

Before heading back to your cabin at Daingerfield, your campsite at Lake o' the Pines, or your cozy corner in Pittsburg, consider another detour, this time to *Winnsboro,* a pleasant hamlet just 22 miles west of Pittsburg on Highway

11. There's another pretty lake here for a dip in summer, but the primary attractions come after the weather begins changing. Fall foliage is a cause for big celebrations, hence the *Autumn Trails Festival,* held every weekend in October. The chamber of commerce hosts an antique car show and a homes tour; driving maps to see the best in fall's color parade are offered, too. And the Christmas season brings folks from all over east and north Texas to choose a special tree from one of the several area Christmas-tree farms; hot apple cider is a bonus offered by the farmers while customers find the prettiest evergreen. For details contact the chamber of commerce at 100 E. Broadway Ave., Winnsboro, or via (903) 342-3666; winnsboro.com.

One of the finest, most praised bed-and-breakfast inns in the state happens to be in Winnsboro. *Thee Hubbell House* (307 W. Elm St., Winnsboro; 903-342-5629; theehubbellhouse.com) is an 1888, 2-acre plantation estate containing a mansion that has 5 luxurious guest rooms and suites and a wonderful carriage house with 6 guest rooms. All have private baths, and all stays include a full plantation breakfast in the mansion.

Other Places to Stay in the Piney Woods

CROCKETT

Warfield House
712 E. Houston Ave.
(936) 544-4037
warfield-house.com
Five guest rooms with private baths; stays include a full breakfast.

JEFFERSON

Benefield House Bed & Breakfast
1009 S. Line St
(903) 665-9366
benefieldhouse.com
A restored 1895 home offers three guest rooms with private baths, in-room coffee stations, beautiful grounds, and a big breakfast.

Old Mulberry Inn Bed & Breakfast
209 Jefferson St.
(903) 665-1945
oldmulberryinn.com

The Claiborne House & Touch of Class Day Spa
312 S. Alley St.
(903) 665-8800 or
(877) 385-9236
claibornehousebnb.com
This restored 1872 home has rooms with private baths named for poets Browning, Yeats, Tennyson, Wilde, Dickinson, and Keats. Ask about the Jacuzzi tubs and king-size beds.

NACOGDOCHES

Hardeman Guest House
316 N. Church St.
(936) 205-5280
hardemanhouse.com
Four guest rooms, each
with king beds and private
baths, are in a historic
home in a quiet, old
neighborhood. Breakfast is
included.

Stag Leap Country Cabins
2219 Farm Road 2782
(936) 560-0766 stagleap
.com
Six cabins near Lake
Nacogdoches are on
property just 10 minutes
from downtown. Each has
its own kitchen and porch.
Choose from 1, 2 and 3
bedrooms.

UNCERTAIN

Hodge Podge Cottages
Route 2
Box 55D, TX 75001
(903) 789-3901
hodgepodgecottages.com
Eleven cottages either on
or close to the water offer
one to three bedrooms,
full kitchen, porches, and
decks. Two-night stay
required.

Spatterdock
Route 2
Box 66B, TX 75661
(903) 789-3268
spatterdock.com
Three guesthouses—
one with 3 bedrooms
and 2 baths, one with 4
bedrooms and 3 baths,
and one with 1 bedroom
and bathroom. All have

fully equipped kitchens.
The hosts offer fishing and
hunting guide services, too.

Other Places to Eat in the Piney Woods

JEFFERSON

Austin Street Bistro
117 E. Austin St.
(903) 665-9700
Tomato basil soup, chicken
salad, lasagna, and pecan-
crusted salmon are among
good choices.

Lamanche's Italian Restaurant
124 W. Austin St.
(903) 665-6177

NACOGDOCHES

The Liberty Bell
422 E Main St.
(936) 622-6425
Libertybellbar.com
In addition to a large wine
and craft beer list, this
gathering place with live
music serves seared ahi
tuna, tacos, enormous
burgers, and chili.

PALESTINE

Pint & Barrel
302 E. Crawford St.
(903) 727-2711
pintandbarrel.com
Starters include roasted
jalapeno-spinach-artichoke
dip, blue cheese fondue
fries and white cheddar
poblano soup; entrees

range from pulled smoked
pork sandwiches and meat
loaf sandwiches to burgers
topped with bacon and
cheddar.

TYLER

The Grove
3500 Old Jacksonville
Highway
(903) 939-0209
thegrovetyler.com
An expansive space with
a wide-ranging menu and
diverse selection of dining
spaces, this pricy-for-Tyler
spot offers a good cheese
board for pairing with wine;
smothered pork chop
special on Thursday; and a
beautiful weekend brunch.

Jucys Hamburgers
2330 E. 5th St.
(903) 597-0660
jucyshamburgers.com
An outpost from Longview,
this much-loved burger
restaurant grinds its beef
on-site each morning and
cuts its fries from whole
russet potatoes daily. The
burger topped with blue
cheese and bacon is a big
hit, and the one blanketed
in cheddar and grilled
onions is another winner.
There's a great chicken-
fried steak on the menu,
too.

North Texas

North Texas mirrors the Lone Star State's uncanny ability to wear a vast number of different hats. Denying any one classification or description, the region exhibits a broad range of personalities. Big D, as Dallas is proudly called in the Southwest, was built largely from the fruits of the oil and banking industries and is known as well as a major fashion, electronics, and motion pictures center. Furthermore, Dallas boasts having more restaurants per capita than any other city in the nation, and the city joins Fort Worth in being home to teams competing in every professional sport. Together the two are called the Metroplex. Fort Worth, 30 miles east, is also called Cowtown, thanks to its ranching heritage, and it is famous for a curious mix of Wild West and world-class fine arts. In addition, Fort Worth has a restored stockyards area where Butch and Sundance hid out and where today you can "scoot a boot" in the world's largest honky-tonk.

Travelers to the north Texas region find that in perfect balance to this unusual cosmopolitan–Wild West mix are the small towns where a simpler way of life is still valued. Communities that gave the world such dignitaries as Sam Rayburn and Dwight D. Eisenhower are special places that continue to

live in yesteryear, where historic houses and pretty lakes—instead of shopping malls and symphonies—are the draws.

Exotic wildlife ranches, a quiet Norse community, a rustic ranch where city folks can play cowpoke for a day, an ancient riverbed where dinosaur tracks are plainly visible—these are the places where people go to escape e-mail and voice mail.

Red River Country

Oldest town in the Red River Valley and home to more than 10,000 residents, the Fannin County seat of **Bonham** was settled in 1837 by a former Arkansas sheriff who brought settlers to a land grant he received from the Republic of Texas. The community was eventually named for James Butler Bonham, the Alamo's courageous messenger, whose statue stands before the courthouse.

But Bonham's greatest claim to fame is Sam Rayburn, the political legend who spent 49 consecutive years, or 25 terms, in the US House of Representatives—17 of those as Speaker of the House. Mr. Sam, as he was fondly called, is remembered at the **Sam Rayburn Library** (800 W. Sam Rayburn Dr., Bonham; 903-583-2455; fannincountyhistory.org/sam-rayburn-library.html), which holds an exact replica of his Capitol Hill office, with all furnishings. A host of his memorabilia is displayed here, including a gorgeous white marble rostrum that was used by every House speaker from 1857 until 1950. Other interesting artifacts are a collection of political cartoons, gavels, and a 2,500-year-old Grecian urn Rayburn received from the Athens Palace Guard. The library was donated to the University of Texas, whose students come to use it for research. It's open Tues through Sun, with several guided tours daily; check website for hour. Admission is free.

Rayburn, who was born in Tennessee in 1882, moved to Texas with his parents in 1887. The **Sam Rayburn House,** 1 mile west of town on US 82 (903-583-5558; thc.state.tx.us or visitsamrayburnhouse.com) is a 14-room home he built for his parents in 1916. Modest but comfortable, it's been restored, along with the grounds, to the look it had upon his death in 1961. It's open Tues through Sat from 8 a.m. to 5 p.m. Admission is free. Rayburn's funeral was attended by President Kennedy, Vice President Johnson, and former presidents Truman and Eisenhower; Rayburn is buried in Bonham's **Willow Wild Cemetery,** on W. 7th Street at Highway 121. The large monument there bears the impression of a gavel and the simple epitaph, Mr. Sam, 1882–1961. The cemetery is never closed, and no admission is charged.

If you happen onto Bonham in October, see if you're in time for the **Fannin County Fair,** a wonderful tradition more than a hundred years old, with livestock shows, baking and other homemaking contests, a carnival, and entertainment (fannincountyfair.com). For more information, call the chamber of commerce at (903) 583-4811 or visit bonhamchamber.com.

Also in Bonham see the ***Fannin County Museum of History*** (1 Main St., Bonham; 903-583-8042; fannincountymuseum.org), housing pioneer furniture, tools, vintage clothing, toys, Native American artifacts, and photographs depicting life in one of the counties of the Republic of Texas. A genealogical and historical library and the Red River Valley Art Gallery are also located here. Open Apr 1 through Sept 1, Tues through Sat from 10 a.m. to 4 p.m. The remainder of the year, it's open Tues through Sat from noon to 4 p.m. Admission is free.

From Bonham follow US 82 west 15 miles, then head north on US 69 another 13 miles to ***Denison,*** a town of nearly 23,000 in Grayson County. It's best known for being the gateway to ***Lake Texoma,*** created from the mighty Red River by the building of Denison Dam, the nation's largest rolled earth-fill dam upon its completion in 1944. The enormous reservoir on the Texas-Oklahoma line covers 89,000 acres and has 50 parks, more than 100 picnic areas, and plenty of recreation facilities along 580 miles of shoreline. Travelers come from a three-state area to the resort hotels and motels and marinas surrounding these waters, and anglers spend time on the lake catching record black bass, striper bass, crappie, and lunker catfish. Many of today's vacationers head for the 14-mile Cross Timber Hiking Trail that hugs the water. Stop by the ***Denison Chamber of Commerce*** at 313 W. Woodward St. for specific information, call (903) 465-1551, or visit denisontexas.us.

Lake Texoma has dozens of places to stay right at the water's edge. The nicest of all is ***Tanglewood Resort*** (903-786-2968 or 800-833-6569;

JUNE'S FAVORITE ATTRACTIONS

Amon Carter Museum Fort Worth	**Inn on Lake Granbury** Granbury
Cafe Modern Fort Worth	**Lake Mineral Wells State Park** Mineral Wells
Davis & Blevins Main Street Gallery Saint Jo	**Mosaics in Hotel Joule lobby** Dallas
Ellis County Courthouse Waxahachie	**Rough Creek Lodge** Glen Rose
Hall of State Dallas	**Sixth Floor Museum** Dallas

tanglewoodresort.com), where accommodations range from hotel rooms to master suites and villas complete with kitchens. Rates are about $100 to $400.

Interesting that the same year the dam was completed, Denison's most famous son became an all-time American hero. Five-star general and two-term US president Dwight D. Eisenhower is remembered at the **Eisenhower Birthplace** at 208 E. Day. The 2-story frame house saw the birth of the great soldier and leader on October 14, 1890, and it's been restored to that period. The family moved a short time later to Abilene, Kansas, but there is an Eisenhower family quilt displayed in the bedroom where Ike was born. His large bronze statue makes a great place for souvenir photos of the family. People interested in taking the "Ike Hike" on the 10-acre reserve should make reservations. Open Tues through Sat from 9 a.m. to 5 p.m. and Sun from 1 to 5 p.m. A small admission fee is charged. For information call (903) 465-8908 or visit thc.texas.gov/historic-sites/eisenhower-birthplace-state-historic-site.

Don't miss Denison's charming **Red River Railroad Museum** (101 E. Main St., Ste. 145, Denison; 903-463-5289; redriverrailmuseum.org). The small museum inside the vintage railroad station is the official repository of historical records and artifacts of the Katy Railroad Historical Association and will delight any train buff. Open Mon through Sat from 10 a.m. to 1 p.m. and from 2 to 4 p.m. Admission is free. Right across the street check out the marvelous inventory at Katy Antique Station (104 E. Main St.).

Sherman, 9 miles south of Denison on US 75, is the Grayson County seat and a city of 35,000 people. Settled in 1846, it was named for Sidney Sherman, a Battle of San Jacinto leader and hero credited with the well-known cry "Remember the Alamo! Remember Goliad!" To see some of the lovely homes and buildings from Sherman's late-19th-century boom, grab a map from the chamber of commerce (307 W. Washington St., Sherman; 903-893-1184; sherman chamber.us), which covers places dating from 1883.

Among buildings of special note in Sherman's downtown are the **Sherman Jazz Museum** (201 E. Lamar St., Sherman), housed in a historic church building; **Kelly Square** (115 S. Travis St., Sherman; 903-868-1771; kellysquaresherman.com), a 3-story complex of antiques shops, art galleries, and charming cafes in the gorgeous Kelly Building, built in 1915; and the **C. S. Roberts House** (915 S. Crockett St., Sherman; 903-893-4067), an Eastlake-style home built in 1886 and maintained today by the Sherman Preservation League.

Austin College (900 N. Grand, Sherman; 903-813-2000; austincollege.edu) is the oldest college in Texas operating under an original charter. Several firsts include being the state's first college to grant a graduate degree, the first to start a law school, and the first to have a national fraternity. A bell hanging in the chapel was a gift from Sam Houston, one of the first trustees of the

JUNE'S FAVORITE ANNUAL EVENTS

Southwestern Stock Show and Rodeo
Fort Worth, mid January through early February

Irish Festival
Dallas, first weekend in March

Fort Worth Food & Wine Festival
Fort Worth, late March

New Vintage Wine and Art Festival
Grapevine, mid-April

Wine Walk
Granbury, late April

Main Street Arts Festival
Fort Worth, third weekend in April

National Polka Festival
Ennis, late April

Scarborough Renaissance Festival
Waxahachie, late April through early June

Mayfest
Fort Worth, first weekend in May

State Fair of Texas
Dallas, late September and early October

college. Plays and concerts are staged by the theater and music departments, and monthly art exhibits are held.

For still another look at history, stop in at the **Sherman Museum,** formerly the **Red River Historical Museum** (301 S. Walnut St., Sherman; 903-893-7623; theshermanmuseum.org), which occupies a wonderful 1914 Carnegie Library building, listed on the National Register of Historic Places. Among exhibits are a room of furnishings and artifacts from Glen Eden, the main house of a grand Red River plantation that was dismantled upon the creation of nearby Lake Texoma; a 1900 country store; and an excellent collection of World War II aircraft models. Open Tues through Sat from 10 a.m. to 4 p.m. A small admission fee is charged.

Now you may want to head west on US 82, stopping 33 miles down the road at **Gainesville,** the Cooke County seat and home to 15,500 people. Some of their ancestors were forty-niners headed to California during the gold rush, and some of these were freethinkers in their day: When most Texans wanted secession in the 1860s, Cooke County folks were against it, and some of them created a secret society supporting the Union.

The surrounding area is now renowned for its rich quarter horse ranches, seen on country drives from town. Downtown, however, is a charming, bricked square with its 19th-century appeal intact, augmented by a cluster of shops, cafes, and boutiques.

Stop in at the local chamber of commerce (311 S. Weaver St., Gainesville; 940-665-2831 or 888-585-4468; gainesvillecofc.com) and pick up a driving tour map of historic Gainesville. There are 34 homes and buildings on the map, including some beautiful homes dating from the 1880s.

Chances are you'll want to spend time exploring the town square, whose centerpiece is the majestic *Cooke County Courthouse,* a 4-wing, 4-story lime-stone work with a polygonal art-glass dome, built in 1910. Look for remaining detail work, such as the mosaic tile in the entryway at Otis Furniture on the west side of the square.

As you make your way around the square, keep in mind a handful of places that deserve a look. Fresh energy fills the space at *Cahoots,* the shop and gallery from local artist Paige Davidson, whose fabulous fabric handbags, watercolor paintings and ceramic creations mix in with gifts of whimsy (205 S. Commerce St., Gainesville; 940-665-2138; cahootshandbags .com). *Sarah's on the Square* claims a plum corner spot facing the court-house. Inside, the exposed brick walls and antique furnishings provide warmth, as does the friendly staff. Wine and beer specials make guests want to linger longer over plates of chicken pot pie, green chile stew, shrimp quesadillas, and slices of homemade pies and cakes (115 W. California St.; 940-612-4782). Next to Sarah's, *The B Hive* is the place to find peasant blouses, jewelry, table top goodies and bath and bed details, along with two lazy shop cats (107 W. California St., Gainesville; 940-665-8566). A few doors down, *Muse* stocks a wide variety of Big Green Egg accessories, plus lots of kitchen and bar tools, as well as nice bottles of wine (103 E. California St., Gainesville; 940-665-7171). Around the corner from Cahoots, find a pleasant diner called the *Fried Pie Co. & Restaurant* (corner of Commerce and Main Streets; 940-665-7641; friedpie.net). Framed stained glass is hanging in the window, and a huge chandelier hangs from an origi-nal pressed-tin ceiling. Burgers, club sandwiches, soups, plate lunches and delicious, homemade fried pies—including peach, cherry, coconut, Dutch apple, and apricot—are offered.

Exploring the whole area for a couple of days is easy if you use Gaines-ville as home base. A lovely place to call home while you do that is a newer bed-and-breakfast option in Gainesville offering such privacy and comfort that you will wish you'd booked it for a week instead of a weekend. Named *205 Melody Lane,* which happens to be the address, the three-bedroom home sits in a pretty neighborhood about three minutes from the downtown square. Recently remodeled, the 1956 house offers a gleaming new kitchen and lots of space for reading and visiting. Décor is mostly modern and stylish. There's even a washer-dryer, as well as a patio and backyard. A full breakfast is left for you in the fridge, and the owners are next door if you need something (205 Melody Ln., Gainesville; 817-403-5980; 205melodylane.com).

Before heading away from Gainesville, make a detour 5 miles north of town on I-35 to the *Texas Travel Information Center.* Here you can pick up hundreds of pieces of free literature, such as state highway maps, colorful guides, and brochures pertaining to every city and nearly every town in Texas. The travel counselors at these centers are especially helpful. Open daily from 8 a.m. to 5 p.m.

An interesting detour in this part of the state is the one to *Muenster,* about 14 miles west of Gainesville via US 82, taking you through rolling Red River Valley landscape. In this minute German town, you'll find a wonderful Germanfest in late April, scheduled when the bluebonnets are in full bloom. But the main reason to get to Muenster is to travel a few miles north to the new *4R Ranch Vineyards & Winery,* opened in 2017 by the Roper family of Dallas. Visit to see the stunning *Wind Shed Tasting Room* high on a ridge overlooking the sprawling family ranch and magnificent Red River Valley beyond. The cantilevered deck provides 270-degree views of the chinquapin oak-covered landscape, a perfect place to sip varietals crafted by sommelier-turned-winemaker Willem Johnson. Some favorites include the estate viognier, among whites, and the Hoof und Hund, a full-bodied red blending Lenoir and grenache grapes, perfect for pairing with brisket, venison and ribeyes (1473 County Road 477, Muenster; 940-736-3370;4rwines.com). Plan to spend a little time and money in the tasting room's fabulous retail space, created by winery co-owner Nicole Dabbert-Roper. Tables and shelves in a corner of the tasting room are laden with wine accessories and lovely gifts for entertaining. If you'd like to stay overnight, the ranch property has a three-bedroom guest house that's perfect for a family or group of friends.

When in Muenster, consider stopping in *Fischer's Meat Market,* (304 N. Main St., Muenster; 940-759-4211; fischersmeatmarket.com) a 1927 landmark stocking beef, pork, German sausages, ham and bacon that's butchered locally in the old world tradition. You'll find plenty of locally made German pastries here, too, plus dozens of different house brand jams, jellies and preserves to take home as souvenirs. There's a decent wine selection in the store, too. On the way to Muenster, slow down in the small town of *Lindsay,* about 3 miles west of Gainesville on US 82. Have a look inside *St. Peter's Church,* ornately adorned with frescoes, stained-glass windows, and carved altars, imparting a distinctly European look. Much of the work was done by Friedolin Fuchs, a Swiss national who was stranded in Texas during World War I. Plan your arrival in Lindsay in time for lunch or dinner at *Dieter Brothers Restaurant,* serving barbecue plates wow with mounds of pork ribs, German sausage, hot links, and brisket with colossal onion rings and superb German potato salad, as well as delicious burgers (401 East U.S. 82, Lindsay; 940-665-5253).

From Muenster, head nine miles west on U.S. 82 to the tiny town of *Saint Jo* to explore the *Davis & Blevins Main Street Gallery* (108 Main St. Saint Jo; 940-995-2786; sjmainstreetgallery.com). It's where you go to see the work of artist Donna Howell-Sickles, famous for her mixed media artworks depicting the contemporary cowgirl and her wild west. Donna's an inductee into the National Cowgirl Museum and Hall of Fame in Fort Worth (read about it later in this chapter), and she's usually around for you to meet here in the gallery, which spreads over three store spaces in a century-old rock building on the cozy town square. Her drawings and paintings command attention, as do the works of fellow western artists whose paintings and sculptures figure into the exceptional art selection. Donna also carried gifts such as beaded necklances, leather bracelets Indian blanket shoulder bags handmade scarves, and other beautiful treasures.

A few doors down, *Lazy Heart* (101 S. Main St, Saint Jo, 940-995-2967; thelazyheartgrill.com) sits next door to the Stonewall Saloon Museum. The welcoming café unfolds within two huge rooms. The creaky wooden floors and rugged rock walls provide both warmth and authenticity, as does the collection of old cowboy boots atop an upright piano. Sometimes, this is the only place in town open at lunchtime, meaning it's packed on a pretty Saturday when adventurers show up, so patience is required, but the café's small, hardworking staff aims to please. Rewards include a solid Reuben sandwich and plate of chicken-fried steak with mashers, green beans and big yeast roll. If you'd like to stay the night, check into *Texas Kings Hotel* (103 S. Broad St., Saint Jo; 940-995-2565). Find five spacious, individually decorated rooms in a vintage building on the town square.

A short drive north of Saint Jo, *Arché* (228 Wagner Rd., 214-536-6330; archewines.com) is a winery set in rolling landscape; its rosé and red wines make for excellent sipping on the winery patio. Nearby, *Blue Ostrich Winery & Vineyard* (5611 FM 2382, 940-995-3100; Saint Jo; blueostrich.net) spreads over a former ostrich farm; today, it's where a good selection of reds and whites are made and tasted and, on Saturday, live music is offered. Blue Ostrich Guesthouse at Fredrick Farms, facing the winery (on Farm Road 2382, Saint Jo; 940-995-3100) is a four-bedroom, three-bath home with a large kitchen and big front and back porches, swimming pool and sweeping views. Be sure to make reservations to eat on weekends at *Ancient Ovens* (857 Childress Rd, Saint Jo, 940-366-4255; ancientovens.com), a BYOB dining destination beloved for exceptional thin-crust pizza. All the food is cooked outside in wood-burning ovens, and the outdoor gathering patio spaces are lovely. When the weather won't cooperate, there are indoor spaces for dining.

Another 13 miles west of Saint Jo along U.S. 82 west, stop in the town of *Nocona* for a look into the past. Long known for its cowboy boot heritage

(Justin Boots was founded here), Long a town known for its cowboy boots, Nocona is home to **Fenoglio Boot Company** and **James Montague Boots,** both made locally and sold at the **Boot Store** (105 Clay St., Nocona; 940-825-3047). Next door, the **Nokona Glove Factory** (105 Clay St., Nocona; 800-433-0957) is the storefront for a baseball glove manufacturer producing handmade gloves since 1934. You'll need a few hours to truly explore the **The Horton Classic Car Museum** (115 W. Walnut St., Nocona; 940-825-1022) with a collection so large that it spreads over more than 37,000 square feet of vintage downtown buildings. The cool rides number about 140, each in pristine condition. The majority of these beautiful American classic and muscles cars—more than 40 of which are Corvettes from nearly every model year the iconic auto has been made—reside in a renovated Ford dealership that's festooned with enough neon to rival that in downtown Las Vegas.

Also in downtown Nocona, find the **Red River Station Inn** (219 Clay St., 940-825-3107), decorated with found objects like old windmills, metal awnings, and aged shiplap boards to add personality and warmth to the interior. You learn a different story from Montague County heritage in each of the room's nine inns; my favorites were the Mose Johnson Room, with a chicken motif that relates to a local poultry ranch, and the Amon G. Carter Room, honoring the Fort Worth Star-Telegram founder (and a good friend to this author's grandparents) who grew up in Nocona. The inn also makes guests feel welcome with its upstairs lounge area, doubling as a breakfast room and afternoon wine-and-snacks parlor; overlooking the street while sitting outside on the balcony is a pleasure at any time of day. Next door, **Red River Pizzeria** (223 Clay St., 940-825-3003) is a good hangout for satisfying food, friendly service and a chance to get to know local folks. Order thin-crust pizzas, delicious, crusty sandwich filled with Italian meats and cheeses, plus a bowl of penne pasta with pesto. Local wines (Arche and Blue Ostrich, among them) are served here, too.

Another North Texas town good for investigating, **Denton**, lying 40 miles south of Gainesville, is seat of the county bearing the same name and home to about 134,000 residents. Besides being home, too, to the University of North Texas, Denton is the site of Texas Women's University (TWU), where you'll find **Little Chapel in the Woods,** at Bell and University Streets. Designed and built in 1939 by noted architect O'Neil Ford, and dedicated by Eleanor Roosevelt it's considered one of the country's finer architectural achievements. Art melds with nature, as the stained-glass window (designed by students) depicts *Woman Ministering to Human Needs*. Open daily from dawn to dusk (call ahead for Saturday and Sunday hours of operation), it's a popular site for weddings. For more information call (940) 898-3644.

Also on the TWU campus, in the TWU Administration Conference Tower (304 Administration Dr., Denton; 940-898-3644), the **DAR Museum** houses the inaugural gowns of the first ladies of Texas. The only one of its kind in existence, the collection features either the original garments or faithful copies. Open Mon through Fri from 8 a.m. to 5 p.m. and by appointment. Admission is free.

Denton's appealing courthouse square earned the town a national designation as a Main Street City. Inside the elaborately designed Denton County Courthouse, built between 1895 and 1897, is the county's **Courthouse-on-the-Square** museum (110 W. Hickory St., Denton; 940-349-2850). Exhibits tell the story of the county's history and 19th-century life with a period country kitchen, farm tools, antiques, textiles, branding irons, guns, dolls, and folk art. Open Tues through Fri from 10 a.m. to 4:30 p.m., and Sat from 11 a.m. to 3 p.m. Two blocks away is the Victorian **Bayless-Selby House,** open Tues through Sat from 10 a.m. to noon and 1 to 3 p.m. Admission to both museums is free.

Shops and sites worth a look on the square include **Recycled Books, CDs, and Records,** a 3-story treasure trove in the old 1901 opera house on the northeast corner (200 N. Locust St., Denton; 940-566-5688; recycledbooks .com). Browse through art galleries, a candy store, boutiques with new and vintage clothing, a jewelry store, a consignment furniture store, shops selling home décor, and plentiful places to eat, such as a donut shop and wine bar.

There's a lot of Denton's favorite dining right on the square, as well. **The Loop Hole Pub** (119 W. Hickory St., Denton; 940-565-0770; loopholepub .com) has a menu written in pseudo-legalese, with appetizers called arraignments, and so on. Just a block south of the square, **Sweetwater Grill and Tavern** (115 S. Elm St., Denton; 940-484-2888) does a dynamite job with grilled vegetable sandwiches, grilled shrimp over greens, toasted tomato salsa, and bountiful burgers with elaborate toppings. A few blocks east of the square is the city's fanciest restaurant, a steakhouse called **Queenie's** (115 E. Hickory St., Denton; 940-442-6834; queeniessteakhouse.com). Owner-chef Tim Love of Fort Worth brought high-style dining to the town where he grew up and where his mom—aka Queenie—still lives. Open for lunch, dinner, and Sunday brunch, Queenie's includes such specialties as spicy lobster salad, grilled oysters, rattlesnake-sage-rabbit gnocchi, dry-aged Kansas City strip, shrimp and grits, and a vegetarian chile relleno. A bonus for late-nighters enjoying live music in the area is Queenie's Back Dough, a donut shop operating from Queenie's kitchen door on Austin Street, from 11 p.m. till about 1 a.m. on weekends. Sweet and savory options are about $5 and serve as a good meal to soak up the adult beverages.

If you are looking to spend time exploring the ***Oak-Hickory Historic District,*** which offers several buildings to be seen on a walking tour as well as a handful of good restaurants and bars, contact the Denton Convention and Visitor Bureau for information at (940) 382-7895. Stay overnight with the ***The Heritage Inns,*** which includes 9 rooms in ***Redbud Inn*** and the ***Locust Inn,*** historic homes with comfortable rooms near downtown (815 N. Locust St., Denton 940-514-1950; and theheritageinns.com and locuststreetinn.com). Stays can include dinner and spa treatments upon request.

Let's hope it's time to eat again, as this ranch country has plenty of good eats to share. From Denton head 4 miles west on US 380, then take FR 156 south another 4 miles to the hamlet of ***Ponder,*** home to an excellent steak joint called ***Ranchman's Cafe,*** right on FR 156 (940-479-2221; ranchman.com). A legendary favorite of north Texans, this family place serves a mean steak dinner. The St. Louis beef is cut when you order your steak, cooked exactly to order, and served with salad and baked potato—if you had the foresight to call ahead and reserve your very own spud. Do not, under any circumstances, get too full for dessert: Ranchman's is famous for its homemade pies and cobblers, good enough alone to draw people from Fort Worth and Dallas, both an hour away. The café is open Sun through Thurs from 11 a.m. to 9 p.m. and Fri and Sat from 11 a.m. to 10 p.m.

A different side trip from Denton is to the town of ***McKinney,*** a straight shot east of Denton on US 380 about 30 miles, then south on Highway 5 about 2 miles. The Collin County seat was once a small farm town but has been going through a growth explosion of late. Now home to about 173,000, the courthouse square has been revived in recent years, with a charming supply of shops providing interest. The Victorian buildings have been renovated and now offer a full day of shop and café browsing.

A favorite dining and lodging spot in McKinney today is the elegant ***Grand Hotel*** (114 W. Louisiana St., McKinney; 214-726-9250; grandhotel mckinney.com), housed in a lovely 1880s building downtown. There are 44 luxurious suites, and the on-site restaurant, Rick's Chophouse, is earning raves for its aged steaks. A block away, ***Patina Green*** (116 N. Tennessee St., Suite 102, McKinney; 972-548-9141; patinagreenhomeandmarket.com) is your destination for lunch and dinner fashioned from farmstand finds and locally sources goods, and it's also a market stocking artistic décor for the home and kitchen. Local history is detailed at the ***Collin County History Museum*** (300 E. Virginia St., McKinney; 972-542-9457; collincountyhistoricalsociety.org), in a 1911 building.

Get a complete guide to the town from the ***McKinney Chamber of Commerce*** by stopping by 2150 S. Central Expressway, Ste. 150, McKinney; calling

(972) 542-0163 or (888) 649-8499; or visiting visitmckinney.com. More than 100 specialty and antiques shops, boutiques, galleries, and cafes are listed.

Sixteen miles west of McKinney, the city of *Frisco* has exploded from a cute little farm town on the prairie to a community with 10 large high schools, the national headquarters for Toyota, a major medical center, and the home offices for the *Dallas Cowboys* of the National Football League. If you're a Cowboys fan, you need to spend several hours exploring *The Star* (One Cowboys Way, Frisco; thestarinfrisco.com), a 91-acre campus that includes the team's enormous practice facilities, the ownership's offices, a hall of fame, the Dallas Cowboys Cheerleaders headquarters, and so much more. Tours are ticketed events and include a look in the warm room, where the Cowboys execute the draft, Super Bowl Memorabilia Station, and more; call (972) 497-4720 for tour details. There's an *Omni Hotel* on the premises (11 Cowboys Way, Frisco; 469-287-0000; omnihotels.com/hotels/frisco) and dozens of restaurants and shops. The Star sits on Frisco's $5 Billion Mile, a stunning collection of developments that is transforming the shape of North Texas (friscoedc .com/5bmile).

The Big D

The way to *Dallas* is easy from McKinney: Drive 35 miles south on US 75 and you're there in the city now boasting some 1.3 million residents. Stay on US 75 all the way into the city and watch for I-30 East, which you'll be upon when you see downtown and the unmistakable *Reunion Tower*—that big silver ball atop a tall tower amidst a ocean of skyscrapers. Take I-30 East, avoiding morning or evening traffic hour if possible, and continue a short distance to the

Take a Tour on the Darker Side of Dallas

Dallas's legends are the stuff of infamy, to be sure. If your sightseeing tastes run a little to the dark side, the *Dallas Historical Society* has tours tailor-made for you. Twice a year you can join in the "JFK Tour: Following in the Steps of Lee Harvey Oswald," which traces the presidential assassin on his route through downtown on November 22, 1963, to his boardinghouse, the theater where he was captured, and the basement where he was killed while in custody. Another pick of the criminal type is the "Legend of Bonnie & Clyde Tour," which takes you to the places where the young outlaws worked, hustled, staged gunfights, and were buried. For more information call (214) 421-4500, ext. 104, or visit dallashistory.org.

exit for *Fair Park.* Follow the directional signs a few blocks until you reach entrances on Parry Street or Cullum Boulevard.

Inside the park your destination is the *African American Museum* (3536 Grand Ave., Dallas; 214-565-9026; aamdallas.org), a $7 million storehouse/ showcase of ethnic artifacts. The only one of its kind in the entire Southwest, the grand building of ivory-colored stone with a huge rotunda and four vaulted galleries contains a library and research center, as well as remarkable changing exhibits that typically include the work of 19th-century black masters: wood carvings, contemporary paintings, photography, and sculpture. The museum is open Tues through Fri from 11 a.m. to 5 p.m., and Sat from 10 a.m. to 5 p.m. Admission is free, except for groups of 10 or more ($5 adults, $3 children).

Nearby are other important buildings worth a look. For example, the *Hall of State* (3939 Grand Ave., Dallas; 214-421-4500; tour.dallashistory.org or hallofstate.com) is one of the fantastic art deco buildings erected for the 1936 Texas Centennial exhibition held at Fair Park. Inside find heroes of Texas's fight for independence honored in bronze, including William B. Travis, Gen. Sam Houston, and Stephen F. Austin. Several fascinating murals illustrate the state's history from the pioneer period to the centennial year. The hall is open Mon through Sat from 9 a.m. to 5 p.m. and Sun from 1 to 5 p.m. Admission is free.

Another attraction that's been a favorite for several generations of Texans is found back in downtown Dallas at the *Farmers' Market,* a rich country tradition deep within the heart of the nation's eighth-largest city. Head back to town on I-30 West and take the downtown exit marked Pearl Street. You'll find the 10-block, mostly open-air market at 1010 S. Pearl St., best if visited early in the day. Some farmers personally bring their produce from around the state, while other vendors are locals who buy from farmers or wholesale nurseries and then sell to the public. Even if you're not in need of fresh fruits, vegetables, herbs, flowers, or plants, the sensory experience is pure invigoration—there are pictures begging to be taken. You're likely to spend a lot of time in a 26,000-square-foot food hall called The Market, where artisan vendors, food booths, and mini-boutiques rub shoulders. Check out an ongoing calendar of classes and festivals there, too. The market is open daily from 7 a.m. to 6 p.m. Call (214) 664-9110 or check dallasfarmersmarket.org for more information. Leave room in your schedule and appetite to eat at *Mudhen Meat and Greens,* the market's restaurant where goods are sourced directly from farmers and vendors on-site. In addition to super-healthy, fresh meals, enjoy craft cocktails, beer and wine (900 S Harwood St., Dallas; 214-698-7000; mudheninthe.net).

Next stop is also downtown, at the *Belo Mansion* (2101 Ross Ave., Dallas). This extraordinarily opulent house was designed by noted architect

Herbert Green and completed in 1900. It's the only residence still existing in the city's Central Business District and was home to Col. Alfred H. Belo, founder of the venerable *Dallas Morning News*. Belo died in 1901, and the family retained ownership of the building, leasing it out as a funeral home from 1926 until 1977, when it was purchased by the Dallas Bar Association. Now open as the Dallas Legal Education Center, it's available for free tours by appointment; just call (214) 220-0239.

Barely a block away, the ***Dallas Museum of Art*** (1717 N. Harwood St., Dallas; 214-922-1200; dallasmuseumofart.org) is a vast facility with collections including pre-Columbian, African, and decorative arts. Upstairs at the museum, an elegant restaurant called ***Seventeen Seventeen*** (214-880-0518 or 214-922-1200) offers lunch and dinner selections including lobster, pasta, roast lamb, Vietnamese chicken salad, and incredible desserts.

Speaking of food, there are close to 100 excellent, nonchain restaurant offerings just north of the museum in the Uptown neighborhood. Breakfast, lunch, and dinner are wonderful at ***Breadwinners*** (3301 McKinney Ave., Dallas) and ***Fearing's*** (inside the Ritz-Carlton, 2121 McKinney Ave., Dallas), the latter from Dean Fearing, a founder of Southwestern cuisine along with colleague, Stephan Pyles, who owns nearby ***Flora Street Café*** (enjoy lunch and dinner by reservation only, 2330 Flora St., Suite 150; 214-580-7000).

A few blocks west of the Dallas Museum of Art find the ***Dallas World Aquarium*** (1801 N. Griffin St., Dallas; 214-720-2224; dwazoo.com), a spectacular offering. Bearing the look of a small European museum, it showcases a 65,000-gallon array of saltwater marine life including sharks, sting-rays, and reef fish in a reconstructed coral reef ecosystem. Then there are tropical blackfoot penguins in their own terrarium world. A restaurant, called the Eighteen-O-One, is open daily for lunch and Sunday brunch. A second restaurant, Cafe Maya, is open for lunch and dinner. The aquarium is open daily from 10 a.m. to 5 p.m. Admission is charged.

Among your downtown destinations should be ***Old Red,*** the imposing red sandstone building that originally was Dallas County's courthouse when erected in 1892 at the corner of Main and Houston Streets. It's quite a spectacle in all its Richardsonian Romanesque glory, complete with scary gargoyles scowling down at you from the corners. This is a great photo opportunity for anybody with a zoom lens.

Right in front of the courthouse, bounded by Houston, Commerce, and Elm Streets, is ***Dealey Plaza,*** a small and very scenic little park with a reflection pool, trees, and a statue honoring early *Dallas Morning News* publisher and civic leader George Bannerman Dealey. Since November 22, 1963, however, Dealey Plaza has been known as the place where President Kennedy was assassinated. No matter the time of day or night when you visit, you won't be alone: Decades after the tragedy people of all ages and nationalities still show up to look around, perhaps wondering if some answer could ever be known.

The life, death, and heritage of President Kennedy are detailed in an educational and historical exhibit across the street from the park, **Sixth Floor Museum: John F. Kennedy and the Memory of a Nation** (411 Elm St., Dallas; 214-747-6660; jfk.org), a remarkable museum on the sixth floor of the former Texas School Book Depository from which Lee Harvey Oswald shot the president. Opened in 1988, the exhibit contains historic pictures, artifacts, 40 minutes of documentary films, and an award-winning audio tour. Open daily from 9 a.m. to 6 p.m. Admission is charged.

texastrivia

The frozen margarita machine was invented in Dallas.

The integrated circuit computer chip (which became the microchip) was invented in Dallas in 1958.

The 52 foot "Big Tex" statue that greets visitors at the annual State Fair of Texas is the tallest cowboy in Texas.

During the winter holiday season, the Galleria Dallas is home to the country's tallest indoor Christmas tree.

The largest permanent model train exhibit in the country is on display in the lobby of Dallas Children's Medical Center.

The Dallas Arts District is the largest urban arts district in the United States.

The Trinity River Corridor Project, when completed, will be more than 10 times the size of New York's Central Park.

Highland Park Village Shopping Center, developed in 1931 has the distinction of being the first planned shopping center in America.

The first convenience store, 7-Eleven, got its start in Dallas and the corporation is headquartered there today.

Lamar Hunt, founder of the American Football League and son of oil tycoon H. L. Hunt, was a noted Dallas resident when he coined the phrase "Super Bowl."

The Dallas area is the largest metropolitan area in the nation not on a navigable body of water.

The Dallas Public Library permanently displays one of the original copies of the Declaration of Independence, printed on July 4, 1776, and the First Folio of William Shakespeare's *Comedies, Histories & Tragedies*.

Don't dare leave downtown Dallas without visiting the retail institution **Neiman Marcus** (1618 Main St., Dallas; 214-741-6911; neimanmarcus.com). The original and still-flagship store is a mecca for serious shoppers, and it's just fun to look around even for those who aren't into spending sprees. Take a trip up to the top floor for lunch in the venerable Zodiac, where chicken salad and popovers with strawberry butter have been in style since the 1950s. A lovely wine and cocktail list are offered, too.

One of the coolest lodgings to open in Dallas in recent years is the **Belmont Hotel** (901 Fort Worth Ave., Dallas; 866-870-8010; belmontdallas.com)—although it's not entirely new. This laid-back, mid-century–modern hotel was opened in 1946 just east of downtown, and it got new life with a magnificent renovation. There are 68 supercool rooms and suites in 4 buildings, some with patio settings and downtown views, along with a swanky lobby lounge and a fabulous restaurant called **Smoke** (smokerestaurant.com).

Dallas's supply of art galleries, theaters, and concert halls is enormous. For a timely schedule of events, pick up free copies of the alternative weekly, the *Observer.* A great online resource for all dining, nightlife, arts, and entertainment offerings, visit guidelive.com. For a complete guide to all attractions, stop by the **Dallas Convention and Visitor Bureau,** located downtown at 325 N. St. Paul St., Ste. 700; or call (214) 571-1000 or go to the website at visitdallas .com to request a visitor kit.

Before leaving the Dallas area, consider a worthwhile side trip. Head exactly 30 miles due south of Dallas on I-35 to **Waxahachie,** the Ellis County seat and home to 21,000 citizens. Waxahachie (WOCKS-uh-hatch-ee) is a charming Victorian town built on the rich cattle and cotton businesses here at the turn of the 20th century. Some 170 of the original, ornate homes with extensive gingerbread detail survive, giving the community its "Gingerbread City" nickname. For a map of historic places on both walking and driving tours, ask at the visitors bureau, 2000 Civic Center Lane, Waxahachie; 469-309-4040; waxahachiecvb.com.

texastrivia

Bonnie Parker was an honor student in west Dallas before going on, with her partner Clyde Barrow, to become one of the country's most famous criminals.

You won't dare miss the **Ellis County Courthouse,** easily the most fabulous of all Texas's many magnificent courthouses. Located at Main and College Streets, the 1896 masterpiece is noted for a spectacular clock tower, balconies, arches, and gargoyles. An intriguing story that's survived the past century says that one of the artisans brought from Italy to craft the stonework became enamored with a Waxahachie beauty and modeled the lovely face above the east entrance after her; she did not return his love, however, and in his anger he created monstrous faces on the rest of the detail.

Waxahachie's celebrated Victorian veneer has appealed to Hollywood in a big way: Among the excellent films shot here are *Places in the Heart, Tender Mercies, The Trip to Bountiful,* and *Bonnie & Clyde.* A brochure outlining the movie sites is available from the visitors office, noted above. For background on local history, we pop into the **Ellis County Museum** (201 S. College St., 972-937-0681; waxahachiccvb.com), sitting just off the southeastern corner of the courthouse. Inside the former Masonic Lodge Hall—the three-story, 1889 building created in a high Victorian Italianate design, one of dozens of lovingly restored structures keeping company on and around the square—the museum occupies a former mercantile store space. Exhibits in the old glass-front cases include vintage military garb worn long ago by local citizens, as well as signage, hardware, décor, and memorabilia from long-gone town businesses. I particularly liked the colorful wartime posters, such as one warning, "Loose lips might sink ships." You'll find the touring maps are available here, as well.

If you're looking for a good lunch, you'll find it at the **Dove's Nest** (105 Jefferson St., Waxahachie; 972-938-3683; thedovesnestrestaurant.com), immediately south of the courthouse square in what was a hardware store, built in 1913. More sophisticated than most places in a town of this size, this charming dining room is a pleasant spot for enjoying gourmet pizzas, antipasto platters, chicken-apricot salad, and a Reuben sandwich. The restaurant is open Mon through Sat for lunch. The Dove's Nest also doubles as a gift store, full of home décor and jewelry.

You'll need the sustenance for all the shopping to be done here on the courthouse square, home to dozens of antiques shops stocking antique and vintage furniture in European, American, Texas, and country designs; Depression glass; fine china; crystal; linens; pottery; lamps; books; dolls; toys; and pictures. The busier shops speak to the current fondness for furnishings and housewares that look old, even if they're not: At **Texas Pearls and Co.** (Texas 313 S. College St., 214-463-5532), just a few doors down from the museum, chairs, tables, sofas, and cabinets bear the Magnolia Home brand, known best to fans of the Waco-based *Fixer Upper* show on HGTV. Besides restored furniture, goodies also include dishtowels, candles, mirrors and more that gave us ideas for things to do in our own century-old home. Across the street, **Farmhouse** (308A S. College St., 972-939-9090) is another store mixing old and new finds, from flower vases and garden birdhouses to a lovely silver tea service and an old dresser made over into a bathroom sink and vanity. It's easy to kill a few hours walking these sidewalks, looking at the profusion of historic markers on nearly every building. There are the oval plaques noting the Waxahachie Heritage Preservation Commission, along with the state historical commission plaques noting a building's background, as well as the rectangular signs that tell the year a building was entered in the National Register of Historic Places.

Be sure to visit the **Webb Gallery** (209 W. Franklin St., 972-938-8085; webbartgallery.com), which adds another dimension of culture to the square. Famous for its folk art collection and exhibits, it's also a friendly place to visit, thanks to the two resident Boston terriers that may come bounding across the painted wooden floors to greet you as soon as you open the blue front door. Among works to take in, check out expansive murals and other paintings hanging on the walls. Listening to the gallery hosts chat with locals about recent trips around Texas makes you feel right at home.

Before departing downtown, wander down to the old railroad depot area for a little pick-me-up at **Fresh Market Coffee** (410 S. Rogers St., 901-647-7742). Besides making all sorts of coffee drinks from freshly roasted beans, Fresh serves cake, cookies, and pastries made in-house, and self-serve refrigerators stock Dr Pepper in old-fashioned bottles, as well as bottled tea and cold-brew coffee. If you like, take home packages of local cheese, yogurt, and tamales, along with fresh flowers for purchase. A happy buzz fills the air, along with the coffee aromas: Throughout the sprawling shop, tables filled with two, four and six guests scatter across the wood floor, and patrons also visit on couches, work on laptops or play bottle cap checkers on vintage wooden boards.

Overnight stays in Waxahachie are luxurious at **The English Merchant's Inn** (717 W. Main St., 254-366-0229; theenglishmerchantsinn.com), where host Mary Baskin has created four guest suites with private baths in the main house and a cottage on the property. Huge and imposing, the handsome red brick home was built by British cotton merchant James Wright Harrison in 1915, and Mary and husband Howard Baskin use décor, books, artwork, and memorabilia to satisfy the anglophile's passion. One of the rooms upstairs is a spacious suite done up with elements from the Union Jack, outfitted with a comfortable king bed and served also by a big balcony overlooking the front lawn and Main Street. Wine is served in the afternoon and a lavish breakfast is set on the formal china in the dining room. The town's architecture is exhibited in grand style annually on the first Saturday and Sunday in June during the **Gingerbread Trail**. The special tour showcases several homes, the courthouse, two museums, and a fine auditorium. For information and tickets call the chamber of commerce at (972) 937-2390 or visit waxahachiechamber.com.

Another annual event that brings throngs to Waxahachie is **Scarborough Renaissance Festival**, a re-created 16th-century English village spread over

35 acres of open countryside. It's an impressive production, consisting of more than 400 actors and musicians portraying royalty, peasants, jesters, knights, ladies, and minstrels. Among activities and entertainment are jousting competitions, juggling, sheep dog demonstrations, magic, and comedy shows. Arts and crafts—some of which aren't entirely Old World—are available, as are all kinds of foods and drink. The fair is held on eight weekends from early April until late May. Admission is charged. Call (972) 938-3247 or visit srfestival.com for details.

Don't fill up on the fair's junk fare, however, because you don't want to miss out on the *College Street Pub* (210 N. College St., 972-938-2062, collegestreetpub.com). Among favorites, try crispy fried green beans, a basket of fish and chips, and the signature French Burger—rather like a patty melt on Texas toast—for a good, casual supper in a convivial bar decorated with more Union Jacks and packed with locals

Around Cowtown

From Waxahachie your destination is *Arlington,* a fast-growing place of almost 400,000 residents living right between Dallas and Fort Worth. You'll find it by traveling 42 miles northeast via US 287.

The stunning *Globe Life Park,* home to the Texas Rangers Baseball Club, is situated on I-30 at the Pennant Drive exit. This masterpiece is crafted from the popular Texas pink granite and redbrick to look like a vintage stadium from baseball's glory days in the 20th century. The stadium boasts multiple tiers as well as friezes around the facade detailed with Texas longhorns and Texas Rangers, the lawmen, and an interior hall of fame honoring baseball greats. Though it opened only in 1994, it's soon to be replaced by a newer, bigger version with a retractable roof. The $1.1 billion new showplace is scheduled to open in 2020. For tour info, for hours, game times, and tickets, call (817) 273-5100 or visit rangers.mlb.com

texastrivia

Big Tex, the official greeter at the State Fair of Texas, was introduced at the 1952 fair. He stands 52 feet tall; boasts a 30-foot chest; and wears a size 90 shirt, size 70 boots, and a 75-gallon hat. The inseam on his western-style jeans measures 15.5 feet.

Next door, NFL owner Jerry Jones built a $1 billion home for his football team. *AT&T Stadium* hosted the 2011 Super Bowl and the 2014 NCAA basketball Final Four, and is a venue for all kinds of events, from monster truck pulls to major rock and country music concerts, along with football games galore. Tours take visitors to see an impressive art collection. There's a restaurant inside, *The Stadium Club* (817-892-5800), open for lunch and dinner daily. Find the stadium at 900 E. Randol Mill Rd. in Arlington; call (817) 892-4626 or visit attstadium.com for tour information.

Less than 10 miles east of Arlington in the town of Grand Prairie, visit *Lone Star Park* (Belt Line Road, just north of I-30, Grand Prairie; 972-263-RACE; lonestarpark.com). Here you'll find world-class thoroughbred and quarter horse racing at the state's top Class 1 track. The Post Time Pavilion is a 36,000-square-foot simulcasting facility with a Las Vegas–style race book, sports bar, and restaurant. Live racing is seen from a multilevel, 280,000-square-foot grandstand with European-style paddock.

And north about 5 miles from Arlington on Highway 360, the *American Airlines C. R. Smith Museum* (Highway 360 at Highway 183; 817-967-1560; crsmithmuseum.org) is a hugely impressive tribute to the history of flight. Among attractions is a film called *Dream of Flight*, which introduces the exhibits; a pre–World War II DC-3, the 1940 *Flagship* **Knoxville;** historical photos and equipment; and a fine museum store with books, toys, videos, models, and travel gifts. The museum is open Thurs through Sat from 10 a.m. to 6 p.m. Admission is free.

From the American Airlines museum, your destination is 10 miles north to *Grapevine,* at the intersection of Highways 360 and 114. The town's roots date to negotiating days between Native Americans and settlers; in fact it was the site of an 1849 treaty signing by Gen. Sam Houston. Don't let its chain

Culture Clash

Several summers ago, a friend from New York called to say that a chum from England was making his first cross-country trek through America. Our New York friend was calling pals all over the States to ask if we would show the Englishman around our towns. Happy to oblige, we received the Brit on a hot August evening and immediately took him for a Mexican-food feast. The place we chose was a little family operation in Fort Worth's historic **Stockyards District,** right on Exchange Avenue, the main thoroughfare. A very good sport, he seemed to genuinely enjoy the spicy salsa, the sizzling fajitas, and the cold Texas beer we ordered. But as he looked out the window next to our table, he looked perplexed. Finally he asked, "Is there a costume party of some sort?" We looked but had no idea what he meant. "Well," he elaborated, "what about all these chaps wearing hats and boots and those big belt buckles?" I told him those were cowboys, probably heading to one of the dance halls or saloons up and down Exchange. "Real cowboys?!" he asked. Yep, the very thing. Our New York friend called us several weeks later to report that after visiting New York, Atlanta, Chicago, Fort Worth, San Francisco, and Los Angeles, our English friend said his favorite stop was our very own Cowtown.

Vestiges of the Wild, Wild West

Every year on February 8, folks gather outside the *White Elephant Saloon* in the Fort Worth National Historic Stockyards District to see a reenactment of what's said to have been the last gunfight in Fort Worth. Legend holds that in 1887, town marshal Jim Courtright shot gambler Luke Short outside the White Elephant. Seems like a good reason for an annual party.

restaurants and close proximity to DFW Airport fool you; Grapevine, which boasts a National Register Historic District, is rich with Texas heritage. Its Main Street is one of the more charming in all of Texas. Pick up a walking-tour guide and list of historic sites at the *Grapevine Convention and Visitors Bureau* (636 S. Main St., Grapevine; 817-410-3185 or 800-457-6338; grapevine texasusa.com) or at the visitor center in the old *Cotton Belt Depot* (705 S. Main St., Grapevine).

The train depot is one end of a popular daily route made from Fort Worth by the *Grapevine Vintage Railroad* (see page 194). The *Grapevine Heritage Center* (817-410-3126) is here, too, with a museum containing castings of dinosaur footprints found at nearby Lake Grapevine. The Heritage Center is home to a blacksmith shop, a railroad foreman's house, and an artisan's shop where old arts and crafts, such as rug hooking, quilting, wood carving, chair caning, and boot making are taught and practiced. In early 2019, the depot is expected to be a stop on the TEXRail commuter rail, a train taking passengers from downtown Fort Worth to Terminal B at DFW International Airport. The development at the depot and throughout the intersection of Main Street and Dallas Road includes a 42,000-square-foot, five-story tall rail station, a six-story, 121-room boutique hotel calle Hotel Vin, and an expansive outdoor plaza. Read more about it at texrail.com.

Grapevine's entertainment includes the Grapevine Opry and other musical events at the *Palace Theatre* (300 S. Main St., Grapevine; 817-410-3100). Shopping includes the *British Emporium* (140 N. Main St., Grapevine; 817-421-2311; british-emporium.com), *Tolbert's Texas Trading Co.* (311 S. Main St., Grapevine; 817-442-8688), and *Off the Vine* (336-A S. Main St., Grapevine; 817-421-1091; offthevinetexas.com), where wines and wine-related gifts are sold. A few doors down, *Main Street Bistro & Bakery* is a delightful place for breakfast, lunch, dinner, and a good bottle of wine (316 S. Main St., Grapevine; 817-424-4333, themainbakery.com).

The wine business is booming in suitably named Grapevine. Among several wineries on the Urban Wine Trail are *Delaney Winery & Vineyards* (2000

Champagne Blvd., Grapevine; 817-481-5668; delaneyvineyards.com); *Messina Hof Grapevine Winery* (201 S. Main St., Grapevine; 817-442-8463; messinahof .com/grapevine); Umbra Winery (415 S. Main St., Grapevine; 817-421-2999; umbrawinery.com). Call for tasting and tour times and for fees. Find the entire list at grapevinetexasusa.com/things-to-do/wineries/urban-wine-trail/. Also check in with the *Texas Wine and Grape Growers Association* at 1 Liberty Plaza in Grapevine, or call them at (817) 421-3201 or visit txwines.org, to learn more about Texas's wine industry, now second in the nation behind California.

Stop for a bite to eat along the main drag in Grapevine at *Tolbert's Chili Parlor* (423 S. Main St.; 817-421-4888; tolbertsrestaurant.com), *Big Fish* (414 S. Main St.; 817-481-2010; bigfishonmain.com), or *Weinberger's Delicatessen* (611 S. Main St., Ste. 100; 817-416-5577; weinbergersdeli.com).

It's time for a megadose of enjoyable culture, so head on into *Fort Worth,* taking Highway 121 south to Highway 183. Stay on 183, then take I-30 west and exit at University Drive, heading north on that street less than a mile to the *Cultural District,* an unexpected place where four unforgettable, very independent museums are clustered within a 5-block area.

From University Drive, turn left at the Lancaster Avenue light and you'll quickly see the *Kimbell Art Museum* (3333 Camp Bowie Blvd., Fort Worth; 817-332-8451; kimbellart.org). Designed by the famous architect Louis Kahn, the museum was founded by industrialist and entrepreneur Kay Kimbell, who left a wealth of art and money to begin the nation's second-richest privately endowed museum, surpassed only by the Getty in Los Angeles, California. Within the beautifully vaulted, gray-white building are vast galleries filled with paintings by El Greco, Velázquez, Rembrandt, Cézanne, Picasso, and others, plus varied pieces of pre-Columbian art. World-class exhibits make appearances here on worldwide tours; for information call the museum or check out the website. Adding to the Cultural District's architectural who's who, the Kimbell continued to turn heads in the art world by opening a Renzo Piano-designed museum expansion in 2013; most special exhibitions are staged in the stunning new building.

The Kimbell is open Tues through Thurs and Sat from 10 a.m. to 5 p.m., Fri from noon to 8 p.m., and Sun from noon to 5 p.m. Admission is free. There's an excellent lunch café inside the museum, the Kimbell Buffet, which is open Tues through Sun.

Just a block west, the *Amon Carter Museum* (3501 Camp Bowie Blvd., Fort Worth; 817-738-1933; cartermuseum.org) is known for its outstanding collection of American art, particularly the western works by Frederic Remington and Charles M. Russell, willed to the city along with a foundation by millionaire Amon G. Carter, the founder of the *Fort Worth Star-Telegram* and dedicated promoter of Fort Worth. An extensive renovation and expansion in 2002 has only improved the museum's stature, long ago established by its collection, which includes works by such noted American artists as Winslow Homer, Grant Wood, and Georgia O'Keeffe. A sensational bookstore is found here, too. And from the front lawn and terrace, you'll see an unparalleled view eastward of downtown. Open Tues, Wed, Fri, and Sat from 10 a.m. to 5 p.m., Thurs from 10 a.m. to 8 p.m. and Sun from noon to 5 p.m.; tours are given at 2 p.m. daily, except Mon. Admission is free.

Fort Worth's beloved **Museum of Science and History** (1600 Gendy St., Fort Worth; 817-255-9300; fwmuseum.org) reopened in 2009 with an entirely new building. A place of great discovery for kids, it holds ample appeal for adults, too, in exhibits that explore natural history, space, regional culture, and much more. There's a planetarium on-site, as well as an IMAX theater. Open daily.

Among the newer arrivals in the Cultural District is the **National Cowgirl Museum and Hall of Fame** (Montgomery at Harley Streets, Fort Worth; 817-336-4475; cowgirl.net), a spectacular, 33,000-square-foot space that honors legendary women whose work epitomized the pioneer spirit of the American West. Among the many honorees are trick riders and rodeo stars, as well as Patsy Cline, Dale Evans, Georgia O'Keeffe, and Laura Ingalls Wilder. A research library is on the premises, and there's a fabulous gift shop. The museum charges admission. Open Mon through Thurs from 9 a.m. to 5.30 p.m., Fri and Sat from 9 a.m. to 8 p.m., and Sun from 11:30 a.m. to 5:30 p.m.

The most famous museum in the district is the magnificent **Modern Art Museum of Fort Worth** (3200 Darnell St., between University and Arch Adam Streets, Fort Worth; 817-738-9215 or 866-824-5566; themodern.org). Designed by Japan's Tadao Ando, the nation's second-largest modern art museum is also the oldest art museum in Texas (formerly located on Montgomery Street). This $60 million, 53,000-square-foot masterpiece of stone, steel, and glass is breathtaking, and possibly even more impressive than the wealth of art inside. Find works by Andy Warhol, Henry Moore, Jackson Pollock, and many others. The museum's **Cafe Modern** is also a stunner, both with an exceptionally interesting menu and a setting in an elliptical space that seems to float over the museum's shimmering pond. Closed Mon, the museum charges a small admission fee.

texastrivia

The small town of Olney, northwest of Fort Worth in Young County, hosts an annual **One-Arm Dove Hunt** in September. An event of international repute, the hunt attracts arm and hand amputees for two days of fun and fellowship.

The entire Cultural District is electrified from mid-January until early February when the ***Southwestern Stock Show and Rodeo*** is held at ***Will Rogers Coliseum,*** facing the Carter and Kimbell Museums at 3301 W. Lancaster Ave., Fort Worth (817-877-2400; fwssr.com). This terrifically Texan event—which includes the world's largest indoor rodeo—celebrated its centennial in 1996. Annual attendance is about 1 million, with attractions ranging from shows of more than 15,000 animals; livestock auctions; and sales of every sort of western wear, western art, Texas souvenirs, and food to pig races, goat-milking contests, and a carnival. Rodeo tickets sell out early, so order in advance if possible. A small admission fee is charged for the grounds. Note that in 2020, the new Dickies Arena opens in Fort Worth, providing a spectacular venue for the rodeo with 14,000 seats and some 87,000 square feet for meetings and other events.

Because so many people make an entire day of touring museums in the Cultural District, it's a good thing there are lots of places to have a great meal within walking distance. Inside the Kimbell Art Museum, there's The Buffet, an upscale place for lunch Tues through Sun and dinner on Fri. Visit ***Righteous Foods*** (3405 W. 7th St., Fort Worth; 817-850-9996; eatrighteously.com) for an upscale but especially healthy meal, suitable for vegans and omnivores alike, open daily for lunch and Mon through Sat for dinner; ***Paris 7th*** (3324 W. 7th St., Fort Worth; 817-489-5300; paris7th.com) for an elegant French dinner Tues through Sat; or ***J&J Oyster Bar*** (612 University Dr., Fort Worth; 817-335-2756; jandjoysterbar.com) for good fish at lunch and dinner daily. Just a couple of blocks east toward downtown, find exceptional burgers, cold beer and live music at ***Fred's Texas Café*** (915 Currie St., Fort Worth; 817-332-0083; freds texascafe.com).

Barely a 3-minute drive south of the Cultural District, find the ***Fort Worth Zoo*** (1989 Colonial Pkwy., Fort Worth; 817-759-7555; fortworthzoo.org), widely rated among the top five zoos in America. Exceptional natural habitats for hundreds of animals plus nature shops and cafés are on the grounds. A miniature train is in the adjacent park, taking a tour alongside the Trinity River. The zoo is open weekdays from 10 a.m. to 5 p.m. and Sat and Sun until 6 p.m. A small admission fee is charged.

Across the street from the zoo, ***University Park Village*** (on University Drive just south of I-30; 817-332-5700) is an upscale complex featuring stores such as Anthropologie, lululemon, Origins, Talbots, The Apple Store, Williams-Sonoma, Pottery Barn, Victoria's Secret, Bath and Body Works, Francesca's, and Starbucks Coffee. Good restaurants here are ***Breadwinners*** and ***EatZi's***.

Now head downtown to ***Sundance Square*** (the center is at Main and 4th Streets), which is undoubtedly the envy of all Texas's other larger cities. This superb and extensive renovation of beautiful Victorian buildings has revitalized downtown Fort Worth to an extraordinary extent. Day and night, the 14-block area with redbrick streets is bustling with folks visiting museums, dining, shopping, and attending plays, concerts, and movies. Special architecture to note is at the Knights of Pythias building—the first such temple ever built—at 315 Main St.

The Circle Theatre (230 4th St., Fort Worth; 817-877-3040; circletheater .com), *Casa Mañana* (3101 W. Lancaster Ave., Fort Worth; 817-332-2272; casa manana.org), and the *Jubilee Theater* (506 Main St., Fort Worth; 817-338-4411; jubileetheatre.org) offer plays and musicals. The largest is the phenomenally grand *Nancy Lee and Perry R. Bass Performance Hall* (4th and Calhoun Streets, Fort Worth; 817-212-4325 or 877-212-4280; basshall.com), the premier performing space for Fort Worth's opera, symphony, ballet, and national touring productions. If you want to catch up on current movies, there's the Palace, at 3rd and Calhoun Streets, with nine screens.

Sundance Square also includes the beautifully expanded and remodeled *Sid Richardson Collection of Western Art* (309 Main St., Fort Worth; 817-332-6554; sidrmuseum.org), with western masterpieces by Charles Russell and Frederic Remington. And you can't miss the *Chisholm Trail Mural* (on the Jett Building at 400 Main St., Fort Worth), a wonderful, enormous artwork honoring the Fort Worth portion of the Chisholm Trail cattle drives from 1867 to 1875. It overlooks Sundance Square Plaza, an expansive courtyard with fountains, stages for live music and free Saturday-morning yoga classes, and places to relax with a date or your kids. Several restaurants and bars surround the plaza. During the holidays, the city's soaring Christmas tree and a wonderfuland of seasonal décor fills the plaza with seasonal cheer.

For cool lodging in Sundance Square, there's *Etta's Place* (200 W. 3rd St., Fort Worth; 817-255-5760 or 866-355-5760; ettas-place.com), a bed-and-breakfast inn named for the Sundance Kid's schoolteacher-girlfriend. All 10 guest rooms are done in period style, with Texas antiques and reproductions, and come with fresh flowers, candies, and cookies. All have private baths with lotions and bath toys. Breakfast is an elaborate 3-course event, complete with sterling silver, china, and crystal. Hosts will assist with theater and dinner reservations.

The beautiful *Tarrant County Courthouse,* 100 Weatherford St. at Main Street, is at the north end of Sundance. The 1893 Renaissance Revival architecture is worth a good look, crafted again from marble and that wonderful Texas pink granite.

The list of Sundance Square's dining options grows all the time. A big favorite is *Reata* (310 Houston St., Fort Worth; 817-336-1009; reata.net), where you can dine on enchiladas and steaks. *Taverna* (450 Throckmorton St., Fort Worth; 817-885-7502; tavernabylombardi.com) is popular for focaccia, wood-oven pizza, and Italian wines. *Piranha Killer Sushi* (335 W. 3rd St., Fort Worth; 817-348-0200; piranhakillersushi.com) makes a mean Caribbean conch salad, as well as a dramatic spider roll.

Restaurants in or within 3 blocks of Sundance Square with lively bar scenes include the *Bird Cafe* (155 E. 4th St., Fort Worth; 817-332-2473; birdinthe.net); *Razzoo's Cajun Cafe* (318 Main St., Fort Worth; 817-429-7009; razzoos.com); and *Mi Cocina* (509 Main St., Fort Worth; 817-877-3600; mycocinarestaurants .com).

About 3 miles north of downtown Fort Worth via N. Main Street, the *Stock-yards National Historic District* supplies a full day or night of history and fun. The district's main intersection is N. Main Street and Exchange Avenue, and the visitor center kiosk (817-634-4741; fortworthstockyards.org) is on E. Exchange Avenue between the White Elephant Saloon and Stockyards Station.

In the Stockyards you can visit *Billy Bob's Texas* (Rodeo Plaza, Fort Worth; 817-624-7117; billybobstexas.com), the "world's largest honky-tonk," where top country performers often include Willie Nelson, the Bellamy Brothers, Pat Green, Patty Loveless, Trisha Yearwood, and Jerry Jeff Walker. There are two dance floors, 40 bar stations, gift shops, and live bull riding inside, too.

At *Cowtown Coliseum* (121 E. Exchange Ave., Fort Worth, 817-625-1025), home of the world's first indoor rodeo, there's a professional rodeo and Wild West Show every Saturday from April through September. Next door at the Livestock Exchange Building (817-626-2334), built in 1904 as offices for live-stock traders, you'll find the *Stockyards Collection Museum,* which chronicles the importance of the Stockyards to Fort Worth's history.

Right across the brick street in *Stockyards Station* (817-625-9715), souvenirs, gifts, clothing, artwork, food, and drink are found in 30 shops and restaurants in what was once the Stockyards's hog-and-sheep pens. It's also a depot for the *Grapevine Vintage Railroad* (call 817-410-3185 or visit grapevinetexasusa .com to get a schedule), a vintage 1896 steam engine making daily excursions to nearby Grapevine (using diesel engines).

Wandering down Exchange Avenue you'll find the *White Elephant Saloon* (817-624-8273; whiteelephantsaloon.com), a century-old barroom named "One of the Best 100 Bars in America" by *Esquire* magazine. It offers a chili parlor, cold beer and margaritas, live music, a lively dance floor, and a breezy beer garden with a good burger stand. Across the street from the White Elephant, the historic Stockyards Hotel (109 E. Exchange Ave., Fort Worth; 817-625-6427; stockyardshotel.com) is a charming 1907 hotel with 52 rooms with period decoration. Just another block west, find *Miss Molly's Hotel* (109½ W.

Exchange Ave., Fort Worth; 817-626-1522; missmollyshotel.com), a bed-and-breakfast inn in a restored 1910 building with 8 guest rooms.

Plenty of good eating goes on in and around the Stockyards area. For an excellent steak and fabulous bottle of wine, with a rattlesnake appetizer and a jalapeño margarita, visit **Lonesome Dove Western Bistro** (2406 N. Main St., Fort Worth, 817-740-8810; lonesomedovebistro.com); for Mexican fare try **El Rancho Grande Restaurante** (1400 N. Main St., Fort Worth; 817-624-9206); **Esperanza's Bakery** (2122 N. Main St., Fort Worth; 817-626-5770); and the famous **Joe T. Garcia's Mexican Dishes** (2201 N. Commerce St., Fort Worth; 817-626-4356), the latter a 1930 institution that now covers a city block with a series of beautiful gardens set with dinner tables that can seat a total of 1,000 guests at once. Lines can be long, so you're advised to go at an off-hour rather that the peak lunch or dinner times.

The hottest district in Fort Worth is the **Near Southside**, immediately south of downtown. The heartbeat of the neighborhood is **West Magnolia Avenue**, a 12-block stretch of restored 1920s buildings now occupied by wine bars, bistros, galleries, and shops. A renaissance of the Fairmount Historic District swept the street in recent years, making this the go-to area for independent restaurants, bars, and other entertainment venues. The entrepreneurial spirit in Fort Worth feels strongest in this neighborhood, with nearly every place a homegrown effort. Among favorite places to eat are Ellerbe Fine Foods, Lili's Bistro, Benito's Mexican Restaurant, Fixture Kitchen, Cane Rosso (a pizza place), Paris Coffee Shop, and, for vegan dining, Spiral Diner. Favorite watering holes include The Bearded Lady (great burgers, too), The Usual, Proper, and two wine bars with good food, Grand Cru and Kent & Co. For details and an events calendar, visit the Near Southside's site, nearsouthsidefw.org.

Visiting the **Fort Worth** information centers are easy to access in Sundance Square at 508 Main Street and in the Stockyards at 128 E. Exchange Avenue. You can also visit the website at fortworth.com. If you want to prowl around town, look for the city's bike-sharing program, **B-Cycle**. The stands are set up in convenient places for you to rent a bike for an hour or a day by using your credit card.

From Fort Worth head west on I-30, then US 180, for about 30 miles to **Weatherford**. The seat of Parker County, Weatherford was established in 1855 and grew in 1857 when the Butterfield Stage was routed through town. Hundreds of lives were lost, however, as pioneers warred with Native Americans

texastrivia

NASCAR's *Texas Motor Speedway* in Fort Worth, which opened in 1997, has seating for 150,061. That makes it the second-largest sports facility in America.

in 1877. One of the lasting monuments to the late 19th century is the Parker County Courthouse, at the center of town on US 180. Made of locally quarried limestone in 1884, the richly Victorian building cost $55,555.55 to construct.

Three blocks east of the courthouse, you'll find a flurry of activity once a month when **First Monday Trade Days** is in progress. Thousands of folks buying and selling junk, antiques, farm animals, puppies, and food converge for the Friday, Saturday, and Sunday prior to the first Monday of each month. Across the street, the stucco Weatherford Public Market is a 1932 WPA building housing an open-air farmers' market, where produce, plants, honey, seeds, jams, and peanuts are sold by the bushel.

Stroll down to the **Weatherford Public Library** (1214 Charles St., Weatherford; 817-598-4269) and see a **life-size bronze of Peter Pan** out front. The sculpture honors Weatherford's late daughter, Mary Martin, who originated the role of Peter Pan in the Broadway musical. The library's Heritage Gallery houses costumes, photos, sheet music, and other mementos belonging to the actress.

Other important sites include a Queen Anne Victorian home at 202 W. Oak St., which was the boyhood home of the late former US Speaker of the House Jim Wright; and the Greenwood Cemetery, at Front and Mill Streets. Here you'll find a state historical site, the grave of Oliver Loving, known as the Dean of Texas Trail Drivers, whose story inspired the Pulitzer Prize–winning novel, *Lonesome Dove,* written by Texan Larry McMurtry. Loving died after being wounded by Native Americans during a trail drive with his close friend Charles Goodnight; Goodnight, along with Loving's son, returned his body more than 600 miles to be buried, as he had wished, in Weatherford.

On or near the downtown square, good dining awaits at **Fire Oak Grill** (114 Austin Ave., Weatherford; 817-598-0400; fireoakgrill.com), where owner-chef Grant Lambdin served beef tenderloin tacos and sea scallops with pork belly, among many things. At **Downtown Cafe** (101 W. Church St., Weatherford; 817-594-8717), chicken fried steak, chicken and dumplings, blackberry cobbler, and omelets keep crowds happy.

Nearby, **Shep's Place** (816 S. Main St., Weatherford; 682-804-5002) is a great stop for burgers and cold beer. **Whistlehill Café** (101 W. Church St., Weatherford; 817-599-4311; whistlehillcafe.com) series a popular breakfast, brunch and lunch.

For information on lodging, dining, historic sites, antiques, and the wonderful Parker County Peach Festival, held every July, contact the **Weatherford Chamber of Commerce,** 401 Fort Worth St., Weatherford 76086; call (817) 596-3801 or (888) 594-3801; or visit weatherford-chamber.com.

Just outside of Weatherford, toward Granbury, you can scratch the itch for a prime glamping experience: **Sundancer on the Brazos** houses you in a spacious luxury tent (complete with central heat and A/C) while you enjoy the great outdoors just outside the canvas walls. This retreat on the 350-acre Double F River Ranch is perfect for giving you a sense of escape—but you're just 10 minutes from civilization. The tent is surrounded by a wraparound pine deck, equipped with comfy lounge chairs where you can nap beneath a shady tree canopy while listening to a waterfall spilling into the adjacent creek. There's a firepit for nighttime solace under the stars, as well as a 1-mile hike down to the Brazos River, over meadows strewn with blooming cactus and wildflowers. At the river, you can use the ranch's kayaks and inner tubes to enjoy the gentle water. At night, sleep in a queen bed made up with posh linens. There's also a sleeper sofa, so the tent accommodates 4. A stocked kitchenette and a large bathroom, complete with a walk-in shower, are all within your tent accommodation. For reservations, call (817) 233-2825 or visit doublefriverranch.com.

Dinosaurs & Hell's Gates

Head on to **Granbury,** a charming 1800s town that was restored in the 1970s to its original Victorian glory. You can reach Granbury by driving south 30 miles from Fort Worth on US 377; note, however, that a slight but most worthy detour can be found 5 miles shy of Granbury. ***Acton State Historic Site*** is just 2 miles away on FR 4, which intersects US 377. The Acton Cemetery holds a lovely monument to Elizabeth Crockett, widow of Alamo hero Davy Crockett, who moved here after he was killed. The statue rising above her grave shows her with her hand to her brow, watching and hoping he will come home. If you arrive during spring, the cemetery—and all this countryside—will be blanketed in vibrant bluebonnets.

Continue then to Granbury, following signs directing you to the historic downtown, which has been listed on the National Register of Historic Places. The town, after its 1890s heyday, fell into a decline but was grandly resuscitated by a town project in the 1970s that became a model for all Main Street renovation projects in the state. The town of 9,000 is the Hood County seat and a charming escape for a day, but most people stay at least a weekend.

The centerpiece of the square is the **Hood County Courthouse,** built in 1890 and containing its original Seth Thomas clock; past that is **Granbury Opera House,** 133 E. Pearl St., built in 1886 and the site of a recent, siginificant renovation. It's home now to the **Granbury Theatre Company,** which stages productions of Broadway shows and musical tributes—think the Rat Pack, Supremes, Blues Brothers; see a full schedule at granburytheatre company.org.

Shopping the square is a primary reason many people come to Granbury. You'll find limestone architecture reminiscent of that in Fredericksburg and other Hill Country hamlets; the timeworn buildings offer a wealth of boutiques and places to sip wine—or both. Recent finds—mixed in with lots of antiques shops—include *St. Helen's* (135 E. Pearl St.), a shop with things for the home, including candles, clocks, and dining table accoutrements; *Home Sweet Home* (130 N. Houston St.), filled with beautiful bedding and gifts like quirky flasks; and *Eighteen Ninety Marketplace* (115 E. Pearl St.), downstairs from the same-named restaurant, a Napa-esque shop stocked with lovely olive oils, vinegars, spices, and kitchen/bar accessories. *Spellbound* (109 E. Bridge St.) stocks plentiful home décor, jewelry, Texana gifts, and comfy sleepwear.

Off the north side of the square, the *Hood County Jail* (400 Deputy Larry Miller Dr., Granbury; 817-579-3316) is an 1885 Old West jail crafted of hand-hewn stone. Used as a jail for 90 years, it's now home to the chamber of commerce, but visitors are welcome to look at the old cellblock and hanging tower. The newest and most impressive place to rest your weary bones in Granbury isn't exactly new. The former Doyle House, a historic cottage

Offbeat BBQ—and lots more

Loco Coyote isn't an obvious place; in fact, you really have to want to find it. But it's an easy reach from the town of Glen Rose: You turn off of US 67, south of Glen Rose, and ride a mile or so down bumpy, twisting Somervell County Road 1004 to the ramshackle joint where pickup trucks, SUVs, and an admirable assortment of fancy motorcycles pull up by a cedar-post fence, as they have for 40 or more years. Under new ownership as of 2013, Loco's barbecue tastes better than ever, and portions are still huge: The Howling Coyote burger resembles a hubcap and comes topped with cheese, chili, bacon, grilled onion, and jalapeño, between halves of a loaf of buttered, toasted bread. It easily feeds four very hungry diners. The massive ribs, with a thick sweet and spicy crust, are part of a three-meat platter weighty with tender, sliced brisket and locally made sausage, all redolent from smoking over oak. There's an appealingly tart barbecue sauce alongside, but this 'cue doesn't require help. In the Loco's cramped interior with its sawdust floor topped with picnic tables, the 106 seats fill up fast. Walls are plastered with Willie Nelson posters and a collection of vintage lunch boxes. There's more seating outside on the deck, where live music plays on Saturday evenings. People-watching is best on Sunday, when the tatted-up bikers and after-church crowd mingle at the community tables, falling into conversation over cold longnecks and tall tumblers of sweet tea. Beware that pretty weekends bring crowds in droves and you may wait a while for a table. You'll meet guests from San Antonio, as well as from Scotland, Germany, and Scandinavia, and everyone agrees this is a really good, really big Texas experience. Find it on 1795 CR 1004, Glen Rose; 254-897-2324; lococoyotegrill.com.

a couple of blocks from the square and one of the early bed-and-breakfast homes in town, has been extensively renovated and remodeled to become the exquisite *Inn on Lake Granbury* (877-573-0046; innonlakegranbury.com), with a scenic bluff-top setting on the lakeshore. It's as comfortable as it is stylish: Each room features a mix of pine, red oak, and maple, as well as elegant linens on a fancy pillow-top mattress, and the baths offer a lovely mix of granite, marble, and tile. The common area has a fireplace, leather couch and chairs, and a help-yourself area with coffee and pastries in the morning and wine and snacks in the afternoon. Outside the back door there's a gorgeous saltwater swimming pool with a waterfall and rock-and-pine landscaping. You can gaze at the lake poolside, or walk down the live oak–shaded lawn to a boat dock. There's an elaborate breakfast, served in a large detached dining room, which typically includes a pancake casserole with sausage and maple syrup, southwestern hominy, eggs with chives, fresh fruit, thick-cut bacon, and blueberry cobbler.

It's an easy walk from the inn to the most popular eatery in town, *Babe's Chicken Dinner House,* found on one corner of the square (114 W. Pearl St., Granbury; 817-573-9777; babeschicken.com). Thick, crunchy crust cloaks the chicken at this landmark, where family-style servings include chicken, mashed potatoes, creamy corn, salad, and biscuits with sorghum syrup on the side. There's also *Ketzler's* (101 E. Pearl St., 682-936-2777; ketzlersschnitzelhaus .com), **a friendly** German bistro on the square serving plates of freshly made bratwurst and knackwurst; and fabulous schnitzel with sides of warm red cabbage (hinting of red wine, cinnamon, and nutmeg); and kraut (with bacon, caraway, and apple). A pretty beer garden out back invites lingering. But best of all is *Eighteen Ninety Grille* (115 E. Pearl St., 817-533-3400; eighteenninety .com), Granbury's showplace for fine dining. Best appetizers include seared ahi, sesame crusted and served in ruby slices over arugula, avocado, and radish in a ginger-soy dressing. For entrees, New York strip with a wild mushroom treatment and a bawdy pork chop with its smoked pear chutney get high marks. A terrific wine list is offered, and local artwork hangs on the aged rock walls; you'll find yourself just wanting to spend an hour or so just relaxing in the lounge, too.

Some of the nation's finest craft beer is made at *Revolver Brewing* (5650 Matlock Rd. Granbury, 817-736-8034; revolverbrewing.com), attracting a few hundred people each Saturday for the noon-till-3 p.m. party. Regulars bring camp chairs, and early arrivals can grab a seat at picnic tables arranged on the huge lawn. A local band entertains the crowd, and a food truck or two serves lunch to soak up the suds. Admission is $10, which includes a 15-minute tank-room tour and four generous pours of Revolver's delicious beers.

The local winery, **Barking Rocks,** is just 10 minutes from downtown (1919 Allen Court, Granbury, 817-79-0007; barkingrockswine.com) and the destination for tastings on Saturday afternoon and on the first Friday evening each month, the latter usually offering live music. Be sure to meet local character Tiberia, the one-name winemaker, who pours wines alongside a helpful staff. Wines here aren't particularly sweet; primo selections include the Roussane Reserve, an oaky white, along with a slightly effervescent rosé, which is used in a refreshing sangria.

To get a list of other lodgings, restaurants, and shops, plus a few good maps, and information, contact the **Granbury Convention and Visitor Bureau** at 116 W. Bridge St., Granbury 76048; call 817-573-5548 or 800-950-2212; or visit visitgranbury.com.

The **Brazos River** cuts its path diagonally across north and central Texas and in Granbury is impounded to make the 8,700-acre **Lake Granbury** that nearly wraps around the city. There are more than 100 miles of shoreline with parks, swimming beaches, and marinas. At City Beach Park, you can rent kayaks and paddleboards for having fun on the water; see **Waterside Sports** (505 E. Pearl St., Granbury, 855-226-2810; watersidesports.net). At **Lake Granbury Marina,** rent pontoon boats, canoes, kayaks and paddleboards (2323 S. Morgan St., Granbury; 817-279-1000; lakegmi.com). At **Sam's Dock,** rent Wave Runners and other boats for exploring Lake Granbury (1003 White Cliff Rd., Granbury; 844-726-7326; samsdock.com).

From Granbury follow Highway 144 south for 17 miles and you'll find the bucolic town of **Glen Rose.** Founded in 1849 as a trading post, it is now the Somervell County seat and home to 2,000 people. From the 1920s through the 1930s, however, this was a thriving health resort for people who came to sanitariums here to take the rejuvenating waters. One still standing has been transformed into a lovely place to stay: the **Inn on the River,** at 205 SW Barnard St., Glen Rose (254-897-2929 or 800-575-2101; innontheriver.com), an extravagantly renovated and decorated 22-room bed-and-breakfast lodge where no two rooms are alike. Built in 1919, the inn backs up to the serene Paluxy River and is a romantic place to spend the weekend. Gourmet breakfasts and dinners are offered to guests, and sometimes to nonguests, by reservation only; note that it's BYOB.

If you're feeling flush, book a night or two at **Rough Creek Lodge** (County Road 2013, Glen Rose; 877-907-0754; roughcreek.com), a resort that melds adventure with luxury on the 11,000-acre Chalk Mountain Ranch, about 20 minutes south of Glen Rose. Hang out in your fabulous room or suite or in one of the cottages, but don't skip the many activities offered here, including a rock-climbing wall, a 200-foot zip-line, a bungee trampoline, a family pool complex, a kids' ranch, a petting corral, horseback riding, a full-service spa, ATV riding, shooting clays, archery, and seasonal bird hunting. Exceptional dining comes from chef Gerard Thompson's kitchen, which offers three meals daily. Ask about family rate packages and good deals in the hottest part of summer.

Glen Rose is best known, though, for something much older—actually prehistoric. **Dinosaur Valley State Park,** 4 miles west of town on FR 205 (254-897-4588; tpwd.texas.gov/state-parks/dinosaur-valley), is the site of the best-preserved dinosaur tracks, some experts say, in the world. In the solid limestone bed of the Paluxy River, just above its confluence with the Brazos River, the unmistakable prints have been found to be those of the sauropod, a gargantuan creature that ate plants, measured longer than 55 feet, and weighed more than 30 tons. Other tracks have indicated that the duck-billed dinosaur and the theropod also lived in this area. Near the river, a fenced off area contains two life-size models of the T. Rex and the brontosaurus, fiberglass models left over from the Sinclair Oil Corporation's dinosaur exhibit at the 1964–1965 New York World's Fair. The park is about 1,500 acres and offers a wild but enchanting shrubby terrain of bluffs and water, ideal for picnicking, camping, and hiking. A dinosaur exhibit at the visitor center is open daily from 8 a.m. to 5 p.m. Park admission is $7 per person.

North Texans also come to Glen Rose in early June for a **bluegrass festival** hosted by Oakdale Park, on Highway 144 about 3 miles south of US 67 (254-897-2321; www.paluxybluegrass.com/). There are camping facilities, cabins, a swimming pool, and a pavilion here, as well.

Three miles southwest of town via US 67 is the fascinating, renowned **Fossil Rim Wildlife Center** (254-897-2960; fossilrim.org). More than 1,000 endangered animals from five continents call this 3,000-acre conservation center home. There's a 9-mile driving tour through the ranch, where visitors see animals roaming at will, among them the white rhino, cheetah, gray zebra, and wildebeest. The scenic overlook near the route's end is an excellent place for photos and reflection, and a restaurant, petting zoo, nature-hiking trail, riding stables, and picnic areas are close by. The ranch is open daily from 9 a.m. to 2 hours before sunset. Admission is charged.

The ranch also offers the **Foothills Safari Camp,** a wildlife safari providing guests with tents and weekend dinners. Five rooms are also available at the lodge and Wolf Ridge Nature Camp bunkhouses. For inquiries and reservations call (254) 897-2960.

From Glen Rose depart on Highway 144 heading south 23 miles, pick up Highway 6 in the town of Meridian, and follow it south another 12 miles. This places you at the tiny community of **Clifton,** settled in 1854 on the banks of the pretty Bosque (BOS-Kee) River, today the largest town—with about 4,000 residents—in Bosque County. Fishing is a popular pastime here on the Bosque River and nearby at Lake Whitney.

Scandinavian traditions are still observed in Clifton by descendants of the original Norwegian settlers. To see the terrain of this heritage, drive into what's known as Norse Country, along FR 219 west from town and FR 182 north from town. Maps and information are available from the **Clifton Chamber of Commerce,** (254) 675-3720; cliftontexas.org. The Norse church, sitting alone in the countryside, is really special.

To explore more of this Norse community, check out the **Bosque County Memorial Museum,** at Avenue Q and W. 9th Street (254-675-3845; bosque museum.org), a small but informative place with exhibits detailing the founding and growth of the Norse Capital of Texas. You'll see excellent examples of "rosemaling," the Norwegian craft of painting or carving intricate floral detail on all sorts of wooden furnishings. The museum is open Tues through Sat from 10 a.m. to 5 p.m. No admission is charged, but donations are gratefully accepted.

It's also worth noting that Clifton is a designated **Texas Cultural Arts District,** thanks largely to the nearby **Bosque Arts Center** (215 S. College Hill Dr., Clifton; 254-675-3724; bosqueartscenter.org) and the community involvement its ongoing programs command. The Bosque Art Center occupies the former Clifton Lutheran College building, dating from 1923, as well as a more modern addition. The old college auditorium has recently been renovated, and it's a venue for concerts like those starring country music greats like Larry Gatlin and Eddy Raven. The art complex is home also to various workshops and shows throughout the year, including the annual Bosque Art Classic, a juried show and sale awarding thousands of dollars to winning artists. Work by local and regional artists, most falling into the category of western art subjects, is seen in the art center's permanent collection, of course. **Treaty Oak Gallery** (126 N. Avenue D) exhibits paintings, sculpture, drawings and wood creations by local artists. On the backside of the gallery, Art Alley is the place to see an assortment of huge, colorful murals, courtesy of area talent.

Across the street from the gallery, find **Market at the Mill** (324 W. Third St.), an impressive renovation of the century-old Dansby Feed Mills building. Inside the sizable retail space, we found a world of goodies for the dining table, kitchen, bar, bath and living areas, plus a few casual wearables. All farmhouse chic in style, it reminded me of the Magnolia silos a few minutes away in Waco—but this one has more fun inventory at mostly better prices. The mill's compound also includes a music venue, featuring country crooners as well as those offering tribute evenings to Frank Sinatra and John Denver, among others.

Just a block away, the ***Bosque County Emporium*** (121 N. Avenue D) occupies an expansive space, housing a beautiful collection of antique furnishings, from Texas primitives to mid-century modern to European pieces, ranging from dining tables and china cabinets to lamps, sofas, silver tea and coffee services, Chinese ginger jars, paintings, china and crystal. Hundreds of books fill a back corner of the store, and there's even a corner of goodies pertaining to local Norse heritage, including books on Norwegian cooking. Another charmer in downtown Clifton is the century-old movie house called the ***Cliftex Theatre*** (306 W. Fifth St., thecliftex.com), showing first-run films in the evening, charging just $5 per ticket. Downtown Clifton's renaissance also includes good lodging and dining, noted at the end of this chapter.

Your next destination from Clifton takes you along roughly scenic prairie and ranch land, gently rolling west. Drive north along Highway 6, 36 miles to the town of ***Hico*** (HY-koe), stopping for a robust breakfast, lunch, or dinner at the ***Koffee Kup Family Restaurant,*** at the intersection of Highway 6 and US 281 (254-796-4839; koffeekupfamilyrestaurant .com). Don't try to resist the extraordinary meringue pies—it's impossible. If you have time, poke around the little town of Hico. There's good shopping for home furnishings, jewelry, books, and gifts at ***Blue Star Trading*** (112 S. Pecan St., Hico; 254-796-2828, bluestartrading.com); for lovingly crafted sweets at ***Wiseman House Chocolates*** (406 Grubbs St., Hico; 866-460-3571; wisemanhousechocolates.com); ***Heartland Atelier*** (102 N. Pecan St.), a flower shop, a place to buy Texana antiques and a studio for learning to work with chalk paint.; and ***Hill Country Dwellings*** (118 N. Pecan St., hillcountrydwellings.com), purveyor of country furniture, home accessories, jewelry, books and a V-neck grey shirt emblazoned with the greeting, "Hico—I Like-O!"

A getaway for romantics in Hico, the ***Upstairs Inn*** (202 N. Pecan St.; 254-796-2230), brings a level of style and comfort not enjoyed before in this town. Downstairs at the inn, the Drink Shoppe is a full liquor store and wine shop, with wine tastings on weekends; its adjacent store is called Eis, a place for ice cream, Texas artisan cheeses, charcuterie, and local artwork. A block away, the ***Midland Hotel*** (103 N. Pecan St., Hico;, 254-796-4426; historicmidlandhotel .com) is a two-story brick landmark dating from 1896 and recently renovated and restored; its 14 rooms each tell a story of Hico and Hamilton County in

texastrivia

Thousands of cyclists from across the US converge in Wichita Falls, northwest of Fort Worth, in late August every year for the ***Hotter 'n Hell Hundred***—to ride 100 miles at the hottest time of the year.

carefully curated décor. Off the lobby, find a steakhouse and saloon that make the stay even more enjoyable.

From Hico drive north on US 281 for 47 miles, touring through more rolling, tree-dotted ranch country, until you arrive in *Mineral Wells,* a pretty old town of nearly 17,000 in Palo Pinto County, a wonderful place to pause in your approach to west Texas. Here's another town that saw a boom—this one in the 1880s—thanks to its mysteriously healing waters. Since no one could explain why this mineral-laden water, which didn't have an appealing scent, would make people feel better, it became known as Crazy Water, and everything in town was named similarly, such as the Crazy Hotel, the Crazy Park, and a radio show called *The Crazy Gang.*

The boom was highlighted by the building of the elaborate, luxurious Baker Hotel in 1929, but the Depression ended the boom, and today the grand Baker Hotel—which was a copy of the famous Arlington Hotel in Hot Springs, Arkansas—stands deserted. Nevertheless, it's a great photo site rising above the skyline in the middle of town. Nearby are a few antiques shops but the main attraction in town is the *Crazy Water* shop (209 NW 6th St., Mineral Wells, 940-325-8870; drinkcrazywater.com), where you can buy the mineral water (it's also sold all over Texas at Central Market stores) or fill up your own gallon jugs with the healing mineral water pulled right from the on-site well. The store sells coffee mugs and skin/body products, as well as T-shirts and hats emblazoned with the Crazy logo. The *Crazy Bath House* is open, too, offering massage, mineral baths and overnight stays in a restored stone cottage (see crazybath house.com).

If a cheap meal is up your alley and you enjoy an old-fashioned pool hall spirit, by all means drop into *Woody's* (6105 Highway 80, Mineral Wells; 940-325-9817). A Mineral Wells legend, this little hole-in-the-wall offers a darned good burger from an old griddle, along with an ice-cold beer.

On beautiful west Texas days, when the sun's out and the rivers aren't too low, you should think about taking a little canoe or kayak excursion on the beautiful Brazos River. *Rochelle's Canoe Rentals* (Highway 4 at the Brazos River; 940-659-3341 or 940-659-2581; rochellescanoeandkayakrental.com) is a friendly outfit that will charge you $30 per canoe, and they'll pick you up at a designated spot.

Hikers and rock climbers will want to spend at least a day at *Lake Mineral Wells State Park* (Highway 180, 3 miles east of town; 940-328-1171; tpwd.texas.gov). Crowded with trees and rocks, this scenic spread with a 650-acre lake is popular with nature watchers, too, in search of white-tailed deer, raccoon, and armadillo. The park is the western terminus of the outstanding *Rails-to-Trails pathway,* a 22-mile connection of Mineral Wells and

Lions, Tigers and . . . Bats, Oh My!

In 1987 Amanda Lollar rescued an injured Mexican free-tailed bat (the state's official flying mammal) on her way to her furniture store. Since then she liquidated her business and turned it into the state's only permanent sanctuary for nonreleasable bats, and she became a state-licensed wildlife rehabilitator. She runs **Bat World Sanctuary** (217 N. Oak St., Mineral Wells; 940-325-3404; batworld.org), where she provides a home to up to 15 bat species, including orphaned bat pups, bats used in lab research, wild bats with permanent injuries, and bats confiscated from the illegal pet trade. Inside you can see several wire-mesh cages with bats hanging upside down from special roosts that she designed and her father built. Lollar says she can tell by the bats' eyes or facial expressions if they're feeling sick, and she has inspired her town to go batty, too. More than 100 bat houses are up on buildings and poles in Mineral Wells; the police department added a roost to its building and painted "Bat Cops" on it, while the bank's bat roost is labeled "Nite Depository." Lollar has also penned two books, *The Bat in My Pocket: A Memorable Friendship*, and *The Crazy Water Town That Went Batty*.

Weatherford, built on an old rail bed and opened in 1997 for hikers, cyclists, and horseback riders to enjoy.

Another great place to spend a few days in this area is at **Possum Kingdom Lake State Park,** reached by driving west of Mineral Wells on US 180 for 38 miles until you reach the settlement of Caddo. Then head north 17 miles on PR 33, which ends at the park entrance; the park's phone is (940) 549-1803 and the website is tpwd.texas.gov. Near the entrance look for some not-too-shy longhorn cattle; they are part of the official state herd.

The massive lake, a 22,000-acre reservoir formed by damming the beautiful Brazos River, has depths up to 150 feet and the clearest water in the Southwest, making it a popular site for scuba diving, waterskiing, and sailing. An extraordinary cliff formation on the southwestern end of the lake is called **Hell's Gates;** it's a great photography subject and is magnificent at sunset. Campsites, cabins, marinas, and cafes sit around the 300 miles of shoreline, but the state park's offerings are generally the best. Sitting on the south shore, the 1,500-acre park has superb hiking trails, nice if small beaches, shady and scenic campsites, a playground, canoe rentals, simple cabins, a small store, a long and lighted fishing pier, and countless good places for bank fishing. A resort on the eastern shores of Possum Kingdom is called **The Cliffs** (940-779-4040 or 888-843-2543; ddresorts.com/the-cliffs/). You'll find it along Highway 16, south of PR 36. There guests can choose between lodge and condo accommodations and take advantage of the resort's 18-hole, championship golf course; health and beauty spa; tennis and swim center; full-service marina; and private, white-sand beach. There are plenty of kid-friendly programs, too, at the Cliffs. There are modest, old-fashioned lake retreats in the form of cabins and apartments on Possum Kingdom, too. Call the **Possum Kingdom Lake Chamber of Commerce** at (940) 779-2424 or visit possumkingdomlake.com for information.

About a half-hour drive northwest of Possum Kingdom Lake, you'll find one of the most appealing retreats to open in Texas in the past few years. **Wildcatter Ranch** (on Highway 16; 888-462-9277; wildcatterranch.com) sits on 1,500 acres about 20 miles from the lake and just 7 miles southeast of Graham, the Young County seat. It's a delightful destination for families and couples in need of a getaway in the hilly, rocky countryside, and you'll find yourself wishing for more than a weekend to squeeze in all the fun offered at the ranch. There's hiking, mountain biking, canoeing, horseback riding, tank fishing, sand volleyball, fossil hunts, cow-pasture golf, birding, scavenger hunts, hayrides, archery, skeet shooting, and ATV touring. Or, if you'd rather, you can just book a massage, followed by a poolside siesta. Sweet dreams are guaranteed in your plush room, with a remote-controlled fireplace and DVD player, and you can relax on your private porch with rocking chairs. Enjoy a great steak and fine bottle of wine at the ranch's restaurant, **The Dinner Bell.**

Set aside time to wander the town of Graham, as well. Nearly everything worth exploring stands chockablock on the downtown square, which claims to be the largest in the United States, as it measures a mile in circumference. The "America's largest downtown square" sign at Third and Oak streets faces a terrific 7Up mural, a replica of the soft drink's old orange-and-green logo on the side of what was originally Graham's Masonic Lodge. That 1900-era building also housed the city hall over time, as attested to the City Hall sign still posted over the doorway. Past the historic National Theater, which still shows first-run films, visit **Pratt's Books** (502 Oak St., Graham; 940-549-5341), occupying an 1890s building that was originally the home of Doty's Grocery Store, where customers once tied their horses to the long-gone hitching posts. Rare and first-edition books are among finds. A few steps away is the **Old Post Office Museum and Art Center** (51- Third St., Graham; 940-549-1470; opomac.net), a 1936 building that now doubles as a center of heritage and culture. Inside, see one of the famous WPA paintings that came to decorate post offices across the nation during the Depression. Completed in 1939 by artists hired as part the government's relief program, "The Old Fields of Graham" features bold scenes of workers against a backdrop of the economy-changing equipment on the landscape. In what was the post office lobby, where mailboxes once stood to serve the local population, the space today offers a museum gift shop and displays of local history. You'll be drawn to a large, glassed-in case holding a sizable collection of ornate spurs, boots, and hats belonging to a local named Dean Smith, who spent his career as a Hollywood film stuntman. The museum's art spaces are hung with changing exhibits throughout the year, often juried events featuring work by artists from Texas and the nation. In a hallway just behind the art exhibit areas, a display of more than 100 framed vintage photos from around Young County tell the story of a growing community.On the museum's lawn, sculpture includes a beautiful copper spiral kinetic piece by a Lake Buchanan artist named Ralph Moresco. And particularly striking is a large piece of a cowboy by his campfire, created by metal artist Joe Barrington from nearby Throckmorton.

From Graham, head north to **Archer City** and Wichita Falls, following TX 16 about 30 miles north of Graham until you reach US 281. Follow US 281 north another 7 miles to Windthorst, deep in dairy country, then turn west on Highway 25 and travel 11 miles until you reach Archer City.

You've arrived in the hometown of author Larry McMurtry, who penned the Pulitzer Prize–winning *Lonesome Dove,* as well as *Terms of Endearment* and *The Last Picture Show,* which was filmed in this very burg. Archer City is home to the old movie house that inspired *The Last Picture Show.* The **Royal Theater,** sitting on one corner of the Archer City town square, was rotting away when locals pitched in to raise money for its restoration. Today the Royal is home to occasional musical performances—often hosted by groups such as the Late Week Lazy Boy Supper Club and the Texasville Opry—and other performing arts. Find out more by calling (940) 574-2489 or visiting royaltheater.org. Also on the town square, **The Spur Hotel** (110 N. Center St., Archer City; 940-574-2501; thespurhotel.com) is a 1928 property that's been carefully restored. It offers rooms and suites and plenty of peace and quiet.

Now turn north on Highway 79, and 25 miles later you'll find yourself in **Wichita Falls,** a city of a little more than 100,000 with an oil-boom heritage, situated on the Wichita River, nearly right on top of the Texas-Oklahoma state line.

Among many historic sites is **Kell House** (900 Bluff St., Wichita Falls; 940-723-2712; wichita-heritage.org), the early 20th-century home of a city founder who entertained lavishly. The restored home features original period furnishings, a baby grand player piano, 7 fireplaces, and hand-stenciled decorations. Open Tues, Wed, and Sun from 2 to 4 p.m. A small admission fee is charged.

At the **Wichita Falls Museum of Art at Midwestern State University** (2 Eureka Circle, Wichita Falls; 940-397-8900; wfmamsu.org), a permanent collection of pre–American Revolution prints are exhibited, and there's a planetarium and a discovery room for kids on-site. Open Tues through Fri from 9:30 a.m. to 5 p.m. and Sat from 10:30 a.m. to 5 p.m. A small admission fee is charged.

Some of the more popular chow palaces in Wichita Falls are the **Bar-L** (13th Street at Travis Street, Wichita Falls; 940-761-3990), a down-home beer-and-barbecue joint that counts McMurtry and sportswriters among its fans; and **McBride's Land & Cattle** (501 Scott St., Wichita Falls; 940-322-2516; mcbrideslandandcattle.com).

Other Places to Stay in North Texas

CLIFTON

Cell Block
120 Clifton Art Alley
(254) 227-5656
stayaththecellblock.com
The tiny, former city jail has been made over into a delightful, intimate accommodation with modern décor. Best for a twosome, it's equipped with a queen bed, full bath, roof-top deck, fire pit, and vintage record player.

The Screen Door Inn
101 N. Avenue D
(254) 675-STAY
screendoorinn.com
In its earlier life, this century-old building housed a boarding house, apartments, beauty shop, a doctor's office and more. Today, its seven guest rooms—six are upstairs on a long hall decorated with archival photos of Clifton's early days—each bear an old screen door original to the building. A different theme is assigned to each of the comfortable rooms.

DALLAS

Hotel Crescent Court
400 Crescent Ct.
(800) 654-6541 or
(214) 871-3200
crescentcourt.com
Elegant, Turtle Creek–area lodging with excellent restaurants, shopping, and sensational spa.

Warwick Melrose
3015 Oak Lawn Ave.
(214) 521-5151
warwickhotels.com/dallas/
A historic property in Uptown offers 184 rooms, fine dining and one of Dallas' best bars, The Library.

FORT WORTH

Ashton Hotel
610 Main St.
(817) 332-0100
theashtonhotel.com
Fort Worth's first boutique hotel is a lovely place for both business and pleasure travelers, smack in the middle of downtown.

Elegant trappings, nice bar, and restaurant downstairs.

Texas White House
1417 8th Ave.
(817) 923-3597 or
texaswhitehouse.com
One of Fort Worth's historic landmarks, the 1910 Colonial Revival home is often the site of weddings and receptions. Three guest rooms in the main house and suites in the carriage house are renovated, modern and filled with local art. Exceptional breakfast is served by the owner, a classically trained chef.

Three Danes Inn & Baking Company
712 May St.
(817) 72-6365
threedanesinn.com
Pretty 1904 Victorian home operates as a charming B&B with five guest rooms filled with contemporary artwork. There's a bakery on-site, so you know the breakfast is excellent.

GRANBURY

Iron Horse Inn
616 Thorpe Springs Rd.
(817) 330-6497
Ironhorsebb.com
Three beautiful rooms in the Craftsman home offer comfort and tranquility. A big breakfast is included.

NOCONA

Veranda Inn
1523 Highway 82
(940) 825-5111
In addition to 29 modern motel-style rooms, including a large one with a Jacuzzi tub, the property offers RV camping.

WAXAHACHIE

The Chaska House
716 W. Main St.
(972) 937-3390
chaskabb.com
The 1900 home offers four large guest rooms in the main house and guest suites in the carriage house.

Other Places to Eat in North Texas

CLIFTON

Corner Drug Café
102 N. Avenue D
(254) 265-7737
Offering breakfast and lunch by a skilled chef, this homey but stylish eatery specializes in biscuits and gravy, lemon-blueberry muffins, shrimp etouffee, baked potato soup, and buttermilk pie on a menu that changes daily.

Sinclair
215 W. Third St.
(254) 675-8888
sinclairrestaurant.com
A former gas station has been beautifully reimagined and is the place for elevated comfort dishes. Fried green tomatoes with pickled vegetables, Gulf shrimp sautéed and served over grits and blackberry-blueberry cobbler topped with a scoop of vanilla from Henry's Ice Cream are among temptations.

DALLAS

Javier's
4912 Cole Ave.
(214) 521-4211
Real Mexican food—meaning from Mexico's interior—includes steak, roasted chicken, fish, and enchiladas with earthy chile treatments. Open for dinner nightly; prices start from about $20 per meal.

Snuffer's
3526 Greenville Ave.
(214) 826-6850
Laid-back bar and grill popular for its cheeseburgers, cheese fries, big beers, and convivial atmosphere.

Sonny Bryan's
Locations all over
(214) 357-7120 for the 2202 Inwood Rd. location
sonnybryans.com
Possibly the best smoked brisket and ribs anywhere in north Texas. Open for lunch only, seven days a week; meals start at about $5.

DENTON

Hannah's Off the Square
111 W. Mulberry St.
(940) 566-1110
hannahsoffthesquare.com
Exquisite steaks, intriguing vegetarian options, fancy sandwiches, and posh desserts make this perfect for dates, families, or business folks.

FORT WORTH

Carshon's Delicatessen
3133 Cleburne Rd.
(817) 923-1907
carshonsdeli.com
The only kosher-style restaurant in town; the sandwiches and pies are outstanding. Open Tues through Sun for lunch. Meals start at about $5.

Paris Coffee Shop
700 W. Magnolia Ave.
(817) 335-2041

Railhead Smokehouse
2900 Montgomery St.
(817) 738-9808
railheadsmokehouse.com
This is the best place in town for smoked ribs, pork, chicken, and cold schooners of beer. Open Mon through Sat for lunch

and dinner; meals start at about $5.

GRAPEVINE

Gourmet Apples & More/ Mrs G's Tacos & More

5013 W. Northwest Highway
(817) 251-8000
gourmetapples.com
A shop selling fabulous Dutch apple pie and dipped apples doubles as a taqueria offering Rio Grande Valley-style breakfast tacos and lunch.

Mac's on Main

909 S. Main St., Suite 110
(817) 251-6227
macsteak.com
Shrimp and grits, spicy crab cakes, a fine burger and a beautiful steak with excellent wine choices make this a favorite.

Meat U Anywhere

919 W. Northwest Highway
meatuanywhere.com
The barbecue is outstanding, but locals know it's also where you get a darned good breakfast taco, too.

WAXAHACHIE

Catfish Plantation

814 Water St.
(972) 937-9468
catfishplantation.com
The delightful 1895 house is said to be haunted, but that seems to simply enhance the good dining experience found here. in addition to signature fresh catfish, enjoy sweet-potato patties, fried corn, fried chicken, black-eyed peas, bread pudding in rum sauce, and cobbler.

WEATHERFORD

Mesquite Pit

1201 Fort Worth Highway
(817) 596-7046
mesquitepit.com
A big favorite for barbecue and grilled steaks.

The Texas Panhandle

Romance and longing? For the Texas Panhandle? Why not? The pioneers who settled here came with a dream that—with plenty of muscle and heart—they made come true. Although the earth and the elements had their hard edges, the South, Staked, and High Plains also offered sweet repose. Anyone who read the Pulitzer prize–winning *Lonesome Dove* will have a sense of déjà vu upon arrival. The *Llano Estacado* (Staked Plains) stretch north toward the Cap Rock Escarpment, later yielding to the High Plains.

The 16th-century Spanish conquistadors were enamored with the endless grasslands and countless buffalo of the Panhandle, as were the Apaches, who were followed by the Comanches and young American pioneers, determined to find a future. Some would-be gold rushers jumped off the Fort Smith–Santa Fe Trail in the Panhandle, and ranchers came sometime after the Comanches were conquered and forced to the Oklahoma Territory. By 1888, 33 ranches spread to occupy a land the size of Ireland.

Yucca plants shoot sharply skyward, nettles sprout white blooms, and challas burst with pink blossoms after a rainy spring. It's not unusual to drive an infuriatingly straight

highway, then find it inexplicably winding and climbing a bluff before the monotonous view suddenly falls off into a green-and-red valley blanketed in yellow flowers. Purple-red firewheels scale rocky hillsides that are also lined by paths etched by the collared lizard, whose skin ranges from neon green to dusty yellow. Watch out for bushes with 3-inch thorns, but rest assured it's okay to eat the tart sumac berries—Native Americans made their version of Kool-Aid from the stuff.

Barbed-wire fences—which originated on ranches in this region—stretch for thousands of miles, attempting to corral this great openness. The sky grows larger every day. A few of the scarce trees have elongated, gnarled arms that surely were loved by those who administered outlaw justice. And hilly rises where there were once no trees are now populated by the tenacious mesquite.

Just a few years after the buffalo hunters and ranchers came to Texas a century ago, the Native Americans and buffalo had been exterminated. Indeed, Panhandle cattle-empire builders were successful in their work; for a period, there were three cows to every person. Poking around the same plains today, it's easy to trace history. Little has changed, for one matter, and the region's children are accomplished at preservation and continuation, for another. You'll come away wondering why all westerns aren't filmed here—it's so utterly Texan that other places in the state seem almost fraudulent by comparison.

Fandangles & Rattlesnakes

Most likely your Panhandle tour will pick up where our north Texas trail left off. But whether you're approaching the northwest section of Texas from Possum Kingdom Lake, just west of Fort Worth, or coming directly from the Dallas–Fort Worth area, you'll want to follow US 180 west from the Metroplex. First stop is *Albany,* seat of Shackelford County and home to 1,900 Texans, 120 miles west of Fort Worth on US 180.

Albany earned the handle "the home of the Hereford" for being the place where the favorite cattle breed was introduced in Texas's young days. The western heritage associated with the town endures: Hereford and other cattle represent some 90 percent of Shackelford County's agriculture business; historians point out that one of Albany's more famous sons was Edwin Dyess, for whom the Air Force base at Abilene is named; and one of its more infamous guests was prisoner John Selman, who later killed gunman John Wesley Hardin in El Paso.

First stop on the Albany tour is the *Old Jail Art Center,* S. 2nd Street near Walnut Street (325-762-2269; theojac.org), which has achieved status as

JUNE'S FAVORITE ATTRACTIONS

Buffalo Gap Historic Village
Buffalo Gap

Old Jail Art Center
Albany

Cadillac Ranch
Amarillo

Palo Duro Canyon State Park
Canyon

Caprock Canyons State Park
Quitaque

Panhandle Plains Historical Museum
Canyon

Fort Phantom Hill ruins
near Abilene

Perini Ranch Steakhouse
Buffalo Gap

Historic Downtown
Canadian

Rancho Loma
Coleman

one of the finer small art museums in the Southwest, having gained a great deal of stature since its 1980 opening. Several wings have been added to the original structure, which was built in 1877. Some of the masons were paid by the stone, and their initials are visible on many of the large rectangles of stone. The jail once housed the keeper's office, cells, and exercise room, also known as a runaround. Today it contains the remarkable pre-Columbian collection donated by a Mineral Wells resident. Of note are the Chinese terra-cotta tomb figures, dating to 206 BC, and a Buddhist prayer book from Cambodia dating to the 16th century.

In the several new wings added to the jail are such interesting items as art deco doors from the Old Town Drug Store; an exceptional jade and amethyst collection; Picasso drawings; Italian ballroom chairs; and small Henry Moore bronzes. There also are exquisite furnishings, such as a grand piano crafted from tiger-eye oak in 1895. The museum's courtyard is a pretty place for reflection and for the myriad parties held there. Commanding attention in the center is a blockish contemporary windmill carved from native stone by artist Jesus Morales. The museum is open Tues through Sat from 10 a.m. to 5 p.m. and Sun from 2 to 5 p.m. Admission is free.

Just a block away in the City Park on S. Main Street at S. 1st Street, the *Georgia Monument* is a touching site. The stark stone memorial commemorates the five companies of volunteers who made the journey from Georgia to fight with the Texans in their revolution. The majority were killed with Col. James Fannin in the famous massacre at Goliad; nearly 20 years later the Georgia legislature invoiced Texas for $3,000 for guns but waived payment if the

Lone Star State would erect a monument to the victims. Thanks to the citizens of Albany, that was finally accomplished in 1976.

Also downtown at City Park, the **Ledbetter Picket House** occupies the corner of S. Main and S. 1st Streets. The restored 1870s frontier ranch has been relocated from near Fort Griffin so people can better inspect the interior, with items from the Ledbetter Salt Works, built in 1860. *Picket* is the term used for the construction style in which walls are built with vertical rather than horizontal boards. It's open during Fandangle, the annual festival held in June.

When it's time for a meal **Beehive Restaurant and Saloon,** just west of the Albany square on US 180 (325-762-3034; beehivesaloon.com), is not only a good place to dine but also a self-contained point of interest. Chef and co-owner Ali Esfandiary is a petite, jovial man who is retired from Dyess Air Force Base, but he originally comes from Iran. Ali is all smiles and jokes, and as he talks with patrons, it's obvious that he's quite a local favorite. The restaurant is all roadhouse upon first impression, but its interior surprises with homey touches such as curtains and antiques. The menu is fashioned after an old-time newspaper, full of noteworthy items and lore from the 19th century. Atmosphere and details aside, the rib eyes are fork-tender and simply the best in memory, the beautiful prime rib is the size of most placemats, and red snapper and fresh zucchini strips are other delights from the mesquite grill.

From town head 15 miles north on US 283 to **Fort Griffin State Historical Park** (325-762-3592; tpwd.texas.gov), occupying 500 acres along the Clear Fork of the Brazos River. The fort was established in 1867 during the federal reoccupation of Texas after the Civil War, and the cavalry stationed here fought Kiowas and Comanches and helped end their domination of north Texas. Some people know the park chiefly as the home of the state longhorn herd, whose story is as impressive as any in the state. Fort Griffin was along one of the routes through which some 10 million head of Texas longhorns were driven north to the beef markets a century ago. The longhorn was nearing extinction around 1920, and western author J. Frank Dobie was among a handful of men who helped preserve the stock. Descendants of the Dobie herd live at Fort Griffin, while other animals in the state herd live at state parks including Possum Kingdom, Palo Duro Canyon, and LBJ. By loan agreement, University of Texas mascots bearing the name Bevo are obtained from the Fort Griffin herd.

The park grounds also hold a restored bakery, replicas of other fort buildings, and some ruins, with a model of the fort and an exhibit on fort history inside the visitor center. In addition, there are nature and walking trails, restrooms, showers, a picnic area, a playground, and campsites, some with water and electricity.

The Chisholm Trail's Western Trail split off and came through Fort Griffin, and, like Fort Worth, this town was one of the West's wildest for gunslingers, gamblers, and outlaws—and that's where the *Fort Griffin Fandangle* comes in. The grand outdoor musical has been staged by locals for more than 50 years and is one of the more endearing annual events in Texas. Lawlessness and the fortitude it took to endure that, as well as isolation and Native American scares, are celebrated in song, dance, and pageantry, with longhorns and horses helping to create the mood. Close to a quarter of the townspeople—about 300—are involved in the spectacle, which takes place the third and fourth weekends in June. The show begins at 8:30 p.m. on pageant nights, with a barbecue dinner taking place earlier. For reservations and information call (325) 762-3838 or visit the website at fortgriffinfandangle.org.

If you've traveled to Albany from the Fort Worth area, chances are you came this way via Interstate 20. If so, there's a worthwhile lunch stop to note in the town of Eastland: *Love Oak Café* (805 W. Main St., Eastland; 254-629-1791; loveoak.com) is a surprise for both its food and shopping offerings. Found in a newly built, family-owned pharmacy, the lunch counter features homemade soups, salads, and sandwiches made with creativity and expertise. The gift selection, which includes décor and educational toys, is also a find. And several shelves in the grocery area carry quality health food items, too.

If you go back through Albany, then west 8 miles on Highway 6 and south 27 miles on Highway 351, you will arrive in *Abilene,* the Taylor County seat and home to 122,000 residents. A sizable stop on I-20, Abilene is best known as the location of *Dyess Air Force Base,* I-20 at US 277 (325-793-2199; dyess .af.mil), which is a closed base requiring you to obtain a pass at the main gate to enter. Having done that, head for Dyess's *Linear Air Park,* where 25 World War II, Korean, and Vietnam War aircraft displayed outdoors include the C-47 Skytrain and B-17 Flying Fortress, plus B-1 bombers for training and combat. The date changes from year to year, but you may be lucky enough to catch an air show featuring the USAF Thunderbirds. Admission is free, and the air park is open during daylight hours.

For another collection head for the *Grace Museum* (102 Cypress St., Abilene; 325-673-4587; thegracemuseum.org), a cluster of three museums. In the Children's Museum, kids learn, in a participatory way, scientific principles and technology's uses and applications in daily life; at the Fine Arts Museum, exhibits generally include classical to abstract art, using various media; and the Historical Museum profiles Abilene's history, with emphasis on the recent past. Numerous traveling exhibits make stops at this museum center annually. A small admission fee is charged; the museums are open Tues through Sat from 10 a.m. to 5 p.m., and for Thursday Family Night from 5:30 to 8:30 p.m.

JUNE'S FAVORITE ANNUAL EVENTS

Rattlesnake Roundup
Sweetwater, second weekend in March

Texas Cowboy Reunion
Stamford, first weekend in July

Buffalo Gap Wine and Food Summit
Buffalo Gap, mid-April

Texas!
Palo Duro Canyon, June through August

Bob Wills Day
Turkey, last weekend in April

XIT Rodeo and Reunion
Dalhart, first weekend in August

Coors Cowboy Rodeo
Amarillo, early June

National Cowboy Symposium
Lubbock, early September

Fort Griffin Fandangle
Albany, last two weekends in June

Punkin Days
Floydada, weekend closest to Halloween

Thanks to a beloved downtown museum called the *National Center for Children's Illustrated Literature* (102 Cedar St. (325) 673-4586; nccil.org) storybooks come to life on the second weekend in June during the annual Children's Art and Literacy Festival. Each year, the celebration honors an author or illustrator whose contributions fit into the growing population of storybook characters in Abilene you see on permanently display on Abilene street corners and in parks. The most popular grouping of whimsical sculptures in downtown sits facing the Grace Museum in *Everman Park,* where the adored stories of Dr. Seuss prompt young and old to recite favorite lines and rhymes. Find The Lorax, Yertle the Turtle, The Grinch, Green Eggs and Ham, Horton Hears a Who, and The Cat in the Hat in larger-than-life form. North 1st & Pine Streets; (325) 677-1161; abilenecac.org.

Be sure the kids get to see the *Abilene Zoo and Discovery Center* (3 miles east of the center of town on Highway 36, in Nelson Park; 325-676-6085; abilenezoo.org.). The plains of Texas and Africa are represented by 500 species of animals, including coyotes, javelinas, zebras, ostriches, and bison. The herpetarium houses more than 70 different species of reptiles and amphibians. At the Discovery Center, visitors can learn more about various biomes. Open daily 9 a.m. to 5 p.m., with extended hours between Memorial Day and Labor Day. A small admission fee is charged.

Don't miss the chance to explore rough-and-tumble Texas history at *Frontier Texas!* (625 N. 1st St., Abilene; 325-437-2800; frontiertexas.com). A state-of-the-art center spreading over several acres, this ultra-interactive destination's high-tech capabilities let you connect with the people who carved a life out of the wilds across the state, putting you inside a herd of stampeding buffalo, a card game gunfight, Indian battles, and scary prairie weather. This is the perfect jumping-off point for wandering the 700-mile-long Texas Forts Trail, and the museum also has a gift shop stocking a wealth of books, toys, clothes, and home decor, all in a western theme.

Before leaving downtown, check out *Abi-Haus* (959 N. 2nd St. (325) 672-7452, good-haus.com) a popular pub and gathering spot for tricked-out burgers and other food compatible with adult beverages. The bar offerings are turning heads, from crafty cocktails to intriguing beer and wine choices. Next door, *Betty & June* (189 Pine St. (325) 672-1522, betty-june-boutique.myshopify .com) invites you to enjoy a glass of bubbly while shopping in this downtown boutique stocking casual-chic frocks, jewelry, and shoes from New York and Los Angeles.

It won't take too long to claim a pair of custom-made boots at *James Leddy Boots* (1602 N. Treadway, Abilene; 325-677-7811; jamesleddyabilene .com), one of the renowned names in Texas cowboy boots. Order now and you should have your eel, snakeskin, calfskin, lizard, or other exotic leather boots within 2 or 3 months. Prices start at around $500 and top out at about $3,500. Don't forget to order a belt or wallet to match. Open Mon through Fri 8 a.m. to 5 p.m.

If you're ready to stick around Abilene for a night or two, consider one of the incredibly comfortable stays at the *Sayles Ranch Guesthouses.* Choose from among nine meticulously renovated private bungalows, all situated in a historic neighborhood in the heart of town, that invite nearest and dearest to unwind together in style; (325) 669-6856; saylesranch.com.

If your palate demands the very best beef with sides of pampering, you'll put *Perini Ranch Steakhouse* (3002 FR 89, Buffalo Gap; 325-572-3339; periniranch.com), situated in *Buffalo Gap Historic Village,* about 6 miles south of the Abilene city limits, on your must-go list. Owner-chef Tom Perini has served his famous beef at the White House in Washington, D.C., and at the James Beard House in New York, so you're assured of something pretty special. In a rustic setting, diners enjoy 16-ounce roast rib eyes with cowboy potatoes and ranch beans, or baby-back ribs cooked over mesquite. You can get margaritas and good wines to go with your steaks, too, but be warned that weekend crowds may mean a sizable wait for a table. Open Wed and Thurs for dinner and Fri through Sun for lunch and dinner. Call (325) 572-3339 for reservations. If you're looking for a big weekend of Texas cuisine, check out the *Buffalo Gap Wine and Food Summit,* held in mid-April at Perini Ranch, where exceedingly comfortable guest quarters are now an option for overnight stays. Lisa Perini, Tom's wife, has opened a great *Country Market* near the

Sweet Old Baird

The town of *Baird,* just east of Abilene via I-20, was settled in 1880 and was named the *Antiques Capital of West Texas* by the state legislature in 1993. In town you'll find the *Old Rock Jail* at 100 W. 5th St., which was moved from the former county seat of Belle Plain; each block was numbered and the jail was rebuilt exactly as it had been. It's now used as a *Boy Grumpe's,* a candy factory at 206 Market St., which is one of only four candy factories in the US that produces lollipops for business advertising, and one of only two that puts messages on both the stick and the candy.

ranch, too, with kitchen wares and gifts, as well as garden and doggy gifts (1042 Litel St., Buffalo Gap; 800-367-1721).

Spend time before dining to explore *Buffalo Gap,* a restored frontier complex that was once a stopping place along the famous Dodge Cattle Trail, containing relocated historic buildings such as the Taylor County Courthouse and Jail, circa 1879; a railroad depot dating to 1881; Abilene's first blacksmith shop; and Buffalo Gap's own Nazarene Church, built in 1902. A charming trip back in time, Buffalo Gap is open mid-Mar through mid-Nov Mon through Sat from 10 a.m. to 6 p.m. and Sun from noon to 6 p.m.; and mid-Nov through mid-Mar Fri through Sun 10 a.m. to 5 p.m. A small admission fee is charged. Call the village at (325) 572-3365 or visit tfhcc.com.

From Buffalo Gap and Abilene, you have a choice to make—go north or south? If you opt for south, head 44 miles down US 84 to *Coleman.* The old ranching town of 4,400 landed quietly on foodies' maps when word spread about *Rancho Loma,* a small, upscale restaurant and contemporary inn on a ranch just outside of town. Four course dinners are served in the main ranch house on Friday and Saturday night and include dishes like steak tartare, baby beets with farro and feta, fresh pasta with walnut pesto, and short rib with parsnip puree. Overnight stays are in one of five modern rooms with a view of fields and vineyards (2969 County Road 422, Talpa; 325-636-4556; rancholoma .com).

The owners now also offer *Rancho Pizzeria* (414 S. Commercial Ave., Coleman; 325-726-9307; ranchopizzeria.com) in the downtown they're helping to refurbish; the contemporary space is where you'll enjoy olive tapenade with burrata cheese drizzled in truffle oil, and roasted, bright red piquillo chiles stuffed with creamy goat cheese, all served with fresh bread warm from the oven. Crisp, thin pizzas come with such toppings as arugula, prosciutto, roasted shiitakes, and Italian sausage. Those are washed down with wines now produced at *Rancho Loma Vineyards* (411 S. Commercial Ave., Coleman;

325-625-1010; rlv.wine), a new winery with winemaking facilities in the back and an ample tasting room in front. The soaring roofline, chic seating areas, wall-size photo images of Paris and soothing lighting invite sitting for long chats over a bottle of wine. While grapevines planted nearly two years ago on Rancho Loma mature, winemaker Kyle Johnston sources grapes from the Texas High Plains for making assorted delicious wines—there's a good choice in whites, reds and a rosé—that are quickly winning awards. The entrepreneurs have also opened an art gallery on the street, giving you more reasons to hang around town.

Be sure to drift down the street to peruse new finds at **Bonneville** (304 S. Commercial Ave., Coleman; 325-625-1500) the store selling mid-century modern furniture and home accessories; a terrific old Phonola stereo radio-record player and a two-tier Heywood-Wakefield end table are among treasures I've seen. That vibe is duplicated a few blocks west of downtown Coleman at the **Terrace Inn** (605 W. Hillside Dr., Coleman, 325-636-3663; terraceinncoleman .com), a handy, inviting place to chill if you're not overnighting at Rancho Loma. The Terrace Inn occupies a 1950s home with smart, stylish suites dedicated to the era's décor and personalities: A favorite is the Frank Sinatra Suite, with its Rat Pack photography and sleek but infinitely comfortable bed, but the Marilyn Monroe is hard to resist, with private patio under a huge old live oak tree. Afternoon cocktails and a full breakfast are included with the stay.

If you're opting to head north from Abilene, drive 14 miles on FR 600, where the **Fort Phantom Hill Ruins** consist of monolithic, cactus-crowded, crumbled masses of stones. These ruins have a particular poignancy about them, especially in the day's first or last light—it's easy to imagine that desertion was a problem here because of monotony and loneliness. Fort Phantom Hill was established in 1851 for protection against the Comanches as the westward settlement spread. The fort was abandoned in 1854, as the water supply was insufficient; although it mysteriously burned shortly afterward, the fort was later used as a Texas Rangers outpost and as a US Army outpost during the Indian Wars of the 1870s. The ruins lie on private property today, but the owner keeps the site open to the public daily from dawn to dusk. Admission is free.

Abilene serves as a good pivot point to reach two more marvelous pockets of the Old West. First is **Anson,** 24 miles northwest of Abilene via US 83/277, the seat of Jones County. The town was long known and widely criticized until a few years ago for banning dancing—except at the Christmas Ball—for religious reasons. Times have changed slightly, but most citizens still choose to go dancin' in Anson only for the three days every December when Anson hosts its historic **Cowboys' Christmas Ball,** usually held the weekend prior to Christmas. Anson has quite a time letting its citizens cut a rug, and western crooner Michael Martin Murphey has put into song and video the century-old poem honoring the ball, written by rancher Larry Chittenden. If you miss the dancin', check out the other element that drew the locals' ire: The Depression-era mural in Anson's post office offended folks at its 1941 unveiling, as some townspeople felt it was wrong to illustrate the fun people were having on the dance floor. (This is the Bible Belt, remember.) See the mural depicting the Christmas Ball in the post office on tiny Main Street (325-823-2241).

Now point your car to our next side trip, to *Stamford,* 17 miles north of Anson on US 277, still in Jones County and with a population of 3,800. You're in true cowboy country here, as Stamford is home to the *Texas Cowboy Reunion* held for three days over the weekend closest to July 4. Begun more than 60 years ago, it hosts unquestionably the world's greatest amateur rodeo, drawing more than 500 competitors and thousands of fans. The festival includes chuck wagon meals, a huge western art show, and lots of music. Call the chamber of commerce at (325) 773-2411 or visit the event site at tcrrodeo.com.

For a better understanding of Stamford's cowboy history, head to the *Cowboy Country Museum,* 113 S. Wetherbee St., Stamford (325-773-2500; stamfordcoc.org/museum.htm). Well-known cowboy artists have paintings and prints displayed here, and other exhibits include ranch and farm artifacts from a century ago, as well as a blacksmith shop. The museum is open Mon through Fri from 9 a.m. to noon and 1 to 4 p.m. Admission is free.

There may not be a better place to capture on film the heritage of this region than at the *Mackenzie Trail Monument,* at the intersection of US 277 and Highway 6. This immense, sand-colored stone marker was hand carved to depict the days of the famous Mackenzie Trail (1874–1900) and the buffalo, Native Americans, pioneers, and early ranchers who figured into this history. Open at all hours.

Now we're off to rattlesnake country: Head west from Abilene on I-20, following it 42 miles to *Sweetwater,* seat of Nolan County and home to 12,000 salty Texans. The community came about when buffalo hunters in the 1870s camped on Sweet Water Creek simply because they preferred the sweet, clear water there over the area's other, gypsum-flavored streams. The humble beginnings continued with the opening of a dugout trading post in 1877; then the town charter—first established in 1884—failed twice due to blizzard, drought, and resulting evacuation. After the 1902 incorporation held, the area grew during World War II, when the Women's Air Force Service Pilots training program was based at the local *Avenger Field.* The world's first and only all-women military flying school produced a little more than 1,000 pilots out of 25,000

We'll Leave the Light on for You

Drive 46 miles east of Abilene via I-20 to the town of **Cisco** in order to visit the **Mobley Hotel,** 309 Conrad Hilton Ave. (also Highway 6). In 1919, Conrad Hilton, who needed a place to sleep, purchased the old hotel. It became the first in a chain of Hilton hotels when Hilton realized he could make a bundle by letting rooms to oil-field workers who would rent by the shift. Today the restored hotel serves as a chamber of commerce office and community center.

applicants. The 39 who died in service are honored with a bronze statue and a walk of fame on the campus of Texas State Technical College–Sweetwater at Avenger Field, on I-20 West at Sweetwater Municipal Airport (325-235-8478). Open during daylight hours.

Plan your arrival in time for lunch, as you wouldn't want to miss a chance to use your boardinghouse reach at **Allen Family Style Meals** (1301 E. Broadway St., Sweetwater; 325-235-2060), not unlike Sunday dinner with a big family. For less than $10 you can eat family-style from a long table spread with a plastic tablecloth and set with unmatched plates. For lunch your table will be filled with plates and bowls weighted down with not only fried chicken but also cream gravy, beef brisket, buttered potatoes, candied sweet potatoes, potato salad, turnip greens, green beans, stewed summer squash, corn, English pea salad, pinto beans, fruit salad, rolls, peach cobbler, and iced tea. The restaurant has been a favorite for more than 60 years and will soon be one of yours. Open Tues through Sun for lunch.

If good fortune was in your planning, you'll have arrived in Sweetwater on the second weekend in March—that's when the town is jumping, thanks to some 20,000 or 30,000 folks who show up for the annual **Rattlesnake Roundup.** Some six or seven tons of rattlesnakes are gathered during this, the world's largest such event. Several other Texas towns have followed suit, but Sweetwater's is the oldest, having begun in 1958 when the Jaycees pitched in to help local ranchers and farmers deal with their tremendous rattlesnake problem. The roundup became a festival, and the rest—as is widely said in the western reaches of this state—is history. The weekend is filled with a parade, the Miss Snake Charmer Queen Contest, real hunts for western diamondback rattlers, professional snake-handling demonstrations, snake-milking for medical research, a 10K run, a dance, a tour of rattlesnakes' natural habitats, and a rattlesnake-eating contest. Fried rattlesnake is available, as are numerous other—and less exotic—snacks. And there's a weigh-in and prize ceremony for the most snakes captured and the largest. All the fun takes place at the Nolan

County Coliseum at the north end of Elm Street. Call (325) 235-5488 or visit rattlesnakeroundup.net for schedules, details, and ticket information.

Now it's time to head into the Panhandle Plains: take I-20 west 8 more miles until you pick up US 84 and follow it 30 miles north to *Snyder,* found right at the US 180 West exit. This is the seat of Scurry County, with a population of 12,000 and—more important—a monument saluting a rare beast, the *White Buffalo Statue,* on the courthouse lawn at College and 25th Streets. One of the many, many buffalo hunters who killed off the valuable herds here claimed that among the 22,000 buffalo he killed was a rare albino, shot near Snyder. To honor the herds Snyder's townspeople put up this life-size replica of the albino buffalo. Some say the beast began as a bull buffalo, but respect for delicate sensitivities rendered it a cow instead.

Cap Rock & Canyons

Now we head into some of the most physically compelling country, if regarded with respect by those who spent lifetimes trying to tame it. Taking country roads at this point is the way to best drink in the often parched land, fascinating to anyone with an eye for prehistoric aesthetics. From Snyder, take Highway 208 north 57 miles to the town of Spur, passing through Clairemont. Now skirting the Cap Rock's eastern edge, head north 20 miles on FR 836 to US 82, then go west just another 6 miles, actually driving onto the famous escarpment. Watch for a roadside park on the left, and you'll have found *Silver Falls Park,* a stop said by many to be the finest of all roadside parks in the vast state. The White River courses through this part of the Cap Rock and its canyon land on its way south to join the Brazos River, and state engineers were wise enough to place picnic tables and carve riverside hiking paths here for journey makers

Horse Heritage

The *American Quarter Horse Heritage Center* at 2601 I-40 East, Amarillo (806-376-4811; aqha.com), explores the magnificence of the quarter horse from its days as the working ranch horse of the American West to the equine competitor of the modern world. Its life is examined from the 17th century, when the breed was developed in the Western Hemisphere, to the present day. The renovated, updated complex is also the international headquarters of the *American Quarter Horse Association,* the world's largest horse registry. Open Mon through Sat from 9 a.m. to 5 p.m. and Sun from noon to 5 p.m. Call ahead for a guided tour. A small admission fee is charged.

Cup of Joe on the Mother Road

Departing Amarillo early in the morning meant finding a really good cup of coffee to motivate us for a long drive. Just west of downtown, we discovered *The 806*, a funky coffeehouse sitting amid the Route 66 stash of antiques stores, tattoo parlors, saloons, and eating joints. A few people sat in pairs outside at sidewalk tables, sipping coffee and reading newspapers, so we ventured in. The interior, straightened up nicely after the previous evening's live music show, held a ramshackle collection of well-worn furniture, as well as nooks and crannies where we could chill as we wished, while reading novels and nonfiction esoterica pulled from myriad shelving. Locally produced artwork includes random paintings, along with a couple of graphic nude studies. A quiet but focused barista turned out perfect cups of caffeine for us, including cafe au lait (made with freshly roasted, fair-trade coffee beans) and green tea chai latte that we enjoyed with toasted bagels. Specialty creations at The 806 include the Mad Hatter, a mixture of espresso and iced Thai coffee, and the Spyder, mixed house-made spiced chai with hot apple cider, topped with whipped cream and caramel syrup. Plans to visit Cadillac Ranch, just west of town, had us on the road again shortly. But we're discussing a return visit for a serving of The 806's veggie pizza and vegan chili, both of which seem rather more healthful than that green chile burger, anyway. Find The 806 at 2812 SW 6th Ave., Amarillo; (806) 322-1806; the806.com.

like yourself. Perhaps you've picked up snacks or sandwiches on the way; this is a perfect place to stretch your legs and take some scenery photos.

It's just another 4 miles west to the town of *Crosbyton,* seat of Crosby County and home to 2,000. It's in the heart of an agricultural land, and the local Associated Cotton Growers is said to be the world's largest cotton-processing plant of stripped cotton, serving more than 500 cotton companies in a 50-mile area. Crosbyton is also home to the *Pioneer Memorial Museum* (101 Main St., Crosbyton; 806-675-2331; cityofcrosbyton.org/site/visitors/pioneer-memorial/). Inside, the pioneer lifestyle is illustrated with home replicas and admirable collections of vintage housewares, arts, and farm equipment. Native American relics and artifacts relevant to the local ecology are exhibited, too. Open Tues through Sat from 9 a.m. to noon and 1 to 5 p.m. Admission is free.

From here head north 23 miles on FR 651 to *Floydada,* seat of Floyd County, home to 3,700 Texans and the undisputed Pumpkin Capital of the US. If it's autumn, you've no doubt seen some awesome pumpkins—they call the hundred-pounders "Big Macs"—at markets and along roadsides in Texas, and you can bet they came from here. The town's annual *Punkin Days* is a festival held on the courthouse square the weekend closest to Halloween. Stop in for some pumpkin bowling, pie tastings, seed-spitting contests, and carving competitions. Most events are free. Find the fun at Main and Missouri Streets; for details call (806) 983-3322.

Now it's time to cross the Cap Rock again, heading east on US 62/70 from Floydada 24 miles to Matador, where you'll pick up Highway 70 north, following it 28 miles to **Turkey,** a Hall County town and site of the **Bob Wills Museum** (on 6th Street at Lyles Street, Turkey; 806-423-1253 or 806-423-1491; churchofwesternswing.net/Turkey), intriguing to anyone with even a passing interest in the music called Western Swing. The museum's collection dedicated to the King of Western Swing—who was born just outside of town and whose daughter has moved back to Turkey to run the foundation—includes fiddles, boots, hats, recordings, sheet music, and photos belonging to or representing the Texas Playboys, Wills's band.

Open Mon through Fri from 8 a.m. to noon and 1 to 5 p.m. and weekends by appointment. Admission is free; however, donations are accepted. Inquire, too, about Bob Wills Day, usually held the last weekend in April, with a parade, fiddlers' contest, dances, and performances by members of the original Texas Playboys.

The town is home to, naturally, the **Hotel Turkey** (3rd and Alexander Streets, Turkey; 806-423-1151; hotelturkeytexas.com). Restored in the late 1980s, the cluttered but comfortable hotel draws plenty of Bob Wills fans, as he played here in the late 1920s, as well as people who simply enjoy old hotels. Guest rooms are filled with original furniture and wallpaper adorned with hand-sewn decorations, while the front parlor downstairs is furnished with century-old sofas, chairs, and tables. The 40-seat dining room is decked out with antique photos of Turkey's residents. A hot breakfast is served to guests, and a modest gift shop sells new and used knickknacks.

From Turkey, turn west on Highway 86 and travel 13 miles to RR 1065, following it north for just over 3 miles until you reach **Caprock Canyons State Park,** just inside Briscoe County and 3 miles beyond the tiny town (population 500) of Quitaque (KIT-a-KWAY). You may want to stock up on some groceries and camping goods in that town or back in Turkey, as this little-known park is an ideal place to kick back a while and savor this rugged country. The views here of mountains, canyons, streams, and indigenous flora and fauna are simply breathtaking, and a visitor center offers an interpretive area plus an archaeological site, with artifacts representing the canyon for some 250 million years. There's a 100-acre lake for swimming, fishing, and boating, but the real draw—besides the vistas, of course—is the hiking trails, 25 miles of paths coursing through the mountainous, 14,000 acres of parkland. Be on the lookout, especially on mountain trails, for buffalo and antelope, among several species of wild animals. Joining you on the paths may be horseback riders, mountain bikers, or campers who brought their own mounts. Camping is in both primitive and improved campsites. The park is always open, and a small admission fee is charged. Call (806) 455-1492 or visit tpwd.texas.gov for more information.

After the relaxation you can get to **Amarillo,** seat of Potter County and home to about 200,000 people, by driving north from Caprock Canyons on Highway 86 not quite 9 miles and taking Highway 256 west another 9 miles until you reach Highway 207 North, which will put you on a scenic route across the majestic **Palo Duro Canyon,** which we'll explore in detail later. For now stay on Highway 207, 48 miles until you reach US 287 at the town of Claude, and follow that highway west 28 miles to the Amarillo city limits.

texastrivia

The world's largest (and oldest) rattlesnake roundup is held every March in Sweetwater.

Amarillo's humble beginnings date to its 1887 establishment as Ragtown, a railroad workers' tent camp. Today it's a mammoth center of cattle trade, and there are wonderful places to buy western artwork and clothing. Some lovely historic homes are on view, as are an art museum and a well-known science and technology museum.

To get a taste of Amarillo's tremendous cattle heritage, make your first stop at the city's **Livestock Auction,** held in the stockyards at 100 S. Manhattan St., Amarillo, every Mon at 11 a.m. As you walk in, the auctioneer's rhythmic patter with odd inflections meets your ears as assorted cows and

The 72-ounce Steak Challenge

The quintessential, Texas-size experience is found in lunch or supper at the **Big Texan Steak Ranch,** 7701 I-40 East at Lakeside exit (806-372-6000 or 800-657-7177; bigtexan.com). Resembling a circus arena, the cavernous interior is fascinating, with a giant wooden Indian, a stuffed grizzly greeting you at the entrance, and big-game trophies covering every wall. Chairs and benches are fashioned from horseshoes, of course. The menu is laden with buffalo, rattlesnake, rabbit, calf fries (the most private of calf parts), chicken-fried steak, and ribeye steak. The fanfare, however, surrounds the presentation of a 72-ounce prime steak dinner that's free if the diner eats the whole thing—with the accompanying salad, shrimp cocktail, baked potato, bread, and butter—in 1 hour. Some do it, but it's a true challenge. There's a craft brewery now operating on-site, too, and there's a gift shop on the premises with plenty of kitschy Texas souvenirs. The restaurant is open daily for lunch and dinner.

bulls are moved quickly for viewing through the main room's bottom, from which rise bleachers for spectators and bidders. Outside, the purchased cattle are herded into pens one at a time, usually by a few no-nonsense cowgirls, who are the only indication that anything has changed in the past 100 years. To understand the significance of this place, note that more than 300,000 cattle are sold here every year, making this the largest individually owned auction in the state. It's the world's largest weekly livestock auction, and annual sales are in the millions. Even if you miss auction day, you can look around the place; admission is always free.

Explore Amarillo's high-tech side at ***Don Harrington Discovery Center and Planetarium,*** in the 50-acre Amarillo Garden Center at 1200 Streit Dr., Amarillo (806-355-9547 or 800-784-9548; dhdc.org). Named for a local oil mogul and philanthropist, the complex presents a number of special films that make science fascinating for kids and adults. The Discovery Center also presents Smithsonian traveling exhibits and several interactive displays for all ages.

And in tribute to Amarillo's standing as chief helium producer in the US, a leggy, four-pronged ***Helium Monument*** stands in front of the Discovery Center. The structure functions as a futuristic sundial, and its limbs are time capsules filled with newspapers, a Sears catalog, and a piece of apple pie sealed in helium. The Discovery Center is open Tues through Sat from 9:30 a.m. to 4:30 p.m. and Sun from noon to 4:30 p.m. Admission is charged. Planetarium shows are included with admission.

Antiques hounds will love the ***Old San Jacinto*** area, located on 6th Street along historic Route 66 (between Georgia and Western Streets). Those in the know think this is becoming the premier antiques center of the Southwest, with dozens of delightful shops selling treasures dating from the turn of the 20th century. While away the morning or afternoon browsing, then stop at any of the several cafés along the strip. Most shops are open Mon through Sat from 10 a.m. to 5:30 p.m. and Sun from 1 to 5 p.m.

Right in the same neighborhood, there's the ***Golden Light Cafe and Cantina*** (2908 W. 6th Ave., Amarillo; 806-374-9237; goldenlightcafe.com), a hamburger joint dating from 1946. This creaky little place gets its atmosphere from neon beer signs and cooking that would never be deemed acceptable by the American Heart Association. Regulars mosey in and plan to sit a spell, waiting on handmade burgers and other

texas*trivia*

Floydada, a Panhandle town, calls itself Pumpkin Capital, USA, and celebrates in late October with ***Punkin Days.*** Fun includes costume contests, pumpkin bowling, pumpkin rolling, pumpkin seed spitting, pumpkin pie relays, and more.

bodacious platters of food, along with cold bottles of Shiner Bock beer. Grab a booth and get ready to travel back in time and enjoy some live music.

After shopping and lunch, treat yourself to the happiest surprise in this dry, flat city. At the renovated and updated Amarillo Botanical Gardens, you'll find the new *Mary Bivins Tropical Conservatory* (1400 Streit Dr., Amarillo; 806-352-6513; amarillobotanicalgardens.org). Within its glass pyramid, you'll roam through more than 6,000 square feet of lush flowers and trees meant to transport you to a South American rain forest. Sit by the rock waterfall and pond and feel stress slipping away. Depending on the calendar, you may stumble upon a horticulture workshop or lecture or perhaps catch an art exhibit on display.

For some of the great outdoors, stretch your legs during a hike at the *Wildcate Bluff Nature Center* (2301 N. Soncy St., Amarillo; 806-352-6007; wildcatbluff.org), a 640-acre retreat on the west side of town. Once part of the Frying Pan Ranch, it's thought to be the location of the last wildcat den in Pottery County. There are traditional hiking trails as well as Libb's Trail, a concrete path with special points of interest for those who walk a little slower or have special needs.

Amarillo's re-energized downtown is a new focal point for visitors exploring this part of the Texas Panhandle. *Center City* is the nonprofit organization responsible for overseeing and promoting the preservation of this historic heart of Amarillo. You'll see *Hoof Prints,* the public art project begun by the American Quarter Horse Association, featuring painted horse statues around town; dozens are in Center City alone. Inquire about downtown walking tours led by Michael Grauer, curator of art and western heritage for the *Panhandle-Plains Historical Museum,* who leads the way on narrated explorations of the city's vintage architecture and heritage sites (Bivins Mansion, corner of 10th and Polk streets, Amarillo; 806-372-6744; centercity.org).

Center City is a dining and nightlife destination now, as well. Among places to eat and drink well and hear live music, check out *Crush* (701 S. Polk St., Amarillo; 806-418-2011; crushdeli.com), a chic wine bar and bistro, noted for its craft beer list, a significant wine selection available by the glass (a pneumatic wine system is employed) and bottle, and an impressive chef-driven menu; *Napoli's* (700 S. Taylor St, Amarillo; 806-220-2588; napolisofamarillo .com), an award-winning, old-school Italian dining spot offering specialties from southern Italy in a friendly setting with a pretty patio; *OHMS* (619 S. Tyler St., Amarillo; 806-373-3233; ohmscafe.com), a café and bar that's long been a favorite for a taste of Santa Fe, Panhandle-style, and a place exhibiting local artwork; and *Six Car Pub and Brewery* (625 S. Polk St., Amarillo; sixcarpub .com), a new craft brewery with rooftop dining and gastropub fare, as well as a Texas wine list. *Esquire Jazz Club* (626 S. Polk St., Amarillo; 806-350-4299;

esquirejazzclub.com) occupies the 1947 Woolworth's building and a former courthouse. Now a place for live jazz, it's a good place to enjoy cocktails, too.

Your opportunities for immersion in the western culture are greater if you're in Amarillo in early June—that's when the ***Coors Cowboy Club Ranch Rodeo*** happens. It kicks off with a weeknight cattle drive on Polk Street, when more than 60 longhorns are pushed along downtown's main thoroughfare, evoking traditions of more than a century ago when cattle were driven to railheads on the north side of town. The weekend rodeo happens at the Tri-State Fairground and involves cowboys and cowgirls from regional ranches in Texas, Oklahoma, New Mexico, Kansas and Colorado; see details at coors ranchrodeo.com.

At any time of year, explore the heritage of the horse that is so vital to the American West with a visit to the ***American Quarter Horse Hall of Fame & Museum,*** a magnificent museum that tells the story of the beautiful animal (1600 Quarter Horse Dr., Amarillo; 806-376-4811; aqha.com).

For more visitor information call the ***Amarillo Convention and Visitor Council*** at (800) 692-1338 or (806) 374-1497, or visit the website at visit amarillo.com.

Just outside of town, 12 miles to the west on I-40—also the epic Route 66—***Cadillac Ranch*** is the unique creation of the late Stanley Marsh 3 (as he was faithfully called), land and broadcasting baron and easily one of the more powerful of all the personalities of modern Texas. Known always for his noteworthy and eccentric ways, he made his contribution to pop culture in a cotton field with a lineup of 10 Cadillacs buried nose-down, exhibiting tail-fin designs from between 1949 and 1963 diagonally into the air. Worth noting is that the cars are buried at precisely the same angle to the ground as the great Cheops pyramids. Graffiti artists have made their own contributions, as the art display—called Amarillo's "bumper crop"—is always open. No admission is charged.

From the ranch take Highway 136 north to ***Alibates National Monument,*** a mostly undeveloped site popular with hikers and archaeology buffs. The area atop a high ridge overlooking Lake Meredith contains an ancient quarry of flint, unique for its amazing colors. Farmers and Native Americans distributed Alibates flint over the Southwest and Great Plains from 10,000 BC until the 19th century. The quarry itself is overgrown with grass and shrubs, so you won't know you've found it until you're in it. The stones are flat, somewhat smooth, and shaded with muted blues and grays, black, maroon, and orange. Nearby, great pits of buffalo bones have been found, along with pottery dating to AD 1250. A Native American village was excavated in a 1938–39 project, and pictographs were found in huge dolomite boulders. Ranger-led walks, extremely helpful for visitors, conclude with flint-chipping instruction. Free tours are offered during summer at 10 a.m. and 2 p.m. and by appointment for the balance of the year. Admission is always free, and the monument is open during daylight hours. Call (806) 857-3151 for information and reservations.

The monument lies on the south shore of Lake Meredith, site of *Lake Meredith National Park.* Fashioned from the Canadian River, the lake is 2 miles wide in places and 14 miles long, offering 100 miles of shoreline. The National Park Service has created eight recreation areas with swimming in a lake and swimming pool, fishing, sailboating, and waterskiing. There are places to play golf and tennis, too. If you've picked up provisions in Amarillo or in nearby Fritch, you can choose a place from several bluffs and canyons around the lake for picnicking and camping. Open at all times, admission is free, but there are fees for boating. Call (806) 857-3151 for information.

Another good sidetrip from Amarillo leads you to *Claude,* a town about 28 miles southeast of the city via US 287. That's where you find the *Charles Goodnight Historical Center* (charlesgoodnight.org), an Armstrong County museum on the edge of the legendary Llano Estacado. It's a magnet for fans of the Emmy Award-winning mini-series "Lonesome Dove," as this is the home of Charles Goodnight, believed to be the person upon whom Larry McMurtry based the character of Texas Ranger Captain Augustus "Gus" McCrae in his Pulitzer Prize-winning novel. Goodnight had a major interest in the JA Ranch, one of the largest ranches in Texas, and he's credited with inventing the chuck wagon, a vital piece of equipment for ranches and cowboys on long cattle drives. He was also close to Quanah Parker, one of the last chiefs of the Comanche Indians, with whom he is credited for saving the Southern Bison herd bloodline that roamed the plains.

Your wanderings from Amarillo might also lead to the town of *Pampa,* a ranching town with a strong oil and agricultural background, 55 miles northeast of Amarillo via US 60. As you follow the highway, you'll see skyscrapers appear on the otherwise bare horizon, but soon you'll realize they're grain elevators that characterize much of the landscape here. Your reason for stopping here is to visit *Coney Island Cafe* (114 W. Foster St., Pampa; 806-669-9137), a simple diner opened in 1933 by Greek immigrants. The chili dogs, chicken and dumplings, homemade pinto beans and cornbread, Frito chili pie, and stew are very popular, but the homemade pies—buttermilk and apricot are among the 16 daily varieties—are outstanding and worth every calorie.

Continuing east along US 60, you'll cross the magnificent, scenic Canadian Breaks, eroded almost to canyons by the legendary Canadian River. Fifty miles beyond Pampa, you'll come upon the marvelous little town of *Canadian,* tucked into a wooded bend of the river, grown from a settlement once known

Adobe Walls

History buffs will want to seek out the site of the *Battle of Adobe Walls,* where two famous Native American battles were fought. In 1864 Col. Kit Carson fought his last fight when his US troops barely escaped defeat by Kiowas and Comanche who had been assaulting wagon trains and settlers. Ten years later, in 1874, Quanah Parker and Lone Wolf led a tribe in an attack on a buffalo hunters' camp, but they were eventually scared away when the famous shot by William "Billy" Dixon took a brave from his horse at a distance of roughly 0.8 mile. The Adobe Walls site is roughly 18 miles northeast of Stinnett, which is northeast of Amarillo and near Lake Meredith. Inquire in Stinnett as to local tours.

only to cavalry soldiers, railroad builders, and cowpokes. Today you'll find a surprising collection of elegant, historic homes, lovingly restored buildings, good dining, bed-and-breakfast lodging, boutiques, and an exceptional art museum and an art center.

If you can't stay overnight in Canadian, allow at least half a day to explore. Be sure your stops in the downtown district include the *W.C.T.U. Building* at 500 Main St., which is the only building in the nation built, owned, or maintained by a local Woman's Christian Temperance Union chapter. Built in 1911, the ornate structure houses the county library today. Other worthwhile stops downtown include the *Palace Theatre* at 210 Main St., opened as a vaudeville house in 1909 and operating as a first-run movie house today; and the *City Drug Soda Fountain* at 224 Main St., a renovated 1910 structure that uses authentic soda fountain equipment and original furnishings today. The *Citadelle Art Foundation* (520 Nelson Ave., Canadian, 806-323-8899; thecitadelle .org) occupies a grand 1910 church building and exhibits a stunning collection of 150 paintings, as well as sculpture and fine antiques, all from around the world. The *Canadian River Art Center* (312 Main St., Canadian; 806-323-8250) exhibits more contemporary art in the way of paintings and pottery. Main Street and 2nd Street are both filled with places for shopping.

Make a quick detour immediately north of town via US 60/83 to see the *Canadian River Historic Wagon Bridge,* originally constructed in 1915, when it was the longest metal truss bridge in the state. Restored in 2000, its wood planking serves as a trail across the river for walkers, cyclists, birders, and other wildlife watchers. Nearby the Gene Howe Wildlife Management Area offers driving tours with beautiful scenery.

You won't go hungry long in Canadian. Barbecued brisket and mesquite-grilled steaks are best at the *Cattle Exchange* (2nd at Main Streets, Canadian;

806-323-6755; cookya.com).Breakfast and daily lunch specials are served up at The Bucket (207 S. 2nd St, Canadian; 806-323-8200).

Among several interesting accommodations choices in and around Canadian, one of particular note is the **Arrington Ranch House Lodge** (9765 County Road 5, Canadian; 806-323-6924; arringtonranch.com). Featured in the final scene in Tom Hanks's film *Cast Away,* the 5-bedroom home was a mail-order house built in 1918. The original owner was a Texas Ranger known as Capt. George Washington Arrington, and his great-grandson owns the home today. Perfect for family reunions, the home is roomy and extremely comfortable, with impressive views of the sunrises and sunsets. For more Canadian information and a full list of shopping, dining and lodging, visit the **Canadian Chamber of Commerce** at 119 N. 2nd St., or call (806) 323-6234; canadiantx.org.

Another good side trip from Amarillo is that to **Dalhart,** seat of Dallam County, home to almost 6,300 residents. To reach it from the north side of Lake Meredith, follow RR 1319 north about 11 miles to Highway 152, follow it west 20 miles to Dumas, and then go west on US 87, 39 miles to Dalhart. The route from Amarillo is north on US 287, 49 miles to Dumas and west on US 87, 39 miles to Dalhart.

The reason for this journey is to explore the heritage of the world-renowned **XIT Ranch** and today's **XIT Museum.** Here you'll discover the considerable history of the XIT, which in the 1880s was the largest ranch in the world under a single fence, which stretches 6,000 miles. It was created when investors from up north were contracted to erect the $3 million granite capitol building in Austin in exchange for this 3 million acres of land. The ranch spread across an area that today covers nine counties and was 27 miles in average width and 200 miles long between north and south fences.

The XIT Museum (108 E. 5th St., Dalhart; 806-244-5390; xitmuseum.com) tells the whole story, which involved 150 cowboys and the running of 150,000 head of cattle. The investors lost interest, however, and sold off the cattle and split the ranch into pieces. The museum lies inside a renovated art deco building and contains photographs, documents, an antique gun collection, and reconstructed period rooms such as a parlor, bedroom, and kitchen. Native American relics and Peter Hurd paintings are exhibited as well. The Pioneer Chapel, created from pieces of Dalhart's first six churches, today is frequently the site of weddings. The museum is open Tues through Sat from 9 a.m. to 5 p.m. Admission is free.

To see more of the XIT legacy, drive to a traffic island adjacent to the underpass at US 87 North and US 385. There you'll find the **Empty Saddle Monument,** honoring all XIT cowboys. The story behind it concerns an XIT cowboy who died just before the annual reunion; his widow requested that his horse be allowed to participate in the parade, and today's parade is always led by a saddled horse without a rider.

Plan your arrival in Dalhart to coincide with the first Thursday, Friday, and Saturday in August, and you'll enjoy the *XIT Rodeo and Reunion,* held in Rita Blanca Park, US 87 South at FR 281 West. This is the world's largest amateur rodeo and features a free barbecue of six tons of beef. The parade, junior rodeo, nightly dance, antique car show, and 5K run add to the revelry. For information and ticket prices, call (806) 244-5646; xitrodeorcunion.com.

The final side trip from Amarillo is a bit ambitious but may be worth it to those who have Irish blood coursing through their veins. *Shamrock,* a town of 2,200 residents, in Wheeler County, is located 86 miles east of Amarillo via I-40. This is the site of Texas's own *Blarney Stone,* in Elmore Park, 400 E. 2nd St. Someone in this town convinced the keepers of the original in County Cork, Ireland, to donate a small piece of their famous rock; it sits on a pedestal and is offered at all hours to anyone who cares to kiss it. Legend holds that those who do are given the gift of eloquence. The Irish celebration of St. Patrick's Day is held annually on the weekend closest to March 17 all over town. There's a carnival, bazaar, old settlers' reunion, beard contest, fiddling contest, chili cook-off, dances, cowboy roping contests, and a Miss Irish Rose pageant. Call the chamber of commerce for information at (806) 256-2501.

Now it's time to make a trek back down the Panhandle, stopping first at *Canyon*—just 16 miles south of Amarillo via I-27—seat of Randall County, home to nearly 13,000 Texans, and site of the exceptional *Panhandle Plains Historical Museum.* Found on the campus of Texas A&M West University, 1 block east of US 87 at 2503 4th Ave. (806 651 2244; panhandleplains.org), the museum holds the honor of being the state's largest historical center. Up

Panhandle's Little Tree

About 5 miles southwest of the town of Panhandle, which is the seat of Carson County, you can visit *Thomas Cree's Little Tree,* the site of the first tree planted throughout the entire Panhandle. On plains that were once a sea of grass, pioneer settler Thomas Cree brought a sapling *bois d'arc* (pronounced "BOE dark") for planting behind his home in 1888. The tree lived until 1969, when an agricultural chemical was accidentally used here; county residents planted a new tree, which sits behind a fence at the south edge of US 60. Be sure to note two State Historical Markers and a medallion from the National Men's Garden Clubs of America.

front, the building's busy 1933 art deco exterior offers friezes depicting an array of Texana designs from spurs to brands. Inside, a time-line approach is used to relate the geological, social, cultural, industrial, and financial development of northwest Texas. Murals in the main hall overwhelm onlookers with an overview, and dinosaurs liven up the geological displays. Pioneer life, Native Americans, and Texas ranching have individual exhibit areas, and the three-floor annex is outfitted with a 1925 cable tool drilling rig. Other oil-patch relics piece together the story of oil and gas discovery and development in west Texas. Several excellent art galleries offer permanent and traveling exhibits, and a good gift shop sells books, games, jewelry, and art. Open Memorial Day through Labor Day Mon through Sat from 9 a.m. to 6 p.m. and Sun from 1 to 6 p.m. From Labor Day to Memorial Day it's open Mon through Sat from 9 a.m. to 5 p.m. and Sun from 1 to 6 p.m. Admission is charged.

Then you'll want to continue east of town 12 miles on Highway 217 to **Palo Duro Canyon State Park.** Here the Panhandle's arid climate, chilly mornings, cool evenings, and clean air are pleasingly exaggerated during spring, summer, and fall in the spectacular chasm, cut 120 miles long by a branch of the Red River. Rich in geological, Native American, and pioneer history, the canyon's rock formations rise and fall a little more than 1,000 feet, showing 90 million years of earth formation, baring brilliant walls colored ocher, red, and coral by the spirits of time. The Coronado expedition took shelter here in 1541 while looking for the fabled Quivira, and they decided *palo duro*—meaning "hard wood"—was appropriate for the tough juniper trees that still flourish here. What's so surprising and invigorating about the Palo Duro Canyon are its green trees and even greener meadows when the rain's been plentiful. Most of the canyon's beauty secrets are revealed in the state park, covering a 16,400-acre portion of the canyon.

An 8-mile paved road takes you rim to floor and affords unforgettable vistas. Hiking, camping, picnicking, and horseback riding are loads of fun. Open in summer daily from 6 a.m. to 10 p.m. and from 8 a.m. to 10 p.m. the rest of the year; admission is charged. Call (806) 488-2227 for reservations and information; paloduro canyon.com. Be sure to visit the park's interpretive center and store, which stocks great gifts and a fine selection of books on pertinent culture and history.

The park's **Pioneer Amphitheater** on the canyon floor is the scene of an outdoor drama called *Texas,* which lights up the sky on summer nights. The story of the Panhandle, its gritty people, and the spirit that helped them conquer the land is told through such characters as Quanah Parker, the last great Comanche chief; Col. Ranald "Bad Hand" Mackenzie, Civil War hero and Parker's main nemesis; buffalo hunters Billy Dixon Jorge and Maria Hinojosa, who celebrate their Mexican heritage every day of their lives; Freedom Jackson, a cowboy from a slave family; and J. C. Travis and Sara Gray, a young couple whose love for each other just might overcome the obstacles between them. An updated dramatic musical score and spectacularly special effects continue a tradition begun in the 1960s on this very stage. For reservations and information call (806) 655-2181 or visit texas-show.com.

To see canyon views from atop a horse, sign up for a horseback ride at **Los Cedros Ranch,** at the rim of Palo Duro Canyon. You can ride for one, two, or three hours and book a sunset ride that includes a light meal. Note that you must wear long pants, long-sleeve shirt, and sturdy shoes. For details, contact **Cowgirls and Cowboys in the West** (806-672-9256; cowgirlsandcow boysinthewest.com).

If you'd prefer a bit more pampering, you can stay in a motel or book a room at the **Hudspeth House,** Canyon's bed-and-breakfast place at 1905 4th Ave., Canyon (806-655-9800 or 800 655 9809; hudspethinn.com). A famous former resident was the late artist Georgia O'Keeffe, who taught at the local university. There are 6 bedrooms, some with private baths and fireplaces, and decor includes beautiful antiques, tins, plates, dolls, grandfather clocks, and musical instruments. The breakfast table is set with linens, china, and crystal, so you'll enjoy a lavish breakfast or brunch in elegance. A spa, fitness room, sundeck, and gazebo are on the property as well. Call well in advance for reservations.

The Staked Plains

From Canyon follow US 60 southwest 30 miles and then take US 385 south 40 miles. At US 70, head west 24 miles to reach **Muleshoe,** seat of Bailey County and home to the peerless **National Mule Memorial**—what else? Found at the intersection of US 84 and Main Street, the memorial to the West's original draft animal is a fiberglass model measuring 15 hands (5 feet) in height. The mule's statue was built in 1965 thanks to donations from people all over the country—even a mule driver from the former Soviet Union sent a 20-cent contribution. Another 20 miles south on Highway 214, you'll see **Muleshoe National Wildlife Refuge,** the oldest such refuge in Texas, founded in 1935. As it is situated on a central flyway between Mexico and Canada, hundreds of thousands of waterfowl stop by during migration between September and March. The park consists of about 5,800 acres of rolling, mostly treeless sandhills planted with sorghum and wheat (bird food) punctuated by lakes, which are occupied during the season by the country's largest concentration of sandhill cranes. Observation areas are available in the refuge, and picnicking and camping are allowed. Admission is free, and the refuge is open Mon through Fri from 8 a.m. to 4:30 p.m. for day visitors. Call (806) 946-3341 for information.

Just south of the refuge, pick up FR 37 and follow it almost 20 miles to US 84, which will lead 46 miles to *Lubbock,* nicknamed "Hub City," or hub of the Panhandle. Seat of Lubbock County, the city is home to 253,000 people and the expansive Texas Tech University. On its campus you'll find the remarkable *Ranching Heritage Center* at 4th and Indiana Streets (806-742-0498; nrhc.ttu .edu), a living, authentic center of ranching in the American West. Each year 100,000 people visit here to tour the 19-acre grounds filled with more than 49 restored structures, dating from 1838 to 1917. Among them you'll find one of seven division headquarters of the XIT Ranch, a century-old schoolhouse, milk and meat houses, a granary, a blacksmith shop, log cabins, a grand Victorian ranch home, a bunkhouse, a barn, and a train depot. There are horseshoeing, bread-making, sheepshearing, spinning, and weaving demonstrations, and changing exhibits include saddles, bronzes, and western art, plus wagons and branding irons. As was the case a century ago, windmills are more plentiful than trees, and the ranching center offers windmills of varying designs. A 44,000-square-foot museum with seven galleries exhibits art, photography and artifacts, including saddles, furnishings, and family portraits. The spread also includes 42 life-size bronze steer scultpures, guaranteed to take your breath away. Open Mon through Sat from 10 a.m. to 5 p.m. and Sun from 1 to 5 p.m. Admission is free.

Among Lubbock's other interests is that of music, since the city gave the world rock 'n' roll pioneer Buddy Holly. You'll find the *Buddy Holly Statue and West Texas Walk of Fame* at 8th Street and Avenue Q, where an outdoor park honors Holly and other west Texans—including Mac Davis, Waylon Jennings, and Jimmy Dean—who made significant contributions to musical entertainment. It's open 24 hours and is free. Holly's grave is found in the Lubbock Cemetery at E. 34th Street at Quirt Street. Marked by a small, plain stone, the site is visited by a steady procession of fans, many from the United Kingdom. There's also a fine collection of Holly memorabilia on display at a nice little museum, the *Buddy Holly Center and J.I. Allison House,* found in the heart of the Depot Entertainment District. You'll learn more about the short life and extraordinary musical career of the city's most famous son and his bandmates. Displays and a documentery film chronicle Buddy's life and his impact on the Beatles, the Rolling Stones and others who would shape the history of modern music (1801 Crickets Ave., Lubbock; 806-775-3560; buddyhollycenter.org). A small admission is charged.

At the **Silent Wings Museum** (6202 North I-27, Lubbock; 806-775-3046) learn about the U.S. Glider Program, known to be an integral part of an airborne strategy helping the Allies conquer foes in World War II. The collection includes a rare Waco GC-4A plane. Head for **Lubbock Lake National Historic Landmark,** N. Indiana Street and Loop 289 (806-742-1116), one of the largest and most productive archaeological excavations in North America and thought to be the continent's only place where deposits relate to all cultures known to have lived on the Southern Plains. Covering the periods of the Clovis Man and the Folsom Man, Texas residents of 10,000 to 15,000 years ago, the site's digs have turned up remains of the mammoth, extinct horse, camel, and bison, plus a giant armadillo. A more recent addition to the park is a pair of sculptures, life-size replicas of a Columbian mammoth and her baby. The mother mammoth weighs 6,800 pounds and has a trunk reaching 15 feet into the air, as she "runs" through Yellowhouse Canyon with her 1,200-pound offspring. Follow a 0.75-mile trail through the 20-acre excavation area and look for interpretive signs along the way. A new interpretive center offers exhibits, a children's center, a gift shop, and an auditorium. Open Tues through Sat from 9 a.m. to 5 p.m. and Sun from 1 to 5 p.m. A small admission fee is charged.

Children also get a kick out of **Prairie Dog Town,** within Mackenzie State Park at 4th Street and Avenue A (contact the **Lubbock Convention and Tourism Bureau,** 800-692-4035 or 806-747-5232). One of the last remaining colonies of its kind in the whole country, it's home to cute little critters who are playful and endlessly amusing and who share their habitat with burrowing owls and a few rabbits.

In the same neighborhood at Mackenzie Park you'll find the impressive **American Wind Power Center** (1701 Canyon Lake Dr., Lubbock; 806-747-8734; windmill.com). Run by a nonprofit organization, the museum land is scattered with dozens of windmills from the 19th and early 20th centuries. Manufactured by more than 700 companies, these windmills—some of which are very unusual—were used throughout the Great Plains. Inside the exhibit hall, you'll see more than 60 windmills, many of which have wheels more than 25 feet in diameter. The museum store has fascinating gifts.

Texas's most award-winning winery is here in Lubbock. Find **Llano Estacado Winery** just over 3 miles east of US 87 at 3426 E. FR 1585 (806-745-2258; llanowine.com). Winery founders discovered ideal conditions in the loose, sandy soil, hot days, and cool nights of the Panhandle Plains. Some 15 or more varieties are grown at a time, and 11 or 12 different wines—plus one sparkling wine—are bottled each year. Plan to spend an hour here touring the winery and tasting four wines. Open Mon through Sat from 10 a.m. to 5 p.m. and Sun from noon to 5 p.m.; tours are free and offered every half hour daily, with the last tour at 4 p.m.

Pheasant Ridge Winery (3507 E. County Road 5700; Lubbock; 806-746-6033; phesantridgewinery.com) is known for the oldest vines in Texas, where grapes are grown to make some of the most acclaimed wines in the state. The tasting room sells wine by the glass and bottle; feel free to bring a picnic to enjoy with wine on the patio. Visit *McPherson Cellars,* winner of more than 600 medals in state, national and international wine competitions, at the historic Coca-Cola Bottling Plant in the city's Depot district (1615 Texas Ave., Lubbock; 806-687-9463; mcphersoncellars.com). The tasting room is a lovely place to hang with friends over wine and to buy wine-related gifts.

Wine bars, naturally, have grown in number in Lubbock. Among them, try *The Wine Nest,* a premier boutique wine and gift store where you can shop, sip wine and hear live music (5217 98th St., Suite 700, Lubbock; 806-368-7964; thewinenest.com); *La Diosa Cellars,* a place for wine and tapas (901 17th St., Lubbock; 806-744-3600; ladiosacellars.com); and the *Funky Door Bistro & Wine Room,* known for fondue, food and wine pairings, and music (6801 Milwaukee Ave., Lubbock; 806-687-0505; thefunkydoor.com).

Among favorite places locals enjoy dining, there's *Cast Iron Grill* (620 19th St., Lubbock; 806-771-7690; castirongrilllubbock.com), a destination for omelets, brisket nachos, bacon cheeseburger and chicken-fried steak; *The Crafthouse Gastropub,* known for pizza, skillet corn bread, chicken curry, stewed venison, and mac and cheese with bacon; (3131 34th St., Lubbock; 806-687-1466; crafthousepub.com); *Triple J Chophouse and Brew Co.* (1807 Buddy Holly Ave., Lubbock; 806-771-6555; triplejchophouseandbrewco .com), with a menu of burgers, steaks, seafood, and whiskey; and *Spanky's*

Buddy Holly's Legacy Lives On

Buddy Holly died before I knew any tunes other than "Jesus Loves Me" and "The Eyes of Texas Are Upon You" (the first songs my mother taught me, in that order). But since I saw the 1979 film *The Buddy Holly Story,* it has remained one of my very favorite films. I find it extraordinary that the son of a very ordinary Lubbock family achieved so much in a career and laid groundwork for landmark artists such as the Beatles before being killed at the tender age of 23. When I visited the 8.5-foot bronze statue of Holly in Lubbock, I felt a great thrill. I was even more moved upon visiting his grave site, as others were before me: There, on top of the headstone engraved with a guitar and musical notes, are flowers and guitar picks left by his fans.

Sandwich Shop (811 University Dr., Lubbock; 806-744-5677; spankys.com), where the Texas Tech faithful line up for great burgers, fried cheese, and ice-cold beer.

For more information on Lubbock and the area, contact the **Lubbock Convention and Tourism Bureau** at (800) 692-4035 or (806) 747-5232 or visit the website at visitlubbock.org.

South Plains wanderers in search of a ranch experience should consider a trip to the **Guitar Ranches,** about 45 miles east of Lubbock at the town of Spur. Established in the late 1890s by John Guitar, the cattle ranch invites groups to explore the land by hiking and mountain biking, while fishing, wildlife-watching, photography, and hunting are popular, too. Guests stay in attractive little cabins that offer beautiful views of the sunset, and meals are cowhand hardy. Book by calling the ranch at 325-673-8329.

Southeast of Lubbock 42 miles on US 84, the town of *Post*—seat of Garza County and one of Texas's more famous speed traps—is located, thanks to cereal magnate C. W. Post, who bought nearly a quarter of a million acres here and founded Post City in 1907 with the intent of developing his own utopia. He built a sanitarium, hotel, business district, cotton gin and textile plant, and farm homes, but his project never saw true success because he couldn't make it rain, and the lack of water during the 1911 drought was devastating. He died in 1914, but his statue on the courthouse lawn keeps his memory alive.

Post is home to **The Hotel Garza** (302 E. Main St., 806-495-3962; hotelgarza.com), a 1915 inn that looks plucked straight out of the Old West. The owners have updated the rooms to make them most comfortable. There's a self-serve kitchen where guests can stash snacks and drinks, and a beautiful garden patio for enjoying a glass of wine, assuming you've brought your own, of course. Free Wi-Fi is available, and breakfast is included with lodging.

About 6 miles southeast of town on US 84, find the **Llano Estacado Marker,** one that helps travelers more easily understand the geography of this remarkable area. It details the flat-topped mountains of the Cap Rock Escarpment and the Staked Plains, or *llano estacado.*

From Post you can trace the lowest reaches of the Cap Rock as it unwinds to the Panhandle's reach into deep west Texas. Follow FR 669 as it meanders along mesas and buttes, about 70 miles south to **Big Spring.** This is the Howard County seat and home to 23,000, and where a nice resting spot is **Comanche Trail Park.** Find this beauty at Whipkey Drive off US 87, immediately south of FR 700 (432-264-2376). A large spring indeed is the focus of this 480-acre park, which offers a swimming pool, lighted tennis courts, an 18-hole golf course, small fishing lake, playground, hiking and biking trails, nature trails, a flower garden, and improved campsites. In summer you'll especially enjoy the huge amphitheater—cut from native limestone during the Depression—which hosts summer concerts. Admission is free, and the park is open daily from dawn to 10 p.m.

Although quite old, the ***Hotel Settles*** (200 E. 3rd St., Big Spring; 432-267-7500; hotelsettles.com) is Big Spring's claim to newfound fame. Originally opened in 1930 during the west Texas oil boom, the hotel has recently been restored to its former magnificence. The art deco opulence of the interior sparkles once again; a grand lobby, 65 exceptionally beautiful guest rooms, a complete spa, a restaurant serving a modern Texas menu, and the swanky Pharmacy Bar make this a destination hotel in a rather surprising location. Packages incorporating romance, golf, or spa elements are offered.

Other Places to Stay in the Texas Panhandle

ABILENE

Courtyard by Marriott
4350 Ridgemont Dr.
(325) 695-9600
marriott.com

ALBANY

Dye Guest House
216 Breckenridge St.
(817) 925-3269
Rock farmhouse built in 1935, this 2-bedroom, 2-bath home includes a full kitchen, two fireplaces, and a large dining room table. Perfect for family getaways.

AMARILLO

The Big Texan Motel
I-40 at
Lakeside Drive
(806) 372-5000
bigtexan.com
Next to the Big Texan Steak Ranch, this 2-story complex has a funny Old West facade, 54 guest rooms, and a swimming pool.

Embassy Suites Downtown Amarillo
505 S. Buchanan St.
(806) 803-5500
A beautiful new property in the re-energized downtown offers a bright, airy lobby with a stunning living wall covered by 4,000 green plants. The lobby bar is especially inviting, and the location is close to good dining. The 226 large guest rooms include studio and two-room suites.

CANADIAN

Canadian Courts Motel
220 N. 2nd St.
(806) 323-8058
canadiancourts.com
A nicely restored motor court with great landscaping, this 2-story complex has 48 rooms with sleeper-car themes.

COLEMAN

The Harbord Kourt
2710 S. Commercial Ave.
(325) 259-1948
theharbordkourt.com
The small 1947 motor court hotel was renovated and reopened in 2017 with four cute little cottages, each with its own patio area, specialty mattress, and private baths stocking Turkish towels. Themes include Rodeo Queens, World War II, Classic Hollywood and Westerns.

LUBBOCK

Arbor Hotel and Conference Center

6401 62nd St.
(806) 771-2420
arborhotelconferencecenter
.com
Newest in the city, this luxury lodging offers 100 rooms, fine linens, outdoor hot tub, fire pits, pool, bar, room service, and much more.

Overton Hotel and Conference Center

2322 Mac Davis Lane
(806) 776-7000
overtonhotel.com
Walking distance to Texas Tech University, this hotel offers huge rooms with luxury appointments, a 14th floor Club Lounge, afternoon happy hour, free breakfast, and a restaurant and bar called the Pecan Grill.

Woodrow House

2620 19th St.
(806) 793-3330
woodrowhouse.com
A newly constructed red-brick home, this 10-room inn was built specifically to operate as a bed and breakfast. Everything at Texas Tech University is in walking distance. A full breakfast is included with your stay.

Other Places to Eat in the Texas Panhandle

ABILENE

Vagabond Pizza

1056 N. 2nd St.
(325) 268-4321
vagabondpizza.com
Wood fired pizzas, burrata cheese with flatbread, inventive salads and a surprising wine and craft beer list make this a must-visit place.

AMARILLO

Acapulco

727 S. Polk St.
(806) 373-8889
acapulcomexicanrestaurant
.net
Serving a blend of classic Tex-Mex with some specialties from within the Mexican interior, this busy place on Polk Street offers combination plates as well as steaks, fajitas, tacos, and seafood. Oh, and the margaritas are good.

Gooney's

705 S. Polk St,
(806) 367-9585
This Asian fusion restaurant specializes in dishes treated to Chinese, Thai, Laotian, and Korean influences. While the kitchen has its fun, the bar gets creative with cocktails like Shogun's Choice, made with Japanese whiskey.

Moondoggy's

626 S. Polk St.
(806)350-1400
The new downtown pizza pub inside an old dime store is quickly winning fans for its scratch-made pizza and pasta dishes, as well as salads. The cocktail, beer, and wine lists add to the fun.

COLEMAN

Amber's Creekside Steakhouse

914 US 84 Bypass
(325) 625-2500
The log cabin exterior doesn't tell you how good the food and service are inside. A big chicken-fried steak, Kansas City strip, BLT and homemade desserts are among good choices. Check out live local music on weekends.

LUBBOCK

Evie Mae's Pit Barbeque

217 US 62 in Wolfforth
(806) 782-2281
eviemaesbbq.com
Scoring in the top 10 best barbecue joints in the big *Texas Monthly* critics' survey, this place just outside the Lubbock city limits brings hungry folks from far and wide for smoked beef brisket, pork ribs, prime rib, smoked beans, jalapeno cornbread, and green chile cheese grits. Open Wed through Sat from 11 a.m. until the

meat runs out—so plan accordingly.

La Sirena
2610 Salem Ave.
(806) 368-7960
ladirenacocina.us
This modern Latin American restaurant in historic Cactus Alley Courtyard specializes in ceviches, empanadas, street tacos, striped sea bass, and grilled beef tenderloin. Find also an excellent wine list and selection of tequilas and mezcals.

West Table Kitchen and Bar
1204 Broadway Ave., Suite 103
(806) 993-9378
thewesttable.com
Tucked into the historic Pioneer Building in downtown, the chef-driven restaurant has changing seasonal menus that utilize fresh, local ingredients. The brunch buffet includes fried chicken, bagels and lox, shrimp and grits, and baked eggs rancheros. Lunch and dinner favorites include crispy frog legs, blue point oysters, steak salad, braised short ribs, and grilled pork porterhouse.

Wildest West Texas

Early life in west Texas wasn't easy, and seeing the land even today is proof. The land is lonely, honest, tough—like the pioneers who conquered it, the cowboys who worked it, and the people who call it home. Everywhere you look, the long histories of Native Americans, cavalry units posted at forts to protect pioneers and settlers, and oil-field discoveries bringing startling fortunes are unfolded.

The country wasn't always harsh. Sixteenth-century explorer Cabeza de Vaca wrote in his diary that he walked around completely unclothed in the soothing surroundings, and the earliest ranchers wrote that grasses here grew as high as cows' bellies. But herds of several thousand head of cattle were allowed to graze uncontrolled, and the ground was left bare. Apaches didn't mind the desolation, and outlaws were grateful for it. The open skies and spaces of west Texas invited pioneers to forge a new existence. Those hardy settlers who didn't find this part of the Rio Grande utterly impassable assigned names to spots like Camp Misery and Murder's Cove. They were preceded, of course, by the Comanches, whose war trails can still be seen. In 1882 the Southern Pacific Railroad connected the Trans-Pecos towns of Alpine and Marfa to

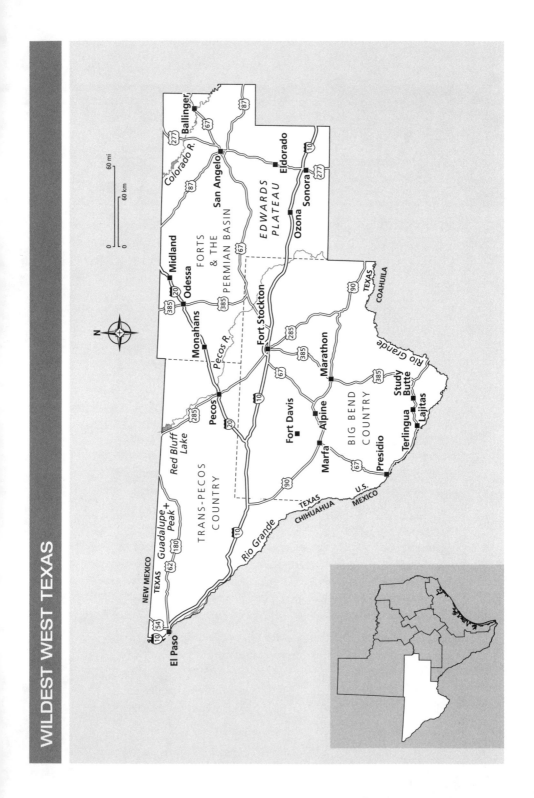

WILDEST WEST TEXAS

its line, and Terlingua, a bit south, became the quicksilver (mercury) mining center of Texas. Faint remains of those and other long-past ventures can be found in the area.

West Texas's great wealth of natural history is defined, revealed, and studied in the sensational form of Big Bend, a name for a region, a national park, and—for many—a state of mind. Within the elbow of the Rio Grande, where it pushes deeper into Mexico, 800,000 acres were set aside by the National Park Service in 1944 for preservation of a complex array of huge canyons, numerous clusters and stretches of mountains, and exotic plant and animal life. Many who live here say it claims a place in the soul, and even geology textbooks found in area shops contain descriptions with mystical undertones; one Native American legend holds that after the Great Creator made Earth with its stars, fish, sea, and birds, he threw all his leftover stony, dusty materials into one heap—the Big Bend. Because it's such a long way from anywhere, the Big Bend is one of the 10 least-visited parks in the nation, and that's what makes it all the more desirable.

So it's time to embrace the Chihuahuan Desert—roll down the windows and smell the cool scent of sagebrush. Walk around, but watch your step and keep quiet so mule deer or even Auodad sheep will appear. Wear sturdy boots for protection and train an eye to the roadsides, as rattlers may dart out and recoil just as rapidly; that other brownish streak of movement into the brush is the regional mascot, the roadrunner. Low slung mountain ranges, bearing names from Christmas to Chisos to Chinati, first appear like little more than bluish shadows nudging the horizon. Broom-weed lies low in oversized

JUNE'S FAVORITE ATTRACTIONS

Chinati Hot Springs Ruidosa	**Front Street Books** Alpine
Cowboy and His Horse Statue Ballinger	**Gage Hotel** Marathon
Davis Mountains State Park Fort Davis	**Hot Springs** Big Bend National Park
El Cosmico Marfa	**McKittrick Canyon** Guadalupe Mountains National Park
Fort Concho National Historic Landmark San Angelo	**Presidio County Courthouse** Marfa

patches of vivid yellow in fall, and robust bluebonnet blooms spring forth with zeal in February. Rafters floating along the Rio Grande marvel at the changing purples, tangerines, and corals in massive canyon walls, and formations of tuff, a hardened ash from volcanic activity millions of years ago, rise like deformed sand castles, followed by layered pink and gray rock cliffs, interrupted with soft carpets of grassy hills. Travelers from as far away as Japan and Germany, as well as those from far-flung corners of Texas, express awe at towering hills of rock, mountain lion warning signs, tough gray-green scrubland, and lush riverside grasses and palms.

Names of places and life-forms often ring of the Spanish-Mexican culture or are pioneer impressions of the land itself: Rosillos Mountains, Mesa de Aguila, Dagger Flat, Dugout Wells, Mule Ear Peaks. And there is such diverse vegetation; most eye-catching are the sotol, century plant, Spanish dagger, and ocotillo, the latter featuring tall spines sprouting bright green, tiny leaves just after the late summer rainy season and brilliant scarlet blooms in spring. The lechuguilla blooms pinkish orange in spring, too, progressing from top to bottom. The Davis Mountains north of the Big Bend wrap comforting arms about you, and the Limpia River is still the crystal, gentle vision it was when settlers arrived 130 years ago. Frontier life is present in a hotel and a distinguished cavalry post. Just don't try to rush through this generous corner of the state, because it takes time to feel and see. West Texas is by turns dusty and sensual, sweltering and refreshing—but always gratifying in a deeply spiritual way.

Forts & the Permian Basin

You'll likely pick up this reach into the Texas "badlands" where you left off at the end of the Panhandle, striking southeast from Big Spring on US 87—better stock the cooler with cold drinks and snacks, as this is the first of several somewhat long but always satisfying hauls. Drive 86 miles on this one highway, leaving Howard County, crossing Sterling and a corner of Coke Counties, to ease into Tom Green County and its seat, *San Angelo.* Home to about 101,000 Texans, the town grew from the exceptional *Fort Concho,* founded in 1867 where the north and middle branches of the lovely Concho River meet. Local lore holds that one of the town's first personalities was the Fighting Parson, who held church in the town's gaming halls; the only time anyone ever objected, the parson gave the protester a knock in the head with the butt of his six-shooter. An early cattle- and sheep-ranching center, San Angelo today is the country's largest primary wool and mohair market and a significant livestock auction site.

Old Fort Concho is one of the state's best-preserved frontier military forts, a 40-acre National Historic Landmark with 23 original and restored buildings quite close to downtown. It served for 22 years for the army, stationed here to keep peace on the frontier. Among the cavalry and infantry forces there were the heroic Buffalo Soldiers, black troops named as such out of admiration by their Native American enemies. The fort today contains three museums featuring frontier life exhibits, officers' quarters, enlisted men's barracks, and a chapel. Throughout the year, special events, demonstrations, and reenactments are held at the fort. Christmas at Old Fort Concho is a particularly colorful event, with artists, dancers, and musicians adding to the celebration. Open Tues through Sat from 10 a.m. to 5 p.m. and Sun from 1 to 5 p.m. A small admission fee is charged. Fort Concho is located at 630 S. Oakes St.; (325) 481-2646; fortconcho.com.

A somewhat unexpected find is the ***San Angelo Museum of Art*** (1 Love St., San Angelo; 325-653-3333; samfa.org), a $6 million masterpiece in its own right. The swooping roofline resembles a saddle, fittingly, and interior works in three large galleries range from classic paintings to contemporary ceramics. The museum maintains a lively schedule of tours, chamber music series, and more.

Still in the frontier vein but more expressive in some ways is ***Miss Hattie's Museum***, 18 E. Concho St., San Angelo (325-653-0112; misshatties.com). One of several bordellos that thrived along this street, it was opened in 1896 and was a successful "gentlemen's social center" until the Texas Rangers closed it in 1946. Still in its original location, Miss Hattie's has been restored to its former glory, complete with furnishings, plus clothing worn by the girls and the cowboys, soldiers, and businessmen who were patrons. Open Tues through Sat from 10 a.m. to 5 p.m. Admission is charged. There's a café and saloon next door, too.

JUNE'S FAVORITE ANNUAL EVENTS

The Pea-Off
Terlingua, New Year's Day

Texas Cowboy Poetry Gathering
Alpine, late February or early March

West of the Pecos Rodeo
Pecos, late June

Viva El Paso!
El Paso, June through August

Davis Mountains Hummingbird Celebration
Fort Davis, late August

Marfa Lights Festival
Marfa, Labor Day weekend

TransPecos Festival of Music and Love
Marfa, late September

Concho Christmas Celebration
San Angelo, throughout December

While you're downtown, check out the **Cactus Hotel** (36 E. Twohig St.; cactushotel.net), Conrad Hilton's fourth hotel—reportedly his most ornate—built in 1929 for $900,000. Rising 14 stories high with lavish ornamentation, the hotel is home to the **Mesquite Bean Café** (open for breakfast and lunch).

The pretty Concho River is the setting downtown for the **River Walk,** a landscaped and lighted stretch of more than 4 miles of river winding beneath huge pecan trees through parks, gardens, gorgeous homes, fountains, and waterfalls.

You'll want to take along a camera to photograph the beautiful **Pearl of the Concho,** a magical sculpture of a mermaid created by the late Jane Charless Beck, found in the Concho River near Celebration Bridge. A bit larger than life size, the bronze mermaid holds in her outstretched hand a Concho pearl, the freshwater gem found only in these waters.

Note that from Celebration Bridge you can walk to historic Fort Concho along **El Paseo de Santa Angela,** a walkway with pecan-tree shade, fountains, historic ranch buildings, and a windmill. The short route follows a footpath used by soldiers at the fort all those years ago.

Inside the restored Historic Orient–Santa Fe Depot, the **Railway Museum of San Angelo** (703 S. Chadbourne St., San Angelo; 325-486-2140 or 325-651-4506 for tours; railwaymuseumsanangelo.homestead.com) offers a changing selection of railroad artifacts and memorabilia, including a permanent model-train layout depicting San Angelo in 1928 when multiple railroads came through town and shared the depot. Other permanent displays include a restored caboose and 4 running displays (1 caboose, 2 locomotives, and a boxcar). The museum is open Sat from 10 a.m. to 4 p.m. A small admission fee is charged.

Two of the outdoor art elements to note in San Angelo are its historic murals and the sheep statuary. The murals are part of a preservation initiative, and the Mural Tour takes you past the Stagecoach Mural, the Chadbourne Street Mural and more. The fiberglass sheeps are placed in front of businesses and painted by local artists to commemorate the area's heritage of a wool-making center. Read more about these at discoversanangelo.com.

First Saturday at the Chicken Farm is a monthly celebration at the **Chicken Farm Art Center** (2505 Martin Luther King Dr., San Angelo; 325-653-4936; chickenfarmartcenter.com). Each of these gatherings features local art vendors, live music, food booths, and artsy activities for kids.

Favorite places to eat in town include **Cork & Pig Tavern** (2201 Knickerbocker Rd., San Angelo; 325-227-7988), great for a Cuban sandwich, Asian chicken salad, and nice wines; and **Armenta's** (1325 S. Oakes St., San Angelo; 325-653-1954), for stacked enchiladas, fajitas, and margaritas. The forever favorite for big slabs of meat, **Zentner's Daughter Steakhouse** (1901

Knickerbocker Rd., San Angelo; 325-284-3376; zentnersdaughter.com) is known for hand-cut T-bones, bacon-wrapped filet mignon and seafood specialties. For more San Angelo information, contact the convention and visitor bureau at (325) 655-4136 or discoversanangelo.com

Just outside of San Angelo, you'll get plenty of peace and quiet at a retreat called **Dry Hollow Hideaway** (RR 380, 7 miles west of Paint Rock; 325-732-4272; dryhollowhideaway.com). Guests have free run of the very nice ranch home, transformed from a historic army barracks, situated on a 700-acre ranch. There are 2 spacious bedrooms, a huge living room and kitchen, and a porch with rockers overlooking a pond that attracts all manner of wildlife. Ask the owners about resident ghosts.

In the tiny town of Paint Rock, you'll find **Texas Handwoven Creations** (formerly Ingrid's Custom Hand-Woven Inc.) (US 83, Paint Rock; 325-732-4370), a shop where crafters hand weave rugs and saddle blankets on old fashioned looms, using alpaca and llama fleece fibers. You can see how the artists finish the items with latch hooks or by hand knotting the fringes. Open Mon through Fri from 8 a.m. to 4:30 p.m. and Sat from 10 a.m. to 5 p.m. If you're hungry, pop into **Paint Rock Grocery** (221 S. Roberts Ave., Paint Rock, 325-732-4759) for burritos, grilled cheese sandwiches, and burgers.

An interesting side trip to make while you're in the neighborhood—relatively speaking, as the neighborhoods out here are pretty big—is one for a photo op at the town of **Ballinger,** 36 miles northeast of San Angelo via US 67 in Runnels County. The county seat and town of 4,000 is worth finding for the **Cowboy and His Horse Statue** on the courthouse lawn, at the intersection of US 83 and US 67. The handsome memorial was sculpted by the acclaimed Pompeo Coppini, who was commissioned by the family of Charles H. Noyes, a local cowboy killed in a range accident.

If nature calls to you, a good retreat is 18 miles south of San Angelo at the town of Christoval: the **Hummer House** is a bed-and-breakfast lodging with a hummingbird wildlife habitat on the premises (21301 Toe Nail Trail, Christoval; 325-255-2254; hummerhouse.com). It's a beautiful place to visit at any time, but in summer, it's home to what's thought to be the state's largest concentration of breeding black-chinned hummingbirds. Migrant birds traveling north and south with the seasons stop by, as well, and deer and wild turkey are frequently seen. Three cottages, surrounded by live oak and pecan trees, are your lodging choices, with breakfast provisions supplied for you to make your own.

About 45 miles south of San Angelo is the town of **Eldorado,** jumping-off point for stays at the **X Bar Ranch Lodge & Nature Retreat,** a 7,100-acre spread at Eldorado (325-853-2688; xbarranch.com). Bring your mountain bike and hiking boots so you can wander the dozens of miles of handmade trails that course through the rocking, rolling terrain. Various seasons bring watchers of birds, butterflies, rabbits, and armadillos, and there are turkey- and dove-hunting packages in fall and winter. In summer you might want to just hang by the pool by day and, at any time of year, study the brilliant sky at night. Accommodations include a cool guesthouse, cabins, and a lodge, all with kitchens where you prepare your own meals.

If your wanderings from Eldorado take you eastward along the San Saba River toward Menard (see Hill Country chapter), you'll notice a lovely, lonely lot of scenery along US 190. Your company will be hundreds of goats, prickly pear cactus, and ancient, crooked live oak trees populating the rocky hills on this scenic drive.

Still another diversion in this neck of west Texas is found in *Sonora,* a 63-mile drive due south of San Angelo on US 277. Go 8 miles west of Sonora on I-10 and take exit 392 to the *Caverns of Sonora* (325-387-3105 or 325-387-6507; cavernsofsonora.com). The founder of the National Speleological Society said of this site, "This is the most indescribably beautiful cavern in the world. Its beauty cannot be exaggerated, even by Texans," which is saying something. Cave experts say some of the delicate crystal growths are "impossible." Ceilings, walls, and floors are covered by phenomenal formations, millions of years in the making, that are seen on guided tours. Do note that the tours can be strenuous for some visitors and that everyone should wear rubber-soled shoes. The park contains picnic grounds, camping areas, shower facilities, and a gift shop. A covered-wagon dinner theater is offered Friday and Saturday evenings from mid-June through mid-August. Open daily, hours vary according to season. For admission fees and tour times, call ahead.

From San Angelo, the next destination is *Midland,* on I-20, 112 miles northwest via US 87 and Highway 158. The seat of Midland County, with a population of about 135,000, Midland lies on the old Chihuahua Trail, the Emigrant Road to California, and the Comanche War Trail. Its name came from its position between Fort Worth and El Paso. Midland was founded in 1885 by Midwestern farm families and supported by agriculture until the 1923 discovery of oil in the region's lucrative Permian Basin. The skies over this incredibly flat land are pointed to by skyscrapers built on the oil booms and by those boom-producing oil derricks.

First stop is *Permian Basin Petroleum Museum, Library, and Hall of Fame* (1500 I-20 West, Midland; 432-683-4403; petroleummuseum.org), a complex devoted to fossil-fuel origins, discovery, and resulting industries. This is where you can understand the significance of the wealthy Permian Basin, told in paintings and exhibits. There's a marine diorama of the prehistoric Permian Sea, containing 200,000 replicas of sea creatures; a re-created 1920s boomtown;

an assortment of antique rigs; and a display on oil and gas well fires. Open Mon through Sat from 9 a.m. to 5 p.m. and Sun from 2 to 5 p.m. Admission is charged.

Midland is also home to the ***American Airpower Heritage Museum and Commemorative Air Force Headquarters,*** at the Midland International Airport (9600 Wright Dr., Midland; 432-563-1000; airpowermuseum.org). Widely considered the nation's best and most complete collection of flyable World War II combat aircraft, this moving museum was founded by dedicated pilots who wanted to make sure future generations would understand the importance of such astounding American air power. The museum is committed to acquiring, restoring, and preserving at least one example of each type of World War II plane. The array today includes—among many—the P-40 Warhawk, P-38 Lightning, P-47 Thunderbolt, P-51 Mustang, P-36 King Cobra, F4F Wildcat, F6F Hellcat, F4U Corsair, plus the British Supermarine Spitfires, a German Messerschmitt, and several Japanese planes. Also find a B-17 Flying Fortress, B-29 Superfortress, and a D-47 Skytrain. The second weekend in October, you can see these craft in flight demonstrations at the CAF "Airsho," and don't miss the museum's 30-minute film on the Ghost Squadron, shown daily at the museum. Open Mon through Sat from 9 a.m. to 5 p.m. and Sun from noon to 5 p.m. A small admission fee is charged.

Another Midland museum to take in is the ***Museum of the Southwest*** (1705 W. Missouri Ave., Midland; 432-683-2882; museumsw.org). Art and archaeology exhibits make up the permanent collection, a children's museum and a planetarium are on-site, and visiting exhibits are of the caliber of Ansel Adams's photography in a 1934 mansion bearing a National Historic Site marker. Open Tues through Sat from 10 a.m. to 5 p.m. and Sun from 2 to 5 p.m. Admission is free.

For tasty time-outs in Midland, here are some considerations: ***Susie's South 40*** (401 S. Marienfield, Midland; 800-221-4442), a factory store for a working confectionery producing handmade chocolates, pralines, and caramels that are shipped to all 50 states and some 37 countries, too; ***Basin Burger House*** (607 N. Colorado St., Midland; 432-687-5696; basinburgerhouse.com), a gourmet burger shop complete with European style breads and cut-to-order French fries; and ***Martinez Bakery*** (206 E. Florida Ave., Midland; 432-683-3100), an old-school Mexican bakery where the tortas (Mexican sandwiches) are filled with your choice of chicken, ham, barbacoa, or fried chicken.

For more information about Midland, call the ***Midland Chamber/Convention and Visitor Bureau*** at (800) 624-6435 or visit visitmidland.com.

Hitting the road again, we go 20 miles west on I-20 to Midland's sister city, ***Odessa,*** seat of Ector County, with a population of 118,000. Established in 1881, Odessa was named by railroad workers from Ukraine for their home city, which this prairie land resembled.

Lest you think oil country is low on culture, Odessa offers its very own **Globe Theatre of the Southwest** (2308 Shakespeare Rd., Odessa; 432-332-1586; globesw.org), on the Odessa College Campus. A nearly perfect replica of William Shakespeare's Globe Theatre in London, this one was built specifically to host plays by the Bard. His works are performed throughout the year, with much celebration made of the Spring Shakespeare Festival, held close to his birthday, April 23. Another replica, the Anne Hathaway Cottage, is home to a Shakespeare library and archives. Branching out, the Globe Theatre now has a live country-and-western program called the Brand New Opree. Open Tues through Fri from 10 a.m. to 6 p.m. and Sat from 2 to 6 p.m. Admission is charged.

texastrivia

The Concho River in West Texas produces freshwater pearls ranging in color from pink to purple.

Odessa has another distinction in its **Presidential Archives and Leadership Library** (in the John Ben Shepperd Public Leadership Intitute at the University of Texas-Permian Basin campus, 4919 E. University Blvd., Odessa; 432-363-PRES; presidentialmuseum.org), the only facility in existence dedicated solely to the office of the US presidency. The campaign and election processes are both studied, and collections of campaign memorabilia, presidential medals, and an array of first-lady inaugural gowns in miniature replicas are all quite interesting. Traveling exhibits are almost always on show, as well. Open Tues through Sat from 10 a.m. to 5 p.m. Admission is charged.

It's hard to resist a visit to the **Odessa Meteor Crater Museum** (5599 Meteor Crater Rd., 432-381-0946), found about 10 miles east of town off I-20. The crater here, measuring 550 feet in diameter and said to be the second largest of its sort in the U.S., dates from an event some 63,000 years ago. The little museum offers exhibits about how mteorites form, where they've hit earth and what happens as a result. A small gift shop is on-site.

Fans of kitsch won't want to leave town without having pictures taken with what is (reportedly) the **World's Largest Jack Rabbit**, a 10-foot-tall statue at 802 N. Sam Houston St., Odessa. You'll see plenty of his ilk in the wild, but none are quite this big.

When you're hungry, head to **Twister Tacos** (3601 Andrews Highway, Odessa; 432-363-1701), a delicious dive where the enchiladas, burritos, quesadillas and tacos bring in a faithful crowd; **Pho House** (1541 John Ben Shepperd Pakway, Suite 2, Odessa; 432-614-2074), a terrific Vietnamese find with shrimp vermicelli and excellent noodle bowls; and *Ed & Tom's Bar-B-Que* (317 E. Murphy St., Odessa, 432-307-6606), where the brisket and pulled pork are best-sellers.

For more information about Odessa, call the **Odessa Convention and Visitor Bureau** at (432) 333-7871 or (800) 780-4678, or visit the website at odessacvb.com.

Before departing this area, take a side trip west via I-20 just 30 miles to *Monahans Sandhill State Park,* immediately north of the interstate (432-943-2092; tpwd.texas.gov). As you're driving west, you'll cross over a tiny corner of Crane County and drive into Ward County. That's when the flat, barren land gives way to hundreds, maybe thousands, of sand dunes, just like those at the coast. You almost think that the beach must be nearby. Wind-sculpted sand dunes resembling those in the Sahara spread over a 4,000-acre park area but also extend into New Mexico. Most of the dunes are still active, growing and assuming various shapes, and are odd also for their proliferating Harvard oak forest, covering 40,000 acres in all. The trees aren't immediately seen, as they grow no more than 3 feet in height, yet their roots reach some 90 feet into the ground. The park's interpretive center offers illustrations of the dunes' history, as well as that of the ranchers, Native Americans, and oil prospectors who once called this area home. There's a 2-mile drive around the dunes leading to picnic and hiking areas and campgrounds, plus a 0.25-mile nature trail allowing you on the dramatic mountains of sand. Inside the interpretive center you can rent huge, flat plastic disks (think of an enormous Frisbee) for $1 for sliding down the dunes. The shop also sells books on area geology, plants, and animals, as well as souvenir T-shirts. The park is open daily from 8 a.m. to 10 p.m., and the center is open from 8 a.m. to 5 p.m. Admission is charged.

In the town of *Monahans*, founded in 1881 as a stop on the Texas and Pacific Railroad and situated today just a couple of miles west of the state park via Business I-20, you'll find a handful of places to grab a bite. Highway 18, a north-south thoroughfare, is the town's main street and home to Emma's Kitchen, Howard's Drive-In, and Hero's Pizza. While you're here, don't miss the *Million Barrel Museum* (US 80/ Business I-20, 432-943-8401; aoghs.org/energy-education-resources/), located

blastfrom thepast

The town of Monahans, famous for its miles of white-sand dunes, is home to the **Butterfield Overland Stagecoach & Wagon Festival,** usually held in late July. The celebration of long-bygone stagecoach days features everything from a parade, live music, and street dancing to bull riding and barbecue.

in the town's 1928 oil storage facility, and an adjacent, relocated railroad hotel. Antique oil-field equipment and other period artifacts are displayed. You can read more about this and the surrounding area at the Texas Historical Commission's Texas Pecos Trail Region site, texaspecostrail.com.

Now it's time to venture south a while, traveling down US 385 for 53 miles to the town of McCamey, where you'll pick up FR 305 for 19 miles, then make a 4-mile jaunt west on US 190 to I-10. Now head back southeast 33 miles via I-10, Highway 349, and a particularly scenic, cactus-lined Highway 290 to **Fort Lancaster State Historic Site.** The site is worth finding if you like ruins, as this briefly occupied fort has a poignancy lingering amid its rubble in a breathtaking little valley carved by the Pecos River. Founded in 1855 to protect the many settlers traveling the San Antonio–El Paso Road, it was abandoned during the Civil War and was only briefly used again after the war's end. It had an important role, however, on the frontier—a story told in the modern interpretive center on-site. Open Mon through Fri from 8 a.m. to 5 p.m. Admission is free. Call (432) 836-4391 or go to thc.texas.gov/ historic-sites/ for information.

If you're a real fort fan, continue east another 30 miles on I-10 to the lonely town of **Ozona,** the Crockett County seat, with a population of 3,500. Unique for being the only town in the county—a county that's larger than the state of Delaware, by the way—and the largest unincorporated town in the nation, Ozona also offers the **Crockett County Museum** (404 11th St., Ozona; 325-392-2837; ozonamuseum.com). Housed there are artifacts and relics pertaining to Native Americans, the Spanish, and pioneers that were found at Fort Lancaster. Open Mon through Fri from 9 a.m. to 5 p.m. and Sat from 10 a.m. to 3 p.m. A small admission fee is charged.

Make time also to explore the park facing the courthouse. A magnificent monument to Davy Crockett bears a dramatic likeness of the hero, with his quote, "Be sure you are right, then go ahead." A bronze honoring the brave pioneers who settled the area sits at the park's center; titled *The Tie That Binds,* it depicts a man, woman, and child in period dress, facing the horizon.

Big Bend Country

West of Fort Lancaster 67 miles via I-10 is **Fort Stockton,** seat of Pecos County. This town of 8,000 residents began with the establishment of Camp Stockton in 1858 by troops forming from the First and Eighth Infantries of the US Army. The town grew into its modern form after the Yates oil-field discovery in 1925 in the eastern part of the county. The massive drilling rigs are still part of the skyline, but historical sites are the reason for stopping.

The first thing to catch your attention in town, however, is the unforgettable **Paisano Pete,** pure Texas kitsch on Main Street immediately south of US 290 at FR 1053. *Paisano* means "companion" in Spanish, and this statue of a roadrunner is 11 feet tall and 22 feet long, making Pete the largest companion of his kind in the world. You'll see these creatures everywhere in west Texas, but you will never see another like Pete, so take this photo now—otherwise, no one back home will believe you.

To explore the admirable local history, have a look around the **Annie Riggs Memorial Museum** (301 S. Main St., Fort Stockton; 432-336-2167; annieriggsmuseum.org). Housed in an 1899 hotel and a popular stop on the Overland Butterfield Stage line, the museum was named for a colorful local figure—a twice-divorced, hardworking woman who ran the hotel for more than 25 years. The building, called territorial in design, features adobe brick and wood with a wraparound veranda and gingerbread trim. The local historical society assembled the collection here, but the salt cedar that Annie planted in the courtyard was already in place. The parlor boasts one of the first pianos brought west of the Pecos River, as well as a giant cranberry-glass chandelier made in Ohio before the Civil War. The hotel's 15 rooms are filled with relics, such as an 1880s baby christening gown, a man's collar box, furniture, lanterns, a profusion of kitchen and outdoor cooking gadgets, as well as artifacts relating to the area's archaeology, geology, ranching, and religion. Open Mon through Sat 9 a.m. to 5 p.m.; closed Sun. A small admission fee is charged.

Immediately adjacent to the Annie Riggs is the **Courthouse Square,** surrounded by wonderfully restored old buildings important to the history of Pecos County. These include the 1883 courthouse, an 1875 Catholic church, the 1883 schoolhouse, and the Zero Stone, a marker placed by a survey party in 1859 that was used as a point of origin for all land surveys in this part of west Texas for many years. There's also the photogenic Grey Mule Saloon, now a private residence.

Mi Casita (405 E. Dickinson, Blvd., Fort Stockton; 432-336-5368) is a favorite Mexican food destination in town, especially for plates of flat enchiladas topped with a fried egg. For sandwiches, pastries, and good caffeine, head to the **Clockwork Coffeehouse** (1608 N. Front St., Fort Stockton| 432-299-1011).

For more information about Fort Stockton, call the **Historic Fort Stockton Visitor Center** at (800) 336-2166 or visit historicfortstocktontx.com.

Now delve deeper into the land of the Big Bend by following US 385 south 58 miles, cutting through the Glass Mountains and arriving in the Brewster County town of **Marathon,** with a population of 500. This is definitely a place to set a spell, as we sometimes say in west Texas. And there's no place better to do that than at the *Gage Hotel,* right in the middle of town on US 90 (432-386-4205 or 800-884-4243; gagehotel.com). This 1927 creation by west Texas architect Henry Trost exudes the Old West in mood and looks, with a contemporary, stylish addition of beautiful landscaping, a gorgeous swimming pool, and all sorts of décor for rooms and public areas, such as branding irons, chaps, saddles, horseshoes, and spurs. The popular adobe wing added rooms, all of which are more luxurious—some have fireplaces and parlors—than those in the original building. Perfect for groups of friends or family traveling together, the *Captain Shepard House* is a beautifully renovated 1890 stucco home sitting just behind the hotel. Within the two-story house, five bedrooms with private baths, dining room, butler's kitchen, living areas, and porch make this a good retreat; a two-bedroom carriage house is also on the site. Three casitas have been added to the mix. Two of these overlook the serene Gage Gardens, and one is found just behind the historic hotel.

The Gage dining room, now called the *12 Gage,* offers southwestern dishes with sophisticated treatment, including the pork chops with chipotle sauce and garlic mashed potatoes, grilled quail, shrimp enchiladas, and rainbow trout. You can also dine in the adjacent *White Buffalo Bar,* enjoying burgers and margaritas. Watch the sun fall from the sky on a front-porch rocker or ask the management to help you arrange a raft, Jeep, or hunting trip. To make this trip even more relaxing, book time in the hotel's spa, where you can indulge in a massage, facial, body wrap and eucalyptus steam room. The Gage also has a nicely equipped fitness room nearby, as well as a lovely landscaped garden with a one-mile walk trail.

Travelers not familiar with Marathon will be surprised at the development in such a tiny town. Since J. P. Bryan of Houston bought the Gage Hotel in 1978 and supervised its marvelous expansion, he has also bought up most all the other buildings in town for renovation as art studios and galleries, boutiques and gift stores, and cafés. Whereas Marathon had been simply a launching point for journeys deep into the Big Bend region, it's now a place where travelers can hang out for a couple of days before continuing.

Bryan's vision for the still-sleepy town—you'll see goats and chickens and windmills in residents' yards, and there are virtually no stop signs or street signs to be found—has resulted in the opening of V6 Collection, which sells artwork, home décor, hats, book bags, shirts, and such with Gage Hotel logos; Klepper Gallery, selling work by E. Dan Klepper, a local artist, writer, and photographer; French Company Grocery, selling gourmet foods and cool hats; and the Cactus Flower, a shop sells gifts, souvenirs, and Marathon craftwork.

These are all within a few steps from the front door of the Gage. In the next block east along US 90, you'll also find beautiful regional art at the James Evans Gallery (jameshevans.com). James' renowned photographic creations include landscapes, portraits, nudes, and more. He also sells his photography books and cool T-shirts bearing his wildlife shots; see desertcritterwear.com.

Chisos Gallery is where you'll inquire about lodging in the fabulous **Adobe Haciendas** (432-386-4200; adobehaciendas.com), expertly restored adobe cottages with full kitchens, living areas, and tiled baths.

Less than a mile west of the Gage, the **Marathon Motel** (432-386-4241; marathonmotel.com) is a wonderfully restored 1940s tourist court on 10 acres with excellent views of sunsets. Motel rooms are basic but very comfortable and clean, with double beds, TV, and showers. At the center of the property, a courtyard offers a large fire pit and a thoughtfully furnished seating area. Also on-site, a guest kitchen lets you cook your own meals

Kicking back in Marathon at a place with an eye toward the future means a stay at **Eve's Garden** (Avenue C and N. 3rd St., Marathon; 432-386-4165; eves-garden.org). This bed-and-breakfast and ecology resource center might serve as a microcosm of what our world would be if it were to function in a purely green manner. Adding onto a pretty, old adobe home, owner Kate Thayer has expanded her holistic hostelry to include 7 guest suites, a lap pool, a wondrous greenhouse, and a coffee-break/Wi-Fi room—all from papercrete blocks, astonishingly lightweight bricks composed of recycled newsprint and Styrofoam, all finished with layers of stucco and paint. You'll feel as though you're wandering through a fairy-tale land with rooms of curved shapes and lines, all cozy, colorful, and rich with texture. The suites, decorated with fabrics from India and appointments like glass chess sets, surround the pond-filled greenhouse, where Thayer grows squash, tomatoes, chard, purple pea pods, sweet potatoes, bok choy, and calla lilies. Eve's Garden is complete with a cartoonish, papier-mâché snake, festooned with colorful pieces of broken glass.

For more information on Marathon lodging, shopping, and dining, call the chamber of commerce at (432) 386-4516 or visit the helpful website at marathon texas.com.

If you'd rather camp nearby and save your money for later Big Bend adventures, consider **Stillwell's Store** (432-376-2244; stillwellstore.com), the only camping option near the park's northern entrance. It's 40 miles south of Marathon via US 385, then 6 miles southeast via FR 2627. The drive itself helps you become even more acclimated to the spreading region; just about 15 miles south of Marathon on US 385, the scrubby, hunchbacked mountains come upon you, huge and enveloping. Here you'll find 25,000 acres for primitive camping, as well as RV hookups. Camping is anywhere from $3.50 to $15 per night, and the store has plenty of provisions. An on-site bonus is **Hallie Stillwell's Hall of Fame,** a great little collection of Big Bend antiques and artifacts from the turn of the 20th century, kept in a building next to the store. Admission is free—you just ask the storekeepers for a key. Stillwell's Store is generally open daily from 8 a.m. to 9 p.m., but you might want to call ahead just to be sure.

Now it's time to explore the incomparable **Big Bend National Park.** The northern entrance is where US 385 reaches its southern terminus, 40 miles south of Marathon. On your drive down, note the Woods Hollow Mountains encroaching on the highway from the east. This image of purplish blue mountains slumping low against the horizon will become very familiar to you as you explore this magnificent region.

Once inside the park boundaries, you'll immediately come upon **Persimmon Gap Visitor's Center,** where you'll pay a $25-per-vehicle entry fee, good for one week. The visitor center has bathrooms, water fountains, books, and park literature. Another 26 miles south, you'll come to Panther Junction, site of **Big Bend National Park Headquarters** (432-477-2251; nps.gov/bibe) and the point at which the park's three main paved roads meet. You'll stop here for a variety of reasons: An abundance of free and inexpensive but vital pamphlets and brochures regarding roads, sightseeing, flora and fauna, hiking, camping, lodging, and ranger-led activities is offered; necessary backcountry permits are issued; and a huge relief map of the park helps you better understand the undertaking ahead of you. This is also the place to inquire about weather, river, and road conditions. Less than a mile west, you'll find a gas station–convenience store where you can buy basic supplies and water. You'd be wise to bring lots of bottled water with you, however.

Having gathered the copious amounts of information that define the park, you are ready to dig in. From Panther Junction, your most immediate option for exploring is to head east on the paved road. It ends at **Rio Grande Village,** near Boquillas Canyon; here you'll find RV camping with full hookups and a shower house, and a store selling snacks, camping permits, and bottled water.

About 3 miles upriver, 2 miles off the main road, is an abandoned resort called **Hot Springs,** a place that was all the rage in the 1920s. The drive down here cuts through dry, white limestone and shale shelves, and the road finally turns to white, powdery sands. The rest can be seen on foot. Out of nowhere appears a long-abandoned, whitewashed stone structure that was the post office for many years and functioned as a concession until 1952. Past that, a vacant rock lodge shaded by a grove of palm trees looks down the sandy path to the river and the therapeutic hot springs on the river's edge. Several healthy cows will probably stare vacantly at you from across the river in Mexico, but pay them no mind and go on exploring the few remains of the bathhouse in the water. When the river is low, those 108 degree waters still soothe tired bones. Ease down onto a small sitting area and feel the gush of hot water—moving at a rate of 250,000 gallons daily—revive your body and spirit.

Boquillas Canyon points up the Sierra del Carmen, rising 8,500 feet into the Mexican sky, blanketed by pine and fir forests. A great 2-hour hike into the canyon delivers sensational views and a wonderful sand dune to play on. Other options to consider exploring in the park's eastern area are those off-road adventures, such as hiking or biking. It's a good idea to make sure your vehicle is ready for the dirt roads first, and rangers can supply you with that information. Some excursions include the trek into **Dagger Flat,** reached from the Old Ore Road that splits off from the main road into the park from the north. It's a little-sought delight on a graded dirt road and an excellent primer to the extraordinary desert vegetation so abundant here. The 7-mile road leads to a strange grove of massive dagger yucca, shooting nearly a dozen feet into the air; these are stunning, especially when topped with blossoms in spring. Hike around here if you're armed with a guidebook. Pick up a 50-cent guide at the road's entry and follow the numbered posts to learn more about the landscape and plants.

Another detour to make off the main road is into **Dugout Wells,** reached by leaving the road that took you to Rio Grande Village. Here is a microcosm of the diverse Big Bend, as hardwoods commingle with all sorts of desert plants, in the company of a windmill and desert critters that are most commonly spied at sunup or sundown. Watch for the marker for the Chihuahuan Desert Nature Trail, a simple 0.5-mile path bearing descriptive signs regarding the odd plants you see.

Heading west to the park's center by paved road, you will reach **Chisos Basin,** situated in a 1,500-foot depression—hence, the basin. It rests right in the middle of the mile-high Chisos Mountains and is the busiest part of Big Bend National Park, since this is where the park's only lodging and dining facilities are. It's also the coolest part of the park, and in summer everyone comes here for relief from the heat. As you drive up the twisting road to the Basin, you'll see a marked change in scenery. Here, there are trees—rich, rare shade is provided by evergreen and deciduous trees. The Basin's **Chisos Mountain Lodge** (432-477-2291; chisosmountainslodge.com) offers lodge rooms and cottages, which are often booked months in advance, and spectacular views are the reason. The restaurant here offers above-average food for breakfast, lunch, and dinner daily. The adjacent store sells candy and basic foods, some camping supplies, drinks, T-shirts and hats, and postage stamps.

The Basin also has lots of campsites up numerous hillsides, but those, too, are often booked far in advance; for spring break, the park's busiest period, reservations are made a year in advance. Unfortunately, there is no longer horseback riding inside the park. Excellent riding opportunities await, however, in Study Butte and Lajitas.

Hikers will enjoy the route from the Basin to the South Rim and to the popular Lost Mine Trail, which can be a 2- to 4-hour hike but the easiest in these mountains. This is an area where extensive wildlife is sighted, including the black bear. Rangers advise hikers to take along 1 gallon of water per person. Photographers will take a special interest in *The Window,* a narrow slit of a gorge through which all Basin drainage flows to a 75-foot fall below. When there is heavy rain in the mountains and rocks rush and bounce through The Window, it's easy to see how the Basin was formed. *Mule Ear Peaks,* southwest of the South Rim, draws both hikers and photo buffs to its twin angular rock fragments and remains of volcanic rock flow. This is a 4-mile hike that takes 3 or 4 hours to complete.

Southeast of the Basin is *Mariscal Canyon,* where the Rio Grande's southernmost dip cuts through 1,600-foot limestone walls of the Mariscal Mountains. You can explore this canyon, which is littered with abandoned quicksilver mining structures, if you're a very serious, experienced hiker. This, along with other canyons pushing against the park from Mexico, is discovered most often on rafting trips. Among the nearby rafting outfitters offering trips lasting from a half day to several days—with hiking, lunch, and camping options—are Far Flung Outdoor Center (800-839-7238; bigbendfarflung.com); Desert Sports (888-989-6900; desertsportstx.com); and Big Bend River Tours (800-545-4240; bigbendrivertours.com). Guides are not only adept at the rowing and navigation of whitewater but also are trained to give you all the information you want regarding history, geology, plant and animal life, photography, and folklore. Exquisite riverside meals and entertainment can be arranged through these rafting companies, too. Tours on land via Jeep are also offered by the same companies. Ask at Desert Sports about guided hike and mountain bike touring in Big Bend, too.

In the park's southwestern section, the village of *Castolon* is reached on a 22-mile paved road branching off from the main park road. Old cavalry barracks sit deserted where a US Army garrison and trading post was active from 1914 until 1916. A little store sells a few basics, such as T-shirts, snacks, books, souvenir coffee cups, and paper products. Grab some sandwich meat, cheese, and a loaf of bread for a picnic at Cottonwood Campground, adjacent to Castolon. There's superb scenery, too, down the 14-mile Maverick Road, but you need to ask a ranger if it's passable.

Morning is ideal for exploring **Santa Elena Canyon,** when the sunlight exposes walls of rose and rust. On the Texas side, the wall of steep cement steps you can ascend is called Mesa de Áquila, and the sheer cliff on the Mexican side is called Sierra Ponce. Santa Elena Canyon is the one most often seen on the shorter raft trips.

This is but a scant overview of a tremendously complex park. If you're itching to explore the lesser-known places bearing names like Devil's Den, Telephone Trail, and Grapevine Hills, ask at the headquarters for appropriate maps and information. The rangers can also provide you with names and phone numbers of personable, knowledgeable guides for hire.

Barely 2 miles west of the western park boundary on RR 170 at Highway 118, **Study Butte** is a 24-mile drive from the park headquarters and has lodging and food. Pronounced STEW-dee B'yewt, this is where travelers relax at the **Big Bend Motor Inn and Mission Lodge** (432-371-2218 or 877-386-4383; bigbend resort.com), offering clean but very plain rooms, RV spaces and campground, gift shop, swimming pool, TV, gas, convenience store, and an above-average diner. Book tours here, too, to explore the River Road and sections of the national park; trips are from five to 12 hours and include box lunches. At the Study Butte Store, you can buy gas, drinks, snacks, and lottery tickets; there's a liquor store adjacent, and the Maverick Rock Shop is facing this on the south side of the road. **Far Flung Adventures** (432-371-2633; bigbendfarflung.com/lodging/) offers casitas with 400 square feet of living space, two queen beds, big bathrooms and with nice towels, kitchenettes, TVs, free Wifi, and porches with rocking chairs.

Just west of Study Butte is a fork in the highway, where RR 170 continues due west and Highway 118 reaches northward to Alpine. At the fork is the Terlingua Post Office and the **Quicksilver Bank** (432-371-2211), with the area's only ATM. Bankers' hours here are serious: Mon through Fri 8 to 11 a.m. and 2 to 4:30 p.m. and Thurs to 6 p.m. Near the fork also is **Big Bend Stables** (432-371-3064, 800-887-4331; lajitasstables.com), where you can book horseback rides to see pictographs and quicksilver mines for an hour to 3 hours or all day.

texastrivia

West Texas was the first viticultural area in what's now the US: In 1662, a century before Junípero Serra planted the first vines in California, Franciscan padres from Mexico established vineyards in the El Paso area to produce sacramental wines.

Just 4 miles west on RR 170 from Study Butte, **Terlingua** (pronounced Tur-LING-gwuh) is called a ghost town—although it isn't anymore. You'll see the turn off RR 170 at the sign announcing Terlingua Ghost Town. Formerly an abandoned quicksilver mining camp, Terlingua generously offers photo ops in ruined houses, a jail, and a rocky cemetery bearing aged wooden crosses. This is where musicians like Butch Hancock (one of the Flatlanders trio, of Lubbock fame) and myriad other poets, authors, and artists have retreated for a life of peace and quiet. Sure, it's anything but quiet the first weekend in November, when thousands of beer-soaked revelers turn out for two world-championship chili competitions, but Terlingua Ghost Town is, nevertheless, the quintessential jumping-off place in Texas.

At the heart of Terlingua, beyond the cemetery, is an aging building that houses the **Starlight Theatre** (432-371-2326; thestarlighttheatre.com), a spruced-up old movie house dating from 1931. Live music is the big draw, as are the bar and restaurant offerings. This is where you load up on suppers of chicken-fried wild boar, chili, filet mignon, quail, burgers, sandwiches, and salads. Check the website for hours.

Next door to the Starlight—past the ubiquitous guy sitting on the porch bench happily drinking his Budweiser, smoking a cigarette, and staring off toward the horizon—is a nice trove of shopping inside **Terlingua Trading Co.** Here you can buy every manner of T-shirt; lots of western, Mexican, and folk music on CD and cassette tape; Mexican glassware; trinkets crafted from rock and stone; and stuffed animals. Also, inside the store is a little museum tucked off in a corner. Here you see old photos and artifacts from the region's early settlement days, when wagon trains from Marathon brought supplies, soldiers, and merchants and huge newspaper ads proclaimed "Presidio—the Coming Metropolis of the Big Bend Country." Behind the store, the **Big Bend Holiday Hotel** (432-201-1177; bigbendholidayhotel.com) offers especially comfortable lodging in what may appear to be dubious dwellings. Inside the primitive-looking buildings are very nice digs of posh western design. Plush bedding, large bathrooms, and seating areas are found in each. You'll have the option to choose from several rooms and suites, as well as private houses, all in the Holiday Hotel collection.

Your other good Terlingua lodging choice is **La Posada Milagro** (432-371-3044 or 432-386-6496; laposadamilagro.net), an artfully crafted, six-room guesthouse sitting in one of the restored dry-stack rock buildings on a scenic hillside. Rustic but lavished with luxurious appointments and well-chosen décor, the inn offers fire pits, sundecks, and outdoor kitchens and spectacular views of the Chisos Mountains.

The Study Butte-Terlingua area is famous also for **La Kiva** (23220 Farm Road 170, Terlingua; 432-371-2250), a restaurant and bar that's reopened, much to the pleasure of all who love this area. Built into the side of a dry river-bank, the semi-subterranean restaurant serves a menu of onion rings and fried

Cooking Weekends in the Trans-Pecos

Chef Lou Lambert, a native of Odessa and a seventh-generation Texan, was raised among cattle ranchers who have been working the West Texas badlands since Stephen F. Austin first sent settlers out west to claim lands for their families. Rather than go to work on horseback, he earned his bachelor's degree in hotel and restaurant management before getting his education at the Culinary Institute of America in Hyde Park, NY. He worked for Wolfgang Puck in San Francisco before returning to Texas, where he owns and runs restaurants in Austin, San Antonio, and Fort Worth. He's the author of *Big Ranch, Big City Cookbook* (co-authored by the author of the book you're reading right now), which is the platform for his celebrated cooking weekends at El Cosmico, in Marfa (see p. 259). (His sister, hotelier Liz Lambert, owns El Cosmico property.) Two or three times a year, Lou illustrates how growing up on those ranches in the Chihuahuan Desert influenced his distinctive cooking style, which blends down-home food with classic cooking techniques. The weekend-long cooking workshops feature menus laden with adobo pork tacos, chiles rellenos, wood-grilled rib-eye steak, leg of lamb, green chile grits, corned beef hash, and griddle lemon pound cake. Call (432) 729-1950 or visit elcosmico.com.

calamari for appetizers, burgers, steaks, and pizzas. The wine list includes good picks from Australia, France, Spain, Portugal, Italy and the U.S.

Another 13 miles west on RR 170, you'll reach the old frontier post town of ***Lajitas,*** which underwent a multimillion-dollar renovation. Now called ***Lajitas Resort and Spa,*** the town has become a very exclusive destination. If you look hard enough, you can find traces of the original site, established by the US Army as a post in 1895 and frequented by Pancho Villa and friends. There's a lovely old chapel, visited on one of the resort's guided walking tours, as well as the old trading post, where you can buy a beer—and all sorts of groceries—and pay a visit to Clay Henry III, the friendly goat whose title is Mayor of Lajitas.

The developers of the contemporary Lajitas have expanded the golf course to include a hole that sits across the Rio Grande in Mexico, which is more than a novelty. There's also a private airport, where the resort's Lear jets are kept, and a very impressive equestrian center. Updating to the resort lodgings has rendered the rooms at the Cavalry Post and in the main hotel very luxurious indeed, with elegant bedding and bath linens, as well as beautiful furnishings. Altogether you have a choice of 101 rooms in five buildings. You can have a massage or facial in the spa, or play a round of golf—as long as you don't mind the high price tags. Daily activities for guests include Jeep touring, horseback riding, zip line adventures, skeet shooting, mountain biking, birding, morning and sunset walks, and putting lessons. For information call (432) 424-5000 or (877) 525-4827 or check lajitasgolfresort.com.

Just shy of **Presidio,** 50 miles west of Lajitas, **Fort Leaton State Historic Site** is on RR 170 (432-229-3613; tpwd.texas.gov). The private fort and trading post was originally a Spanish mission founded in 1759 but was taken over in 1848 by frontiersman Ben Leaton, who monopolized profitable trade with the Native Americans in the area. The adobe fortress now holds a museum covering Leaton's controversial personal and business ethics, along with the area's Mexican, Native American, and pioneer heritage. Exhibits offer bilingual signage and include natural history, along with chronology of commerce, settlement, and cattle and silver industries. A slide show covers the desert ecology. Open daily from 8 a.m. to 5 p.m. Admission is charged.

Presidio, settled in 1683 by Franciscan missionaries, sits in some of the most rugged land Texas can offer, an isolated Rio Grande settlement that's often mentioned in the news as having the hottest temperature in the country. Besides that, it's the self-proclaimed Onion Capital of the World and a good jumping-off place for travelers wishing to journey southwest into Mexico to tour the magnificent Copper Canyon.

If you arrive in Presidio hungry, head right to **El Patio Restaurant** (513 O'Reilly St., Presidio; 432-229-4409), an inexpensive, family-run spot serving fajitas, enchiladas, tacos, and other Mexican specialties, as well as salads, soups, and ice cream. It's open daily for breakfast, lunch, and dinner.

For more Presidio information and help with planning trips into Mexico, contact the **Presidio Chamber of Commerce** at (432) 229-3199. You'll want to stock up at a grocery store in town if you're heading to Chinati Hot Springs.

If you're in pursuit of something more remote than you ever dreamed possible, continue west from Presidio via RR 170 about 36 miles down a teeth-rattling road to the speck of a town called Ruidosa. From there you'll veer onto rough Hot Springs Road for another 7 miles until you reach **Chinati Hot Springs** (Pinto Canyon Road, 432-229-4165; chinatihotsprings.net), one of the most restorative places on Earth. Towering cottonwood trees line a running stream, and hot mineral baths will help work out your troubles. People don't come here to party, although you'll see plenty of guests who have brought a cooler of beer or several bottles of wine for their stay. Some folks will grill steaks outside the community kitchen, which is surrounded by cactus and bougainvillea, while others heat up stew inside. The community kitchen is for everyone to share. Try to book the adobe hut called Patron, a little charmer with a private toilet and sink, plus a minifridge and comfy queen-size bed and a tiny patio with a deep tub, fashioned from an old trough. Light candles and soak under the stars while listening to the desert's silence. Note that there's no cell phone or Wifi service, but you can drive down the road to a general store for connectivity.

Beer-Guzzling Goat

Whether or not cows can fly, it's certain that goats can drink beer. Proof is found at the *Lajitas Trading Post,* (432) 424-5000, where the mayor—a goat named Clay Henry Jr.—once guzzled beer on a daily basis. His predecessor, Mayor Clay Henry, was a huge hit with tourists who would stop in for a beer and see the mayor's pen littered with beer cans and bottles. When the curious would ask, someone at the trading post would kindly put a beer up to the goat's mouth, whereupon the goat would get a grip on the bottle with his mouth, tip his head back, and down the whole thing. It's said that old age, rather than liver problems, finally took Clay Henry a few years ago, but C. H. Jr. and C. H. the third have filled his shoes. Or hooves, as it were. Today the goats are just for show and photo ops.

From Presidio, follow US 67 north 61 miles, looking first to the west along the drive at the slumping Chinati Mountains, followed by the Cuesta del Burro Mountains. Keep an eye out for the sign indicating Lincoln's profile in a mountain formation to the west; sure enough, there's a clear profile of a reclining Abe's face. Soon after that look to the east side of the highway for Shafter Ghost Town. A turn from the highway will take you into a small, nearly abandoned historic mining town with scenic stone building ruins. Be sure you have a camera on hand.

Another turn to watch for from US 67—about 25 miles north of Presidio—is that to Cibolo Creek Ranch, a luxury resort (see Other Places to Stay, at end of chapter, for details). Watch carefully and you'll spot some pronghorn antelope hopping and bounding along in the tall grasses to the east. You'll wind up in the ultra-western town of *Marfa,* seat of Presidio County and home to 2,400. The town is becoming well-known for a mysterious phenomenon called the *Marfa Ghost Lights.*

If you're around for Labor Day, you'll get to help celebrate the *Marfa Lights Festival,* which includes a fun run, street dance, food and arts booths, parade, evening concert, Mexican folkloric dancers, and mariachi musicians. For details call the chamber of commerce at (432) 729-4942 or (800) 650-9696; visitmarfa.com.

By daylight, Marfa shows off its beautifully restored *Presidio County Courthouse,* at the north end of Highland Street, a stone-and-brick creation in the Second Empire design, built in 1886. The view of the surrounding land is stunning from the dome up top, which is open Mon through Fri from 8:30 a.m. to 4:30 p.m. Admission is free.

A few yards away, the *Hotel Paisano* (207 N. Highland Ave., Marfa; 432-729-3669; hotelpaisano.com) is a beautiful example of Trost architecture dating from 1927; it has hosted Franklin D. Roosevelt, Harry S. Truman, and John F. Kennedy, among other dignitaries. Bearing state and national historical markers, the hotel is beloved by movie buffs for having been the home of Elizabeth Taylor, Rock Hudson, James Dean, and Dennis Hopper, plus all the other actors who appeared in the epic film *Giant,* shot close by. Past the fountained courtyard, inside the Spanish-detailed hotel lobby, there are glass-fronted cases of *Giant* memorabilia, including signed photos of the cast, clippings from *Life* magazine, and numerous news clippings regarding the shoot.

A much-needed and painstaking renovation has made the Paisano grand again. Rooms and suites are pretty and comfortable, and there's a TV in a little room off the lobby that plays *Giant* continuously. Perhaps best of all, the restoration included the addition of an attractive restaurant called ***Jett's Grill*** (432-729-3838), named for the movie's James Dean character. Among good choices for dinner are the pistachio-crusted chicken-fried steak with chipotle gravy, penne with spinach and goat cheese, and creamy, rich shrimp bisque.

New lodgings of note include the ***Hotel Saint George*** (105 S. Highland Ave., Marfa; 432-729-3700; marfasaintgeorge.com), with 55 rooms and suites, local artwork, restaurant and bar; and ***105 Lincoln*** (105 West Lincoln St., Marfa; 105Lincoln.com or airbnb.com), a collection of 11 guest suites with full kitchens in historic buildings, houses, apartments, and even a 1950s bomb shelter.

One of the gathering spots in town is the ***Marfa Book Company*** (105 S. Highland Ave., Marfa; 432-729-3906; marfabookco.com), a bookstore that would be at home in Manhattan, San Francisco, or Chicago. An emphasis on art books makes a lot of sense here, naturally. Find it off the lobby of the Saint George. Up and down Highland and around most corners, you'll find an assortment of art galleries. See the list of thest at visitmarfa.com/arts/.

Across the street from the Saint George, dine on exceptional cooking at ***Stellina*** (103 N. Highland Ave., Marfa; 432-729-2030; stellinamarfa.com), where Mediterranean-inspired specialties include items like blistered shisito peppers, grilled bread with roasted tomatoes, fried zucchini cakes, pasta with wild boar ragout, braised lamb shank and ratatouille. Seating is communal; best is a seat at the bar. Open Tues through Sat for dinner only.

If you're staying in a casita, you'll want to stock up on food and drink good at ***The Get Go*** (208 S. Dean St., Marfa; 432-729-3335; thegetgomarfa.com). This is where you can find imported cheeses, organic eggs and produce, lovely chocolates, Asian foods, a good wine selection, and more.

Marfa's blend of raw landscape and pure solace have long made it a magnet for creative forces. The late American sculptor Donald Judd moved to Marfa in 1972 and created the ***Chinati Foundation*** in 1986 as an art museum dedicated to permanent installations of very large works of art in 15 buildings and scattered around the grounds of the former army post called Fort D. A. Russell. The museum is about a mile south of town and is open Wed through Sun from 9 a.m. to 5 p.m. For information call (432) 729-4362 or visit chinati.org.

Adjacent to the Chinati Foundation property is a cultural center, **El Cosmico** (US 67, a few blocks south of US 90; 432-729-1950; elcosmico.com). A lodging site with numerous, magnificently restored travel trailers, this has become a magnet for artists, musicians, and people who embrace a lifestyle that blends sophistication with bohemian sensibilities. Your reservation includes all bedding, bath linens, cookware, and more. El Cosmico offers several special events throughout the year, including culinary classes and music gatherings, including the very popular **TransPecos Festival of Music and Love** in late September.

If you get high on golf, head 2 miles east from downtown on Gold Course Road and you'll find the **Marfa Municipal Golf Course** (432-729-4043), the highest golf course in Texas, sitting almost a mile in elevation above sea level. There are nine holes open to the public, and greens fees are $10.63 on weekdays and $15.94 on Fri, Sat, and Sun. Open Tues through Sun 8:30 a.m. to 7:30 p.m.

The most daring visitors may want to take to the skies on a ride with the **Marfa Gliders** at the Marfa Airport (4 miles north of town on Highway 17; 432-386-5505; flygliders.com). Owner Burt Compton, an FAA-certified flight

Ghost Lights of Marfa

Nobody seems to know why, but there have been some strange lights appearing off the horizon near Marfa since the late 1800s. Various stories and theories circulate about what the **Marfa Ghost Lights** are, but not even the scientists who have studied them have come up with a sure explanation. Most people who have observed them say the lights sometimes glow softly and then brighten to the intensity of a searchlight. You can see for yourself by driving (after dark, of course) east from Marfa on US 90/67 about 8 miles.

Pull over on the south shoulder of the road where a visitor center and viewing station await. Look southwest toward the Chinati Mountains and just wait. You'll probably wait just a little while, then—poof! There's the first one, a little ball of light in the distance, bobbing just the tiniest bit. Then—poof! It splits into two slightly wavering, shimmering spheres. More will likely appear, but maybe not. Ask the folks around town about all the theories, and decide for yourself. The Marfa Chamber of Commerce has information at (432) 729-4942.

instructor, will take you up in the wild blue yonder, and he can teach basic piloting and advanced soaring techniques. It's open year-round.

For a more in-depth look at the region, head west on US 90/67 for 26 miles to **Alpine,** seat of Brewster County and home to 6,000 west Texans and Sul Ross State University, right on US 90. On the campus you'll find the **Museum of the Big Bend** (432-837-8143; museumofthebigbend.com), relocated in its original but renovated WPA rock building. Drink in the west Texas cowboy history and buy any number of books about Texas. Open Tues through Sat from 9 a.m. to 5 p.m. and Sun from 1 to 5 p.m. Admission is free, but donations are accepted.

Stick around a while and maybe rest up at **Holland Hotel** (209 W. Holland Ave., Alpine; 800-535-8040 or 432-837-2800; thehollandhoteltexas.com), a historic, 3-floor hotel with 12 restored rooms and 2 suites. Recently and lavishly restored, the Holland is smack in the middle of historic downtown. Even high in the hotel's tiny "penthouse"—a cute little hideout for those who don't mind a steep staircase—you can still hear the train whistling by every couple of hours. A tiny sign on the nightstand, accompanied by two little packages of earplugs, reads, We Think Our Train Is Very Quaint. But If Ears It Pains, Plug 'Em And It Cain't. The restaurant and bar at the Holland are popular, to say the least.

In this charming downtown neighborhood is a host of shops and galleries. Among these, find **Front Street Books** (121 E. Holland Ave., Alpine; 432-837-3360; fsbooks.com), an excellent bookstore selling plenty of Big Bend and west Texas titles, maps, natural history guides, rare and out-of-print books, as well as notecards, books on tape, the *New York Times,* and used books. It's open Mon through Sat until 7 p.m. Just a few blocks from the bookstore, **Plaine** (215 E. Holland Ave., Alpine, 432-837-5157), is a busy coffee shop with beautiful locally made pastries. The Cow Dog food truck is frequently parked next to Plaine.

Have no doubt: Crowds still flock to the original **Reata** (203 N. 5th St., Alpine; 432-837-9232; reata.net), a mainstay in Alpine and the place to find filling goodies like beef tenderloin tamales, shrimp enchiladas, and grilled quail. Low-key and affordable, **Los Jalapenos Cafe** (102 W. Murphy St., Alpine; 432-837-5101) serves good green chile–chicken enchiladas and posole.

Baseball fans and lovers of historical architecture are sure to be fond of **Kokernot Field** (Loop Road; 432-837-5180), a scaled-down version of Yankee Stadium and a beloved memorial to the game of summer. Home to the Sul Ross Lobos, the stadium was built for the semipro Alpine Cowboys, who play on only in memory.

To celebrate Alpine's growing arts community, there's an annual **Gallery Night** held in November, during which more than 20 galleries keep special evening hours and invite you to stroll and peruse special exhibits. For details on this event, and to get a wonderful walking-tour map of Alpine, visit the chamber of commerce at 106 N. 3rd St. in Alpine, call (432) 837-2326, or check out the website visitalpinetx.com.

If you're ready for more adventure, head out for Jeff Davis County and its county seat, **Fort Davis,** north 26 miles via Highway 118. A cavalry post was established in 1855, the town later became a haven for sufferers of respiratory problems, and commercially grown Delicious apples eventually became a primary industry. The highest town in Texas at just over 5,000 feet, Fort Davis is cool enough to warrant wearing at least a sweater 11 months out of the year.

A good home base in town is the **Hotel Limpia,** on the square in the middle of the tiny town (432-426-3237 or 800-662-5517; hotellimpia.com). The hotel was built in 1912 by the Union Trading Company, was remodeled, and is a member of the Historic Accommodations of Texas. There's an upstairs balcony and an enclosed veranda full of rocking chairs, potted flowers, and oak tables—plus a lovely view of the sunset. The front desk's stained-glass detail and an old ranch house door add to the period mood. High-ceilinged rooms and suites are filled with antique oak furnishings, and the big main lounge has a native-stone fireplace. The Limpia's lodgings have been expanded to include—in addition to the main hotel and the annex out back—the Mulhern House, a renovated adobe home built in 1905, now offering 3 suites; Limpia Cottage, with its back pressed to the mountains; and the Dr. Jones House, a 1903 home that has been restored.

The Limpia's Blue Mountain Bistro features Spanish cuisine (think shrimp with garlic, prosciutto croquettes, potato omelet), steaks, veal scallopini, whole mountain trout, and a good wine list. Also part of the Limpia are Sutler's Club, a friendly little place to wet your whistle; the Hotel Limpia Gifts, a pretty store specializing in glassware and home furnishings; and Javelinas to Hollyhocks, an artistic boutique selling books and maps, candles, pewter photo frames, and sweatshirts.

A few blocks north of the Limpia, find **Cueva de Leon** (611 Highway 118, Fort Davis; 432-426-3801), a friendly, no-frills café famous in the area for handmade chiles rellenos and cheddar cheese enchiladas in red chile sauce.

The best orientation to the area's wonders is found by driving the **74-Mile Scenic Loop Road,** beginning and ending in Fort Davis. An array of mountain vistas, Madera Canyon, and roadside parks bounded by ancient boulders are the rewards for following Highway 17 south of town just 2 miles to Highway 166 west to Highway 118, then southeast back to Highway 17 and Fort Davis.

Then it's time to see the reason Fort Davis came into being: As Indian raids increased with the numbers of settlers arriving or traveling through this part of the state, usually en route from San Antonio to El Paso, a cavalry post was built in 1855. **Fort Davis National Historic Site** is the restored site, named for US Secretary of War Jefferson Davis, who ordered the army's posting here. Active from 1854 until 1891, with lapses during the Civil War, when fire destroyed the fort, it was home to 12 cavalry and infantry companies—numbering up to 800 men—stationed here in 50 buildings. The renovated stone-and-adobe remains sit in a scenic box canyon, sheltered on the west by towering cliffs, and are as complete and impressive as any in the Southwest. This indoor-outdoor museum was also the post for black troops from the Ninth, Tenth, Twentieth, and Twenty-fourth US Cavalries. As was the case at Fort Concho, the enemy Comanche and Apache soldiers named these men the Buffalo Soldiers, which has been interpreted as a term of respect.

texastrivia

Nine of the giant **Texas Ruby Red grapefruit** (the state fruit) equal the volume and mass of 12 regular grapefruit.

During the summer a living-history program demonstrates pioneer and fort life with costumed participants; the fort's Labor Day celebration draws as many as 2,000 spectators, and a special Black History event is a February highlight. Otherwise the place is easily seen on self-guided tours with a slide-show introduction. A bugle sounds twice daily, starting the audio of a formal ceremony on the parade yard. Images of hundreds of mounted and marching soldiers in full dress are easy to see in the mind's eye. The commander's house was occupied the longest by Col. Benjamin H. Grierson, and his original furnishings show luxury's spotty hand in a usually mundane frontier post life. Antiques, silver, and linens decorate the parlor and dining areas; giant beds and ornate wardrobes are characteristic in the over-size bedrooms. A museum in the main building contains a display illustrating Trans-Pecos frontier days, the overland gold rush, stagecoach and Indian raiding routes, plus artifacts such as an officer's scabbard, pistol, and musket. A gift shop sells books and more books, including Old West cookbooks, art books, and children's coloring books.

Fort Davis is open daily from 8 a.m. to 5 p.m. A small admission fee is charged. The fort is situated immediately north of town on Highway 118; call (432) 426-3224 for more information.

You can be enveloped in the area's solitude and natural beauty by a stay in **Davis Mountains State Park,** 4 miles north of town on Highway 118 (432-426-3337; tpwd.texas.gov). Sandwiched ideally between the grassy desert plains and the fragrant, woodsy mountains, this 2,700-acre park offers numerous hikes, from easy to challenging, as well as a rewarding Skyline Drive. Camp if you like, or call ahead for a room at the nicely renovated **Indian Lodge,** a pueblo-style motel with plenty of amenities, plus the hand-carved cedar furniture fashioned by Civilian Conservation Corps workers, who also built the lodge in the 1930s. The park is open daily for day use from 8 a.m. to 5 p.m. and at all hours for campers. Admission is charged. The Black Bear restaurant inside the lodge has been recently upgraded, and the chef offers plentiful plates of seasonal and—when possible—local provisions.

Or hang your hat at the **Prude Ranch,** also just north of town on Highway 118 (432-426 3202 or 800-458-6232; prude-ranch.com). A working ranch run by the same friendly west Texas family and open to guests since 1921, it offers bunkhouse and motel-style lodging, horseback riding, tennis, a Jacuzzi, and plenty of ranch-hand chow. To honor the ranch's centennial (it was founded in 1897), the Texas State Historical Commission bestowed a historical marker in 1997 that details the ranch's history.

Stargazing travelers will want to drive up to the **McDonald Observatory,** a University of Texas operation reached by driving from Fort Davis 17 miles northwest on Highway 118, then 2 miles southeast on Spur 78. Sitting atop 6,800-foot Mount Locke, the observatory features a 107-inch telescope, plus tours for visitors to see its 160 tons of moving parts. Programs at the spectacular visitor center include solar viewings, and star parties are staged Tuesday, Friday, and Saturday evenings for looking at celestial objects through small telescopes. Even if you're not in time for a viewing, pay a visit anyway to see the fascinating 30-minute video on the universe, produced by NASA. A great gift shop with unusual goods and the Stardate Cafe are on-site. The visitor center is open daily from 9 a.m. to 5 p.m. Solar viewing programs are offered. Call (432) 426-3640 or (877) 984-7827, or visit mcdonaldobservatory.org, for information and times. Admission is charged.

If you're hungry, belly up to the soda fountain called **The Drug Store** (113 N. State St., Fort Davis; 432-426-3118; fortdavisdrugstore.net). The burgers and root beer floats are the stuff of your childhood dreams. Upstairs, there's an inn, too.

Next door along the boardwalk, facing the Hotel Limpia, is the **Harvard Hotel** (109 State St., Fort Davis; 432-426-2500; harvardhotelandlodge.com). Every room is a suite with microwave, refrigerator, TV/DVD player, Wi-Fi, pillow-top mattresses, and western décor. Book well ahead and you'll get one of the suites with a great balcony overlooking the street. The hotel owners offer similar suites on their ranch, along with a rock cabin, outfitted with a full kitchen and washer-dryer. At the ranch you can sit in a hot tub, shoot skeet, take a Jeep tour in the beautiful and scrubby Davis Mountains, or arrange a guided hunt for elk, mountain lion, deer, antelope, javelina, and birds.

For more lodging and dining information, contact the **Fort Davis Chamber of Commerce** at (432) 426-3015 or (800) 524-3015 or log onto fortdavis .com.

Trans-Pecos Country

Driving north from Fort Davis along Highway 17, the gorgeous winding road courses through slumping rock formations as it follows Limpia Creek; if you take along some snacks, you can stop at one of several roadside picnic sites and enjoy the scenery in relative quiet, as there isn't a lot of traffic along the route. Watch on the east side of the road for a 1956 Texas Historical Marker, noting Wild Rose Pass.

From Fort Davis the next stop is **Balmorhea State Park,** north on Highway 17, 39 miles away. Truly unusual in this modern day is a pool like the one here: Said to be the world's largest spring-fed swimming pool, Balmorhea's measures nearly 2 acres, is 30 feet deep, and contains 3.5 million gallons of water. Talk about cool—the water is between 72 and 76 degrees year-round, so your only swimming opportunities fall between the end of May and Labor Day. In addition to a vintage bathhouse and concession stand, you'll find tent and RV campsites and a small hotel, called San Solomon Courts, on-site. The grounds are green and roomy, so even if you miss the pool season, this is a delightful place to kick back and plot your next move down the road. Call (432) 375-2370 for reservations or visit tpwd.texas.gov/state-parks/balmorhea. Open daily from dawn until dusk. Admission is charged for park entry and pool use.

If the San Solomon Courts in Balmorhea State Park are full, look for a room in the town of Balmorhea at a lodging called the **Eleven Inn** (504 S. Main St., Balmorhea; 432-375-2263; theeleveninn.com). There are—you guessed it—11 rooms in this renovated motor court, all spanking clean and updated with iron or wood beds, cool antique or retro furnishings, and flat-screen TVs. No two rooms are alike; two have microwave ovens and minifridges. The grounds have picnic tables, grills, a fire pit, and clotheslines where scuba divers hang their wetsuits after exploring the depths over at the park's spring-fed pool.

Keep your eyes peeled in this area for some of the purely Texan things that make this part of the world something you won't forget. On the section of Highway 17 that is the main street in Balmorhea, for example, there's a yellow road sign with just a turkey on it—as in, turkey crossing. And on Highway 17 between Balmorhea and Pecos, look at the tops of telephone poles. More than likely, you'll see a hawk perched on high, looking for lunch in the fields.

If you've come at the right time, this is the point at which to make a detour 33 miles north on Highway 17 to **Pecos,** home in late June to the world-famous **West of the Pecos Rodeo.** The massive affair has been held annually since June 1883, when cowhands from the Hashknife, W, Lazy Z, and NA ranches argued in Red Newell's saloon over which one had the best ropers and riders among its brethren. Ever since, the summer holiday has been set aside for competitors in saddle-bronc riding, steer roping, bulldogging, and plenty of other tough events. Things have progressed considerably since that first rodeo, when 1,000 spectators showed up to watch the cowhands compete for a $40 prize—the numbers have increased by the thousands. Pecos, known far and wide also for its cantaloupes, hosts its **Night in Old Pecos & Cantaloupe Festival** in late July, as well as a **Sheriff's Posse Championship BBQ Cook Off** the first weekend in October. For tickets and information call the tourism office at (432) 445-2406, or stop by at 111 S. Cedar St.

Should you decide to stick around and explore Pecos for a spell, pay a visit to the **West of the Pecos Museum** (1st Street at US 285/Cedar Street, Pecos; 432-445-5076; westofthepecosmuseum.com), occupying the old Orient Hotel. You can see bullet holes from the last gunfight in town, which took place more than 120 years ago, and explore 50 rooms on 3 floors filled with area relics, as well as period exhibits pertaining to such folks as the local sheriff, doctor, rodeo queens, Rotarians, and so on. A popular exhibit is the replica of the Jersey Lilly Saloon, where Judge Roy Bean reigned as "the Law West of the Pecos" down in the town of Langtry. Another exhibit honors Clay Allison, the gentleman gunfighter who "never killed anybody who didn't need killing." The museum is open Tues through Sat from 9 a.m. to 5 p.m.

All this is bound to work up a hunger, so it's a good thing the **La Nortena Tortilla Factory** (211 E. 3rd St., Pecos; 432 445 3273) is right around the corner. It's nothing fancy, but the homemade tamales and tortillas are rewarding.

Sorry, No Muppets Here

The Winkler County seat of **Kermit** became a boomtown in 1926, when oil was discovered nearby in the Permian Basin. If you're passing through, stop to see the town's oldest structure, the **Medallion Home,** built in 1907 about 5 miles south of town. It was dismantled and moved into Kermit in 1910 and was occupied until deeded to the city in 1967. Find it in Pioneer Park. For details call (432) 586-2507.

Whatever the season, your path from Balmorhea is northwest to *Guadalupe Mountains National Park.* You can reach it by driving west for 71 miles, through parts of Reeves, Jeff Davis, and Culberson Counties to the town of Van Horn. Here you'll turn north on Highway 54 and go 55 miles to the park. Note that once inside the park, you've entered Mountain Time. This former ranch land is blessed with 80 miles of hiking trails, assorted mountains (some up to 8,700 feet high), breathtaking overlooks, ancient canyons colored in ridges of brilliant oranges and reds, abandoned ranches, springs, and spectacular foliage in autumn—all of it a photographer's delight. Because of its remote position, this isn't ever a crowded park; those mountaintop pine-and-fir forests are usually just yours to relish. The only company you might have is that of mountain lions, elk, wild turkeys, and black bears. More tame in the way of wildlife are cacti blooming with purple, pink, and ruby flowers. Stop at the visitor center first and inquire about ranger-guided hikes, programs in the amphitheater, and the best places to view or photograph McKittrick Canyon, El Capitan, and Guadalupe Peak. Camping is available at Pine Springs and Upper Dog Canyon campgrounds in the park. The headquarters visitor center is open Mon through Fri from 8 a.m. to 4:30 p.m. Call (915) 828-3251 or visit nps.gov/gumo for more information. The entrance fee (payable at any trailhead) is $8 per person (good for seven days).

If you head west on US 62/180, 70 miles to FR 2775, then make a turn north and follow it 8 miles to *Hueco Tanks State Park,* you'll find odd, blobbish rock formations with caves and cliffs containing some 2,000 ancient Native American pictographs, some from the Apaches, as well as ruins of an old Butterfield stage station. The park's name comes from the vast, natural rainwater basins, or *huecos* (WHAY-coes) in Spanish, making this spread a giant oasis for dwellers and travelers for as long, some studies reveal, as 10,000 years. Camping, picnicking, rock climbing, nature study, and rock art tours are offered. Open daily 8 a.m. to 6 p.m. (until 5 p.m. for campers). Admission is charged. Call (915) 857-1135 or visit tpwd.texas.gov for information.

Your final area for west Texas exploration is *El Paso,* 30 miles west of the Hueco Tanks turnoff, via US 62/180. Jammed into a pass of the mile-high Franklin Mountains, the ancient city clings to and curves around the mountains' base. Inspirations all around are as Native American and pioneer as they are Mexican and Spanish. Combined with Juarez, El Paso's twin across the Rio Grande, the population pushes 1.5 million—and some days there's the smog to prove it. In spite of all those people, El Paso feels wide open and very much a part of the Wild West. The purple and orange–layered sunsets soften the craggy mountains, giving them a blue cast and the city a somber backdrop. Annual visitors number around 15 million, due in part to the sunshine, which brightens at least 300 days each year. The story goes that World War II servicemen stationed at massive Fort Bliss discovered the margarita, but they were preceded in discoveries by the 16th-century Spanish conquistadors who found this pass to the north from Mexico, and so named the place for its use.

Older even than California's, ***El Paso's historic missions*** occupy a lower valley along El Camino Real, or the Royal Highway used by the missionaries and conquistadors and the longest historic road in the US. The first to explore is the ***Ysleta Mission,*** situated at Zaragosa and Alameda, next to the Tigua Indian Reservation. Founded by Franciscan padres in 1680, this mission has been rebuilt several times and is thought to be the nation's oldest mission and possibly the oldest continuously used parish in the nation. Don't be confused, but the church's official name is Our Lady of Mount Carmel, yet there's a St. Anthony statue on the outside, as he is the patron saint of the Tigua Indians, who fled New Mexico during the Pueblo Revolt in the 17th century. All missions are open daily from 8 a.m. to 5 p.m. Admission is free.

Socorro Mission, 3 miles southeast of Ysleta Mission on FR 258, was also founded in 1680. This one is of the classic, stark adobe design, and its ornate, hand-hewn roof beams are the oldest in Texas. Travel 5 miles southeast to ***San Elizario Presidio Church,*** also on FR 258, to see the 1770s architecture in a lovely courtyard. This is still an active Catholic church. Note that drives to the missions are prettiest in autumn, when cotton fields are overrun with white bolls, pecan groves stretch without end, and row upon row of chiles and onions burst in reds and greens. Farmers are usually found on roadsides tending their stands, selling roasted chiles or big, fat ristras, those hanging bunches of chiles that are very fashionable in southwestern décor. For more history and information on the missions, visit visitelpasomissiontrail.com.

For a deeper look into history surviving to the modern day, visit the ***Tigua Indian Reservation*** (119 S. Old Pueblo Rd., El Paso; 915-859-7913; ysletadelsurpueblo.org). Also called Ysleta del Sur Pueblo, this is the home of descendants of those Tiguas who fled during the Pueblo Revolt in New Mexico more than 300 years ago. There's a living-history pueblo, with demonstrations of pottery, jewelry, and weaving crafts, plus bread baking in dome-shaped ovens. Tribal dances are performed during special events, while the 21st century threatens to impose itself, as the Tiguas prepare to bring high-stakes gambling to the reservation to increase tourism income. In the Cultural Center, you'll find handcrafts for sale. There's a wellness center on the reservation, too. Open daily from 8 a.m. to 5 p.m. Admission is free, but donations are accepted.

Of El Paso's two scenic drives, the ***Scenic Road*** is shorter and easier to access. Drive behind the Sun Bowl and wind between formidable walls of rock for 2 miles west to east, from Rim Road to Richmond Avenue. From Murchison

Park at the road's apex 4,200 feet high, your vista includes two cities, three states, and two countries. You can see a stone peg that marks the end of the Rocky Mountains, a giant Christ statue on Sierra del Cristo Rey, and several war memorials. Sadly, you may also see a fair amount of graffiti and trash.

don'tyou walkonby . . .

In *Wink* there's the *Roy Orbison Museum,* named for the native son and rock 'n' roll legend who became famous for "Pretty Woman," "Only the Lonely," and many other popular songs. See memorabilia from his youth and his career, including albums and singles and his trademark sunglasses. For tours call (432) 527-3545.

The other route is the more lengthy *Transmountain Drive,* a highway cutting through Smugglers Gap in the North Franklin Mountains. The summit is almost a mile above sea level, and the Wilderness Park is up there with great Chihuahuan Desert hiking trails. A nature trail passes replicas of a Pueblo ruin, kiva, and pithouse. The view of mountains reveals geologic history—gray shades indicate where ancient inland seawaters lapped, and reds are the leavings of volcanic lava flows.

The *Franklin Mountains State Park* is in this area, too. The 24,000-acre wilderness offers mountain bikers, hikers, rock climbers, and horseback riders more than 100 miles of trails. After $1.5 million in improvements, the park is now open to overnight campers, too. Guided tours led by park rangers are given the first and third weekends of each month, and there is an aerial tramway to ride. Call (915) 566-6441 for reservations, or visit tpwd.texas.gov for information.

Downtown El Paso showplace for more than a century has been the *Camino Real Paso Del Norte Hotel* (101 S. El Paso St., El Paso; 915-534-3050; camino-real.elpasobesthotels.com/en/), built in 1912 and listed on the National Register of Historic Places. The 80-year-old Tiffany glass dome is a commanding sight in the hotel's elegant Dome Bar. Guests here over the years have included Pancho Villa, President Taft, and "Black Jack" Pershing.

Three fine museums are *El Paso Museum of Art* (1 Arts Festival Plaza, El Paso; 915-532-1707;epma.art), featuring the Kress Collection of European Art, with masterpieces from the 13th to the 18th centuries; *El Paso Museum of History* (510 N. Santa Fe, El Paso; 915-351-3588; elpasotexas.gov/history/) has a new, beautiful home in downtown El Paso, where colorful exhibits detail the history of Native Americans, conquistadors, vaqueros, cowboys, and cavalrymen who played a role in taming the Southwest; and the *Magoffin Homestead* (1120 Magoffin St., El Paso; 915-533-5147; thc.texas.gov/historic-sites/magoffin-home-state-historic-site), a state historical park featuring the adobe

Evolutions in the High Desert

The first time I visited Marfa, it was yet undiscovered by the throngs of art aficionados who would eventually come from New York, Los Angeles and the world. It was still a quiet ranching town, where everyone was either paying a bill at the electric company on Highland Avenue, picking up supplies at a hardware store or eating lunch at the Capri. I was doing the latter, enjoying a massive chicken-fried steak at the popular café where all the other diners were in cowboy boots, some jangling with spurs, just in from whatever ranch they called home. The Capri went away as Marfa's explosion as a chic art destination grew, but I didn't forget that home-cooking and friendly vibe. Just recently, the owners at the fashionable Thunderbird, a hip motel in town, revived the *Capri,* rebuilding on the same site but making it a place for today's hip visitor. Instead of chicken-fried steak and big tumblers of iced tea, guests enjoy foie gras terrine, squash soup, Island Creek oysters with prickly pear mignonette, and a 50-ounce Akaushi ribeye steak. With swanky cocktails. While I miss the Marfa I first knew, it's nice to enjoy martinis and the high desert air on a pretty patio—a pleasure that never goes out of style.

hacienda built by settler Joseph Magoffin in 1875, with some original period furnishings.

Two more museums, the **Fort Bliss Replica Museum** (915-568-4518) and the **US Army Air Defense Museum** (915-568-5412), are found at Fort Bliss on Pleasanton Road, near the airport. The largest air defense center in the world, the base was founded as an army post in 1849 and named after Lt. Col. William Wallace Smith Bliss. Both museums are wonderful in detail. Call for hours. Admission is free, but donations are accepted.

At the **Border Patrol Museum** (4315 Transmountain Rd., El Paso; 915-759-6060; borderpatrolmuseum.com), visitors learn about the US Border Patrol's history since the days of the Old West. Exhibits include aircraft and vehicles used by the patrol, surveillance equipment, confiscated items, and more.

You can find a little bit more history at **Concordia Cemetery** (just northwest of the intersection of I-10 and US 54), a graveyard begun in 1856. Find the section that was El Paso's "Boot Hill," where illustrious gunfighter John Wesley Hardin is buried.

People drive from all over west Texas and southern New Mexico to while away days just eating and shopping in El Paso. Among the favorite places to eat is the **H&H Car Wash and Coffee Shop** (701 E. Yandel Dr., El Paso; 915-533-1144), an old-fashioned institution where you can have your car hand washed while the kitchen staff inside makes you an unforgettable meal. Best bets are the carne picada, or sautéed beef tips with tomato, onion, and jalapeño, or the amazing huevos rancheros and other spicy breakfast treats.

Long considered the town's most romantic restaurant, ***Cafe Central*** (109 N. Oregon St., El Paso; 915-545-2233; cafecentral.com) is also thought to be the best. A blend of contemporary and classic cuisines, the menu offers smoked salmon paired with crab and caviar, as well as tender osso buco in red wine.

It's possible to do nothing for days but shop for wonderful Texas and Mexican gifts and goods in El Paso. The first two of several stores of special note is ***Justin Boot Factory Outlet*** (7100 Gateway East at I-10, El Paso; 915-779-5465; justinboots.com), a superstore selling a complete line of boots as well as belts, hats, and all kinds of western accessories; and ***Lucchese Boots*** (6601 Montana Ave., El Paso; 915-778-8060; lucchese.com), the factory store for the famous bootmaker, established in 1883. You'll find boots at up to 50 percent off retail prices, as well as cool old photographs, boot casts, and memorabilia of famous people who have boasted a pair of Luccheses. ***Tony Lama Factory Stores*** (call for directions to three locations, 915-772-4327) sell leather western boots made right in El Paso.

For a look at the Texas-Mexico connection, visit the ***Chamizal National Memorial*** (800 S. San Marcial, El Paso; 915- 532-7273; nps.gov/cham). Built on land that became part of the US when the Chamizal border dispute with Mexico was settled in 1963, the grounds cover 55 acres and feature a museum and amphitheater. Open daily from 8 a.m. to 5:30 p.m. Admission is free.

Other Places to Stay in Wildest West Texas

ALPINE

Maverick Inn
1200 E. Holland Ave.
(432) 837-0628
themaverickinn.com
A contemporary ranch-style makeover of an old motel; sand-colored stucco walls, Saltillo tile floors, heavy Mexican furniture, Indian rugs, flat screen TVs, Wi-Fi, Egyptian cotton bed linens, and cushy down bedding make for a chic stay.

BALMORHEA

San Solomon Courts
inside the state park
tpwd.texas.gov/state-parks/balmorhea/fees-facilities/motel-rooms
(432) 375-2370
All 18 adobe units are within a few steps of the celebrated pool. Some have kitchenettes.

EL PASO

Hotel Indigo
325 N. Kansas St.
(915) 532-5200
ihg.com
A renovated 1960s hotel brings a retro option to downtown El Paso with décor that mixes modern American with Mexican influences.

FORT DAVIS

The Veranda

1 block west of courthouse
(432) 426-2233
theveranda.com
Opened in 1883 as the
Lempert Hotel, this adobe
building with 2-foot-thick
walls has wood floors, high
ceilings, period furniture,
porches, courtyards,
and gardens. There are
7 rooms, all with private
baths, ranging from
the large bedroom with
2 double beds and a
fireplace inlaid with quartz
to the 2-room king suites
with mountain views.
There's also a private
carriage house in an
orchard of apricot and
peach trees. Breakfast is
included with stay.

MARFA

Cibolo Creek Ranch

30 miles south off
Highway 17
(432) 229-3737
cibolocreekranch.com
This 25,000-acre working
ranch offers tours of
lands where bison, elk,
and longhorn roam. The
ranch consists of 3 lavishly
restored, 19th-century
forts named El Cibolo, La
Cienega, and La Morita. El
Cibolo, the largest, has 11
guest rooms, which start at
$250 and top out at $500
or so (meals are included),
and has a heated pool,
Jacuzzi, stocked reservoir,
and an exceptional
museum. Décor in all areas
is a tasteful, stylish blend

of western and Mexican
designs.

Thunderbird Hotel

601 W. San Antonio St.
(432) 729-1984
thunderbirdmarfa.com
Renovation of an old motel
has delivered a desirable,
contemporary oasis in
west Texas. This hotel
has 24 rooms, some with
private patio or balcony.
Features include flat-screen
TV, DVD player, fabulous
appointments, nice pool,
and outdoor fireplace.
Dogs allowed. Rates start
at $125.

Other Places to Eat in Wildest West Texas

ALPINE

Judy's Bread & Breakfast Bakery

113 W. Holland Ave.
(432) 837-9424
Coffee, cinnamon rolls,
pancakes, biscuits and
gravy are among good
ways to start your day.

BALLINGER

Lowake Steak House

about 6 miles south via US
67 and FR 381
(325) 218-4025
This legendary steak joint
has unbeatable T-bones,
rib eyes, filets, and strips,
plus the best onion rings

and baked potatoes. Open
Tues through Sun for lunch
and dinner, meals average
$10.

EL PASO

Doña Lupe Cafe

2919 Pershing Ave.
(915) 566-9833
A former 1960s drugstore
soda fountain in the
historic Five Points district
has been a mainstay
for homemade chiles
rellenos and other Mexican
specialties for nearly 50
years. Open daily for lunch
and dinner.

MARFA

Cochineal

107 W. San Antonio St.
(432) 729-3300
Cochinealmarfatexas.com
Exceptional food that you
might find in New York or
San Francisco includes
handcrafted pastas and
salads made from locally
produced ingredients. Very
nice wine list, too.

Food Shark

909 W. San Antonio St.
(432) 207-2090
foodsharkmarfa.com
A lunch truck and gathering
spot for locals, this eatery
dispenses an always-
changing menu of Middle
Eastern–inspired dishes
and some unforgettable
baked goods. Friday-night
dinner features a changing
menu.

Pizza Foundation
305 S. Spring St.
(432) 729-3377
Exceptional pizza topped
with such goodies as feta,
ricotta, spinach, fresh
basil, local tomatoes,
and chorizo. Don't miss
the tomato-bread salad.
BYOB.

MIDLAND

**Manuel's Country Store
& Deli**
3905 TX 349 South
(432) 682-2258
Homemade tortilla chips,
burritos, brisket tacos,
and chicken enchiladas
are great reasons to come
here. Open for breakfast
and lunch.

Sedona Grill
2101 W. Wadley St.
(432) 570-9600
sedonamexicancantina
.com
Shrimp tacos, green-
chile empanadas (savory
turnovers), and tortilla soup
have patrons panting at
this southwestern cuisine
hot spot. Lunch and dinner
are served, and prices are
moderate.

ODESSA

**Permian Basin
Hamburger Co.**
520 N. Grant St.
(432) 333-4971
This quaint diner in the
heart of old downtown
serves breakfast and lunch
Mon through Fri.

Rockin' Q Smokehouse
3812 Penbrook St.
(432) 552-7105
Delectable pork ribs and
beef brisket are smoked
over a hickory fire for tasty
delights. Open for lunch
and dinner daily; moderate.

PECOS

Abi's Kitchens
425 W. 3rd St.
(432) 447-0475
Serving American and
Mexican food. Closed Sat.

Index

A

Abbott, 5
Abi-Haus, 210
Abilene, 206, 208, 232, 233
Abilene Zoo and Discovery Center, 209
Abi's Kitchens, 272
Abri Gallery, 22
Acapulco, 233
ACL Live at The Moody Theater, 16
Acme Dry Goods, 81
Acton State Historic Site, 189
Adams Extract Co., 13
Adobe Haciendas, 249
African American Museum, 173
Alamo Irish Festival, 111
Alamo, The, 109
Albany, 205, 206, 209, 232
Alibates National Monument, 221
Allen Family Style Meals, 214
Allens Boots, 17
Alpine, 237, 239, 260, 270, 271
Amarillo, 206, 209, 218, 232, 233
Amarillo Convention and Visitor Council, 221
Amber's Creekside Steakhouse, 233
American Airlines C. R. Smith Museum, 180
American Airpower Heritage Museum and Commemorative Air Force Headquarters, 243

American Quarter Horse Association, 215
American Quarter Horse Hall of Fame & Museum, 221
American Quarter Horse Heritage Center, 215
American Wind Power Center, 229
Amistad National Recreation Area, 120
Amon Carter Museum, 163, 182
Ancient Ovens, 168
Anderson, 28
Angelina National Forest, 137
Annie Riggs Memorial Museum, 247
Anson, 212
Antiques Capital of East Texas, 149
Antiques Capital of West Texas, 211
Antlers, 78
Antone's, 19
Ant Street Inn, 31
Aplomado falcons, 65
Apple Capital of Texas, 99
Apple Store, 99
Aquarena Springs, 102
Aquarium, 45
Aransas National Wildlife Refuge, 54
Arbor Hotel and Conference Center, 233
Arbor House, 201
Arché, 168
Archer City, 199
Arlington, 179

Armadillo/Christmas Bazaar, 4
Armadillo Palace, 43
Armadillo Palace, The, 43
Armand Bayou Nature Center, 45
Armenta's, 240
Armstrong Browning Library, 3, 7
Arp, 134
Arlington Ranch House Lodge, 224
Arrowhead Resort, 31
Art Museum of South Texas, 58
ArtPace, 114
Ashton Hotel, 200
Ashton Villa, 47
Asian Cultures Museum, 59
Athens, 135, 149
AT&T Stadium, 179
Attwater Prairie Chicken National Wildlife Refuge, 45
August E's, 106
Auntie Skinner's River Boat Club, 155
Austin, 3, 4, 12, 30, 31
Austin City Limits, 14, 16
Austin College, 164
Austin Motel, 18
Austin Nature and Science Center, 14
Austin Street Bistro, 159
Autumn Trails Festival, 158
Aveda Institute, 115
Avenger Field, 213
Azalea and Spring Flower Trail, 135

B
Babe Didrikson Zaharias
Museum, 35
Babe's Chicken Dinner
House, 191
Backstreet Cafe, 70
Baird, 211
Baker Boys BBQ, 23
Balcones Distillery, 8
Ballinger, 237, 241, 271
Balmorhea, 270
Balmorhea State
Park, 264
Bandera, 73, 75, 96, 105
Bandera Convention &
Visitors Bureau, 99
Bandera ProRodeo, 75
Bar D Brewhouse, 83
Barking Rocks, 192
Bar-L, 200
Baron de Bastrop, 23
Barton Springs Pool, 14
Basin Burger House, 243
Bastrop, 3, 22, 30
Bastrop County Historical
Museum, 22
Bastrop State Park, 22
Battle of Adobe
Walls, 223
Battleship *Texas*, 44
Bat World Sanctuary, 197
Bay Area Houston
Convention and
Visitor Bureau, 45
Bayless-Selby House, 170
Baylor University, 7
Bayou Bakery and
Café, 156
Bayou Bend Collection
and Gardens, 36, 41
Bayou City Art
Festival, 39
B-Cycle, 187
Beaumont, 35, 36
Beaumont Convention
and Visitor Bureau, 39
Becker Vineyards, xii, 89

Beckmann Lane Guest
House, 105
Beehive Restaurant and
Saloon, 207
Beer Can House, 42
Beeville, 61
Belle-Jim Hotel, 137
Bell's Farm to
Market, 126
Belmont Hotel, 176
Belo Mansion, 173
Bending Branch
Winery, 96
Benefield House Bed &
Breakfast, 158
Benini Foundation
Galleries and
Sculpture Ranch, 76
Bentsen–Rio Grande
Valley State Park, 125
Bernard Mediterranean
Cuisine, 144
Betty & June, 210
Bevers Kitchen, 32
B Hive, The, 166
Biga on the Banks, 130
Big Bend Holiday
Hotel, 254
Big Bend Motor Inn and
Mission Lodge, 253
Big Bend National Park,
237, 250
Big Bend National Park
Headquarters, 250
Big Bend Stables, 253
Big Cypress Tours of
Caddo Lake, 152
Big Fish, 182
Big Pines Lodge, 152
Big Spring, 231
Big Tex, 179
Big Texan Motel,
The, 232
Big Texan Steak
Ranch, 218
Big Thicket National
Preserve, 36, 37

Big Tree of Lamar, 52
Billy Bob's Texas, 186
Bird Cafe, 186
Bishop's Palace, 47
Bi-State Justice
Center, 156
Blackchalk Home and
Laundry, 92
Blackchalk Laundry &
Home, 73
Blair House Inn, 103
Blanco, 77, 105
Blanco Bowling Club
Cafe, 77
Blanco County
Courthouse, 77
Blanton Museum of
Art, 14
Blarney Stone, 225
Blissmoor Valley Ranch
Company Store, 151
Blue Bell Ice Cream, 26
bluebonnet, 24
Bluebonnet Cafe, 78
bluegrass festivals, 193
Blue Hole, 103
Blue Ostrich Winery &
Vineyard, 168
Blue Star Contemporary
Art Center, 114
Blue Star Trading, 195
B. Naylor Morton
Research and
Collections, 112
Boardwalk Inn, 45
Bob Bullock Texas State
History Museum, 15
Bob Wills Day, 209
Bob Wills Museum, 217
Boca Chica, 125
Bodacious Barbecue, 150
Boerne, 99
Bogel, Philip Hendrik
Nering, 23
Bonham, 162
Bonneville, 212
Boomerang Billy's, 67

Boot Store, 169
Border Patrol
    Museum, 269
Bosque Arts Center, 194
Bosque County
    Emporium, 195
Bosque County Memorial
    Museum, 194
Botanical Gardens, 14
Boy Grumpe's, 211
Bracken Cave
    Colony, 116
Brackettville, 109, 119
Brady, 75, 83
Branch on High, 96
Brazos Belle, 32
Brazos Island State
    Park, 128
Brazos-Republic Trail,
    xiv, 1
Brazos River, 1, 192
Breadwinners, 174, 184
Brenham, 4, 26, 31, 32
Brewster County, 64
Briscoe Western Art
    Museum, 113
Briscoe Western Art
    Museum, The, 113
British Emporium, 181
Brownsville, 111, 127,
    129, 130
Bryan–College Station, 28
Bryan Museum, 48
BT Longhorn
    Steakhouse, 27
Buchanan Dam, 75, 81
Buckhorn Saloon and
    Museum, 111
Buddy Holly Center and
    J.I. Allison House, 228
Buddy Holly Statue and
    West Texas Walk of
    Fame, 228
Buffalo Gap, 206,
    209, 211
Buffalo Gap Historic
    Village, 206, 210

Buffalo Gap Wine
    and Food Summit,
    209, 210
Burnet, 75, 79
Busbee's Bar-B-Q, 105
Butterfield Overland
    Stagecoach & Wagon
    Festival, 245
Buttermilk's On the
    Square, 148
Buu Mon Buddhist
    Temple, 39

C
Cabernet Grill, 106
Cactus Hotel, 240
Caddo Lake, 134, 152
Caddo Lake State
    Park, 152
Caddo Lake Tours, 152
Caddo Outback
    Backwater Tours, 152
Cadillac Ranch, 206, 221
Cafe Central, 270
Cafe Modern, 163, 183
Café on the Beach, 70
Cahoots, 166
Caldwell, 10
Caldwell Zoo, 143
Camel Corps, 95
Camino Real Paso Del
    Norte Hotel, 268
Camp Comfort, 73, 95
Camp Ford, 151
Camp Verde, 95, 96
Camp Verde General
    Store & Restaurant, 96
Canadian, 206, 222, 232
Canadian Chamber of
    Commerce, 224
Canadian Courts
    Motel, 232
Canadian Historic
    Downtown, 206
Canadian River Art
    Center, 223

Canadian River Historic
    Wagon Bridge, 223
Candlelight Posada,
    111, 126
Cantaloupe Festival, 265
Canton, 135, 148
Canton Visitors
    Bureau, 148
Canyon, 206, 225
Canyon of the Eagles
    Lodge & Nature
    Park, 80
Capitol Complex Visitor
    Center, 15
Capri, 269
Caprock Canyons State
    Park, 206, 217
Captain Ron's Swamp
    Tours, 152
Captain Shepard
    House, 248
Carnegie Center of
    Brazos Valley
    History, 29
Carol Bolton Hicks
    Antiquities, 92
Carshon's
    Delicatessen, 201
Carthage, 151
Casa de Palmas, 109
Casa Mañana, 185
Cascade Caverns, 100
Cast Iron Grill, 230
Castolon, 252
Castroville, 118
Catfish Plantation, 202
Cattle Exchange, 223
Cavalry Court, 29
Caverns of Sonora, 242
Cave Without a
    Name, 100
Cedar Street, 19
Cell Block, 200
Centennial House, 59
Center City, 220
Central Station, The, 150

Central Texas Area
Museum, 10
Chamizal National
Memorial, 270
Chantilly Lace Country
Inn, 76
Chappell Hill, 3, 4,
27, 32
Charles Goodnight
Historical Center, 222
Charlie's Corona, 130
Charlotte Plummer's
Seafare Restaurant, 54
Charro Days Fiesta, 111
Chaska House, The, 201
Chicken Farm Art
Center, 240
Children's Museum of
Houston, 42
Chinati Foundation, 258
Chinati Hot Springs,
237, 256
Chisholm Trail
Mural, 185
Chisos Basin, 251
Chisos Mountain
Lodge, 251
Chloe Dao Boutique, 42
Cibolo Creek Ranch, 271
Cinnamon Shore, 68
Circle Theatre, The, 185
Cisco, 214
Cisco's, 13
Cisco's Bakery, 21
Citadelle Art
Foundation, 223
City Cemetery
(Uvalde), 119
City Drug Soda
Fountain, 223
Claiborne House &
Touch of Class Day
Spa, 158
Claude, 222
Cleveland Armory Black
Beauty Ranch, 149
Cliffs, 197

Cliftex Theatre, 195
Clifton, 193, 200, 201
Clifton Chamber of
Commerce, 194
Clockwork
Coffeehouse, 247
Coastal Bend Audubon
Society, 60
Cochineal, 271
Coleman, 206, 211,
232, 233
College Street Pub, 179
Collin County History
Museum, 171
Collin Street Bakery, 4
Colorado Bend State
Park, 82
Colorado River, 1
Coltivare, 43
Comanche Trail
Park, 231
Comfort, 94
Comfort Pizza, 96
Comstock, 109
Concho Christmas
Celebration, 239
Concordia Cemetery, 269
Coney Island Cafe, 222
Congress Avenue Bridge,
17, 20
Connor Museum, 63
Conservation Plaza, 100
Contemporary Austin/
Jones Center, The, 16
Continental Club, 19
Cooke County
Courthouse, 166
Cooper's Barbecue, 82
Coors Cowboy Club
Ranch Rodeo, 221
Coors Cowboy
Rodeo, 209
Copano Bay, 52
Coppersmith Inn, 50
Cork & Pig Tavern, 240
Corner Drug Café, 201
Corpus Christi, 57, 68, 69

Corpus Christi Visitor
Office, 59
Corpus Christi Yachting
Center, 59
Corsicana, 4
Costa Messa
Restaurant, 126
Cotton Belt Depot, 181
Country Market, 210
Country Tavern, 147
Courthouse-on-the-
Square, 170
Courthouse Square, 247
Courtyard by Marriott
(Abilene), 232
Cowan Center, 143
Cowboy and His Horse
Statue, 237, 241
Cowboy Country
Museum, 213
Cowboys' Christmas
Ball, 212
Cowgirls and Cowboys
in the West, 227
Cowtown Coliseum, 186
Crafthouse
Gastropub, 230
Crafthouse Gastropub,
The, 230
Crazy Bath House, 196
Crazy Cajun, 57
Crazy Water, 196
Crockett, 136, 158
Crockett County
Museum, 246
Crosbyton, 216
Crush, 220
Crystal City, 122
Crystal River Inn, 105
C. S. Roberts House, 164
Cueva de Leon, 261
Culinary Institute of
America, 115
Cultural District (Fort
Worth), 182
Cured, 130

Cypress Creek
Cottages, 105
Czech Stop, 5

D
Dagger Flat, 251
Daingerfield, 157
Daingerfield State
Park, 157
Dalhart, 209, 224
Dallas, 163, 165, 172,
200, 201
Dallas Convention and
Visitor Bureau, 176
Dallas Cowboys, 172
Dallas Historical
Society, 172
Dallas Museum of
Art, 174
Dallas World
Aquarium, 174
DAR Museum, 170
Das Peach Haus, 92
Davis & Blevins Main
Street Gallery,
163, 168
Davis Mountains
Hummingbird
Celebration, 239
Davis Mountains State
Park, 237, 262
Davy Crockett National
Forest, 136
Day the Wall Came
Down, The, 29
Dealey Plaza, 174
Deep in the Heart
Foundry, 22
Delaney Winery &
Vineyards, 181
Del Rio, 109, 120, 129
Delta Street Inn, 155
Denison, 163
Denison Chamber of
Commerce, 163
Denton, 169, 201
Depot Museum, 156

Devil's Backbone, 104
Diamond Back's, 8
Diamond Bessie Murder
Trial, 155
Dichotomy Coffee &
Spirits, 8
Dickens on the
Strand, 39
Dieter Brothers
Restaurant, 167
Diggs Restaurant &
Club, 83
Diner, The, 144
Dinner Bell, 198
Dinner Bell, The, 198
dinosaur tracks, 118,
162, 193
Dinosaur Valley State
Park, 193
Dirty Al's, 70
Dirty Martin's Place, 21
Discovery Green, 36, 41
Dixie Dude Ranch, 97
Doc's BBQ, 137
Doc's Seafood &
Steaks, 60
Dofflemyer Hotel, 83
Dogleg Coffeehouse, 105
Dogwood Trails Festival,
135, 141
Dolphin Research and
Sea Life Nature
Center, 66
Doña Lupe Cafe, 271
Don Harrington
Discovery Center and
Planetarium, 219
Dove's Nest, 177
Downtown Cafe, 188
Dream of Flight, 180
Driftwood, 73, 104
Dr Pepper Museum
and Free Enterprise
Institute, 7
Drug Store, The, 263
Dry Hollow
Hideaway, 241

Dugout Wells, 251
Dye Guest House, 232
Dyess Air Force Base,
207, 208

E
Eagle Pass, 122
East End Historical
District, 46
East Texas Oil
Museum, 146
Easy Tiger, 17
EatZi's, 184
Edinburg, 126
Edom, 145
Ed & Tom's Bar-B-
Que, 245
1848 BBQ, 130
1895 Tarlton House, 4
Eighteen Ninety
Grille, 191
Eighteen Ninety
Marketplace, 190
814· A Texas Bistro, 96
8th Street Market, 95
806, The, 216
Eisenhower
Birthplace, 164
El Chile Café y
Cantina, 21
El Cosmico, 237,
255, 259
Eldorado, 241
Elephant Story, 95
Elephant Story, The, 95
Eleven Inn, 264
11th Street Cowboy
Bar, 98
El Guapo Records, 145
Elisabet Ney Museum, 13
Elissa, xiii, 48
Ellis County Courthouse,
163, 176
Ellis County
Museum, 177
El Paseo de Santa
Angela, 240

El Paso, 239, 266, 270, 271
El Paso Museum of Art, 268
El Paso Museum of History, 268
El Paso's historic missions, 267
El Patio Restaurant, 256
El Pato, 128
El Rancho Grande Restaurante, 187
Embassy Suites, 129
Embassy Suites Downtown Amarillo, 232
Empty Saddle Monument, 224
Enchanted Rock State Natural Area, 73, 93
English Merchant's Inn, The, 178
Ennis, 165
Esperanza's Bakery, 187
Esquire Jazz Club, 220
Etta's Place, 185
ETX Brewing Co., 143
Everman Park, 209
Eve's Garden, 249
Evett's Barbecue, 130
Evie Mae's Pit Barbeque, 233
Excelsior House, 154
Ezekiel Airship, 156
Ezekiel Cullen House, 138

F
Fair Park, 173
Falcon State Park, 123
Fall Creek Vineyards, xii, 73, 81, 104
Fannin County Fair, 162
Fannin County Museum of History, 163
Fannin Park Plaza, 61
Far Flung Advenures, 253

Farley Girls Café, 50
Farmers' Market (Dallas), 173
Farmhouse, 177
Farm Road 337, 73
Faust Hotel, 95
Faust Hotel & Brewing Company, 101
Fearing's, 174
Fender, Freddie, 128
Fenoglio Boot Company, 169
Festival Hill, 26
Fiesta San Antonio, 110, 111
Fiesta Winery, 82
Findery, The, 7
Fins to Feathers, 65
Fire Ant Festival, 135, 139
Fire Museum of Texas, 36
Fire Oak Grill, 188
First Monday Trade Days (Canton), xiii, 135, 148
First Monday Trade Days (Weatherford), 188
First Presbyterian Church, 39
Fischer's Meat Market, 167
Fischer & Wieser, 92
Flagship *Knoxville*, 180
Flora Street Café, 174
Floydada, 209, 216
Floyd's Cajun Seafood and Texas Steakhouse, 38
Flying L Hill Country Resort, 97
Folk Festival, 75
Fonda San Miguel, 21
Food Shark, 271
Foothills Safari Camp, 193

Fort Bliss Replica Museum, 269
Fort Clark Springs, 109, 119
Fort Concho National Historic Landmark, 237, 238
Fort Croghan Museum, 80
Fort Davis, 237, 239, 261, 271
Fort Davis Chamber of Commerce, 264
Fort Davis National Historic Site, 262
Fort Duncan Museum, 122
Fort Griffin Fandangle, 208, 209
Fort Griffin State Historical Park, 207
Fort Lancaster State Historic Site, 246
Fort Leaton State Historic Site, 256
Fort Mason, 84
Fort Mason Outpost Guest House, 84
Fort McKavett State Historic Site, 86
Fort Phantom Hill Ruins, 206, 212
Fort Stockton, 246
Fort Worth, 163, 165, 182, 187, 200, 201
Fort Worth Food & Wine Festival, 165
Fort Worth Zoo, 184
Fossil Rim Wildlife Center, 193
4R Ranch Vineyards & Winery, 167
Foxfire Cabins, 87
Francisco's Restaurant, 106
Franklin Mountains State Park, 268

Fredericksburg, 73, 75, 90, 105, 106
Fredericksburg Brewing Company, 92
Fredericksburg's Main Street, 92
Fredericksburg Visitor Information Center, 90
Fredonia Hotel, 140
Fred's Texas Café, 184
French Legation Museum, 13
Fresh Market Coffee, 178
Fried Pie Co. & Restaurant, 166
Frisco, 172
Frontier Texas!, 209
Frontier Times Museum, 98
Front Street Books, 237, 260
Fulton, 36, 39, 53, 69
Fulton Mansion State Historical Structure, 36, 53
Funky Art Café, 26
Funky Door Bistro & Wine Room, 230

G
Gage Hotel, 237, 248
Gaido's, 50
Gainesville, 165
Gallery Night (Alpine), 260
Galveston, 36, 39, 46, 68, 69
Galveston Island State Park, 49
Galveston Visitors Center, 47
Garner Museum, 118
Garner State Park, 86
Gathering of the Scottish Clans, 10

George Bush Presidential Library Center, 28
George's, 32
George, The, 29
Georgetown, 11, 32
Georgetown Convention and Visitors Bureau, 11
George Washington's Birthday Celebration, 123
George West, 121
Georgia James, 43
Georgia Monument, 206
Get Go, The, 258
Gingerbread Trail, 178
Gladewater, 149
Gladys Porter Zoo, 128
Glen Rose, 163, 192
Globe Theatre of the Southwest, 244
Golden Light Cafe and Cantina, 219
Golden Triangle Faith Trail, 38
Goliad, 36, 60
Goliad State Historical Park, 61
Gonzales, 23, 31
Gonzales Memorial Museum, 23
Gooney's, 233
Goose Island State Park, 52
Gorman Cave, 82
Gourmet Apples & More/Mrs G's Tacos & More, 202
Governor's Mansion, 15
Grace Museum, 208
Granbury, 163, 165, 189, 201
Granbury Convention and Visitor Bureau, 192
Granbury Opera House, 189

Granbury Theatre Company, 189
Grand 1894 Opera House, 48
Grand Hotel, 171
Granite Mountain, 78
Grape Creek Vineyards, 78
Grape Juice, 106
Grapestomp, 75
Grapevine, 165, 180, 202
Grapevine Convention and Visitors Bureau, 181
Grapevine Heritage Center, 181
Grapevine Vintage Railroad, 181, 186
Great Storm, The, 47
Great Texas Balloon Race, 135, 150
Great Texas Birding Classic, 39
Great Texas Coastal Birding Trail, 37, 60
Great Texas Mosquito Festival, 66
Gristmill, 102
Groove, The, 70
Grove, The, 159
Gruene, 101
Gruene Hall, 102
Gruene Historic District, 102
Gruene Mansion Inn, 102
Guadalupe Mountains National Park, 237, 266
Guadalupe Peak, 81
Guadalupe River, 88
Guadalupe River State Park, 100
Guenther House, 114
Guitar Ranch, 231
Gulf Coast, xiii, 33
Gumbo Cook-Off, 39

H
Habitat, 52
Hallie Stillwell's Hall of
  Fame, 250
Hall of State, 163, 173
Hamilton Pool Nature
  Preserve, 19
Hamilton Shirts, 42
Hanging Tree, 61
Hannah's Off the
  Square, 201
Harbord Kourt, The, 232
Harbor Lights Festival, 39
Hardeman Guest
  House, 159
Harlingen, 109, 127
Harry Ransom
  Humanities Research
  Center, 14
Harry's, 83
Harvard Hotel, 263
Hasse House, 84
Haute Goat
  Creamery, 150
Hay Merchant, 43
Heartland Atelier, 195
Heart of Texas Historical
  Museum, 83
H-E-B Body
  Adventure, 112
Helena, 117
Helium Monument, 219
Hell's Gates, 197
HemisFair Park, 111
Henkel Square, 25
Heritage Inns, 171
Heritage Park, 58
Heritage Village
  Museum, 136
Hester's Café & Coffee
  Bar, 69
H&H Car Wash and
  Coffee Shop, 269
Hico, 195
High Hill Farm, 134, 146
Highland Lakes, 77
High's, 96

High Street, 95
Hill Country, xiv, 71
Hill Country Cupboard,
  The, 106
Hill Country
  Dwellings, 195
Hill Country Equestrian
  Lodge, 98
Hill Country State
  Natural Area, 98
Hill County Cell Block
  Museum, 3
Hill County
  Courthouse, 3
Hillsboro, 3
Hippodrome, The, 8
Historic Fort Stockton
  Visitor Center, 247
Historic Homes Tour, 46
Historic Pilgrimage, 135
Hodge Podge
  Cottages, 159
Holland Hotel, 260
Holocaust Museum, 42
Homestead Craft
  Village, 6
Homestead Heritage
  Visitor Center, 6
Home Sweet Home, 190
Hondo, 118
Hondo's on Main, 92
Hood County
  Courthouse, 189
Hood County Jail, 190
Hoof Prints, 220
Horseshoe Bay
  Resort, 79
Horton Classic Car
  Museum, 169
Horton Classic Car
  Museum, The, 169
Hotel Contessa, 129
Hotel Crescent
  Court, 200
Hotel Derek, 68
Hotel Ella, 3, 18
Hotel Emma, 115

Hotel Galvez, 49
Hotel Garza, The, 231
Hotel Granduca, 68
Hotel Havana, 117
Hotel Indigo, 270
Hotel Limpia, 261
Hotel Paisano, 257
Hotel Saint Cecilia, 18
Hotel Saint George, 258
Hotel San Jose, 18
Hotel Settles, 232
Hotel Turkey, 217
Hot Springs, 237, 250
Hotter 'n Hell
  Hundred, 195
Houston, 36, 39, 40,
  68, 70
Houston Convention and
  Visitor Bureau, 42
Houston Heights, 43
Houston Livestock Show
  and Rodeo, 39
Houston, Sam
  (statue), 134
Howard House
  Museum, 141
Hudspeth House, 227
Hueco Tanks State
  Park, 266
Hummer House, 241
Huntsville, 133, 134
Hut's Hamburgers, 21
Hygieostatic Bat
  Roost, 94

I
IMAX Theatre (San
  Antonio), 110
Independence, 27
Independence Plaza, 44
Indian Lodge, 263
Inks Dam National Fish
  Hatchery, 79
Inks Lake State Park, 80
Inn at Chachalaca
  Bend, 67
Inn at Fulton Harbor, 53

Inn at Fulton Harbor,
The, 53
Inner Space Cavern, 11
Inn of the Hills
Resort, 89
Inn on Baron's Creek
Spa & Conference
Center, 105
Inn on Lake
Granbury, 163
Inn on the River, 192
Institute of Texan
Cultures, 109, 112
International Festival-
Institute, 3, 26
Irish Festival, 165
Island Adventure
Park, 65

J
Jacksonville, 134,
135, 141
James Leddy Boots, 210
James Montague
Boots, 169
Janis Joplin's Birthday
Bash, 39
Jasper, 137
Javier's, 201
J.C. Campbell
Mercantile, 83
Jefferson, 134, 135, 154,
158, 159
Jefferson and Cypress
Bayou Railroad, 154
Jefferson General
Store, 155
Jefferson Ghost
Walk, 155
Jefferson Historical
Society Museum, 155
Jefferson Pilgrimage, 155
Jett's Grill, 258
J&J Oyster Bar, 184
Joe T. Garcia's Mexican
Dishes, xiii, 187

John Jay French
Museum, 36
Johnson City, 73, 75, 106
Joseph's Riverport
Barbecue, 155
Jubilee Theater, 185
Jucys Hamburgers, 159
Judge Baylor House, 31
Judge Roy Bean Visitor
Center, 121
Judy's Bread & Breakfast
Bakery, 271
Junction, 85
Junk Gypsy Store, 25
Junque Queens, 7
Justin Boot Factory
Outlet, 270
J Wilson's, 69

K
Kell House, 199
Kelly's Irish Pub, 67
Kelly Square, 164
Kemah Boardwalk, 45
Kermit, 265
Kerrville, 73, 75, 88, 106
Kerrville Convention &
Visitor Bureau, 88
Ketzler's, 191
Kiepersol Estates,
134, 145
Kilgore, 146
Killen's Barbecue, 70
Kimbell Art Museum, 182
Kingfisher Flyfishing
Company, 65
King Ranch, 36, 62
King Ranch Museum, 63
King Ranch Saddle
Shop, 63
Kingsland, 75, 78
Kingsland House of Arts
and Crafts, 78
Kingsville, 36, 62
King William Historic
District, 114, 117

King William Manor,
The, 129
Kitchen's Hardware &
Deli, 147
Kitchen & Yard, 22
Koffee Kup Family
Restaurant, 195
Kokernot Field, 260
Kolache Festival, 10
kolaches, 5
Kreische Brewery State
Historical Site and
Monument Hill, 24
Kreuz Market, 21
Kuebler-Waldrip Haus
B&B, 105
Kuhlman Cellars, 78
Kuhlmann–King
Historical House, 99

L
La Borde House, 124
La Carreta Carnes
Asadas, 123
La Condesa, 31
La Diosa Cellars, 230
Lady Bird Johnson
Wildflower Center,
3, 18
Lady Bird Lake, 17, 20
La Finca, 123
Lafitte's Landing Guest
Quarters, 134, 153
Lafitte's Landing Guest
Quarters, 134
La Fogata, 116
La Fonda on Main, 130
La Gloria, 115
La Grange, 24
Laguna Atascosa National
Wildlife Refuge,
65, 67
Laguna Madre Nature
Trail, 66
Lajitas, 255
Lajitas Resort and
Spa, 255

Lajitas Trading Post, 257
Lake Amistad, 109, 120
Lake Austin Spa
    Resort, 20
Lake Buchanan, 73
Lake Buchanan Dam, 78
Lake Fork, 148
Lake Fork Lodge, 148
Lake Granbury, 192
Lake Granbury
    Marina, 192
Lake LBJ, 79
Lake Livingston, 135
Lake Marble Falls, 77, 79
Lake Meredith National
    Park, 222
Lake Mineral Wells State
    Park, 163, 196
Lake o' the Pines, 157
Lake Palestine, 142
Lake Sam Rayburn, 137
Lake Texoma, 163
La Kiva, 254
La Lomita Chapel, 124
La Maison in
    Midtown, 68
Lamanche's Italian
    Restaurant, 159
Lambert, Lou, 255
Lamberts Downtown
    Barbecue, 16
Lampasas, 75
Landmark Inn State
    Historic Site, 118
Langtry, 121
La Nortena Tortilla
    Factory, 265
La Posada Hotel, 123
La Posada Milagro, 254
La Quinta Rockport-
    Fulton, 69
Laredo, 111, 122,
    129, 130
Larryland Music, 22
La Sirena, 234
La Torretta Lake
    Resort, 46

La Villita, 115
Lazy Heart, 168
Lazy Hills Guest
    Ranch, 89
LBJ Library and
    Museum, 12
Leakey, 86
Leaning Pear, 106
Leaning Pear, The, 106
Ledbetter Picket
    House, 207
Leon's World's Finest
    In & Out BBQ
    House, 69
Liberty Bar, 130
Liberty Bell, The, 159
lightning whelk, 56
Lil Rita's Grill House, 127
Lincoln Street, 91
Lindsey, 167
Linear Air Park, 208
Lions Club Tube
    Rental, 103
Little Chapel in the
    Woods, 169
Livestock Auction, 218
Llano, 75, 81
Llano County Chamber
    of Commerce, 81
Llano County
    Courthouse, 81
Llano Estacado
    Marker, 231
Llano Estacado
    Winery, 229
Llano Fine Arts Guild
    Gallery, 82
Llano Grande
    Plantation Bed and
    Breakfast, 140
Llano Uplift, 81
Local Fix, The, 130
Loco Coyote, 190
Locust House, 171
Lodge at Sanders
    Point, 120

Lodge at Sanders Point,
    The, 120
Lonesome Dove Western
    Bistro, 187
Lone Star Hiking
    Trail, 135
Lone Star Park, 180
Longhorn Cattle
    Company, 127
Longhorn Caverns State
    Park, 80
Longview, 135, 150
Loop Hole, The, 170
Los Asados, 127
Los Barrios, 116
Los Cedros Ranch, 227
Los Ebaños Ferry, 124
Los Jalapenos Cafe, 260
Lost Maples Cafe, 87
Lost Maples State Natural
    Area, 75, 87
Lost Pines Art Bazaar, 22
Lost Pines Art Center, 22
Louie Mueller BBQ, 12
Love Creek Orchards, 99
Love Oak Café, 208
Love's Lookout Park, 142
Lowake Steak
    House, 271
Lubbock, xii, 209,
    228, 233
Lubbock Convention
    and Tourism Bureau,
    229, 231
Lubbock Lake
    National Historic
    Landmark, 229
Lucchese Boots, 270
Luckenbach, 73, 94
Luckenbach General
    Store, 73
Lufkin, 137
Lula Jane's, 8
Lyndon B. Johnson
    National Historic
    Park, 75

Lyndon B. Johnson State Park, 75

M

Mackenzie Trail Monument, 213
Mac's on Main, 202
Magnolia Market at the Silos, 6
Magoffin Homestead, 268
Main Street Arts Festival, 165
Main Street Bistro & Bakery, 181
Malaquite Beach, 60
Manuel's Country Store & Deli, 272
Marathon, 237, 247
Marathon Motel, 249
Marble Falls, 75, 77
Mardi Gras, 39
Mardi Gras Museum, 48
Marfa, 237, 239, 257, 271
Marfa Book Company, 258
Marfa Ghost Lights, 257, 259
Marfa Gliders, 259
Marfa Lights Festival, 239, 257
Marfa Municipal Golf Course, 259
Marine Military Academy and Texas Iwo Jima War Memorial, 127
Mariscal Canyon, 252
Market at the Mill, 194
Market Square (San Antonio), 112
Marshall, 135, 150
Martinez Bakery, 243
Mary Bivins Tropical Conservatory, 220
Mason, 84
Mason Burger, 85
Mason Square Hotel, 85
Matagorda Bay, 51

Matagorda Bay Nature Park, 51
Matagorda County Birding Nature Center, 51
Matt's El Rancho, 21
Maxine's on Main, 22
Mayan Dude Ranch, 97
Mayfest, 165
Mc Allen, 130
McAllen, 109, 111, 125, 129
McAllen Convention and Visitors Bureau, 126
McAllen International Museum of Art & Science, 125
McBride's Land & Cattle, 200
McDonald Observatory, 263
McFaddin-Ward House, 36
McKinney, 171
McKinney Chamber of Commerce, 171
McKinney Roughs, 3, 19
McKittrick Canyon, 237
McNay Art Museum, 113
McPherson Cellars, xii, 230
Meadows Center for Water and the Environment, 102
Meadows Center for Water and the Environment, The, 102
Meat U Anywhere, 202
Medallion Home, 265
Medina, 99
Melissa Guerra Tienda de Cocina, 115
Menard, 85
Menger Hotel, 116
Menil Collection, 42

Mermaid & Dolphin Resort, 68
Mesquite Bean Café, 240
Mesquite Pit, 202
Messina Hof Grapevine Winery, 182
Messina Hof Wine Cellar, 30
Mexic-Arte Museum, 16
Meyer Bed & Breakfast, 95
Mi Casita, 247
Michelson Museum of Art, 151
Mi Cocina, 186
Midland, 242, 272
Midland Chamber/ Convention and Visitor Bureau, 243
Midland Hotel, 195
Migel House, 8
Millard's Crossing, 139
Million Barrel Museum, 245
Mill Pond Park, 83
Mineola, 147
Mineral Wells, 163, 196
Miss Hattie's Museum, 239
Mission, 109, 111, 124
Mission Chamber of Commerce, 124
Mission Espiritu Santo de Zuñiga, 61
Mission San Jose, 110
Miss Molly's Hotel, 186
Mi Tierra, 112
Mobley Hotel, 214
Modern Art Museum of Fort Worth, 183
Mokara Hotel and Spa, 129
Monahans, 245
Monahans Sandhill State Park, 245
Monument Cafe, The, 32
Moody Gardens, 47, 49

Moondoggy's, 233
Moondog's Seaside
    Eatery, 69
Moon Rivers
    Naturals, 145
Mosaics in Hotel Joule
    lobby, 163
Mosquito Cafe, 50
Mother Neff State Park, 9
Mount Gentilz
    Cemetery, 118
Moye Center, 118
Mrs. Lee's Daffodil
    Garden, 133
Mrs. Sam Houston's
    Home, 27
Mudhen Meat and
    Greens, 173
Muenster, 167
Mulberry's, 98
Mule Ear Peaks, 252
Muleshoe, 227
Muleshoe National
    Wildlife Refuge, 227
Municipal Rose
    Garden, 134
Munzesheimer
    Manor, 147
Muse, 166
Museum of Fine Arts, 42
Museum of Fine Arts,
    Houston, 41
Museum of Science and
    History, 183
Museum of the Big
    Bend, 260
Museum of the Gulf
    Coast, 38
Museum of the
    Southwest, 243
Museum of Western
    Art, 88
Mustang Island State
    Park, 55

N
Nacogdoches, xiii,
    134, 135, 136, 137,
    138, 159
Nancy Lee and Perry
    R. Bass Performance
    Hall, 185
Napoli's, 220
National Center for
    Children's Illustrated
    Literature, 209
National Cowboy
    Symposium, 209
National Cowgirl
    Museum and Hall of
    Fame, 183
National Mule
    Memorial, 227
National Museum of the
    Pacific War, 91
National Polka
    Festival, 165
Navajo Grill, 92
Nave Museum, 53
Neal's Vacation
    Lodges, 86
Near Southside, 187
Neiman Marcus, 176
New Braunfels, 75,
    100, 105
New Vintage Wine and
    Art Festival, 165
New Witte Museum, 112
New Zion Missionary
    Baptist Church, 135
New Zion Missionary
    Baptist Church
    Barbecue, 134
Night in Old Pecos
    & Cantaloupe
    Festival, 265
903 Handmade, 134, 145
Nocona, 168, 201
Nokona Glove
    Factory, 169

Nolan Ryan Foundation
    and Exhibit Center, 40
North Texas, xii, 160

O
Oak Grove Cemetery,
    134, 139
Oak-Hickory Historic
    District, 171
Oaks Restaurant, The, 32
Obregon's, 130
Odessa, 243, 272
Odessa Convention and
    Visitor Bureau, 245
Odessa Meteor Crater
    Museum, 244
Off the Square
    neighborhood, 145
Off the Vine, 181
Oge House, 117
O. Henry Museum, 17
OHMS, 220
Oktoberfest, 75
Old 300 BBQ and Back
    Forty Event Hall, 77
Old Baylor Park, 27
Old Bayview
    Cemetery, 58
Old Jail Art Center,
    205, 206
Old Llano County Jail, 81
Old Man Scary
    Cellars, 82
Old Mulberry Inn Bed &
    Breakfast, 158
Old Post Office Museum
    and Art Center, 198
Old Red, 174
Old Rock Jail, 211
Old San Jacinto, 219
Old Seabrook, 45
Old Stone Fort, 138
Oliver & Co., 83
Omni Corpus Christi, 68
Omni Hotel, 172

Omni La Mansion del Rio, 129
One-Arm Dove Hunt, 183
105 Lincoln, 258
Orange, 39
OST, 97
Osteria Il Sogno, 115
Otto's German Bistro, 92
Our Lady of Guadalupe Church and Shrine, 39
Outlot 201 Guest Houses, 105
Overton Hotel and Conference Center, 233
Oysterfest, 39
Ozona, 246

P
Pace Park, 11
Padre Island Brewing Company, 67
Padre Island National Seashore, 36, 59, 64
Paint Rock Grocery, 241
Paisano Pete, 247
Palace Theatre, 181, 223
Palestine, 134, 135, 141, 159
Palmetto State Park, 24
Palmito Ranch Battlefield, 128
Palo Duro Canyon, 209, 218
Palo Duro Canyon State Park, 206, 226
Pampa, 222
Panhandle Plains Historical Museum, 206
Panhandle-Plains Historical Museum, 220
Paradise Key Dockside Bar & Grill, 70

Paris 7th, 184
Paris Coffee Shop, 201
Paseo del Rio (River Walk, San Antonio), 114
Patina Green, 171
Peach Tree Tea Room, The, 106
Pea-Off, The, 239
Pearl Brewery, 115
Pearl of the Concho, 240
Pearl, The, 109
Pecan Street Inn, 30
Pecos, 239, 265, 272
Pecos River Canyon scenic overlook, 122
Pedernales Falls State Park, 73, 76
Pedernales River, 75
Peggy's On the Green, 99
Perini Ranch Steakhouse, 206, 210
Permian Basin Hamburger Co., 272
Permian Basin Petroleum Museum, Library, and Hall of Fame, 242
Perot Theatre, 156
Persimmon Gap Visitor's Center, 250
Peter Pan statue, 188
Pheasant Ridge Winery, 230
Pho House, 244
Pickett House (Woodville), 136
Pine Creek Lodge, 140
Pine Mills Pottery, 148
Piney Woods, xiii, 131
Pint & Barrel, 159
Pioneer Amphitheater, 226
Pioneer Memorial Museum, 216
Pioneer Village, 4

Piranha Killer Sushi, 186
Pittsburg, 157
Pittsburg Hot Link, 157
Pittsburg Hot Links Restaurant, 157
Pizza Foundation, 272
Plaine, 260
Ponder, 171
Popeye the Sailor (statue), 122
Po Po Family Restaurant, 99
Port Aransas, 36, 55, 68
Port Aransas Chamber of Commerce Tourist and Convention Bureau, 57
Port Arthur, 38, 39
Port Isabel, 64
Port Isabel Lighthouse State Historic Park, 64
Possum Kingdom Lake Chamber of Commerce, 198
Possum Kingdom Lake State Park, 197
Post, 231
Prairie by Rachel Ashwell, The, 25
Prairie Dog Town, 229
Pratt's Books, 198
Presidential Archives and Leadership Library, 244
Presidential Museum, 244
Presidio, 256
Presidio Chamber of Commerce, 256
Presidio County Courthouse, 237, 257
Presidio La Bahía, 36, 60
Prince Solms Inn, 101
Prude Ranch, 263
Punkin Days, 209, 216, 219

Q
Queenie's, 170
Queen Isabella
  Causeway, 64
Quitaque, 206

R
R. A. Apffel Park, 49
Railhead
  Smokehouse, 201
Rails-to-Trails
  pathway, 196
Railway Museum of San
  Angelo, 240
Rainforest Pyramid, 49
Ranching Heritage
  Center, xiv, 228
Ranchman's Cafe, 171
Rancho Cortez, 105
Rancho Loma, 206, 211
Rancho Loma Vineyards,
  xii, 211
Rancho Pizzeria, 211
Rangerette
  Showcase, 146
Rangers Ballpark, 179
Rao's Bakery, 36
Rattlesnake Roundup
  (Sweetwater),
  209, 214
Razzoo's Cajun Cafe, 186
Real Cajun Seafood
  Restaurant, 38
Reata (Alpine), 260
Reata (Fort Worth), 185
Recycled Books, CDs,
  and Records, 170
Redbud Café, 77
Redbud Inn, 171
Red River Historical
  Museum, 165
Red River Pizzeria, 169
Red River Railroad
  Museum, 164
Red River Station
  Inn, 169

Renaissance Casa de
  Palmas, 129
Resaca de la Palma
  Battlefield, 128
Residence Inn
  (Brownsville), 129
Reunion Tower, 172
Revolver Brewing, 191
Rice Village, 42
Righteous Foods, 184
Rio Frio Lodging, 86
Rio Grande City, 123
Rio Grande Village, 250
River Bend
  Restaurant, 153
River Haven Cabins, 86
River Walk (Paseo del
  Rio, San Antonio), 114
River Walk (San
  Angelo), 240
Roast Social Kitchen, 144
Robert J. and Helen C.
  Kleberg South Texas
  Heritage Center, 112
Rochelle's Canoe
  Rentals, 196
Rockbox Theater, 92
Rockin' Q
  Smokehouse, 272
Rockport, 53, 70
Rockport Center for the
  Arts, 53
Rockport-Fulton
  Chamber of
  Commerce, 55
Rockwall County, 64
Rose Hill Manor, 105
Rose Mansion, 11
Rosevine Inn, 143
Rough Creek Lodge,
  163, 192
Round Top, 3, 4, 25, 32
Round Top Music
  Festival, 4
Royal Theater, 199
Royer's Round Top
  Cafe, 25

Roy Orbison
  Museum, 268
RR 1340, 89
Rudy and Paco, 50
Ruidosa, 237
Rusk, 134, 140

S
Sabine Lake, 39
Sabine National
  Forest, 137
Sabine Pass Battleground
  State Historic Site, 39
Sadler's Kitchen, 142
Saint Jo, 163, 168
Salado, 9, 32
Salado Chamber of
  Commerce, 11
Salt Lick BBQ, 104
Salt Lick BBQ, The, 104
Salt Lick Cellars, 104
Saltwater Grill, 50
Salvage Sisters, 7
Sam Houston
  Homesite, 27
Sam Houston
  Memorial Museum
  Complex, 133
Sam Houston National
  Forest, 135
Sam Houston Park, 40
Sam Houston Sanders
  Corps of Cadets
  Center, 29
Sam Houston's Grave
  and National
  Monument, 134
Sam Rayburn House, 162
Sam Rayburn
  Library, 162
Sam's Dock, 192
San Agustín Plaza, 122
San Angelo, 237,
  238, 239
San Angelo Museum of
  Art, 239

San Antonio, 109, 111, 129, 130
San Antonio Children's Museum, 111
San Antonio Convention and Visitor Bureau, 117
San Antonio Museum of Art, 113
San Augustine, 138
Sand Castle Days, 39
San Elizario Presidio Church, 267
San Gabriel House, 11
San Jacinto Battleground State Historical Park, 44
San Jacinto Monument, 44
San Jacinto Museum of History, 44
San Jose Island, 56
San Marcos, 102, 105, 106
San Saba, 82
San Saba River Nature Park, 83
San Solomon Courts, 270
Santa Ana National Wildlife Refuge, 126
Santa Cruz de San Saba, 85
Santa Elena Canyon, 253
Sarah's on the Square, 166
Sara's Bed & Breakfast Inn, 44
Sayles Ranch Guesthouses, 210
Scarborough Renaissance Festival, 165, 178
Scenic Road (El Paso), 267
Schlitterbahn, 101
Scholz Garten, 31
Schooner Restaurant, The, 38

Screen Door Inn, The, 200
Seafood & Spaghetti Works, 57
Seaquist House, 84
Seaquist Ranch, 85
Sea Ranch Restaurant and Bar, 67
Sea Rim State Park, 39
Sea Turtle Inc., 66
Second Bar + Kitchen, 17
Sedona Grill, 272
Seminole Canyon State Historical Park, 109, 121
Seminole Indian Scout Cemetery, 119
Serenity Farmhouse Spa, 103
Seventeen Seventeen, 174
74-Mile Scenic Loop Road, 261
Shady Glade, 153
Shamrock, 225
Shangri La Botanical Gardens and Nature Center, 37
Shed, The, 145
Shell's Pasta and Seafood, 57
Shep's Place, 188
Sheriff's Posse Championship BBQ Cook-Off, 265
Sheriff's Posse Rodeo, 126
Sherman, 164
Sherman Jazz Museum, 164
Sherman Museum, 165
Shiner, 3, 24, 31
Shiner Beer, 24
Shiner Country Inn, 31
Shrine of La Virgen de San Juan del Valle, 126

Sid Richardson Collection of Western Art, 185
Silent Wings Museum, 229
Silk Stocking Historical District, 46
Silver Falls Park, 215
Sinclair, 201
Sirena, 10
Six Car Pub and Brewery, 220
Sixth Floor Museum, 163, 175
Slovacek's, 5
Smoke, 176
Snoopy's Pier, 60
Snuffer's, 201
Snyder, 215
Socorro Mission, 267
Sonny Bryan's, 201
Sonny's Place, 50
Sonora, 242
Sophienburg Museum, 101
South by Southwest Music & Media Conference, 4
Southern Hotel, 81
South Llano River State Park, 85
South Padre Island, 64, 70
South Padre Island Convention and Visitor Bureau, 65, 68
South Texas, xiv, 107
Southwestern Stock Show and Rodeo, 165, 184
Southwestern University, 11
Southwest School of Art, 109, 114
Space Center Houston, 44
Spanish Governor's Palace, 109, 112

Spanky's Sandwich Shop, 230
Spatterdock, 159
Spellbound, 190
Spindletop–Gladys City Boomtown, 35
Spoetzl Brewery, 3, 24
Spur Hotel, The, 199
Square Dance Capital of the World, 127
Stadium Club, 180
Stadium Club, The, 180
Stagecoach Inn, 10
Stag Leap Country Cabins, 159
St. Agustín Church, 123
Stamford, 209, 213
Stanley-Fisher House Bed & Breakfast, 52
Stanley's Famous, 134
Stanley's Famous Pit BBQ, 144
St. Anthony, 117
St. Anthony Roman Catholic Cathedral Basilica, 38
Stark Museum of Art, 37
Starlight Theatre (restaurant), 254
Star of the Republic Museum, 3, 27
Star, The, 172
State Capitol Building, 3, 15
State Fair of Texas, 165
State Parks Pass, xix
Stella Hotel, 29
Stellina, 258
Sterne-Hoya House, 139
Steves Homestead, 114
Stewart Beach, 49
St. Helen's, 190
Stillwater Inn, 156
Stillwell's Store, 249
St. James Inn, 31
St. Louis Catholic Church, 118

Stockyards Collection Museum, 186
Stockyards Hotel, 186
Stockyards National Historic District, 180, 186
Stockyards Station, 186
Stonewall, 75
Stout's Trattoria, 78
St. Peter's Church, 167
Strand, 36, 46
Stubblefield Lake, 135
Stubb's Bar-B-Que, 21
Study Butte, 253
Sundancer on the Brazos, 188
Sundance Square, 184
Sunflower Bakery & Café, 69
Susie's South 40, 243
Sweetwater, 209, 213
Sweetwater Grill and Tavern, 170

T
Tack Room, 123
Taco Palenque, 130
Tanglewood Resort, 163
Tarpon Inn, 36, 56
Tarrant County Courthouse, 185
Taverna, 186
Taylor, 12
T. C. Lindsey and Company General Store, 153
Temple Emanuel, 38
Terlingua, 253
Terlingua Post Office and the Quicksilver Bank, 253
Terlingua Trading Co., 254
Terrace Inn, 212
Texarkana, 156
Texas!, 209

Texas Basket Company, 134, 141
Texas Blueberry Festival, 135
Texas Citrus Fiesta, 111, 124
Texas Country Music Hall of Fame, 151
Texas Cowboy Poetry Gathering, 239
Texas Cowboy Reunion, 209, 213
Texas Cultural Arts District, 194
Texas Department of Transportation, xix
Texas Energy Museum, 35
Texas Folklife Festival, 111
Texas Forestry Museum, 137
Texas Forever, 44
Texas Freshwater Fisheries Center, 149
Texas Handwoven Creations, 241
Texas Hill Country Distillers, 96
Texas Iwo Jima War Memorial, 109, 127
Texas Kings Hotel, 168
Texas Motor Speedway, 187
"Texas, Our Texas ", 45
Texas Panhandle, xiv, 203
Texas Parks and Wildlife Department, xix
Texas Pearls and Co., 177
Texas Prison Museum, 134
Texas Ranch Life, 3, 28
Texas Ranger Hall of Fame and Museum, 7

Texas Reds Steak &
  Grape Festival, 4
Texas Reds
  Steakhouse, 106
Texas Rose Festival, 143
Texas Ruby Red
  grapefruit, 262
Texas Seaport
  Museum, 48
Texas Sports Hall of
  Fame, 8
Texas State Aquarium, 57
Texas State Parklands
  Passport, xix
Texas State Railroad,
  134, 141
Texas State Travel
  Guide, xix
Texas Travel Information
  Center, 167
Texas White House, 200
Texas Wine and
  Grape Growers
  Association, 182
Texas Wine Tours, 90
Texas Zoo, 52
Tex Ritter Museum, 151
Tex Ritter Park, 38
T.G. Canoe Livery, 103
Thee Hubbell
  House, 158
Thomas Cree's Little
  Tree, 225
Threadgill's, 31
Three Danes Inn &
  Baking Company, 200
Three Oaks Bed and
  Breakfast, 151
Thunderbird Hotel, 271
Tia Juanita's Fish
  Camp, 69
Tigua Indian
  Reservation, 267
TJ's at the Old
  Forge, 105
Tolbert's Chili Parlor, 182

Tolbert's Texas Trading
  Co., 181
Toledo Bend
  Reservoir, 137
Tomato Festival, 135
Tony Lama Factory
  Stores, 270
Tow, 73, 81
Traditions Club, 29
Transmountain
  Drive, 268
TransPecos Festival of
  Music and Love,
  239, 259
Treaty Oak Gallery, 194
Tremont House, The, 49
Triple J Chophouse and
  Brew Co., 230
Turkey, 209, 217
Turning Basin Riverboat
  Tours, 134, 154
Turquoise Door, The, 18
12 Gage, 248
Twister Tacos, 244
205 Melody Lane, 166
Two Street, 9
Tyler, 134, 135, 142, 159
Tyler Museum of Art, 143

U
Uncertain, 153, 159
Uncertain Inn, 153
Uncle Fletch Hamburger
  Festival, 135, 149
University of Texas, 12
University of Texas
  Marine Science
  Institute, 56
University of Texas Pan
  American Coastal
  Studies Lab, 66
University Park
  Village, 184
Upstairs Inn, 195
US Army Air Defense
  Museum, 269
USS *Lexington*, 58

Utopia, 87
Uvalde, 118, 130
Uvalde Grand Opera
  House, 119

V
Vagabond Pizza, 233
Val Verde County
  Courthouse, 120
Val Verde Winery,
  120, 122
Vanderpool, 73, 87
Vanishing Texas River
  Cruise, 73, 80
Veranda Inn, 201
Veranda, The, 271
Vera's Backyard Bar-
  B-Q, 128
Victoria, 52
Vintage Round Top,
  The, 25
Viva El Paso!, 239

W
Waco, 3, 6, 9, 31, 32
Wander'n Calf Espresso
  Bar & Bakery, 96
Wanna Wanna Beach
  Bar & Grill, 67
Warfield House, 158
Warwick Melrose, 200
Washington, 3
Washington County
  Convention and
  Visitor Bureau, 27
Washington-on-the-
  Brazos, 27
Washington's
  Birthday, 111
Watermelon Thump, 125
Waterside Sports, 192
Waxahachie, 163, 165,
  176, 201, 202
W.C.T.U. Building, 223
Weatherford, 187, 202
Weatherford Chamber of
  Commerce, 188

Weatherford Public
Library, 188
Webb Gallery, 178
Wedding Oak Winery, 82
Weinberger's
Delicatessen, 182
Weisman, 151
Weisman, The, 151
Welfare, 106
Welfare Cafe, 106
West, 5
Westcave Preserve, 76
Westfest, 4, 5
West Magnolia
Avenue, 187
West of the Pecos
Museum, 265
West of the Pecos
Rodeo, 239, 265
West Table Kitchen and
Bar, 234
West Texas, xiv, 235
Whaling Wall No. 53, 66
Whispering Palms
Inn, 129
Whistlehill Café, 188
White Buffalo Bar, 248
White Buffalo Statue, 215
White Elephant Saloon,
181, 186
Whitney, 31
Wichita Falls, 199
Wichita Falls Museum
of Art at Midwestern
State University, 199
Wildcate Bluff Nature
Center, 220

Wildcatter Ranch, 198
Wildflower Tours, 4
Wildseed Farms, 93
Willow Creek Café, 85
Willow Wild
Cemetery, 162
Will Rogers
Coliseum, 184
Willy Burger, 69
Wimberley, 73, 103,
105, 106
Wimberley Pie Co.,
73, 103
Windberg Art Center, 11
Window, 252
Wind Shed Tasting
Room, 167
Wind & Wave Water
Sports, 59
Winedale Historical
Center, 26
Wine Nest, 230
Wine Nest, The, 230
Wine Shoppe, The, 8
Wine Walk, 165
Wink, 268
Winnsboro, 157
Wiseman House
Chocolates, 195
Witte Museum, 112
Woerner Warehouse, 92
Woldert-Spence
Manor, 144
Wonderland of Lights,
135, 151
Wonder World, 103
Woodrow House, 233

Woodville, 136
Woody's, 196
World Birding Center,
109, 125
World Championship
Barbecue Goat Cook-
Off, 75, 83
World's Largest Jack
Rabbit, 244
World's Richest Acre, 146
Wurstfest, 75, 101
Wyland, 66

X
X Bar Ranch Lodge &
Nature Retreat, 241
XIT Museum, 224
XIT Ranch, 224
XIT Rodeo and Reunion,
209, 225

Y
Ye Kendall Inn, 99
Y.O. Ranch, 73, 88
Y.O. Ranch Hotel, 89
Ysleta Mission, 267
Yummie's Bistro, 70

Z
Zachry Family Acequia
Garden, 112
Zapata, 123
Zentner's Daughter
Steakhouse, 240
Zilker Park, 14